DEADLY SEAS

David J. Bercuson
and Holger H. Herwig

DEADLY SEAS

The Duel between the St Croix *and the*
U305 *in the Battle of the Atlantic*

Vintage Canada
A Division of Random House of Canada

Published in 1998 by Vintage Canada, a division of
Random House of Canada, Limited. Originally published in
hardcover in 1997 by Random House of Canada, Toronto.

Canadian Cataloguing in Publication Data

Bercuson, David Jay, 1945 –
    Deadly seas: the duel between the St. Croix
and the U305 in the Battle of the Atlantic

Includes index.
ISBN 0-679-30927-6

1. World War, 1939-1945 — Campaigns — Atlantic Ocean.
2. St. Croix (Destroyer).   3. U-305 (Submarine).   4. World War, 1939-1945 —
Naval operations, Canadian.   5. World War, 1939-1945 — Naval operations,
German.   I. Herwig, Holger H.   II. Title.

D770.B47 1998   940.54'21   C97-932287-1

Printed and bound in the United States of America

10 9 8 7 6 5 4 3 2 1

Contents

Acknowledgements

We could not have told the story of Harry Kingsley, Andrew Hedley Dobson, Rudolf Bahr, *St Croix*, and *U305* without much help and encouragement. Our agent, Linda McKnight, offered important advice and guidance from the start. Robert Mitchell of Ottawa tracked down the personnel records of Harry Kingsley, A.H. Dobson, and many other former officers of *St Croix* as well as other important information. Brian Murza, Marc Milner, Roger Sarty, Bill Wilson, and Peter Chance were more than generous with their advice and time. Bill Wilson, Peter Chance, Michael Hadley, and Wilhelm Deist of Freiburg read large portions of the manuscript. Tom and Caroline Dobson helped us gain valuable background information on their father, A.H. Dobson, and his family. Jim Sterret was a great help in researching the Admiralty records at the Public Record Office in London. Archivists at the PRO, the National Archives of Canada, the National Archives in Washington, and the U-boat Archive in Cuxhaven gave generously of their time and their ideas, and we are eternally grateful. As always, the errors in this book are ours alone.

Prologue

At mid-afternoon on 15 September 1943, HMCS *St Croix*, a destroyer built in the United States during the First World War, steams out of Plymouth as part of Escort Group (EG) 9. The Senior Officer of the Escort is aboard HMS *Itchen*, a Royal Navy frigate specifically built to hunt U-boats.

It is a beautiful sunny day but, after leaving the calm waters of the harbour, the escort vessels begin to rise and fall on a heavy swell. The wind picks up. The men aboard the *St Croix* wonder where they are going. Some say the Mediterranean, others the Bay of Biscay. No one but her Captain, Lieutenant-Commander Andrew Hedley Dobson, Royal Canadian Naval Reserve, really knows. After passing Land's End, the group shapes course for the Western Approaches. Dobson tells his officers that EG9 is due to rendezvous with inbound convoy HX256 some 500 miles west of Ireland.

At dawn on the 17th, EG9 sights HX256. *St Croix* and the other escorts sweep the flanks of the convoy, making sure that all is right aboard the plodding merchantmen. She then assumes her assigned place in the escort screen. Just before midnight, new orders flash to EG9 from the Commander-in-Chief Western Approaches: If HX256 is not threatened, leave at dawn on 19 September and proceed to support westbound convoy ONS18. Signals intelligence strongly indicates there is a large group of U-boats in its path.

Precisely at dawn, *Itchen*'s signal lamp blinks out a message to *St Croix* and the other vessels of EG9: "Execute course change on my signal." A signal flag is hauled up on her yardarm, and similar flags soon flutter on the other ships. At precisely 6:45 a.m., the flags snap down and the escorts heel over and pull away from the convoy. They head north at 12 knots, with *Itchen* in the lead. At 3:50 p.m. the Admiralty informs *Itchen* that EG9 is being tracked by the Germans and suggests that she and her consorts approach the convoy by an evasive route.

EG9 changes course and steams ahead into nightfall. Aboard *St Croix*, Dobson warns his officers that something big is up, but he decides not to call the ship to action stations. He knows there will be many long hours at full alert in the coming hours of darkness, and he does not want to disturb the ship's routine until he absolutely has to. But he doubles the watch, tells anti-submarine officer Lieutenant John F. Gallagher to pay close attention to the asdic, and checks that the radar set is working properly. What Dobson does not know is that the Admiralty has ordered ONS18 to rendezvous with ON202, a somewhat faster convoy steaming westward on a parallel course some miles to the north. This order is issued as evidence mounts of a major submarine attack against one or both of the convoys.

Soon *St Croix* spots convoy ONS18 and takes up a position on its outer screen. At 9:45 a.m. five very long-range B-24 Liberators of the Royal Air Force 120 Squadron from Iceland fly over. Aircraft X120 makes the first positive spotting of a 'grey wolf' 15 miles north of ON202. From noon until nightfall of the 20th, the two convoys try to join together. It is a slow and difficult process when it is done this way, at sea and en route, and has its share of confusion and chaos. But it is done, and the combined convoy ONS18/ON202 is made up of eighty-eight merchant vessels guarded by seventeen escorts. It is among the largest convoys of the war.

Four days earlier, at midnight on 15–16 September 1943, Grand Admiral Karl Dönitz, Commander-in-Chief of the German navy, the Kriegsmarine, had ordered the formation of Group Leuthen, a concentration of twenty U-boats, against what he suspected was a westbound convoy. All the submarines in this wolfpack are equipped with the new acoustic *Zaunkönig* ("wren") torpedo. In the middle of the line is *U305*, commanded by Lieutenant Rudolf Bahr. Shortly before midnight on

19–20 September, one of the submarines sights convoy ONS18. The "Great Lion," as Dönitz is idolized throughout the u-boat service, knows that the moment has arrived. "To Leuthen," he radioes, "At 'em!"

Bahr's *U305* is on the surface at 12:48 a.m. when a lookout spots an aircraft with Leigh Lights approaching fast. Two minutes later, the boat next to him, *U270*, spies several dark shadows to the north. It is a second convoy! Just before 3 a.m., *U270* draws first blood: its WREN torpedo blows off the stern of the Royal Navy frigate HMS *Lagan* at a range of 1.8 miles. It is a triumphant inauguration for Dönitz's new "destroyer cracker," which the Allies quickly dub the "gnat."

Dönitz now orders all Leuthen boats to concentrate against ON202. At 4 p.m. on 20 September about six submarines charge the enemy cavalry style, flak firing furiously, in an attempt to break through both air cover and escort screen to get inside ON202. Forty ships in ten serried columns: a target-rich environment! Dönitz urges the u-boats on: "Remain surfaced and proceed to convoy at full speed."

Bahr is frustrated. The battle is raging all around him, but *U305* just can't get a fix on any hostile target. He searches the vast expanses of the ocean for ON202. At 5:20 p.m. one of *U305*'s lookouts spots an aircraft approaching. There are no German Luftwaffe planes way out here, so the alarm is called: "Captain to the bridge! Aircraft approaching. West by northwest at 12,000 metres."

Bahr springs into action: "Emergency! Dive! Dive! Chief, level off at 100 metres!"

U305 plunges beneath the surface. "The bastard hasn't seen me," Bahr gloats, as no bombs crash around his boat. At 5:45 p.m. he resurfaces and rushes to the bridge. He later records: "Freighter at 2500 metres. I approach. Soon discover a destroyer screening the freighter." Bahr dogs the smoke clouds on the horizon, hoping to get a good shot in later under cover of darkness.

Suddenly, the hunter becomes the hunted! "Aircraft at 250° attacking out of the eastern sun. Range 5000."

Damn it, the spotters must be asleep! Sons-a-bitches! Bahr bawls them out: "Clear the machine-gun! Hard a port! Open up with the Flak!" The old twin 2-cm guns on the port side fire eighty well-placed rounds at the intruder. Still, he can "detect no effect." The Liberator's cannons spit out a deadly stream of fire and its pilot releases four depth-bombs.

They fall to the starboard side, "without particular effect," Bahr records laconically in his war log. Close call!

"Contacts bearing dead ahead! 010°. Getting louder!" Radioman Herbert Ballmann has picked up a destroyer's propellers. "Radar impulses increasing sharply!" he yells, beside himself with anxiety. "Impulses amplitude four!"

"Periscope depth!" Bahr barks out. And to the Chief Engineer: "Switch to e-motors, Chief!"

Asdic pings bounce off U305's hull like a thousand small hammer blows. The sound of thrashing blades is audible throughout the boat. Bahr slowly rotates the periscope 360 degrees. "Destroyer in sight. Bearing zero degrees. Range 6–8000."

Then he commands: "On periscope depth, Chief! Action stations! All torpedo tubes ready for action!"

Normally, Bahr would order a fan shot from the bow tubes. Not now! It's time to test the destroyer cracker. "Correction: Distance 1500 metres! Estimated speed 12 knots! Angle left 060 degrees! Depth 4 metres!"

"Tube 2: Ready . . ." It is 9:33 p.m.

Up above, the Liberator circles the spot where U305 disappeared. The crew is bone tired and hungry. They have been in the air for almost eleven hours. "There!" The co-pilot points to two destroyers that are apparently attacking a contact, and a third that has just turned away. The pilot banks the aircraft into a tight circle over the departing destroyer. The navigator flashes his signal light at the "tin can." "Have depth charged submarine 15 miles astern. Can you follow me?"

St Croix leaps into action. "Chief, give me 250 revolutions," Dobson orders. "Cox, starboard 15 to 045. Follow that plane, man."

In the boiler room, stokers rush to flash the two after boilers. The old destroyer slowly builds a head of steam and races eastward into the darkening sky. Dobson is going in for the kill. "If that bastard's still afloat," he says between clenched teeth, "he'll be back at periscope depth by the time we get there." St Croix is slicing through the Atlantic at 24 knots.

"Contact dead ahead, sir, range 1200 yards," Gallagher shouts.

Once again, the lethal cat-and-mouse game pitting destroyer skipper against U-boat captain begins. Death to the loser.

1

A Destroyer
Goes to War

HARRY KINGSLEY was born in the International Settlement of Shanghai, China, on the last day of September 1900. Located on the west bank of the Huangpu branch of the mighty Yangtze River, Shanghai is the largest and busiest port in China. The trade of almost half the country flows to the East China Sea on the broad waters of this river. It is a river that periodically floods, destroying the homes of millions of Chinese peasants while depositing the rich silt that is the basis of their lives.

Shanghai was of little note or importance until the middle of the nineteenth century. In 1842 Britain defeated the Middle Kingdom in the first Opium War and, with the signing of the Treaty of Nanjing, forced China to open its borders to British and other foreign traders. The treaty designated Shanghai and four other ports as entry points for previously barred foreign commerce. By 1900 no other port in China rivals the great trade that flows through Shanghai each day.

The sights and sounds of dockside Shanghai form a colourful and noisy backdrop for the commerce that is carried out there. The ships of dozens of nations tie up along the river wharfs and jetties, their holds loaded or unloaded by thousands of Chinese labourers. The older of these vessels, caught between two eras, are driven by both wind and steam power, but the newer freighters are dominated by the straight tall stacks that exhaust the smoke from their coal-fired scotch boilers and

triple-expansion steam engines. Junks ply the river waters and bring in
the products of the coastal trade. Sampans and small steam lighters vie
for space in the river's main channel with arriving and departing ships.
At dockside, the singsong voices of street hawkers and beggars mingle
with the hubbub of men going about their business in the narrow
streets. Near the river are large warehouses and smaller, squat buildings
housing brokerage and insurance offices. There is a constant din from
the chuffing of gasoline donkey engines, the groans of cranes slinging
cargoes into and out of ships' holds, the shouts of the stevedores, and
the honky-tonk music of dozens of riverside bars. In those bars, foreign
sailors blow their pay on the clear, fiery liquid the Chinese call *maotai*
and fondle slight black-haired girls in tight cheongsams.

The International Settlement, which lies in the heart of Shanghai
astride Soochow Creek, is young Harry Kingsley's world. The Soochow,
really a small river, empties into the Huangpu from the west. The settlement, like the busy port around it, is also a legacy of the Opium War
and other humiliations visited on the Chinese by European powers
more advanced in the science of war. There are three such settlements
on the west bank of the river, one administered by the Japanese, one
by the French, and one by the British. The settlements are governed by
Europeans, for Europeans, and according to European law. The Chinese
who live there are refugees who have slipped into this European sanctum of jobs, food, and shelter. The lot of these Chinese is not happy,
but they live better than the millions of poor peasants in the small rural
villages to the south and west.

Harry Kingsley and his family may be foreign to the soil of China,
but in the International Settlement they live like the masters that guns
and great power politics have made them. Their homes and office buildings are constructed of stone and brick in the style of England, France,
or the United States, on quiet tree-lined streets. At their opulent tennis
and lawn-bowling clubs, they are served drinks by white-jacketed Chinese servants who would not otherwise be allowed on the grounds.
Many of Kingsley's friends will still be living like this four decades later
when the armed forces of Japan extinguish the Settlement and consign
its foreign inhabitants to concentration camps.

Kingsley is born into this Shangri-La of European power just as
China is beginning to recover from the Boxer Rebellion. Centred in

northern China, the Boxer uprising is launched in late June 1900 by the Society of the Righteous and Harmonious Fists, a secret organization dedicated to driving foreigners out of China. Its members kill thousands of foreigners and Chinese Christians, and destroy their houses and churches. When the Europeans, the Japanese, and the Americans bring in troops to put the rebellion down, the Chinese government declares war and besieges the foreign embassies and legations in Beijing. Foreign military power prevails, but unrest seethes below the surface.

Kingsley soon longs for a life at sea. He goes to the harbour to watch the ships coming and going. He is particularly fascinated by the warships. He sees the gunboats as they swing into the mainstream, smoke pouring from their funnels, awnings shading their low-slung main decks from the searing sun of southern China. He watches the sailors coiling rope, fixing and cleaning their vessels, strolling the decks, or looking at the passing shore as their boats begin their journey upriver. He wonders what it is like to live aboard a gunboat. By modern warship standards they are not well armed. Kingsley can see a Maxim machine-gun fixed here or there on the superstructure, or a small breech-loaded cannon fore and aft. He doesn't yet realize that it is not the boats but their flags which are the real portents of their power.

Sometimes Kingsley sees an ocean-going warship. They are much larger and more modern. The newer of these vessels sport large gun turrets fore and aft and amidships. Their superstructures are dominated by tall funnels, and their midships wells and quarterdecks by high masts sprouting wireless antennas held in place by rigging lines. Their prows jut forward at the waterline. Their bilge pumps spew a steady stream into the filthy water of the harbour. Usually they anchor in mid-river, their sides streaked with rust from the salt water that has poured through their scuppers in a heavy sea. Kingsley soon learns to identify heavy cruisers and light cruisers, as well as the new torpedo-boat destroyers, fast vessels of 200 tons or more carrying self-propelled torpedoes. He reads all he can about these ships, and about the famous captains who have commanded men-of-war to protect the British Empire since the time of the Spanish Armada. He admires the Royal Navy officers he sees ashore, their blond hair tucked neatly under peaked caps and their tanned faces dark against tropical whites. By the time he is twelve, Harry Kingsley decides to be one of them.

In August 1914 war breaks out in faraway Europe. The tensions are felt in China and in the waters of the south Pacific, as German raiders sailing from ports in Germany's Pacific island possessions attack British and French commerce. Kingsley is now almost fourteen and keen to share in this great adventure. As each dispatch from overseas tells of great battles fought in the fields of France and Belgium and of momentous encounters at sea, he grows more determined to pursue a naval career. He follows the newspaper reports about the Battle of the Falklands, fought in early December 1914 when four German cruisers are destroyed by British guns. In May 1916 he waits anxiously for the latest news of the great battle at sea between the Royal Navy's Grand Fleet and the German High Seas Fleet off the coast of Denmark. It is the Battle of Jutland, perhaps the greatest surface-to-surface battle in the history of naval warfare. The British lose more ships, but the Germans retreat to their home ports, more intent on survival than victory. Kingsley sees only glory in these accounts, the honour of the British Empire at stake. He knows nothing of the searing agony of war at sea, of men blasted on the bridges of their ships, roasted in their turrets, broiled in their boiler rooms and stokeholds by clouds of superheated steam, or drowned in freezing waters.

Kingsley wants to join the Royal Navy, but his family's move to Canada puts an end to that idea. An ocean crossing to the United Kingdom for a young man in wartime is out of the question. German u-boats are attacking passenger vessels such as the *Lusitania*, torpedoed off the coast of Ireland in May 1915 with the loss of one thousand lives. So, in the spring of 1916, Kingsley writes the competitive examination for entrance to the Royal Naval College of Canada in Halifax. The college had opened its doors in January 1910 to prepare Canadian midshipmen for the fledgling Royal Canadian Navy, born at the same time. For the next few weeks, Harry nervously awaits the results of the exam. Then the envelope with the official navy stamp arrives. The news is good. He has passed, and he is expected at the college at the beginning of August. On 3 August 1916 Kingsley is appointed a cadet in the Royal Naval College of Canada. His navy career is beginning.

Halifax is no Shanghai, but it has a long history as a key part of the Royal Navy's Atlantic defences. Founded as a naval base in 1749, the "warden of the north" once provided a firm base for the Royal Navy as it went to sea to battle the French, the Spanish, the Americans, and other enemies of the Britannic Majesties. In 1910 the great base passed to Canadian hands. Canadians, as always, neglected their own defence during peacetime, and the base's obsolescent facilities were allowed to deteriorate. Royal Navy ships continued to call, but the once-bustling naval base was in a state of decline when war was declared in August 1914. Then, once again, it soon came into its own as a western terminus for the new convoy system, organized by the Admiralty to protect British and Allied shipping from the newest German menace, the u-boat.

Located in an old hospital building on the grounds of the Halifax naval base, the Royal Naval College of Canada accommodates forty-five cadets in the main building. Nearby are a small electrical laboratory, an engineering shop, a mechanical drawing classroom, a gym, a sick bay, and a small boathouse. The cadets play sports on a field to the west of Admiralty House on Gottingen Street. Kingsley and his thirteen classmates, all between fourteen and sixteen years of age, will spend the next three years studying a mixture of academic and practical seamanship. The academic curriculum consists of mathematics, physics, chemistry, engineering, physical and recreational training, geography, history (including naval history), English, French, and German. The cadets also learn navigation, mechanics, and pilotage. The curriculum is not much different from that of the Royal Naval College in the United Kingdom, but the facilities are not as good and the course of study is shorter. At the end of the academic course the successful candidates will graduate as Midshipmen (not yet commissioned officers but, in theory, higher in rank than the ratings) and go to sea on a Royal Navy cruiser to gain practical experience.

The atmosphere at the Royal Naval College of Canada is distinctly English public school. The boys wear uniforms to class, salute their officer instructors, and learn drill. They are taught comportment fitting for young officers-to-be. There is a major emphasis on sports. Rugby, soccer, and baseball teach teamwork, keep bodies taut, and imbue the boys with a spirit of cooperation, fair play, and the will to win. In their few off-hours, the boys walk the wharfside streets of Halifax and engage in the usual horseplay that teenagers everywhere indulge in. They are eager. They do everything with dash and determination, to show their instructors they are made of the right material to be naval officers.

The business of preparing boys for a naval career is a serious one, especially in wartime. Harry Kingsley and the other cadets spend as much time learning how to behave as officers as they do improving their academic and practical skills. The Royal Canadian Navy barely exists on paper, but its traditions, values, and history will be those of the venerable Royal Navy, the Empire Senior Service. The instructors pound the message in daily. A British naval officer does his duty. He does not complain. He leads by example. He is compassionate and he is fair, but he is also very much in command when he needs to be. He is a superb seaman. He has five hundred years of history and tradition to uphold. He serves the greatest empire the world has yet known and he brings civilization to the darkest corners of that empire. He protects the sea lanes along which British laws and institutions flow. He never lets the side down. Already, four college graduates have given their lives for the empire. They are killed in action when the RN cruiser HMS *Good Hope* is sunk by the German Pacific Squadron off the western coast of South America on 1 November 1914. The four midshipmen are the first Canadians killed in the war.

—————————

The instructor walks through the classroom door promptly at 9 a.m. on the morning of 6 December 1917. The second class of the day is about to begin. It is cold outside and the winter sky is its usual grey. There is frost on the inside glass of the large wooden-framed windows. The radiator pipes tick and knock as the steam rushes through them. The students take pens in hand as the teacher begins to put the day's lesson on the blackboard. Suddenly a massive explosion rocks the room. The window glass is blown in; furniture, chalk, bits of plaster, glass from lightbulbs, and the bodies of students and instructors are tossed about like so much trash. The clockface is shattered; the hands stand at 9:05.

The building, the base, and much of Halifax has been devastated as the French ammunition ship *Mont Blanc* blows up in the harbour. The shock wave expands rapidly out from the epicentre of the explosion and, in seconds, virtually the entire north end of the city is levelled. Fires break out all over the devastated area. The college's main building is solidly built and doesn't collapse, but almost every wooden structure on the base is flattened. The cadets are protected from the blast by the thick stone walls. They are stunned, but as they get to their feet they realize that none of them is seriously hurt, even though sixteen hundred Haligonians have been killed and some nine thousand injured. Kingsley and his classmates run outside and immediately pitch in to help, despite the danger that fire will touch off the naval magazine. They search for bodies in the smouldering rubble. They dig out the injured and help cart food and blankets to the homeless. They see death at first hand. The war has come home to them dramatically, but their first role in this war is to save lives, not take them.

The blast damages the college beyond immediate repair. Within days, Kingsley and his classmates load their belongings onto a train and journey to Kingston, Ontario, where their classes will be continued on the grounds of the Royal Military College. In the fall of 1918 they move again to larger and better facilities at the Royal Canadian Navy base at Esquimalt, near Victoria, for their last year of study. After they move west, the sea war moves closer to Halifax. In the spring and summer of 1918 the German navy sends its large U-cruisers to the coast of North America. There they find ships sailing alone, and sinkings mount. *U156* destroys two large schooners off Sable Island in July, and a third off the Fundy shore at the beginning of August. The schooner's crew row ashore and the news quickly flashes up and down the Nova Scotia coast. Halifax is rife with rumour. Seven more schooners go down. Convoy sailings are delayed. The Americans, in the war since the spring of 1917, send small submarine-chasers to strengthen the convoy escorts. On 5 August a British tanker is stopped and then sunk only 17 miles from Sambro Light.

On 8 August the Canadian and the Australian Corps on the Western Front spearhead the Allied attack as the Battle of Amiens is launched in eastern France. It is a major defeat for the German army and the beginning of the end of the war. The Allies push eastward. The Germans fight hard at first, but then start to surrender in droves. In Germany, soldiers and sailors revolt. A social-democratic government takes power and sues for peace, and the guns stop firing on 11 November 1918. The First World War is over, but few of the major issues of European power politics are settled.

Harry Kingsley graduates from the Royal Naval College three and a half months after the war ends. He is now a Midshipman in a small navy no longer at war. He has grown into a young man. He is of average height and slightly built. He has a shy smile, but he keeps his own company much of the time. He faces a long journey to Portsmouth and his first assignment aboard a British warship. The war may be over, but the promise of the sea, of warships, of the comradeship of navy men, and of exotic foreign ports lures him on.

On 10 September 1918 the keel for destroyer Hull 252 is laid at the Fore River shipyard in Quincy, Massachusetts. At Fore River, just outside Boston harbour, the Bethlehem Steel Corporation is building thirty-six destroyers for the United States Navy. These vessels are part of a 273-ship destroyer flotilla rushed into production when the United States entered the war in March 1917. Only a handful have yet taken to sea, but the type is already distinctive. Although the ships vary somewhat in size, equipment, and performance, those of the Clemson Class, of which Hull 252 is one, are almost all 1190 tons displacement, a little over 314 feet long, and a mere 30.5 feet wide. Their maximum draft, always shallow for destroyers, is 12 feet.

The most distinguishing feature of these vessels is their flush decks: the forecastle is part of the main deck, which is laid on one unbroken plane from stem to stern. The forward superstructure that houses the bridge, the wheel-house, the chart-house, the captain's sea cabin, and the radio room divides the forecastle from the forward well-deck, which is not really a well-deck at all but the area between that superstructure and the midships deck-house. In most other destroyers—indeed, in most ships—the forecastle is higher than the main deck. This configuration gives the forward part of the ship more buoyancy, allowing it greater capacity to rise over a rough sea. The flush-deck design is intended to give higher freeboard at the bows to better take a heavy sea, but with a lower profile in the rear to better launch torpedoes, and greater strength amidships than in conventionally designed vessels.

The flush deck will make Hull 252 a "wet" ship. She will slice through oncoming waves rather than ride over them. Many more tons of water will crash over her forecastle in a heavy sea than will be true of other types of ships. Inevitably, some of the water will find its way along the deck and into open hatches and vents before it runs out the scuppers. The other main distinguishing feature of Hull 252 and almost all her sisters is their four tall stacks. The four-stack design is simple and straightforward, but it is obsolescent and adds additional top weight.

Hull 252 sits in dry dock as men lay the keel, attach the ribs, rivet the hull plates together and to the skeleton of the ship, and build the bulkheads, instal the watertight doors, and construct the main deck, the lower decks, and sections of the superstructure and other deck parts. The four White-Foster boilers and two Westinghouse geared turbines that will power the vessel are lifted in, made fast, and connected up. Each turbine develops some 27,000 shaft horsepower. When steaming on all four boilers and with the turbines at full speed, the destroyer will be capable of 35 knots. Hull 252 and the other Clemson Class vessels are different from earlier US-built flush-deck destroyers in that she displaces from 100 to 160 tons more than they do. The extra displacement is needed for her larger tanks, which have a capacity of 375 tons of fuel oil. At her optimum cruising speed of 14 knots, she will burn 2 tons of fuel per hour. At 10 knots, she can steam some 4000 nautical miles; at double that speed, her range drops to about 2500 nautical miles. Very high speeds will reduce that range considerably.

In January 1919 twin shafts and screws and outrigger-type screw-guards are installed on Hull 252, one guard on each side at the stern. By 31 January 1919 she is ready for the water. The champagne bottle smashes into her bow, she is christened USS *McCook*, and sent down the ways into the waters of the Fore River. As with most of the flush-deck destroyers, she is named for a notable figure in US naval history. Commander Roderick S. McCook served in the United States Navy in the mid-nineteenth century, capturing slave ships off the coast of Africa and participating in the American Civil War. After the war he commanded US warships on the West India and Asiatic stations.

After *McCook* settles into the water, she is towed, pushed, and nudged into place alongside her sisters, all in various stages of completion. The four stacks are constructed, one for each boiler, and the remainder of the deck structures are completed. The crew quarters, officers cabins, wardrooms, and galley are fitted out. Voice tubes and telephone lines are installed. The masts go up and the wireless equipment is put into place. A searchlight tower is constructed on the aft deck-house. Deck vents are included to pull air below decks, especially to the boiler room, which is to be pressurized to prevent flashbacks. In the last stages of construction, the armament is installed. There are four 4-inch guns, one on the forecastle, one on the quarterdeck, and two high on the midships deck-house, one on each side. That deck-house contains the galley and sits in between numbers 2 and 3 stacks. The front gun has a partially enclosed gunshield; the others do not. A 3-inch high-angle gun is installed atop the rear deck-house. Inside that structure are the torpedo shop and the crew's head (toilets).

McCook's main armament is not her guns but her torpedoes. Four batteries of three 21-inch torpedo tubes are installed on her main deck, two on each side staggered fore and aft. The torpedoes are her *raison d'être*. Like the other destroyers taking shape beside her, *McCook* is designed as a fast, light, torpedo-launching ship. Her major purpose in life is to accompany the main fleet into battle, rush ahead at the first sign of the enemy, and, in echelon formation, deliver high-speed torpedo attacks against the enemy's capital ships. The four torpedo batteries add yet more top weight. The length of its hull compared with its narrow beam width means that *McCook* will be a lively ship in a heavy sea, but she is not intended to hunt submarines or to escort convoys through the wildly heaving seas of a North Atlantic winter. She is designed primarily to operate in the warm and usually placid waters of the Caribbean.

McCook and her sister ships have evolved from the small 200-ton torpedo-boat destroyers of the late nineteenth century. These destroyers were originally designed to defend capital ships against small, fast torpedo boats built to launch the Whitehead self-propelled torpedo. Usually no more than 50 to 60 tons, the torpedo boats were capable of neutralizing capital ships that were far larger and more expensive to build. They were so fast that modern cruisers or battleships could not bring their larger guns to bear on them during an attack. The problem was partly solved by the mounting of quick-firing guns on the beams of the larger warships and partly by the invention of the turbine-driven torpedo-boat destroyer. These latter vessels mounted both guns and torpedoes and were capable of speeds fast enough to catch and destroy torpedo boats. By the outbreak of the First World War, virtually all sea-faring powers had torpedo-boat destroyers. The newest, called simply "destroyers," displaced 1000 tons and mounted multiple gun and torpedo batteries.

As *McCook* nears completion, Lieutenant-Commander G.B. Ashe, USN, is assigned to command her and a crew is gathered to be delivered dockside before she sails. Early on the morning of 21 April 1919 *McCook* is towed to an oiler, made fast, and loaded with fuel oil. Then Ashe noses her carefully downriver to Boston harbour, just a few miles away. *McCook* carries a young and inexperienced crew. Aboard are representatives of Bethlehem Steel. Her fresh grey paint is broken only by the large "252" pendant numbers painted on her bows and the black tops of her funnels. A wisp of white smoke follows her as she eases her way past river craft and makes for a mooring buoy at President's Roads. She comes up smartly, with not too much way on, and is quickly shackled to the buoy. Her boarding ladders are lowered and a navy launch carrying Rear-Admiral George W. Kline, Captain John G. Tawresey, and Commander John M. Schelling noses up to her side just a few minutes after 9 a.m. These officers are the examination board. They and the contractor's agents will watch carefully as Ashe puts *McCook* through a standard set of tests designed to measure her performance. *McCook* will not be officially commissioned until the US Navy is satisfied that Bethlehem Steel has delivered her as specified.

The trial begins as the navy launch pulls away. Ashe orders his executive officer to take *McCook* into Massachusetts Bay. Within three-quarters of an hour, they arrive at their start point. Ashe orders "all ahead full," and *McCook* leaps forward as her screws bite into the waters of the bay. It is a beautiful sunny day, not too hot and with barely a breeze rippling the water. With the bridge revolution counter showing 420, *McCook* carves the waters of the bay, her bow plume spraying almost as high as her main deck, then trailing away into an ever widening wake. Less than two hours into the run she suddenly loses steam pressure and her speed decreases rapidly. Someone has forgotten to watch the fuel levels and neglects to ensure that the pumps in the second tank are started up when the first runs dry. The problem is quickly fixed. Again, *McCook* rushes forward at high speed.

For almost six hours, the navy board puts the destroyer through her paces. She is run full ahead and full astern. Her steering gear is tested at full power. Her emergency hand-wheel steering is tested. Her right shaft is run forward and her left in reverse. Then her left is run forward and her right in reverse. How low does her stern dip as she accelerates?

What is her freeboard at the bow in a high-speed turn? What is her displacement with half her fuel gone? How quickly does she respond to manoeuvring orders from the bridge? What happens when full-speed astern is ordered when she is racing ahead at 35 knots and her turbines are turning her shafts at more than 400 revolutions? Everything is carefully noted as Ashe heads her back to her mooring in Boston harbour late in the afternoon. For the most part, she fits the bill, but the board notes that there are still many difficulties with her steering gear. The most serious problems are a slackness in the chains that connect the rudder wheel to the steam-driver steering engine and a looseness in the clutch mechanism on the steering engine. The manufacturer undertakes to fix the problems, and the navy declares *McCook* sound and ready for sea. On the last day of April, the US flag is hoisted on her quarterdeck and she becomes the latest destroyer to join the lists of the US Navy.

The US Navy has got what it wanted: a fast, graceful, fair-weather ship, capable of delivering more torpedoes in two salvos—one from port and one from starboard—than any destroyer in service with any navy. To the Americans, that advantage outweighs any disadvantages *McCook* might suffer as a result of her design or quick construction. But in truth those disadvantages are many. Her paint flakes off too easily, leaving bare metal exposed to salt water and the salt sea air. The steering problems noted by the navy board are not completely fixed. She heels over too much in a tight turn or in a heavy beam sea. Her low stern is easily crashed by a following sea, and her quarterdeck is small and cramped. Her wide turning circle is more akin to that of a small cruiser than a destroyer, and her screws are too close together for easy manoeuvring in close quarters. She ships tons of sea water in an ahead sea. Her steering mechanism is an engineer's nightmare; the helm is connected to the steam-driven steering engine by wires that run unprotected through the engine and boiler rooms. This arrangement may be adequate for fleet work, but is not reliable for the constant manoeuvring that is a necessary part of convoy escort duty. The subdivision of the hull, designed to create twelve separate watertight compartments, is poor. A large hatchway through the weather deck leading to the crew's quarters isn't even watertight. Missing and corroded rivets in her hull and her tanks pose a constant danger that sea water will adulterate the fuel in her bunkers.

McCook is first assigned to Destroyer Force, Atlantic Fleet, and cruises the Atlantic coast and the Caribbean. Once the war is over, however, the US Navy has too many destroyers. In the spring of 1922 *Mc-Cook* is selected for decommissioning. Towards the end of June, she noses into a berth at the Boston Navy Yard, where tens of her sister ships are lashed to each other. Her boilers are shut down and her crew debarks. A special team boards her to close her up and prepare her for her long sleep. Her hatches and scuttles are sealed; her vents and funnels are covered over. The gunshield from the forward 4-inch gun is removed and placed on her forecastle. Her torpedo batteries are removed. The water is drained from her steampipes, and the oil from her tanks. Delicate instruments such as her gyrocompass are landed. Most of her weather surfaces are covered in thick grease to combat corrosion. On 30 June 1922 the US Navy takes her name off the list of commissioned vessels. *McCook* joins the reserve fleet of almost forgotten vessels and begins her hibernation.

———————

On 5 July 1919 Midshipman Harry Kingsley can barely conceal his excitement, but he must. He is a naval officer-in-training and he should behave like one. An officer of the Royal Canadian Navy must be unflappable. Being calm, controlling one's emotions, is something all men who aspire to command one of His Majesty's warships must learn.

Kingsley has been at the great, historic naval base of Plymouth since the previous April. The sights and sounds of the base are like nothing he had ever imagined. In the harbour, some of His Majesty's largest and most powerful warships lie moored. Kingsley knows them by heart. There is HMS *Benbow*, a pre-war Dreadnought mounting 13.5-inch guns, late of the 4th Division, 4th Battle Squadron, of Lord Jellicoe's Grand Fleet. She is a veteran of Jutland. There is the newer HMS *Royal Sovereign*, a battleship carrying massive 15-inch main guns. She is moored near HMS *Iron Duke*, Jellicoe's flagship at Jutland. To Kingsley, the massive main guns of these monster ships signify the power and the majesty of the British Empire. He is moved by the very sight of them.

All over the harbour, battleships, battle cruisers, heavy cruisers, light cruisers, and destroyers lie shackled to their moorings. Alongside the docks are smaller vessels—lighters, tugboats, and fleet oilers. Small craft churn up the waters—whalers and motor launches from the ships, mail boats, and civilian bum boats with goods for sale. In the massive dry docks are ships in various stages of refit or construction. One is the former battle cruiser *Courageous*; its heavy guns have been stripped away and it is being rebuilt into an aircraft carrier with an offset superstructure and flight-deck. It towers over the dock. The sounds of ships under refit—rivet hammers, drills, and saws—mingle with the harbour sounds of bosuns' pipes, motor launches, ships' horns, and bells clanging the end and beginning of watches. Kingsley absorbs it all and breathes in the salt air, with its smell of tar, fuel oil, and seaweed.

For three months Kingsley has sat in his classroom at HMS *Excellent*, the RN gunnery school, and concentrated on his lessons. Sometimes he stares out the window, watching as a great warship slips its moorings and heads out to sea. But today he takes the first big step on the road to a full commission; he boards HMS *Erin*, a battleship veteran of Jutland, and, like all new Midshipmen, he is assigned to the battleship's gunroom.

"Come on, Snotty, haven't you ever been on a real warship?" the Sub-Lieutenant chides Kingsley as they head to the *Erin*'s stern. Snotty is naval jargon for Midshipman. Kingsley and the "Sub" have come across the harbour on a motor launch, climbed the boarding stairway rigged against the grey-slabbed side of the battleship, and been admitted to the main deck by the officer of the watch. The sub relishes this part of his duty; Midshipmen are the only men aboard, apart from ratings, who he can lord it over. Besides, Midshipmen are meant to be chided, and colonials like Kingsley make such good foils.

The gunroom is partitioned from the rear main guns messdeck by a canvas curtain. It is home to Midshipmen who have been assigned to *Erin* to begin their sea training. The experience is especially crucial for the handful of Royal Canadian Navy Midshipmen who can get big-ship experience in no other way than to serve with the Royal Navy. They are expected to learn the basics of their trade and, just as important, to soak up the culture and traditions of the Royal Navy at sea. Should the RCN ever go to war again, it will function once more as an adjunct to the RN.

Gunroom living teaches Midshipman Kingsley how to fit in. At first there is constant hazing from the subs, whose lives seem dedicated to making things miserable for the snottys. Sometimes that hazing is physical and downright brutal. One of the more notable trials of endurance visited on the Midshipmen is "running torpedoes." That's when some unfortunate newcomer is launched off the gunroom mess table as hard and fast as his messmates can manage. The boy who tries to shield his head or break his fall is beaten up. The more senior officers rarely engage in this sort of physical abuse; most use sarcasm and stinging personal criticism when a snotty makes a mistake, doesn't know the answer to some obscure question about the ship or its equipment, or performs some task poorly. Kingsley knows his mettle is being tested as well as his skills and knowledge, and he is determined to pass the test. He bears the physical harassment with nary a sound, and the verbal humiliation with a poker face. Being at sea on a great battleship is more than he ever imagined it would be. He is resolved to stay.

HMS *Erin* is like a self-contained floating city. Completed in 1914, she was designed and built for the Turkish navy, but appropriated by the Royal Navy at the outbreak of war. At 23,000 tons, she is protected by shipside armour-plate one foot thick; her turrets have plate almost as thick. She is wide in the beam and carries five twin turrets, each with two 13.5-inch guns. She never leaves port without her attendant cruisers and destroyers, the latter dashing madly about simulating torpedo attacks or anti-submarine sweeps. Most destroyers are now equipped with the new asdic system for sound ranging and detection of submarines under water. Asdic sends out a directed sound pulse. When it is reflected off an object and picked up by a sound-head mounted on the keel of the vessel, it indicates where that object might be. Some naval men claim that asdic renders submarine warfare obsolete. Few of them care to train on it. Anti-submarine warfare is not glamorous and holds no promise for the star-crossed who want to command big ships in a big navy.

Kingsley and the other Midshipmen are rotated through the battleship's many divisions to learn how a large ship functions. They spend time on the bridge, in the signals room, and on all types of guns. Mostly they run errands for the officers and take care of odd jobs. They are expected to pick up practical seamanship knowledge aboard ship and to learn most of the scientific skills they will need at the RN shoreside schools such as *Excellent*, *Vernon*, where the torpedo trade is taught, or *Dryad*, where they learn navigation and pilotage.

Kingsley serves aboard *Erin*, *Royal Sovereign*, *Courageous*, and *Benbow*. He is fastidious and quick to learn. He develops a clipped British accent and he is immensely proud of being a part of this mighty navy. Towards the end of June 1921 he is notified of promotion to Acting Sub-Lieutenant, a probationary rank. He spends three months learning the art of big-ship navigation at HMS *Dryad* and a year aboard the cruiser HMS *Cairo*, and is promoted to Lieutenant at the end of April 1923. The promotion has come remarkably quickly for peacetime.

In the fall of 1923 Kingsley sails back to Canada. He now sports the two gold stripes and the executive curl of a Lieutenant RCN on the sleeves of his navy-blue double-breasted jacket. At the beginning of July 1925 he is assigned to HMCS *Patrician*, one of two British destroyers built during the Great War that were handed over to the RCN by the Royal Navy in late 1920. The other destroyer is *Patriot*, and the cruiser that accompanies them is *Aurora*. *Patrician* is based at Esquimalt and cruises the Pacific coast. Each winter she heads south with her sister ship, passes through the Panama Canal, and enters the Caribbean to exercise with the Royal Navy's Atlantic and West Indies Squadron. The sun-baked Mexican ports of call such as Ensenada or Manzanillo provide some shore amusement for Kingsley and the other officers and ratings when *Patrician* stops to oil. But the Mexican towns pale beside Kingston in Jamaica, Hamilton in Bermuda, or Nassau in the Bahamas. The gaiety at these ports seems unending. There is cheap overproof rum, island music, and attractive, brightly clad girls.

For the RCN, the annual Caribbean exercises are a chance to show the flag in an area that is increasingly significant in Canadian commerce; more important, they are also a chance to exercise alongside the Royal Navy. Kingsley's specialties of communications and navigation are particularly useful as the Canadian destroyers practise high-speed torpedo attacks against the larger vessels of the main British squadron. Kingsley spends no time learning anti-submarine countermeasures or the tricks of the asdic trade.

For ten days in 1926, Kingsley gets a brief taste of command. He is temporarily placed in charge of the First World War–vintage Battle Class trawler HMCS *Armentières*, based at Esquimalt. She is small, slow, obsolete, and lightly armed, but she is a first command. Command of any ship is a most important position. As captain, Kingsley has the last word on everything on board his vessel. The men and the ship in his charge are his responsibility alone. There is no one else to seek guidance from, or to lean on, when at sea. For the first time Kingsley learns that command is lonely, even on a small vessel, and wonders what it must be like in charge of a larger, more complex, and more important warship. He spends only one week aboard *Armentières*, then returns to administrative and staff work ashore. Even in a small navy, there are reports to write, forms to complete, personnel to manage, and repairs and supplies to oversee. Harry would much rather be at sea, but he has learned not to complain and he does his work diligently. Besides, spending summer and fall in Victoria is not a hardship. The city is small, but the parks, golf courses, and tennis courts are green and well kept in the English fashion, and Kingsley has many friends and companions living on or near the base. The weather is usually ideal for late afternoon cocktail parties, and life ashore is a constant round of dinner, drinks, and dancing, especially when a British warship comes calling.

In 1928 Kingsley returns to Portsmouth for more training and more sea duty. He serves aboard the battleships *Benbow* and *Iron Duke* and the cruiser *Lucia*. He does well in the torpedo course and begins to learn the rudiments of asdic and submarine detection. He continues to specialize in signals and communication, and successfully completes the long course given at HMS *Victory*. From now on he is considered a qualified signals and communications specialist. When not standing his regular watch on a bridge, he will be responsible for the welfare and discipline of the men of the signalling trades and for all communication to and from the ship. He's an expert in the various methods of visual signalling with code flags, semaphore, and signal lamp, as well as in short- and long-range radio transmission.

Kingsley performs well enough in this task and in other jobs, but he almost never impresses his superiors as being especially talented. Throughout the decade his all-important, semi-annual, fitness reports almost always describe him as "average" or "satisfactory." His superiors think of him as "quiet" or "pleasant" or "studious." One finds little more to say about him than that he is a "good dancer." Almost no one describes him in anything other than general terms. He is being damned with faint praise. He does not show superior leadership qualities. The fitness reports change little as the new decade dawns. He is careful, perhaps too careful. He always consults his superiors before making an important decision. He may well make a good staff officer, the navy seems to be saying, but whether he will be able to command a ship at sea is still an open question.

The RCN is in a state of crisis when Kingsley returns to Halifax at the end of 1930. The service barely survives the first years of the Great Depression. In April 1931, however, Kingsley is promoted to lieutenant-commander and posted to Esquimalt as signals officer on the brand new RCN River Class destroyer HMCS *Saguenay*. He serves two years aboard *Saguenay*, then leaves Esquimalt for another stint with the Royal Navy, where he is eventually assigned to the battleship HMS *Rodney*. Completed in 1927, *Rodney* is by far Britain's mightiest ship. She displaces almost 34,000 tons, and carries nine 16-inch guns as main armament. Kingsley is put in charge of the battleship's communications division. He commands a department of two other officers, two petty officers, and twelve ratings. His chief responsibility is the large radio room, with its many different radios of varying frequency ranges used for keeping in touch with other ships and shore stations. In the event of war, *Rodney* will carry an Admiral's flag and be the nerve-centre for a fleet. Kingsley runs a tight department. He is a strict disciplinarian with the ratings, though he fits in easily with the other officers in the wardroom. He soon develops a reputation for his quick wit and dry sense of humour. He is now a senior RCN officer with heavy responsibilities on Britain's most important warship. He has made the grade.

While in England, Kingsley sees at first hand the gathering of the war clouds in Europe and the slow but steady expansion of the British fleet. Like most military men, he has a decided distaste for politics and politicians. He cannot decide if Adolf Hitler is crazy, power mad, or simply good at bluffing. He has nothing personal against the Germans and, in fact, believes they were given a raw deal at the end of the Great War. But like most RN officers, he knows that if war comes, Germany will be the main antagonist, and that he and his colleagues must do their duty no matter how right or wrong the Germans may be. He gives little thought to the great issues of power politics.

Kingsley returns to Canada at the end of 1936 and, in the spring of 1938, takes command of the recently commissioned Fundy Class minesweeper HMCS *Nootka*. He has now spent more than twenty years learning his trade, and the RCN has invested much in him. But he does not yet feel comfortable in command. Although his two officers are RCN regulars, with big-ship time in the Royal Navy, the other thirty-five members of *Nootka*'s company are almost all Canadians. They are not as deferential as the highly class-conscious British. He feels that discipline is too loose on his ship, and he tends to take his frustrations out on his junior officers. As the diplomatic crisis deepens in Europe, he wants to get back to the United Kingdom. He asks for transfer and, after five months, he is reassigned to shore to join the staff of the Commanding Officer Pacific Coast as a signals specialist. His plans to return to Britain are cut short a day later when Hitler invades Poland. The Canadian armed forces are on a state of alert, and not a single man of the small navy can be spared.

McCook sleeps as the world drifts towards war. Some of her sisters remain in service with the United States Navy as destroyers, fast minelayers, even radio-controlled target ships, but most sleep in the harbours of San Diego, New York, Portsmouth, Norfolk, Charleston, Philadelphia, and Boston. In 1931 *McCook* is towed from Boston to Philadelphia when the US Navy decides to mothball most of its east-coast destroyers in one or two places so as to simplify the routine maintenance and inspection it performs on these vessels. By the end of the year some sixty flush-deck destroyers are secured alongside each other at the Philadelphia Navy Yard.

On the afternoon of 6 July 1933 six navy officers board *McCook* for a routine inspection. They constitute a board of inspection and survey charged under USN regulations with ascertaining *McCook*'s condition and reporting to the navy on her state of suspended animation. With clipboards in hand, they work their way systematically from bow to stern. They open her inspection hatches, shine their flashlights into her fuel tanks and boilers, and check her steampipes, steering gear, and living quarters. What is the state of her hull above and below the waterline? What is the condition of the water in her bilges? Are her fuel tanks dry, as they should be? Is there inordinate leakage of water anywhere? How are gaskets, seals, and watertight doors holding up? Do the officers' heads work? Is the electrical system still functioning? It is a long day, hot and humid in the Navy Yard, but by nightfall the job is done. For a ship almost fifteen years old, decommissioned for more than a decade, *McCook* is judged to be in good shape. She will, however, need a new set of radios to replace her obsolete spark-type transmitter, and she will also need sound-detection and ranging gear (asdic to the British, sonar to the Americans) for anti-submarine work.

When the Second World War opens in Europe, the United States is officially neutral. Within hours of the outbreak of war, German submarine *U30* sinks the British-registered passenger liner *Athenia* 240 miles west of Ireland. Washington is quickly reminded that US neutrality on the high seas must ultimately be protected by the US Navy. Since the rise of the fascist powers in the early 1930s, the United States has been building modern destroyers to add to, and ultimately to replace, the aging four-stackers launched between 1917 and 1919. Some sixty of the new Farragut, Porter, Mahan, Somers, Gridley and Bagley Class destroyers have come sliding down the ways. Almost forty more destroyers of the Sims, Benham, and Benson Class are under construction. But *McCook* and her sisters are still badly needed; the United States has two long coastlines and is a major maritime power. In Philadelphia Navy Yard and other yards around the country, men begin to walk the main decks of the First World War destroyers once more. Like the men who came in the early 1930s, they too have clipboards in hand and carry flashlights, and they too poke into boilers, inspection hatches, and fuel tanks. Unlike those earlier inspectors, however, these men are not only interested in fulfilling naval inspection regulations. They are selecting sixty-eight of these old destroyers to be brought back to life to play a role in this newest conflict.

The US government calls it the "Neutrality Patrol." Its avowed intention is to cruise the waters of the Atlantic coast to ensure the safety of US shipping and the free passage of US commerce. Its real intention is to keep the Germans away. The job is perfect for the obsolescent flush-deck destroyers because, for the most part, they will simply need to show the flag to signify the US presence and the willingness of the republic to protect its interests. They are not expected or intended to fight. The plan is to select the sixty-eight most seaworthy, bring them back into commission, fix their ailments, modernize whatever basic equipment (such as

radios) needs updating, and add submarine-detection gear before form-
ing them into new destroyer divisions (DesDivs) and sending them to
sea. *McCook* gets the call on 18 December 1939. She will become part of
DesDiv 73 and proceed to the sprawling US Navy base at Norfolk, Virginia, after refitting at New York Navy Yard. She arrives in New York on
15 April 1940; she is due to sail in early June.

McCook needs lots of work. She has no major engineering defects,
but she cannot operate at speed; she needs bearings and journals replaced in both her turbines and in her reduction gearing. She also needs
sound-detection gear, a new searchlight tower, remounting of her aft 4-
inch gun, repairs to her fire-fighting system, additional bunks for her
crew, more lockers, modernized cooking equipment for her galleys, and
many other improvements. The navy has allocated about $20,000 for
each ship. It is not enough. *McCook* sits high and dry on blocks in her
dry dock as the Navy Yard scrambles to make do. She is not ready until
August; by then, the war has taken a nasty turn for the Allies.

––––––––––––

At the very outbreak of the war the Admiralty institutes a convoy system to protect transatlantic shipping. Convoys had been critical in
blunting the German u-boat campaign during the First World War,
and Prime Minister Winston Churchill has been an avid advocate of
convoying since 1916. The convoys soon develop a routine. Early in the
war, they average about forty merchant ships arrayed in six to ten serried columns; after 1943, convoys of ninety or more ships will become
common. Operational experience will eventually teach the Admiralty
"the law of convoy size": whereas escorts protect the convoy's perimeter
and not the individual ships within, and whereas the perimeter of a
large convoy is only slightly larger than that of a small convoy, "the area
occupied by the ships increases as the square, while the perimeter is directly proportional to the length of the radius." In plain language, what
counts is not the ratio of ships to escorts, but the ratio of the attack area
around a convoy to the number of close escorts. The greater the number of ships to be convoyed, the further the Admiralty can spread the
number of warships then available. Westbound North Atlantic convoys
are code-named ON (fast) and ONS (slow); eastbound convoys HX (fast)

and SC (slow). Later in the war United States to Gibraltar convoys will be code-named UGS; Gibraltar to United States convoys GUS. Gibraltar to Great Britain convoys will become MKS; and Great Britain to Gibraltar KMS.

The Royal Canadian Navy helps by controlling ship movements out of east-coast Canadian ports and assigning as much of its small destroyer fleet as it can to escort the convoys. On 16 September 1939 HMCS *Fraser* and *St Laurent* depart Halifax to escort convoy HX1 to the Grand Banks off Newfoundland. The Admiralty is well aware of the threat that U-boats pose to Allied shipping, but in the first eight months of the war they believe that German surface raiders are an even greater menace. And so they are. Most of Germany's still small fleet of submarines are of the Type VIIC variety. There are only forty-six of them. They have a limited range of 6240 miles and can reach the Atlantic from their Baltic Sea ports only by sailing north around Scotland. Since one-third are either going to or from their bases at any given time, and one-third are in port to be rearmed and replenished, the German navy can deploy an average of fewer than seven boats in the Atlantic at any given time. That number is even further reduced when Hitler decides to invade Norway in April 1940, and most of the U-boat fleet is sent to Norwegian waters. All that soon changes, however. On 10 May 1940 Germany invades France; by mid-June, France is defeated and its Biscay Bay ports are open to the Germans. From St Nazaire, Brest, Lorient, and La Rochelle, the U-boats can now sail directly to the mid-Atlantic. *U30* enters Lorient on 6 July, inaugurating a new and much deadlier phase in the German war against Allied shipping. Tonnage lost to submarine attack virtually doubles to some 700,000 tons in the third quarter of 1940.

Five days after Germany attacks France, British Prime Minister Winston Churchill approaches US President Franklin D. Roosevelt to request direct US aid for the British war effort. He specifically asks the United States to loan Britain forty to fifty destroyers until UK warships then being built are ready for service. Roosevelt at first refuses, citing congressional opposition, but Churchill persists. On 1 August Roosevelt relents. With the fall of France, the intensification of U-boat attacks in the Atlantic, and the Democratic Party nomination for an unprecedented third term under his belt, FDR sends a message to London suggesting that the United States make fifty destroyers available to the United Kingdom in return for rights to bases on British possessions from the Caribbean to Newfoundland. This initiative launches several weeks of intense negotiations which formally culminate in an agreement that Britain will lease bases in Newfoundland, Bermuda, British Guyana, and the West Indies to the United States for ninety-nine years in return for fifty flush-deck destroyers.

As the talks proceed, the Admiralty approaches the Royal Canadian Navy to ask for help. The Royal Navy has too few trained crew to operate fifty additional destroyers and wants the RCN to man as many of the vessels as it can. The RN also approaches the Australians and other Allies with the same request. It seeks Canadian permission to use the RCN base at Halifax to effect the transfer of these ships from the US Navy to the Royal Navy, should it take place. The RCN is in a quandary at the first request. Having entered the war with only ten modern vessels, it is at the start of a massive expansion program of its own based mainly on the construction and manning of single-screw Flower Class corvettes. It is rushing raw recruits through its own training establishments as fast as it can, and it is literally throwing crews together as soon as new ships are ready to sail. The RCN is calling every available Royal Canadian Naval Reserve (RCNR) officer to command these ships. These RCNR officers are usually men with extensive deep-sea experience in merchant vessels. The navy even places officers from the Royal Canadian Naval Volunteer Reserve (RCNVR) in command of its smaller vessels. These "wavy-navy" types (so-called because of the wavy gold stripes on their sleeves) generally have little more than short stints of reserve duty at sea under their belts. Almost none of the escort ships the RCN sends to sea receive any operational training experience whatever.

Despite the severe shortage of suitable officers and crew, the RCN initially agrees to man four of the old destroyers and, in mid-August, six. It will do so only if the ships are transferred outright to the RCN, instead of being owned by the Royal Navy and manned by Canadians. The RCN also promises to send four of the destroyers to UK waters, to increase the Canadian destroyer flotilla operating there to eight. These other four ships are River Class destroyers. The Admiralty quickly agrees.

By late August the plans for the transfer are in place. After being readied for the turnover, the fifty destroyers will be sailed by US crews to Halifax in groups of eight every two weeks, or as UK or Canadian crews are made ready, then decommissioned from the US Navy. UK crews will then man the vessels and commission them into the Royal Navy or the Royal Canadian Navy. The Admiralty decides to rename the ships after towns common to Britain, the United States, or the British colonies where the US-leased bases will be established. The Canadians decide to name their destroyers after five rivers that cross the Canada–US border (the Columbia, Niagara, St Clair, St Francis, and St Croix rivers) and one that is common to both countries—the Annapolis Rivers of Nova Scotia and Maryland. (Two further flush-deck destroyers will be transferred to the RCN from the RN in 1941 and 1943.) All fifty vessels will be known as Town Class destroyers. Canada pays nothing for its ships, but assumes full costs of repairs, alterations, and the fitting of new equipment. As far as the Admiralty is concerned, these ships are so old that their only real monetary value is for scrap; the cost of their upkeep will probably prove equal to their book value.

In late August the one thousand officers and men of the Royal Navy chosen to man the US-built destroyers sail from Portsmouth for Halifax. At the same time, the US Navy selects fifty of its flush-deck destroyers for transfer. Like *McCook*, the great majority have been recommissioned, but six are still in mothballs and two have actually been consigned for scrap. Everything possible is done to prepare the ships for transfer. All repairs are hurriedly completed. The ships' superstructures are painted, as are the hulls above the waterline. Everything is thoroughly cleaned, the galleys are stocked with provisions, and electrical systems, depth-charge and torpedo systems, asdic gear (twelve of the ships are to be transferred without this equipment), boilers, engines, and galleys are carefully checked. Spare parts are loaded aboard. Even the china in the officers' wardrooms is cleaned and carefully stacked away.

At 8 a.m. on 31 August 1940, eight ships from DesDivs 65 and 67 sail from Norfolk, Virginia, for Boston. After stopping at Philadelphia and Newport to take on torpedoes and additional supplies, they arrive in Boston harbour between 2 and 4 September. Someone in the new Bureau of Ships (BUSHIPS) in Washington suddenly discovers that a number of the destroyers have not been recently dry docked, and seven ships from this first contingent are removed for a quick hull scraping and painting. All eight ships then sail for Halifax, arriving on 6 September at almost the same hour as the British sailors. The destroyers are accompanied by the flotilla leader USS *Russell*, a Sims Class destroyer, and the destroyer tender USS *Denebola*. The *Denebola* is a floating supply base and destroyer repair facility. Its machine and repair shops and its parts shelves are well stocked, and its crew of technicians, mechanics, and specialists is ready to render last-minute assistance. The *Denebola*'s presence is crucial, because many of the repairs and modifications the destroyers will need are beyond the knowledge or the capacity of the RCN.

The eight US destroyers rest on the north side of Pier B and are given a careful once-over by the British crews that will man them. With their enclosed bridges, four stacks, and narrow hulls, they look strange to the British sailors. Few of these men have had any real sea experience. Most of the officers are either elderly or very young, and almost all are Royal Naval Volunteer Reserve. They quickly pitch in to help the US sailors ready the ships for transfer. The Americans remove the confidential code-books, ships' logs, and equipment that the British will not need or want. Everything taken off the destroyers is transferred to the *Denebola*. The American sailors give the British sailors instruction in the use of equipment that is not familiar to them, such as the US-designed asdic equipment. They go over long lists of weapons, ammunition, food stocks, and other supplies to be handed over. They point out the foibles and possible failures of the ships. They work fast, because the Admiralty has sent word that the modifications it wants carried out to the destroyers cannot be done in Canada, so the destroyers must sail for the United Kingdom as soon as possible. All goes quickly and the sailors of the two nations get on well together.

In a simple ceremony at 10 a.m. on 9 September, the captains of the US destroyers order the US flag hauled down on all eight vessels while most of their officers and men stand at attention on the piers beside the ships. Many of the American crew members have lumps in their throats as Old Glory is lowered. The flags are carefully folded and handed to the captains, who then lead their men off the pier to a train waiting at the Halifax railway station. Within the hour they leave for Boston, as the British crews march onto the piers, take formal possession of the destroyers, and hoist the White Ensign.

As soon as the Americans leave, a team of RN officer inspectors under the command of Captain Taprell Dorling scrambles aboard. They find the ships exceptionally clean and well stocked, with full supplies of stores and ammunition, navigation instruments, electric coffee makers in the wardrooms, blank log books, pens, ink, mattresses, sheets, pillows and pillow cases, and even mechanical pencil sharpeners. To their amazement, the ships' storerooms are chock full of canned meats, fruit, and vegetables far superior in both quality and quantity to the usual RN fare. But they also find that the ships need major modifications before they can function as modern warships. Some of the ships still lack modern radios and sound-detection equipment. The asdic sets on the vessels so equipped are much different from those used by the Royal Navy. The bridge structure is not thought strong enough to endure a heavy North Atlantic sea. The ships are top heavy and the steering gear is frail. Some hatch covers are defective. There are corroded spots on the superstructure, especially on the stacks. The fresh-water tanks and delivery system need repair. The darkening-ship arrangements have to be modified. Hull corrosion and missing rivets are allowing water to leak into the fuel tanks. There are machinery and electrical defects, and the telegraph controls need repair.

Some immediate improvements have to be made to lessen top weight. Among them, the main mast will need to be replaced by a short stump rigged to carry the wireless antennas. The foremast must be shortened and the searchlight platform attached to it taken off. Portions of the bridge must be cut away. Fifty tons of pig-iron ballast have to be loaded in the hull as low down as possible. Later, in the United Kingdom, much more will need to be done to these ships, including the removal of three of the four torpedo batteries, three of the four 4-guns, and the cutting down of the three aftermost stacks. After all, these ships are to be used as anti-submarine escort vessels, not torpedo-firing fleet destroyers.

The six flush-deck destroyers originally selected for transfer to the Royal Canadian Navy are from DesDivs 69 and 73. *McCook* is attached to the latter. She is one of only two "long-legged" Town Class ships with a 375-ton bunker capacity given to the RCN. Under the command of Commander J.K. Davis, USN, she slips her mooring in Boston harbour on 19 September and heads to sea with her five consorts, USS *Mackenzie*, USS

Haraden, USS *Thatcher*, USS *Bancroft*, and USS *Williams*. Early the next morning the six vessels, moving in line-ahead formation, steam past the Sambro Light, anchored in the southeast approaches to Halifax harbour. As they close the harbour entrance, they exchange signals with the boarding-service vessel, which then approaches alongside the lead destroyer so that a pilot and a liaison officer can clamber aboard. The boom defence gate is opened and the ships slide through into the harbour itself. To the starboard is Dartmouth; to port lies Halifax; ahead is the Narrows. It is a harbour at war; the merchant ships moored in Bedford Basin are gathering for the next transatlantic convoy. The RN and RCN destroyers, corvettes, and minesweepers in the inner harbour are awaiting orders to escort this soon-to-be-born convoy or other convoys. They are anchored in the harbour or berthed alongside dockyard wharfs and jetties. Lighters, power boats, harbour craft, and ferries cross the cold waters, which are fouled with fuel oil, tar, and effluent from ships and land. The harbour resonates with the sounds of gulls, ships under repair, ships loading, ships arriving and departing, bells and horns and bosuns' pipes.

The six US destroyers anchor in the South Basin. Harbour craft carrying five RCN officers and fifty ratings for each ship nose alongside. As soon as the Canadian sailors are aboard, the destroyers weigh anchor and turn back out to sea for a four-hour familiarization run at 15 knots. Then they return to harbour and secure alongside Pier 40, just astern of the *Denebola* and the *Russell*. The Canadians disembark and return to their barracks at HMCS *Stadacona*, the RCN's shoreside Halifax establishment. Many of these men have been waiting in Halifax for months for a sea berth. They have come from across the country for basic training and they want to get into action, but there are just too few new RCN ships to accommodate most of them. So they spend the eventful summer of 1940 watching warships come and go, while they load and unload warships, clean warships' boilers, and scrape warships' bottoms. Other men are withdrawn from Canada's three armed merchant cruisers, HMCS *Prince Robert*, HMCS *Prince David*, and HMCS *Prince Henry*, for service in the six destroyers. Almost nine hundred of these men will soon find new homes aboard the old four-stackers.

The American officers and men work hard alongside the Canadians to effect the transfer. They are welcomed with open arms by the people

of Halifax and they are on their best behaviour. The officers are enter-
tained at Admiralty House on the 21st, and the ratings in the base gym-
nasium the next day. But the work goes on. *Denebola's* machine shops
are busy night and day making repairs to engine parts, pumps, hatch
covers, and other defective equipment. The Americans familiarize the
Canadians with the vessels. At 8 a.m. on 24 September the destroyers
slip from Pier B and move up harbour to No. 5 Jetty in the RCN dockyard. The US sailors' personal gear is carried off and brought to a waiting train. At 3 p.m., the US flags are hauled down on all six ships, and
the US crews leave the base and walk a few hundred yards to a train
waiting on a new nearby siding. The Canadian crews then board the
vessels. Just after 4 p.m., with flags flying and massed buglers blowing a
salute, the Union Jack and the White Ensign are raised. USS *McCook* is
no more; a successor destroyer of the Bristol Class will be commissioned into the USN in mid-March 1943. In this way, HMCS *St Croix* joins
the active list of His Majesty's Canadian ships. Her captain is Morson
Alexander Medland, RCN. A Lieutenant, Medland is a gunnery specialist and a ten-year veteran of the navy. Like most RCN officers, he has cut
his teeth on the big ships of the Royal Navy and has taken instruction in
navigation, gunnery, and other essential skills at the RN's various shoreside establishments in the United Kingdom.

Not long after the fall of France, Naval Service Headquarters in Ottawa
orders Kingsley and a large number of Esquimalt's RCN officers to Halifax. Every experienced man who can be spared is needed on the east
coast as the crisis in the North Atlantic mounts. Kingsley will join HMCS
Prince David as that ship's First Lieutenant-Commander. Kingsley
knows he will not likely return to Esquimalt any time soon, and takes
time to make arrangements for his family to transfer also. It is a bad
time to move. The government has decided to send the 20,000 soldiers
of the 2nd Canadian Infantry Division overseas. The division is based
primarily in western Canada and, throughout the late spring and summer of 1940, the trains rumbling east are packed with soldiers. The
United Kingdom is in danger of invasion, and the soldiers have first priority. Kingsley doesn't arrive in Halifax until early September. His new

ship is a 5700-ton converted Canadian National Steamships vessel taken over from that company by the RCN at the outbreak of war. It and two sister ships, *Prince Henry* and *Prince Robert*, have had their upper decks removed and have been armed with four 6-inch and two 3-inch guns and fitted with warship bridges and superstructures. Their role is to provide convoys with a modicum of protection against German surface raiders. In truth, however, if a well-armed German cruiser or pocket battleship should attack one of those convoys, *Prince David* could do little more than commit suicide by engaging her foe while her merchant charges slips away. That is precisely what happens to the British armed merchant cruiser *Jervis Bay* on 5 November 1940 when the pocket battleship *Admiral Scheer* attacks convoy HX84. *Jervis Bay* is sunk in less than half an hour, but most of the convoy escapes.

Kingsley has just enough time to begin familiarizing himself with his new vessel and shipmates when new orders arrive. He is to leave *Prince David* and report aboard HMCS *Annapolis* as an Acting Commander to assume the position of Senior Officer, Group C2 Destroyer Escorts. For the time being he will be in charge of the initial flotilla of Canadian Town Class ships. His first mission is to arrange a work-up for the six destroyers in Shelburne, Nova Scotia, 100 miles to the southwest of Halifax. Kingsley oversees a six-hour speed and steering trial for the vessels on 27 September; four days later, he leads them into Shelburne harbour.

The destroyers take to sea for basic manoeuvring tests for Commanding Officers and Officers of the Watch on the 3rd. In the next few days the crews are drilled on the basics of ship routine: watches at sea; watches in port; action stations; close up for leaving and entering harbour. Special sea-duty men are selected. There are depth-charge and torpedo exercises, and gunnery practices against surface and air targets. Over the weekend, *St Croix*'s new pendant number "I-81" is painted on both her bows. There is no time to make any extensive alterations to her superstructure, other than to convert the upper open-air bridge into a working bridge. That is done by the installation of a sound-powered telephone, a gyrocompass repeater, and a magnetic compass. A rudder inclination indicator, two engine telegraphs, and two revolution counters are also put in. A captain's chair is attached to the deck, and the voice pipes are extended from below. Heavy coco matting is attached to the upper-bridge railings for protection against shell splinters. There is no time to give the crew extensive training in anti-submarine warfare, and no practice submarine is available. The asdic specialists and the depth-charge crews have learned their trade by the book. With the exception of the very few among them who have served aboard a corvette on actual escort duty, they have not had any practical experience.

On 9 October Medland is suddenly rushed to hospital with acute appendicitis. *St Croix* must sail for Halifax in two days, so Kingsley is assigned to command. It is a logical choice for the navy. Earlier doubts about Kingsley's leadership ability have largely disappeared. He has shown himself to be hard-working and dedicated in whatever post he was assigned to. His commanding officer in Halifax is especially impressed by the "initiative and administrative ability" Kingsley demonstrated as commander of the Town Class flotilla in its working-up.

Kingsley boards *St Croix* the next day and stows his meagre luggage in his day cabin on the starboard side of the ship, just aft of the wardroom. It is furnished with a comfortable bed, a bedside table, a desk and chair, and a reading lamp. This will be Kingsley's home while his ship is in harbour. At sea, he will sleep in his small sea cabin behind the wheelhouse, just below the upper bridge. He has orders to take *St Croix* to sea for an overnight run to the Sambro Light, where she will meet a tug and target, and to conduct gunnery practice the next morning.

It is pitch dark by 10 p.m. Kingsley sits at his desk and fills out reports and forms. Over the ship's loudspeaker he hears the call "Hands to station for leaving harbour. Close all watertight doors and scuttles. Stand by wires and fenders." Then there is a knock at his door. The First Lieutenant enters Kingsley's cabin and reports that *St Croix* is ready for sea. This man is Kingsley's executive officer, his "Number One." He will stand the first of each day's regular four-hour watches beginning at midnight. Officers of the Watch will each stand the same watches every day. When they do, they run the ship while the captain is sleeping, eating, or otherwise engaged. When *St Croix* enters or leaves harbour, Kingsley will take command on the bridge. He will also take it during action stations. Although Kingsley is responsible for all phases of the ship's operation at all times, the routine operation of the ship is the responsibility of the First Lieutenant. He answers directly to the captain.

The captain of a Royal Canadian Navy man-of-war is a veritable God on his vessel. His authority is unchallenged, no matter what his ability. It is his duty to set the standard for the behaviour of the ship's officers and ratings, to enforce the King's Regulations and Admiralty Instructions, to make the final decisions on all important questions, and to fight his ship as he sees fit. In these matters, he answers to no man alive. His power is supreme, but he pays a supreme price for that power and position. He has no friends aboard his ship at sea. He lives in a state of isolation. He eats alone in his sea cabin. He never enters the officers' wardroom while the ship is at sea, and rarely at other times. He does not allow any of his officers, even his First Lieutenant, to address him in anything but the most formal manner. He holds himself at a distance from the rest of the ship's company, even as he conducts Sunday services or does an occasional round of inspection. He is in no way a shipmate; when he is at sea, he is the lord and master of all he surveys.

It is a lonely business, this being in command, made more so by the requirement that he also act like a God. He must not display emotion on his bridge—no doubt, no fear, no loss of control. He is a rock, no matter how he may quiver inside. But at the same time, he must inspire confidence in his ship's company by showing that he is a master seaman, a superior navigator, a brilliant tactician, and that, despite his lofty position, he is aware of his ship and cares deeply about the men serving under him. It is a tall order.

Kingsley slips on his sea boots, his cap, and his thick naval-issue duffle coat. He climbs to the bridge, his binoculars hanging around his neck. *St Croix*'s engines are vibrating the deck. Down below, two of the four boilers are at pressure feeding steam to the turbines. The turbine blades whirl, but the transmission is in neutral and the shafts and screws are still as the Engineer Officer, "the chief," awaits orders from the bridge. The ship is closed up for sea, the Coxswain at the wheel in the wheel-house below, the First Lieutenant and other officers on the bridge or on the stations on deck. The Coxswain, a chief petty officer, is *St Croix*'s senior non-commissioned rating. In all matters of the ship's regular operations and discipline, he will be the link between the ratings who operate the ship and the officers who manage it. He is the most experienced seaman on board. All the chief petty officers or petty officers report to him on those matters that fall within his bailiwick. As the ship's most experienced helmsman, he will take the wheel whenever the ship enters or leaves harbour and during action stations. Kingsley barely

knows the men on the bridge or in the wheel-house. They barely know
him or even each other. He seems rather old to be in command of a
warship these days. But then, he is regular navy, and they know he has
had extensive sea time on the big ships of the Royal Navy.

Kingsley quietly takes in the scene. Ratings stand by each telegraph.
The Yeoman of Signals stands on the right of the bridge. The First Lieutenant is at the front of the bridge just behind the dodger. Kingsley
stands next to the captain's chair. This is not his first time in command
of a warship and it is only a drill, but it is his first night run in command
of a destroyer and he is nervous. The full weight of this ship and her
crew is on his shoulders, and this is wartime. He must not fail now. On
the outside, he struggles to appear calm and confident. He must show
these men standing expectantly around him that he is worthy of the
trust of command. He knows well the complex drill for getting a ship
under way. He begins quietly: "Single up all lines."

The First Lieutenant leans over the dodger and repeats the command; on the main deck below, the special sea-duty men single up the
three sets of lines securing *St Croix* to the jetty.

"Let go aft." The aft line is removed from the jetty and hauled
aboard.

"Slow ahead port." The rating assigned to the port engine telegraph
rings the lever to the "slow ahead" position, and the port screw begins to
churn the waters of Shelburne harbour. With her bow still attached to
the jetty by a single line, and the midships spring still secured, *St Croix*'s
stern slowly swings away from the dock. When she is at a 45-degree
angle from the jetty, Kingsley orders the remaining lines cast off and
calls for "slow astern both engines." *St Croix* backs away from the pier.

"Slow ahead starboard, port ten." The port screw is still turning in
reverse, but the starboard screw now begins thrusting ahead. From the
steering room the Coxswain answers "Port ten," and the First Lieutenant reports "Ten of port wheel on, sir." *St Croix* begins to swing her
bow towards the harbour entrance.

"Slow ahead both engines, midships," Kingsley commands. The
port screw now begins thrusting ahead to match the starboard screw, as
the Coxswain tugs the wheel back over to the right so the twin rudders
are pointing straight aft. The two telegraph men repeat the order as
they ring their instruments, "Slow ahead both engines, sir." The First

Lieutenant calls out, "Both telegraphs are slow ahead, sir," and the Coxswain reports that he has placed the wheel amidships.

"Starboard five." Kingsley orders the rudders to starboard for a few moments to correct *St Croix*'s swing to port. He watches the engine revolution counters. "Midships." The Coxswain puts the wheel midships again. *St Croix* is moving slowly to the harbour mouth.

"Take in fenders, secure the upper deck." The deckhands haul the fenders up and begin securing the lines as *St Croix* sends out a small bow wave that now begins to lap at the shore.

"Half ahead both engines." *St Croix* picks up speed, her bow wave grows.

"Hands to station for leaving harbour." The bosun's pipe whistles and all hands not assigned to duty muster in straight lines on the main deck. It is an age-old custom. It shows all who watch that *St Croix* is closed up and secure, and that her crew is ready for whatever they will meet. As *St Croix* moves through the opening in the anti-submarine net and pushes out to sea, Kingsley orders the Navigating Officer to set course for the Sambro Light off Halifax harbour. It has been a long day and this turns out to be a routine trip. He decides to grab whatever sleep he can while he can get it. He nods to the Officer of the Watch who is standing by "She's all yours" and climbs down to his sea cabin. He throws his coat over the chair and slips off his boots, placing them carefully beside the bunk. He lies down, feeling the ship rising and falling on the gentle swell. He can hear the ping of the asdic repeater and the voices of men going about their business. The voice pipe to the bridge is just above his head. He'll be called the moment he is needed. He falls asleep.

On the bridge above, the First Lieutenant stands just to the rear of the Officer of the Watch. He'll be taking his turn in less than an hour and he decides to stay on the bridge until then. The Officer of the Watch whistles into the voice pipe leading to the engine room and tells the chief what speed to maintain. He usually does this by calling for so many revolutions, or propellor revolutions, per minute, to give him the speed he desires. He knows how many revolutions to call for by consulting a conversion table that tells him how many revolutions equals how many knots. The table also compares knots with the instructions embossed on the engine telegraphs ("Full Ahead," "Half Ahead," and so on).

Ship and crew steam into the night on a gentle sea, and the stars guide their way, the air crisp and cold. Ahead and to the east, a band of light grey appears on the horizon, a portent of dawn. The ship wakes as hands are called to their duty stations. The smells of the galley signal bacon frying and bread baking, and watches change. At 9 a.m. they draw near to the Sambro Light. The tug and target is on time and the shoot soon begins. It is a good practice and, when it is finished, *St Croix* sets course for Halifax.

Refreshed after an uneventful night, coffee mug in hand, Kingsley stands on the bridge and watches the grey sea and the cloud that has moved in since dawn. There is a swell from the north. Somewhere out to sea, a storm is raging, testing men and ships with all the raw power nature can muster. For now, however, Kingsley is mindful only of entering harbour smartly with his new command shipshape. There is still much work to be done to prepare *St Croix* for sea. For the next ten days she lies alongside the jetty as cohorts of her "libertymen" haunt the streets and bars of Halifax, looking for something to do. There is no rest for Kingsley, however. He is the man ultimately responsible for the seaworthiness of his charge. For the next nine days he lives and works in his sleeping cabin and in the dock office, where he oversees much-needed repairs and minor modifications. On 19 October he is handed a message from the Senior Officer Halifax Force. Kingsley has expected it for the last two days. "Being in all respects ready for sea, HMCS *St Croix* will sail in consort with HMCS *St Francis* to join convoy HX82 for local escort leaving Halifax at 0800 20th October 1940. Senior officer of escort is in *St Francis*. Acknowledge." Kingsley dictates a short reply; he and his ship will sail on the morrow. It is time. The war at sea awaits.

2

Rudolf Bahr
Goes to Sea

RUDOLF HERMANN ROBERT BAHR was born on 1 April 1916 at Landsberg on the Warthe River, one of the inland backwaters of the Baltic Sea trade. He shares a birth date with the German Empire's founder, Otto von Bismarck, and as a child he revelled in the annual fêtes he was convinced were designed to honour "his" special day. Landsberg was the capital of the New Mark in the historic province of Brandenburg, a bastion of Hohenzollern royal power.

The sparsely populated, gently undulating land had been bitterly contested between Poles and Pomeranians before falling to the Teutonic Knights in 1402. Markgrave Johann I of Brandenburg had given the city its charter in 1257 and had granted it the right to establish a modest riverine shipbuilding industry. Landsberg quickly grew into a busy transshipping site for Baltic trade bound for the Polish hinterland. Hanseatic traders put in at Stettin and then sailed south down the Oder River; near the Prussian fortress town of Küstrin they came about east to enter the Warthe estuary. At Landsberg they unloaded their precious cargoes, which were then hauled further east either by small boats and barges down the Warthe and Kladow rivers or by oxen and horse carts along Poland's dusty roads. Flax, hemp, lumber, beets, potatoes, and *Schnaps* made up the return ballast. Patricians from Hamburg and Lübeck exchanged goods and money with Brandenburg nobles and Galician Jews along Landsberg's narrow, bustling docks. A small theatre, a stout red-brick Protestant church called the Marienkirche, and several Prussian trade and technical schools proudly attested to the city's growth.

But the Thirty Years' War after 1618 brought the Swedes, who took control of the Oder River trade, and war and pestilence. Protestant and Catholic armies criss-crossed and ravaged the land. Prussia's great king, Frederick II, forcefully recruited the New Mark's young men between 1740 and 1763 and confiscated its coffers for his three Silesian wars with Maria Theresa and Joseph II of Austria. Napoleon I's French forces after 1806 plundered the land for recruits and war supplies. In 1815 Landsberg proudly adopted Brandenburg's red eagle as its coat of arms after being incorporated into this historic Hohenzollern province.

Yet the city did not recover economically until the middle of the nineteenth century, when modest industrialization revitalized the erstwhile river trade. Shipyards, docks, rope and cable factories, a brickyard, jute and cloth mills, leather tanneries, and lumber yards brought new prosperity to the city. By the turn of the century, the Prussian Crown had blessed Landsberg with several research facilities—most specifically, an agricultural and forest research institute as well as an experimental potato seed farm. Not surprisingly, Landsberg's political, social, and economic tone was dictated by the landed gentry, the *Junkers*, set off from the merchants and lesser breeds by the participle "von" between their birth and family names.

The Bahrs belong to the lesser breeds. Of modest bourgeois origins, they are part of the solid middle class of civil servants and tradesmen. Rudolf's father, Fritz Bahr, is a merchant with a small store at Nr. 2 Karl Teiske-Platz; his mother, Margret née Bahr, keeps a decent, Protestant home. Like many a young German lad, Bahr is fascinated by the sea. He reads countless stories of windjammers and luxury liners, of naval battles and heroes. The scows and prams that ply the Kladow and the Warthe only whet his appetite for the mysteries that lie beyond: the Oder River, its bustling port of Stettin, the Baltic Sea, the Danish Belts, the North Sea, and, somewhere far beyond dour northern Scotland and the Shetlands, the great Atlantic Ocean. Rudolf reads voraciously: tales of the Hanseatic League that once dominated trade from London to Riga; histories of the great Venetian galleys; accounts of the mighty High Seas Fleet built in his father's day by Grand Admiral Alfred von

Tirpitz, and of its scuttling at Scapa Flow in the summer of 1919; and strident calls for the fleet's rebirth.

Born in the depths of the Great War on the eve of the terrible "turnip winter" of 1916–17, Bahr belongs to the postwar generation caught between the Scylla of chronic unemployment and the Charybdis of national humiliation. The Reich collapses in defeat and revolution in November 1918. The Kaiser goes into voluntary exile in the Netherlands, ending 504 years of Hohenzollern rule in Brandenburg-Prussia-Germany. The new republic, founded at Weimar, is saddled with the twin burdens of war guilt and reparations. The once invincible Prussian army is reduced to a long-service policing force of 100,000 men, its General Staff declared illegal, and its arsenal stripped of tanks, heavy guns, and aircraft. The once proud Imperial Navy consists of a few antiquated cruisers and one or two pre-Dreadnought battleships; its submarines are scrapped and forbidden by the Treaty of Versailles.

Political violence and murder, black marketing and hunger, bankruptcies and stock-market crashes, and finally occupation by an Allied Military Control Commission are among Bahr's first memories as a child. At the age of eight he sees Germany plunged into the great inflation, which reduces the Reichsmark to scrap paper: four *billion* to one American dollar by November 1924! Belgian and French troops invade Germany's industrial heartland, the Ruhr. The Communists try to seize power in Thuringia and Saxony; the monarchists in Bavaria. The Bahrs lose their meagre savings. Bahr hears his family and friends tell stories at the local beer gardens of the way Chancellor Gustav Stresemann's policy of "fulfilling" the Versailles Treaty is "enslaving" his generation—as well as the next. At school his teachers daily recite the litany of Germany's lost lands as a result of the Versailles *Diktat*—northern Schleswig, Eupen-Malmédy, Alsace-Lorraine, parts of Silesia, West Prussia, Danzig—and drive home the lesson with a pointer that glides effortlessly along a wall map of Bismarck's once-proud Reich.

Bahr does well at school. He attends elementary school from Easter 1922 until Easter 1926, and a special Reform High School that features modern languages rather than Latin from Easter 1926 until Easter 1935. But a savage depression in 1929 ravages Landsberg's fragile shipping trade and light manufacturing. Unemployment soars. Political violence becomes the norm. In April 1932 Frankfurt an der Oder, the electoral

district that includes Landsberg, divides its ballots almost evenly between former Field Marshal Paul von Hindenburg (48%) and former
Corporal Adolf Hitler (46%). In the breakthrough elections of July 1932
Hitler's National Socialist German Workers' Party (NSDAP) tops the
vote with 48.1 percent.

On 30 January 1933 Bahr, now a teenager, learns that Hitler, the
Austrian-Bavarian veteran of the Great War, has been handed the reins
of power in Berlin by Germany's greatest living soldier, Hindenburg,
the second and last President of the Weimar Republic. Hitler has made
no secret of the fact that he wishes to restore the Reich to military great-
ness. In the elections of March 1933 Frankfurt an der Oder gives Hitler
an absolute majority of 55 percent of the vote.

There is no time to lose. Bahr passes the high school tests required for
admission to the Naval School, fulfils his compulsory National Labour
Service, and then, on 5 April 1935, packs his bags and says goodbye to the
48,000 burghers of Landsberg/Warthe. At the age of eighteen, he is
bound for Mürwik-Flensburg, a proud recruit of the Crew of 1935.

The Marineschule, Germany's equivalent to the United States Naval
Academy at Annapolis or the Royal Naval College at Greenwich, is alive
and vibrant in 1935. Mürwik received its first major postwar class of 277
cadets in 1934; this time round, under Rear-Admiral Wolf von Trotha, the
corps of cadets has grown to almost 450 in anticipation of general rearmament and the rebirth of naval power. The *Seekadetten* do not have long to
wait. In rapid succession, Hitler, in January 1935, brings the Saar "home
into the Reich," and, two months later, declares unilaterally that he will
create an air force (Luftwaffe) and build an army (Wehrmacht) of thirty-
six divisions through universal male conscription. The cadets at Mürwik
rejoice: Germany is on the move again, and Hitler is the man of the hour.

Organizationally, the naval aspirants of the Crew of 1935 are broken
down into three Kompanien, and these, in turn, into several Züge, each
led by an executive officer. The Züge are then subdivided into eighteen
Korporalschaften of about a dozen cadets each and commanded by
petty officers. The daily regimen is Spartan, in the best Prussian tradition of unquestioned discipline.

But before Bahr can wear naval blue, there is the matter of three
months of basic training at Stralsund along the Baltic coast. On the
Dänholm, across from the island of Rügen, the day begins at 5:30 a.m.,

when the cadets are piped out of their bunks. In short order they make beds, shower and shave, eat breakfast, endure room and barracks inspection, and participate in early morning sports, followed by three hours of gruelling infantry drill in field-grey uniforms, jack boots, 60-pound backpacks, and steel helmets. Army sergeants take special delight in introducing future naval officers and would-be gentlemen to the basics of spit and polish in general and to the intricacies of the sixty-seven interlocking parts of the Mauser rifle 98 in particular. Lunch is followed by more sports and drill as well as by formal education in naval history, regulations, terminology, flags, and salutes. The only relief from the seemingly endless infantry drills comes on 16 March 1935, when the cadets assemble on the parade square to receive the news that Hitler unilaterally has "cancelled" the Versailles Treaty.

On 1 May 1935, Germany's traditional labour day and now the Nazi Day of Labour, Bahr takes the oath of loyalty as a naval cadet. The Crew of 1935 assembles on the sports field in parade uniform and steel helmets. The command "Attention!" rolls across the field. The youngest cadet in each company stands front and centre, clutches the naval war flag in his left hand, and raises his right hand: "I swear by God and this sacred oath that I will render unquestioning obedience to the Führer of the German Reich and Volk, Adolf Hitler, and that I am prepared as a brave soldier to lay down my life at any time for this oath." Thirty days later the ceremony is repeated on the nineteenth anniversary of the Battle of Jutland (1916).

A brief first visit home at Whitsuntide is followed by a formal inspection by the navy's Commander-in-Chief, Admiral-General Erich Raeder. A gala review and parade on 17 June 1935 marks the end of seventy-four days of infantry drill on the Dänholm. The cadets, being lowest in the military pecking order, lustily wash down the dust of the past ten weeks at the slightly seedy Mutti Holst pub in Stralsund.

Next comes a three-month cruise aboard the 1500-ton square-rigged windjammer *Gorch Fock* (soon to be renamed the *Horst Wessel*, and decades later the US Coast Guard tall ship *Eagle*). Launched in May 1933 and named after a naval artist and poet who had died at the Battle of Jutland, the three-master boasts 1800 square yards of sail. Only future executive officers go aboard; designated engineer, artillery, and administrative officers instead pound the books at the Naval School. Rudolf

Bahr quickly learns the routine aboard the "swan of the Baltic Sea": wash decks, polish brass, eat, sleep, wake, learn knots, hoist sail, clear ship. At least the sparkling white flannel suits are a welcome change from infantry grey. The 2000-mile trip between 17 June and 26 September 1935 goes through the Baltic Sea from Kiel to Swinemünde to East Prussia—with a land tour to visit the infamous Polish Corridor that divides the Reich in half—and finally into the North Sea and the Shetlands, Helgoland, Bremerhaven, and then, in September, back to Kiel.

On 18 June 1935, the 120th anniversary of the Anglo-Prussian victory over the French at Waterloo, the cadets cheer wildly at the news that Berlin has signed a formal treaty with London whereby the Reich can build up to 35 percent of the surface tonnage and, eventually, 100 percent of the submarine strength of the Royal Navy—a task that would have taken until the mid-1950s at least to complete. Versailles is dead. Promotions, decorations, and commands to plum cruiser and capital ship positions beckon for the officers and cadets of what, on 1 July, officially becomes the new Kriegsmarine of the Third Reich. Few cadets, if any, take notice of the regime's anti-Semitic "Nürnberg racial laws" promulgated in September 1935.

On 27 September Sea Cadet Bahr and about 150 of his mates report to Wilhelmshaven. On 23 October they board the 5600-ton light cruiser *Emden*, skippered until June of that year by Commander Karl Dönitz, Bahr's future U-boat chief. The Crew of 1935 is headed for the most exciting and satisfying part of naval training—an eight-month tour overseas. Mixed emotions and pride run through the cadets: high adventure at sea and visits to exotic venues while representing the new fatherland, learning the seaman's trade, and showing the flag.

The journey does not disappoint. The *Emden* sails under blue Atlantic skies through the Bay of Biscay before dropping anchor at Portuguese Angra do Heroismo. There, in accordance with Hitler's order of 31 October 1935, the crew ceremoniously hauls down the black, white, and red imperial ensign and hoists the swastika, "the sign of the future," as the yearbook crows. *Emden* is the first German ship to show the world "the direction of things to come." Hamilton in Bermuda and Port-au-Prince in Haiti are the next ports of call, followed by Venezuela, the Panama Canal, and Christmas in the Pacific Ocean. After a brief stop at Guatemala, Bahr and the *Emden* steam into Portland, Oregon. It is the first contact with Americans for the cadets. The galley produces special swastika cakes for the American visitors to the ship, and the crew offers their best rendition of the NSDAP's anthem, the "Horst Wessel Lied." The cadets are especially fond of the promissory lines: "Millions already look with hope upon the swastika/The day of freedom and of bread is dawning!"

But the cadets are bitterly disappointed in America. "Money! money! money!" seems to be the national passion. "Time is money!" Money dominates culture as well as public and private life. Businessmen seem utterly ignorant of the "new Germany," and even immigrants from the former Fatherland have been thoroughly assimilated and know little about "things German"—beyond a German glee club and bowling club. Few seem proud of their "German blood" and "racial superiority." "A lost German century?" the cadets wonder. Hawaii offers typical "American amusement and entertainment." Then the return trip takes the *Emden* back through the Panama Canal to the West Indies, which seem little more than "Negro ports." The cadets stand watch, take astronomical readings, sight the ship's eight 15-cm guns, and familiarize themselves with radio and hand signals. A cool reception awaits the ship at Easter 1936 at British Jamaica: Hitler has just reoccupied the demilitarized Rhineland without firing a shot.

The *Emden* then turns north and for days on end ploughs through waters that Bahr will later revisit as a U-boat commander. The Führer's birthday is celebrated in grand style at sea on 20 April. The Crew finds Baltimore to be worse than Portland: "impersonal, hectic, aggressive; this is eastern America, the centre of Jewish world finance." By contrast, the Naval Academy at Annapolis is a delight: clean, crisp, disciplined. Next comes New York, with its "so-called culture and art." It is ugly, unfriendly, cold, and sunless, with no sense of *Volk* or of blood: "A facade of a farce." There, also, the German colony has been amalgamated into a nondescript melting pot, forever lost. And a cadet can do little in New York on a shore allowance of fifteen devalued Reichsmarks!

Still, there is something new in the air: "Will [Franklin D.] Roosevelt find the way; Is he the future; Is his 'New Deal'?" Last but not least, the *Emden* carefully makes her way through the fog banks off Newfoundland and then gingerly steers through loose ice floes in the St Lawrence River as far as Montreal. "Through dark forests, snow-crowned peaks, and the first spring buds in the valleys—that is Canada as we experience it in May." A quick trip by rail to Niagara Falls completes the Canadian leg of the journey. Thereafter, *Emden* navigates her way out of the St Lawrence and re-enters the Atlantic via the Strait of Belle Isle. Little could Bahr appreciate that six years later he will hunt in these very waters off Canada.

Emden heads home in the spring of 1936 via Spain, France, and the English Channel. Bahr and his mates write their Midshipmen exams on board ship under the watchful eye of her skipper, Captain Johannes Bachmann, and are then allowed to slip into double-breasted blues. Ahead of them lie months of serious study at the Naval School. The Crew of 1935 has spent eight months at sea, time to develop a sense of camaraderie and unity; fewer than 5 percent of the original corps of cadets have fallen by the wayside because of mental or physical handicaps. *Emden* steams past Helgoland Island and, on 19 June 1936, docks in Wilhelmshaven, where a military band and thousands of well-wishers anxiously await her return. The cadets are formally welcomed home by a most surprising visitor: Adolf Hitler. The Summer Olympic Games are in full swing and the Führer has come to the North Sea to bless some of the yachting events. Heady stuff for a young lad from the Warthe region of the New Mark!

Once again, few midshipmen are even aware that the Kriegsmarine has issued special instructions to its officers not to "frequent Jewish pubs or to buy in Jewish stores" during the Olympics, as this would "damage" its public image. And just a handful may have discovered while on furlough that "Negroid music in the hot style" has been decreed as inappropriate for a prospective officer and gentleman. Most midshipmen concentrate on the coming term at Mürwik. The laying down of two battleships and several destroyers under the terms of the Anglo-German Naval Agreement of the previous year augurs well for their future careers. And Hitler's support of General Francisco Franco's uprising against Republican Spain in July 1936 is hailed by the midshipmen as a crusade against socialism and Bolshevism. They proudly, if enviously, follow the dispatch of the two pocket battleships *Admiral Scheer* and *Deutschland* to blockade Communist ports in Spain.

Flensburg in 1936 is a city of about 70,000 people. On its northern edge, hard by the Flensburg Fjord and within sight of Denmark, stands the Naval School. Opened at Flensburg-Mürwik in October 1910, it consists of a sprawling complex of barracks, administrative buildings, boat houses, officer quarters, and sports fields. In the centre stands the main educational building—a towering edifice built with red bricks and affectionately dubbed the "red monastery on the fjord," or simply "the castle." It is to be Rudolf Bahr's home from June 1936 until March 1937.

In nine months of intensive study, the Crew of 1935 has to learn what it takes American cadets at Annapolis years to do. Thirty hours per week are divided into classroom learning in the mornings and hands-on training and sports in the afternoon. Navigation, seamanship, and English are core courses, followed by mathematics, natural science, electronics, naval architecture, oceanography, naval tactics, marine engineering, and naval history. Gymnastics, boxing, fencing, horseback riding, dancing, sailing, soccer, and swimming dominate the afternoons. There is little in the way of socializing or cultural life in Flensburg, where mothers carefully shield their daughters from the Midshipmen.

Indoctrination in National Socialist ideology—two hours per month—entered the curriculum on 30 January 1936 by order of the War Minister, General Werner von Blomberg. By and large, Bahr and his fellow Midshipmen are content to hail Hitler as a friend of the navy, as the architect of a successful revisionist foreign policy, and as the guarantor of rearmament. Bahr concentrates on his profession. As an officer-to-be, he is not allowed to join either the party (NSDAP) or one of its auxiliary organizations. The popular saying that Hitler has a Prussian Army, an Imperial Navy, and a National Socialist Air Force is more myth than reality.

Bahr, like all his mates, rotates through a series of theoretical courses and practical experience: navigation on the tug *Hecht*; torpedo and artillery practice at Mürwik; intelligence and communications instruction at Mürwik; and mine-sweeping practice in the Flensburg Fjord. More intensive specialization will come later. He is required to purchase and to read Siegfried Sorge's book *The Naval Officer as Führer and Educator*; it is a primer on the concepts of honour, professionalism, pride, comradery, and duty.

The Crew of 1935 takes its main officer candidacy exams in March 1937. Marks range from 1 (utterly insufficient) to 9 (excellent), and then are multiplied by factors of 3, 2, or 1 according to the importance of the course; the resulting numerical score determines the midshipmen's placings within the Crew in terms of seniority and future promotion. Rudolf Bahr takes fifth place among the 400 officer candidates of his class. The new ensigns leave the castle in March 1937, bound for six months with a special service branch—in Bahr's case, the Naval Artillery School at Kiel-Wik and anti-aircraft or Flak (*Flugzeugabwehrkanone*) training at Wilhelmshaven. This instruction is followed by six months on board a warship—in Bahr's case the *Admiral Graf Spee*. The Crew of 1935 as a unit is promoted to the rank of Sub-Lieutenant (Leutnant z. S.) on 1 April 1938—Rudolf's twenty-second birthday.

Ship and shore commands alternate every six months beginning in May, when Bahr reports back to the *Graf Spee* as a Flak specialist. He is keenly aware that Nazi Germany is escalating both its domestic and its foreign policies. At home, the "Crystal Night" of 9 November 1938 brings about an orgy of looting and burning of synagogues and Jewish stores throughout the Reich. "Non-Aryan" civil servants and officers disappear from government agencies almost overnight. Concentration camps begin to fill. At the time of Bahr's commissioning, Hitler occupies his erstwhile homeland, Austria; in September 1938 at Munich he annexes the Sudetenland in Czechoslovakia. The rest of Czechoslovakia is transformed into two German puppet states, Bohemia and Moravia, in the spring of 1939. The Baltic port of Memel again becomes German. Bahr will later experience it as the home of the 24th U-boat Flotilla.

Sometime between September 1938 and August 1939 it becomes clear that war in Europe lies just over the horizon. The fleet is kept at constant readiness, manoeuvres follow one another in rapid succession, live ammunition replaces practice shells, and dockyards in Hamburg and Kiel work overtime not only to complete the capital ships already on the slips but also to mass produce the new Type VII and IX submarines.

The honour of launching the Second World War in the early morning hours of 1 September 1939 falls to the old battleship *Schleswig-Holstein*, when it shells the Westerplatte near Danzig. The Crew of 1935 has enjoyed one year of peace. Fresh-baked lieutenants, Bahr and his mates are hastily assigned commands with the naval air wing, shore batteries, and on light as well as heavy craft; about 10 percent of the Crew find themselves on Captain Dönitz's U-boats. With lightning speed, Hitler's Wehrmacht crushes Poland and links up with Joseph Stalin's Red Army at Brest-Litovsk in late September. Denmark and Norway fall during Operation Weserübung in April 1940—but at the cost to the navy of ten destroyers. The Low Countries and France experience *Blitzkrieg* in May 1940. With the extension of German power to Norway and France, Admiral Raeder finally has access to the broad sweeps of the Atlantic.

Rudolf Bahr is bitterly disappointed by the outbreak of the war. Apparently not in need of every available lieutenant, the Kriegsmarine detaches him to Kiel for almost three months of further training in anti-aircraft warfare. He is promoted to the rank of Lieutenant (Oberleutnant z. S.) on 1 October 1939. Almost as if to add insult to injury, he is awarded the "Memel Campaign Medal" in October and the "Sudeten Campaign Medal" in November 1939—two campaigns he did not take part in! Then, to Bahr's great delight, on 1 August 1940 he is assigned to the heavy cruiser *Prinz Eugen*. It is a plum command, the best that could be expected by a Lieutenant.

After a brief furlough at Landsberg, Bahr reports on board the cruiser at Gotenhafen by Danzig in the Baltic Sea. The *Prinz Eugen* is a dream come true. Just completed by the Germaniawerft at Kiel at a cost of 104 million Reichsmarks, the 18,400-ton cruiser has a best speed of 20 knots and a range of 7200 nautical miles. Her oil-fired Brown, Boveri turbines develop 132,000 horsepower. The main armament consists of eight 20.3-cm guns; her complement, of forty-two officers and 1340 ratings. Weeks of frenetic and nerve-racking sea trials lie ahead before the *Prinz Eugen* can be certified seaworthy and combat ready. Bahr, placed in charge of a detail of anti-aircraft guns and men, now adds practical experience at sea to more than thirty months of book learning at the Naval School.

On 21 May 1941 "The Day" is at hand: the *Prinz Eugen* is to accompany the pride of the fleet, the new battleship *Bismarck*, on a raid on British shipping in the Atlantic. Bands play and thousands of onlookers wave handkerchiefs as the two gleaming ships slip out of Gotenhafen. They are about to put into practice Admiral Raeder's "double-pole" strategy, whereby the Kriegsmarine will deploy two groups each of three battleships overseas, and four heavy units in the North Sea; each is to be augmented by support craft. British agents, with the help of Swedish intelligence, report to London the passage of the *Bismarck* and the *Prinz Eugen* through the Danish Belts. The Royal Navy is placed on ready alert.

As the Kriegsmarine's two newest vessels steam north of Scotland and the Shetlands, they are sighted by the battle cruiser HMS *Hood* and the battleship HMS *Prince of Wales*. An artillery duel at the incredible range of 20 miles ensues almost immediately. The British, close to their bases and supply depots, fire 15-inch broadsides in square patterns—shells the size of Volkswagens—that soon straddle the wake of the *Bismarck*. The latter, far removed from any base and resupply, carefully calibrates each 35-cm salvo. Bahr can see the British broadsides splash ever closer to the *Bismarck*; her demise is just a matter of time. And then a thunderous cheer goes up: the *Hood* explodes in a flash of fire and smoke. *Bismarck* next concentrates her fire on the *Prince of Wales*, which is damaged but manages to limp off to fight another day. The date: 24 May 1941. The site: just west of Iceland. Bahr has experienced his first "kill" in these northern waters.

Prime Minister Winston Churchill is livid. The Royal Navy's reputation is on the line, and all available heavy ships and aircraft of Home Fleet and Force H are alerted to find the *Bismarck* and her escort. The deadly hunt is on: "Sink *Bismarck*!" Fleet Commander Admiral Günther Lütjens and Captain Ernst Lindemann of the *Bismarck* have but one choice—to make a run for the German-occupied port of Brest at the northern edge of the Bay of Biscay. Aided by rudimentary radar and good luck, British Swordfish planes from the aircraft carrier HMS *Ark Royal* on 27 May damage the *Bismarck*'s rudder with air-launched 1600-lb torpedoes. The mighty battleship flounders aimlessly in the seas 400 miles west of Brest, awaiting the inevitable *coup de grâce*. Lütjens immediately realizes the hopelessness of his situation and releases the *Prinz Eugen*, thereby saving her from certain destruction. *Bismarck* is last reported in grid square BE65. U-boat Command sends out an urgent message to all units in the area: "Bismarck victim of concentrated enemy fire. All U-boats in vicinity to search for survivors." The *Prinz Eugen* makes Brest on 1 June 1941, leaving Bahr to the vicissitudes of magnanimous fate. On 26 June he is awarded the Iron Cross 2nd Class for the Atlantic sortie.

Bahr is not impressed by Brittany's largest port. The brackish waters of Brest's non-tidal inner basin are ringed by dull grey cliffs that rise behind the French Navy Arsenal; the entire harbour as well as the Crozon Peninsula that stretches out to the south of it are dominated by the massive granite edifice of the hundred-year-old École Navale. It reminds Bahr all too much of the castle in Flensburg. The ambiance in Brest is one of grey on grey: grey sea, grey sky, grey rock, grey ships, grey buildings.

But the port is a beehive of activity. Since September 1940 Vice-Admiral Hans Stohwasser and an army of engineers and construction workers from Organization Todt, as well as about 8000 French labourers, have toiled to transform Brest into the home port for the 1st and 9th U-boat Flotillas. Bahr is amused by the sight of the slender 700-ton submarines lying like metal cigar tubes row upon row at the southwestern edge of the French Navy Arsenal on the site of a former seaplane station. The submarine shelter, when completed at the end of 1941, will cover a record area of 62,400 square yards, measuring 366 yards wide, 219 yards long, and 18.7 yards high. Thirteen pens (A to E and 1 to 8) are being readied for the U-boats. Across the way, the modern harbour houses destroyer moorings as well as docks and dry docks for the capital ships. There the tides rise and fall 26 feet during spring floods.

Nor does Bahr find the town itself picturesque. Supply sheds, warehouses, shipyards, repair shops, cranes, and anti-aircraft batteries dominate the landscape. The smell of tar and oil, salt and fish, seaweed and paint is almost overpowering. Yet the bistros, cafés, and shops bustle with German soldiers, sailors, and airmen—and their female companions. These are the "happy times" for submariners, when they feast on easy pickings at sea and lobster and champagne in port. Brothels for every taste and price range abound. Who knows how long the New Order will last? *Carpe diem* is the motto of the men in the silent service. Rumours of espionage and sabotage by the Maquis, the French resistance movement, lend the place an aura of mystery and intrigue. At the Casino Bar, Lieutenant Bahr catches wondrous tales of the U-boat "aces" and their officers and the way they celebrate their "kills" at the medieval Châteauneuf, further inland. He longs for a chance to experience their lusty lifestyle himself.

But Bahr is not allowed time to savour the sights and smells of Brest. Hardly has he set foot on land and enjoyed his first meal on shore in France when new orders arrive: after a brief furlough he will undertake U-boat training in the Baltic Sea starting on 1 July. Bahr takes a special express train—the "Admiral u-boats Train"—to the Gare de Montparnasse in Paris, and from there an evening train to the Stettiner station in Berlin. It is while visiting with family in Landsberg that he hears the shocking news: the German army, the Wehrmacht, invaded the Soviet Union at dawn on 22 June 1941. As in 1914, Germany is now engaged in a two-front war, and one that will probably be as prolonged. It is with mixed emotions concerning the future that Bahr retraces his steps to Berlin, where he catches an express that rolls across the heather and pines of the Pomeranian Plains to Königsberg. The train is filled with soldiers bound for the northern flank of Operation Barbarossa, most likely en route to Leningrad. A local shuttle drops Bahr off at Pillau, where he secures temporary quarters on board the luxury liner *Pretoria*, his initial base with the 1st u-boat Training Division.

Rudolf Bahr in the summer of 1941 enters a new and final career: Admiral Karl Dönitz's submarine service, better known as the Dönitz Volunteer Corps. Bahr has exchanged the glamorous world of an 18,400-ton heavy cruiser for that of a 700-ton "pig boat." The grand view from the bridge of the *Prinz Eugen* has yielded to one of greasy gauges and endless rows of pumps and levers. Crisp summer whites have given way to shabby grey and black fatigues. But his new commander, Dönitz, has the edge in the new German naval strategy, and is soon affectionately dubbed "the Great Lion" (*der grosse Löwe*) by his loyal band of submariners.

Pillau harbour becomes a living hell for Bahr. Under the watchful eyes of Captain Hans Ibbeken, Bahr goes out on mock patrols by day and night, alternating the roles of captain and chief engineer with fellow officers also tapped for submarine duty. Experienced u-boat commanders specially detached to the 1st and 2nd Training Divisions teach the prospective skippers, executives, and chiefs the latest tricks of surface attacks at night and submerged attacks by day. They use their old war logs to initiate the novices into the intricacies of actual combat—substitute "on-the-job training." Next comes a brief stint with the 25th Training Flotilla at Danzig and Memel, where, with the guidance of other veteran submariners, the would-be future aces of the Kriegsmarine hone their attack skills.

Then, on 30 August, it is off to the Torpedo School at Flensburg-Mürwik—an old and familiar haunt from midshipman days. Classroom instruction and practice shooting in the Flensburg Fjord teach Bahr the latest secrets of Dönitz's assault tactics. A veteran of the U-boat force of the First World War, Karl Dönitz is a man of simple yet iron faith in the U-boats. He imbues his submarine force with two well-known military tenets: concentration and surprise. Additionally, he teaches his U-boat skippers to operate in groups of fifteen to twenty like young "wolfpacks" (*Rudeltaktik*): to use stealth to approach a hostile convoy silently and undiscovered, and then to hit it with full force from every angle. Dönitz orchestrates every aspect of the U-boat war with mathematical precision from his lair at Kernevel near Lorient.

Unbeknown to Bahr, orders are already being cut for his first submarine assignment: Executive Officer—literally, First Watch Officer—aboard *U69*. As such, he will serve as the boat's torpedo officer and, in the informal atmosphere of a submarine, be addressed simply as *Eins WO*. But first comes the final shakedown training with Commander Hans Eckermann's 8th U-boat Flotilla at Danzig. There Bahr receives new instructions on how to shoot on the surface by day and submerged by night. Day after day, he puts out to sea from Gotenhafen at 7 a.m. and, within the hour, fires dummy torpedoes at tramp steamers standing in for Allied convoys. When all the torpedoes have been expended, the training boats race back to port, reload, and return to practise firing by night. It is usually midnight before an exhausted Bahr tumbles into bed in his modest quarters by the U-boat pier. There is no time to make formal acquaintances and to go courting: after all, women are available in abundance at the luxurious Casino and the various cafés of Zoppot, a famous sea resort across Danzig Bay, only twenty minutes by tram. There one can win and lose—money and women—before returning to the reality of war.

Above all, Bahr is immersed into the mysteries of Dönitz's submarine strategy. The material is partly familiar from the classes at the Naval School and the practice sessions in the Flensburg Fjord. But there is much more to be learned. Dönitz's single, obsessive, all-consuming passion is simply to destroy the enemy's gross tonnage (*Tonnagekrieg*). He rejects all suggestions that the U-boats prey on certain selected vital targets such as tankers, troopships, and ammunition carriers, or that they target convoys bound for critical theatres of the war. The war against "perfidious Albion," as far as Admiral U-boats is concerned, can only be won in the Atlantic; it is critical that "the noose be tightened around England's neck."

Instead, Dönitz demands that ships found at sea be destroyed ruthlessly, methodically, and efficiently—regardless of their function, location, or destination. Body counts in the war on land find their parallel in tonnage count at sea. If the U-boats can sink more tonnage—Dönitz in February 1942 will set that figure at 600,000 for Germany and Japan—than Britain and the United States can build, the war will be won in two years. Dönitz reduces strategy to simple addition and subtraction.

Experienced U-boat commanders quickly teach Bahr the new wolfpack tactics that Dönitz established for the Atlantic in the summer of 1940. About fifteen boats depart from their bases in France, Germany, and Norway at intervals of several days. When the U-boats from Brest, La Rochelle, St Nazaire, and Lorient exit the Bay of Biscay or when those from Germany and Norway pass the Iceland-Faeroes gap, they report by radio to Admiral U-boats in France and receive a "heading point" instructing them to rendezvous at a digraph, or quadrant, on the top-secret German naval grid map (*Quadratkarte*). Using information on convoy sailings gathered by his radio intelligence service (Funkbeobachtungsdienst, or simply xB-Dienst), Dönitz deploys his patrol line in codenamed groups at right angles to the expected arrival. The boats stand about 15 to 20 miles apart as the "prongs" of a 180- or 240-mile-wide "rake" designed to comb the largest possible area of water. The boats have no radar, nor can they communicate while submerged.

Once a convoy is sighted, Admiral U-boats devises a time and place for the pack to attack in unison at a given radio signal. One boat always acts as a shadower, keeping Dönitz apprised of any change in position, course, or speed by the convoy and sending out beacon signals to home the other U-boats in on the intended victim. Dönitz's favourite tactic is to attack on the surface at night—using the U-boats' low profiles and relatively high surface speed to advantage. The pack's objective is to elude the escorts, penetrate their radar screen, and create chaos by attacking the merchant ships from within the convoy. Once the operation is broken off—or in case no convoy is sighted—Dönitz simply relocates his patrol line north or south, east or west of the original site, and repeats the procedure until the boats are out of fuel or torpedoes.

But how to coordinate the pack attacks? Dönitz rejects another idea tried in 1917: control by an at-sea pack leader such as a large U-cruiser. Rather, he seeks both to macro- and micro-manage the war from a central point on shore. There, the xB-Dienst and submarine operations group can be brought together—under Dönitz's personal command. This super headquarters proposes to move the submarines about the Atlantic like pieces on a chessboard. Dönitz's staff initially sends the U-boats to predetermined operational meeting points by latitude and longitude in the short signal book, but later, for greater security, it divides the world's major waterways into square grid coordinates that bear double letters, such as CB. Each double-letter grid, 486 nautical miles on a side, is then divided like the numbers on a touch-dial telephone into a nine-by-nine matrix of eighty-one smaller squares, each 54 nautical miles on a side and identified by two digits, such as CB94. These double-letter and double-number quadrants are then subdivided into smaller grids of nine squares each; and, finally, these grids are subdivided into yet smaller grids again of nine squares each, 6 nautical miles on a side. Theoretically, Dönitz, from Kernevel, Paris, or Berlin, will be able to pinpoint and direct any U-boat to a precise location.

To find convoys, Dönitz by April 1941 forms groups of twenty and later of forty or even sixty boats into patrol lines—"rakes"—with which he will furrow the vast expanse of the Atlantic. The U-boats are instructed to sweep their assigned sectors no more than 20 or 30 miles apart, optimum visibility in summer. As soon as a U-boat sights a convoy, it reports its position to Dönitz as ordered and then shadows the enemy rather than attack, all the while transmitting the convoy's course to the control centre on shore. From there, Dönitz orchestrates the precise time and place of attack, preferably on the surface by night to deny the convoy and its escorts a clear shot at the tiny craft in the dark of night. Only thereafter are the grey wolves permitted to submerge in order to evade the escorts' expected counterattacks. *Rudeltaktik* becomes the norm by June 1940.

At first, the advantage lies with the grey wolves, since the Allies have few weapons in their arsenal to defend against the U-boats. The British Type 286 radar can spot submarines on the surface only at a range of 2 to 3 miles. Asdic, an underwater sound-ranging system, is limited to about half a mile. Shore-based radio direction-finders, when used in tandem, can locate u-boats 500 or 1000 miles out at sea—but only within an area of 25 to 60 miles. And air patrols out of Newfoundland and Northern Ireland leave much of the central Atlantic south of Greenland and Iceland unguarded. Even when Allied aircraft are based on Iceland after May 1940, London and Washington put most of their air power into the bombing campaign against Germany rather than against Dönitz's grey wolves.

But this initial advantage is soon negated by a new and perplexing problem: the incredible amount of shore-to-ship and ship-to-shore radio traffic generated by Dönitz's rigid command and control system between a central shore command and possibly a hundred u-boats at sea. Admiral u-boats demands constant and precise data not only on the location of his boats but also on such matters as the state of their provisions, fuel, sightings, sinkings, and weather as well as sea conditions. German radio traffic increases from 319 messages per day in 1940 to 2563 per day by 1942. Bahr quickly appreciates that signal traffic analysis—the study of message characteristics, frequencies, and addresses—constitutes a critical component of the Battle of the Atlantic.

Admiral Dönitz relies for information on enemy movements at sea on cryptographic intelligence derived from Allied transmissions in Naval Cypher No. 3. This is the job of the 900-man, English-language section of the xB-Dienst. Headed by former radioman Wilhelm Tranow, who cracked the Royal Navy's code in the First World War, the xB-Dienst tackles the job of breaking the Royal Navy's four-digit Naval Cypher. In fact, the Royal Navy uses three primary crypto-systems—dubbed "Cologne," "Munich," and "Frankfurt" by the xB-Dienst—based on a combination of codes and ciphers. The British superencipher code groups by a long digit series (long subtractor system) that is changed every two months, and later twice a month. Obviously, the longer one system is in use, the greater the likelihood of its being broken by the xB-Dienst.

But the radio intelligence service is beset by numerous problems. First and foremost, without computers it can tackle only one intercepted transmission at a time. Second, it takes too long to decrypt Allied signals for the information to be operationally useful. The xB-Dienst manages to crack only about 10 percent of intercepted messages, and of these it gets only one in ten to the front in time to be of operational use; overall, a success ratio of one in a hundred! At its best—for example, from January to June 1943—the XB-Dienst manages to get information from decrypts to Dönitz roughly ten to twenty hours in advance of Allied convoy movements. Third, the radio intelligence service can provide only an overall picture of convoy cycles and procedures. It never decrypts Cypher No. 3 messages—much less those of the "stencil subtractor" Cypher No. 5 introduced in June 1943—fast enough to provide U-boat commanders with hard information on convoy diversions. And at no time does the XB-Dienst even begin to penetrate the security of the US Navy electric cipher machine.

Given that his radio intelligence service is reading the enemy's signals traffic, Admiral Dönitz naturally is concerned about the security of his own. Moreover, he knows that the British had captured the German radio code as well as naval grid maps in the First World War and that, at its famous Room 40, the Admiralty had read all German naval radio traffic. Thus, Admiral U-boats develops a system whereby the U-boats report to the central command and control centre with short signals, based on a code-book that reduces all vital information such as sightings, kills, positions, fuel levels, numbers of torpedoes, damage reports, and weather updates to a few four-letter groups. The groups are superenciphered by the daily key of the navy's cipher machine and sent off in a matter of seconds—never more than thirty. And to clear the air waves on a given frequency in the short-wave band, Dönitz and his U-boat commanders begin by sending out the Greek letters *beta-beta*, or "b-bar" as the Allies call it. Finally, the daily settings of the cipher machine, radio manuals, wireless logs, and codes are printed on water-soluble paper, to protect the system against boarding by the enemy in case a boat has to be abandoned after serious damage.

During his final days with the 8th U-boat Flotilla at Danzig, Bahr is given detailed knowledge of Dönitz's most prized and top secret possession: the German cipher machine. He learns that Arthur Scherbius, an electrical engineer, had by 1918 developed a sample machine featuring a cryptographic principle called the rotor. The eventual *Schlüssel M* machine, better known as "Enigma," looks like a cumbersome electric typewriter. It operates roughly as follows. It mounts three rotors, each with twenty-six contacts; each rotor is wired to connect the twenty-six contacts in pairs in a different pattern. When the Enigma operator types a letter at the keyboard, an electrical impulse is sent to the appropriate contact on the first rotor; output goes through the connected contact to the second rotor, and from there to the third rotor. The final output shows up as a light that comes on under one of the letters in a panel of letters on a "keyboard" located above the input keys. The Enigma M machine of 1939 has, in addition to the three active rotors (and five in reserve), a sequence of ten jacks and plugs to add additional variability to the system's circuitry.

The naval cipher—code-named "Hydra" until February 1942—has four different settings. The two interior settings are made by "officers only" every forty-eight hours; choosing to activate three out of eight cipher rotors allows 336 different combinations. Each rotor's revolving ring has 26 positions, which translate into 16,900 positions for three active inset rotors. The two exterior settings also are changed every twenty-four hours by cipher clerks, which permit 1547 possible connections on the plug board. And even before beginning to encipher, the Enigma operator can set each active rotor to twenty-six different positions, rendering another 17,576 possibilities. Multiplying all these factors, Dönitz's brains trust comes up with a theoretical total of 160 trillion possible settings for a complete transmission. No human brain, Bahr is assured by German naval intelligence, can possibly unravel such staggering combinations. No mathematical calculators exist—as far as Dönitz knows—to assist in the task of deciphering trillions of possibilities. Above all, none can do so sufficiently fast to allow the decrypted material to be of operational use.

Last but not least, Bahr is informed that each U-boat commander on heading out for patrol is given a sealed envelope that contains bearing and distance from one of the "reference points" provided. And that Dönitz now encodes the two large letters, or digraph, of the German grid map—for example, AK—by two other letters, which he changes every forty-eight hours. Bahr's brain fairly buzzes each night as he digests this ocean of electronic and cartographic intelligence. It will be his task as Executive Officer of U69 to master this information for his Captain.

3

Hard-Luck Destroyer

THE TASK facing Kingsley and *St Croix*, and all the other Allied men and warships struggling for mastery over the western ocean, is to safeguard the cargoes bound for Britain. The aim of Dönitz and his growing coterie of U-boats and crews is to destroy as many of those cargoes as they can. The food, textiles, lumber, ores, and fuel oil from the United States, Canada, the Caribbean, and Latin America must reach Britain. If they do not, Britain's people will starve and the fires of Britain's war factories will die out. Now, with France gone and Germany perched on the very shores of the Atlantic Ocean, the Allies have one more major task. They must bring to the United Kingdom the soldiers and airmen, the planes and tanks and guns, and the reinforcements from overseas that will some day allow them to attack and breach Hitler's Atlantic Wall. That is the essence of the Battle of the Atlantic.

To win that battle, the Allies must push enough ships through to Britain to sustain the island and its people while, at the same time, they build the strength they will need when D-Day is at hand. They will lose that battle if the Germans sink Allied ships and kill Allied seamen in sufficient numbers. Both sides mould their strategies according to these goals. The Germans deploy as many U-boats as they can at concentrated points across Allied shipping lanes; the Allies try to avoid those U-boat concentrations. By late 1940 the Germans are winning. They are destroying three merchant ships for every new one built in Allied shipyards, and they are launching eight submarines for every one they lose.

During the Kaiser's war, the Admiralty learned that convoys were still the best way to protect merchant shipping from attack. Convoys were easier to protect with fewer escort vessels than ships travelling alone. If U-boats missed a single vessel at sea, then one cargo arrived safely at its destination. If U-boats missed an entire convoy, then forty or sixty cargoes got through. Even if a convoy was detected, however, a well-mounted defence by the convoy's escort could ensure that some, even most, of the merchantmen survived. In September 1939 the Admiralty wastes no time instituting convoys.

The best defence a convoy can have is not to be found. Throughout the Second World War the Admiralty's main aim in the Battle of the Atlantic is to fool Dönitz by sending the convoys where he least expects them to go. Even when the Germans begin to deploy patrol lines up to 200 miles long across the main shipping routes, there is still a lot of ocean left for the convoys to plod through, much more ocean than the eyes of U-boat lookouts can scan. At first the Admiralty's ability to send convoys around the German patrol lines is strictly limited. It is mostly done by guesswork derived from sinking reports and the occasional sighting of a U-boat, and by tracking U-boat radio transmissions from shore-based stations.

High-frequency direction-finding, or "Huff Duff," had its roots in the First World War when the Allies learned they could roughly determine the position of German submarines at sea by plotting the location of their radio transmissions using two or more shore-based detection stations. The more stations they built, the more accurate the plots became. Even though they could rarely fix a U-boat's position closer than 50 miles to its actual location, Huff Duff did help the Royal Navy sink a number of German submarines by the end of the war. At the start of the Second World War, the Allies resort to Huff Duff almost immediately. Dönitz's tactics make it necessary for his submarine captains to make frequent transmissions. Those transmissions are picked up by Huff Duff, plotted, and immediately reported to the Admiralty, which then guesses where the U-boats are and where the convoys ought not to be.

In the last half of 1941 the Admiralty's ability to outwit Dönitz improves tremendously when the British break the naval code used by the German navy. That gives the British the ability not only to plot the whereabouts of enemy submarines through their radio transmissions but also to listen to Dönitz instructing his captains where to concentrate.

In the early years of the war, Royal Navy escort groups usually consist of two destroyers and four corvettes; Royal Canadian Navy escort groups rarely have more than one destroyer and three corvettes. The Senior Officer of the Escort (SOE) is the senior destroyer captain. His ship is larger, faster, and better armed than the corvettes and is usually manned by more experienced officers and ratings. The SOE's job is to plan convoy defence and to command the escort vessels during actions. At sea he answers to the Convoy Commodore, usually an ex-naval officer with much experience at sea who sails in a ship in the front row and in the middle column of the convoy. The Commodore issues instructions for course, speed, and alterations of course.

The destroyer's normal station is in front of the convoy, where its speed and range allow the SOE to sweep across the front of the advancing columns. In action, he can go swiftly to the scene of an attack to back up one of the corvettes. The corvettes are much slower. Their top speed is 15 knots—actually less than a u-boat's top speed on the surface. They are disposed on the convoy's beams and in the rear. The hindmost escort is the "tail-end Charlie." All the escorts zigzag as they sweep the ocean with their asdic. This path allows them to cover more area. By day they sweep at maximum visibility from the convoy; by night they close up to it. Each evening, just before dusk, the destroyer sweeps far ahead of the convoy to force down any waiting u-boats while the trailing corvette sweeps far astern to detect submarines that might be following.

Convoys are either "slow" or "fast." At the end of 1940, slow outbound convoys (SC) usually depart for the United Kingdom from Sydney, Nova Scotia. They consist of ships with maximum speeds of from 6 to 8 knots. Fast outbound convoys (HX) leave from Halifax. They consist of ships with maximum speeds of from 8 to 11 knots. Very fast troop ships such as the *Queen Mary* or the *Queen Elizabeth*, with top speeds in excess of 30 knots, sail on their own. A surfaced submarine has more than enough speed to shadow either a slow or a fast convoy and report its position, or to join other members of the pack that are already in contact with a convoy. Underwater, however, the submarines can manage a bare 5 to 7 knots. When they are forced below periscope depth, they are blind.

In the first three and a half years of the Battle of the Atlantic, it is not the job of the convoy escorts to actively seek out and destroy submarines. In the official language of the Royal Navy's Western Approaches Command Convoy Instructions (WACCI, or "Wacky" for short), the main aim of the escorts is to ensure the "safe and timely arrival of the convoy." Although escorts will sink a submarine if they can, they are primarily interested in forcing their foes down deep, where they can do little harm. There are so few escorts that neither the Royal Navy nor the Royal Canadian Navy has the luxury of detaching a corvette or a destroyer from the convoy screen to hunt a sub to the death. Escorts may spend a few hours searching and depth charging a contact, but rarely do anything more than that. There are to be no wild-goose chases. Escorts are under strict instructions to stay with the convoys and to keep the screen as tight as possible.

In the early part of the war, shore-based Allied aircraft are too short ranged to seriously impede submarine attacks, break up wolfpacks, or damage or sink submarines. They can, however, force them under when they do see them. In the waters off the United Kingdom, the Royal Air Force's Coastal Command tries to do that as it works under the operational control of the Admiralty. In the waters off the east coast of Canada, the Royal Canadian Air Force's Eastern Air Command does the same job. Most of the mid-ocean is unprotected by aircraft, however, and that is where the Germans gather their forces. The merchant seamen and the men manning the escorts call that area "the black hole." It is a hole into which men and ships enter and are never seen again.

———————————

On the morning of 20 October 1940 *St Croix* stands out from Halifax. In company with another Town Class destroyer, HMCS *St Francis*, she proceeds to escort convoy HX82 to the waters off Cape Race. The Royal Navy's 3rd Battle Squadron, operating out of Halifax, will then take the merchantmen eastward to the United Kingdom. There, the two most important escort bases are Greenock on the Clyde and Londonderry in Northern Ireland. *St Croix* joins what will soon be known as the Western

Local Escort Force, which is assigned the job of guarding the convoys from an east coast port to the Grand Banks. There is little danger from U-boat attacks on this side of the Atlantic, so the hard-pressed Royal Canadian Navy assigns its Town Class destroyers, armed yachts, motor launches, and a handful of corvettes to provide the escort. At this early stage of the war, it is a job without glamour or public notice, and with long days of sailing in bad weather, near treacherous coasts and shoals, and perilously close to that graveyard of ships known as Sable Island.

Winter is descending on the North Atlantic. The hours of daylight are shrinking, the air is colder, there is snow in the weather forecast, and the seas are starting to heave with the perpetual storms that batter the western ocean at this time of year. *St Croix* passes out of Halifax harbour under a lowering sky. Kingsley is on the bridge and orders his navigating Officer or "pilot" to take up station on the merchant ships as they exit the safety of Bedford Basin one by one. The two destroyers then begin to dash through the rising swells to shepherd the ships into rows and columns. Each master knows his assigned place, but the intricate business of assembling a convoy is always time-consuming. The tankers must go in the middle, and the ships with less volatile cargoes are on the outside.

As the ships form up in columns, the two destroyers careen through the water, their signal lamps flashing messages of cajoling, of urgency, of remonstrance:

"Make [send a message] to *Empire Scout*: You are making too much smoke."

"Make to *Esso Trader*: Make your best speed to your station."

"Make to *Federal Raven*: Close up on *Norwegian Soldier*."

Even though this is a "fast" convoy, most of the merchantmen are long-time veterans of the ocean. Their sides are streaked with rust. Heavily laden, they move sluggishly in the rising seas. Laundry snaps on clotheslines. Livestock can be heard on the Greek-registered ships. The Greeks like to bring their fresh meat supply on the hoof. The convoy is a small floating city. The merchantmen communicate with each other by signal lamp. "Have you a doctor aboard? We have a man with a broken ankle" flashes from a tanker to a nearby ore carrier.

By afternoon, the convoy is assembled and moving northeast through a heavy swell. As darkness falls, a driving snow whips across the seascape.

The watch keepers on the bridge of *St Croix* peer through their glasses. They look for signs of submarines, but mostly to make sure their charges don't get too close; the narrow hull of a destroyer is easily sliced in two by the plunging bow of a heavily loaded merchantman. The crew of HMCS *Margaree* discovers that two days after *St Croix* sails from Halifax. *Margaree* is escorting convoy OL8 when she is cut in two by the freighter *Port Fairy* some 600 miles south of Iceland. Her captain and 140 men go down with her.

On the evening of 21 October, lookouts aboard *St Francis* spot the ocean escort vessels of the Royal Navy. Her signal lamp stabs through the darkness: "Newfoundland escort sighted bearing 040." On the bridge of the *St Croix*, glasses are trained to the northeast and eyes strain in the gathering gloom. The ships are sighted and signals are flashed as the handover is arranged. Then *St Croix* and *St Francis* turn westward into the full fury of an early winter storm.

The two destroyers plunge ahead into the rising seas. With their narrow hulls and flush decks, they slice into the oncoming waves rather than ride over them. Water sweeps across *St Croix*'s forecastle and pours into the ship through ventilators and hatches. On the bridge, Kingsley, the Officer of the Watch, and the rest of the bridge crew are soaked by seas smashing high over the dodger. Below decks, the crew tries to carry on. Life cannot stop in a ship at sea. The watches must be kept, the engines tended, the boilers checked, and the food prepared. But each job becomes more difficult with each passing minute. Men move slowly about from handhold to handhold. The men on deck grab the wire lifelines that run on both sides of the main deck from under the bridge to the rear deck-house. Though swathed in oilskins and sea boots, they are soaked to the skin only moments after dashing onto the weather decks.

On the bridge and in the wheel-house, the Officer of the Watch and the quartermaster struggle to keep *St Croix*'s bows pointing in the direction of the wind and seas. The struggle between storm and ship is always the same. The wind tries to push the ship into the troughs of the waves, to force her to present her beam to the sea. This is the quickest way to kill her and her crew. Hit beam on by a heavy blow, some ships roll over too far to recover and plunge to the bottom—a fate even more true for these narrow Town Class destroyers. To survive, the mortals whose lives depend on the cockleshell of steel between them and the deep must keep their ship's bows pointing into the maelstrom so that wind and water come from straight ahead. Then they can maintain some control over what direction she takes and try to ensure that the seas pound her from fore to aft. The ship is steered by her twin rudders and her twin screws. When the wind presses against the port bow, the helm is put over to port, and vice versa.

The storm rages through the night. Kingsley knows his steering gear is delicate at best and worries about losing steerage. He orders revolutions for 10 knots, which he thinks will be enough to keep headway but not so fast as to bore directly into the oncoming seas. Visibility drops sharply. Thunder rolls over the seascape and lightning illuminates the mountainous waves. Tons of sea water sweep over *St Croix*'s forecastle. The guard-rail stanchions are carried away. The ship rolls heavily. This is the first big storm *St Croix* has been through under Kingsley's command. He is distressed at the violence of her rolls and the green seas that break over her forecastle, but he knows he must keep calm. Even the slightest hint that he is worried will set off a chain reaction of fear among his crew.

"How are things below, Number One?"

"There's some water in the petty officer's mess, Captain, but everything seems to be holding up well. Should I order the men into their life-belts?"

"I don't think that will be necessary, Number One. I've been through much worse than this. We needed to paint those stanchions; now we'll just get new ones."

It is idle chitchat, meant to reinforce calm. What Kingsley is really doing is sizing up his charge, seeing how she rolls and bucks in a heavy sea. He is trying to get the measure of her amid mountainous waves and high winds.

The storm passes. On the afternoon of 22 October, *St Croix* re-enters Halifax harbour in a light drizzle. Kingsley noses her to the side of a harbour tanker, where she is refuelled, then guides her to her berth. The libertymen prepare for an evening ashore; Kingsley tells his First Lieutenant to report to him as quickly as possible on the defects the storm has uncovered. Repairs and improvements will have to be made promptly because *St Croix* is due to cross to the United Kingdom for a major refit before taking up escort duties in UK waters. The most serious problem is that sea water continues to seep through the hull plates and into the fuel tanks. There is more water than fuel at the bottom of the tanks. The problem is made worse by the need to switch manually from one tank to another to maintain a constant flow of fuel. If the stoker responsible is not on his toes and fails to switch before the tank is down to its last few tons, the fuel intake hoses suck in the water at the bottom of the tank and spray it into the boilers. When that happens, the ship loses way quickly. Some of the boiler tubes are leaking, and the fresh-water condensers work only intermittently. Kingsley decides there will be strict rationing of fresh water at sea from now on. *St Croix* has suffered only minor damage. She is lucky. One British Town destroyer caught in a vicious storm suffers major damage to her superstructure and bridge, and her captain is killed in his sea cabin when a massive green sea sweeps over her forecastle.

For the next three weeks, workmen swarm over the ship installing new equipment, fixing old gear, and working to get *St Croix* shipshape for the long mid-winter crossing that lies ahead. The aft 4-inch gun and the main mast are removed. Other more significant alterations will be done in the United Kingdom. At mid-month Kingsley receives his orders: *St Croix* will sail for the United Kingdom via St John's, Newfoundland, at the end of the month in consort with *St Clair* and *Niagara*. *St Croix* will carry Captain C.R.H. Taylor, who is designated Captain (D) (or flotilla commander) of the three Town Class destroyers. When he reaches his destination, Taylor will become Captain Commanding Canadian Ships in European Waters.

Preparations for the crossing are speeded up. The boilers are checked, especially the safety valves during high-speed runs. The steering gear is given a workout. The gyrocompass is tested, the magnetic compass is swung. The three 4-inch and the aft 3-inch high-angle guns are all test fired. The ship's ancient Lewis machine-guns rattle off several dozen pans of ammunition. The radios are tested and adjusted. On 29 November the three ships secure alongside the harbour tanker and fill their tanks. Fresh water is pumped aboard. At 11 a.m. the next day they leave Halifax harbour and set course for Newfoundland.

The little flotilla runs northeastward at 13.5 knots all day and into the early subarctic darkness. The watches change every four hours. Lookouts scan the horizon and the submarine detectors listen to their asdic sets. The constant ping of the asdic echoes on the bridge repeater.

They do not expect to encounter subs in these waters. In the wheel-house, the Quartermaster stands watch while the helmsman grips the wheel. Every now and then an adjustment in the ship's heading is ordered to compensate for wind and waves. Kingsley keeps close to the bridge all day; after nightfall, he stays in his sea cabin, saying little but listening to the sounds of the ship around him. The messmen are called to the galley to pick up their evening meals. From somewhere in the bowels of St Croix comes the sound of a harmonica; from elsewhere the voices of laughing men. Though deep in his own thoughts, Taylor provides company for Kingsley. Every now and then he checks the progress and state of his other two charges. The two ships keep station on St Croix's beams. Course alterations are ordered from St Croix's bridge by signal flag. The flotilla must maintain strict radio silence.

The ships steam into the morning watch of 2 December. There is no dawn, however, just a faint lightening of the sky to the northeast. The glass is falling and low, scudding clouds skim the seascape. Meteorological reports indicate a storm to the southeast of Cape Race. A heavy swell and a freshening wind signal that St Croix and her consorts will soon run into foul weather. The Officer of the Watch sends the Coxswain to check that all openings are closed tight and that loose gear is lashed down. As they steam past Cape Race, a mix of rain and snow begins to pelt the three destroyers. They are soon heaving and rolling in the mounting seas. Their bows slice into 30-foot waves piled up by the force 7 near gale. With every plunge of their bows, water floods back along their forecastles. Aboard St Croix, a green sea sweeps the forecastle, swirls around "A" gun, and smashes into the base of the superstructure. It is impossible to peer directly ahead for more than a few moments; the driving sleet hits the officers and men on the bridge like birdshot.

Taylor orders flotilla speed reduced to 8 knots while he tries to keep track of the two plunging consorts. Aboard St Clair, the wheel-house steering gear breaks down and the aft steering position is manned. Her captain orders his First Lieutenant to have a crew member stand by near the tiller flat in case the emergency manual steering gear needs to be used. The storm delays the flotilla for five hours. The three destroyers approach St John's harbour in late afternoon as night begins to fall.

Going into St John's is always dangerous in darkness and heavy weather. The harbour entrance is narrow and difficult to find. New masters find it unnerving to steer directly for what appears to be an iron-bound coast; even experienced masters feel uneasy about the approach. Once inside the fjordlike harbour, however, the water is suddenly calm. On the north side, where the city is found, the hill climbs steeply to the colonial legislative building at the top. The houses are mostly clap-board, painted in reds and greens and blues. On the south side, the bur-geoning naval facility never sleeps; jetties are being built for harbour tankers and destroyer tenders, for corvettes and destroyers and other es-cort vessels. The three destroyers secure alongside the Imperial Oil Jetty to embark fuel and fresh water and to effect minor repairs. Taylor is under orders to proceed as quickly as possible, but has discretion to leave only when he deems his three ships to be ready. When he leaves the sanctuary of St John's, he is to steer northeast to a point roughly 800 miles south of Reykjavik, Iceland, and from there to UK waters.

———————

At 11 a.m. on 4 December *St Croix* leads her two consorts to sea. Kings-ley orders his Navigator to maintain a course of 040 at 12.5 knots. It is very cold. Soon the sea spray begins to freeze on the metal surfaces of the superstructure, the deck-houses, the guns, the depth-charge racks, and the ventilators. The coating of ice grows thicker by the hour. The Officer of the Watch orders all hands not on watch to turn out for ice chipping. Hour by hour the men hack, chop, and chip at the ice. *St Croix* is top heavy to begin with. In a rough sea, the additional weight of a few tons of ice can make the difference between survival and death.

On the first day out, *St Croix* suddenly loses way; her fuel pumps have sucked water from one of the tanks. The stokers quickly switch over and the turbines begin to whir once again. But just as *St Croix* starts to recover speed, *St Clair* falls astern. She signals that she, too, has lost pressure in her steam lines. Taylor tells Kingsley and *Niagara* to re-duce speed to enable *St Clair* to catch up. All three destroyers are having trouble with their forward steering gear, and all three close up men in the tiller flat should it be necessary to steer the ships manually.

In the early hours of 7 December, Kingsley is sleeping in his sea cabin when a whistle comes through the voice pipe above his head. It is the First Lieutenant:

"Sir. You'd better get up here. It's looking a bit nasty up ahead."

Kingsley shakes the sleep from his head and looks at his watch dial. It is just past 3 a.m. and he can feel *St Croix* rising and falling on a heavy swell. He slips into his sea boots and dons his duffle coat. He remembers to wrap a towel around his neck and stuff it inside his hood. He'll need it when the spray starts coming over the bridge dodger.

It is dark and cold on the bridge, with low cloud holding the promise of rain. There is a heavy swell from the south. The glass is falling sharply and the wind is blowing from the southeast against the starboard beam.

"Pilot, have we picked up any met. reports in the last hour or so?"

"No, sir, but there haven't been any of ours through here in the last day or so. I reckon there's a low crossing our track to the east somewhere ahead and moving south."

"I'm afraid you're probably right. We'd better get the SOE up here. Bosun, see to it." Kingsley has seen the signs many times before. The low-pressure area ahead has very steep gradients, he reasons, and counter-clockwise winds bear against the ship's beam. Over hundreds of miles of open ocean the winds are piling up a heavy swell. They'll be into it before long.

Kingsley takes the bridge from the Officer of the Watch. He is not a man to delegate authority. He asks the pilot for regular reports on the barometric pressure. If the glass keeps falling, they are drawing nearer to the storm centre; if it begins to hold steady, the system is passing them by. Taylor is still buttoning his duffle coat as he joins Kingsley. "Blow shaping up, eh? Seems to be tracking south somewhere ahead of us. From the size of the swells, I'd say we're in for it."

Kingsley nods. The two men keep watch into the dawn hours as the seas mount and the wind shifts to their starboard quarter. The wind whips the white tops off the waves as soon as they curl over and hurls the spray horizontally across the seascape.

Kingsley has rarely seen the sea in such a state. He knows he must conceal his concern even as *St Croix* pitches and rolls violently in the quartering sea. The dodger is banging in the wind. The howling storm makes it impossible to hear a human voice. *St Croix* creaks and complains with every roll. From below comes the sound of crashing equipment, breaking dishes and utensils, men swearing loudly. The wind rips at the mast and yardarm and groans through the wires.

"Coxswain, you'd better go round and check everything you can, then get back here and take the wheel."

Kingsley and Taylor lose their footing as the ship twists savagely beneath them. Taylor shouts into Kingsley's ear: "Make to *St Clair* and *Niagara* to execute a 90 degree turn to starboard. We can't head into this thing much longer. We're not going to outrun it either. I think we'd better try to find calmer water to the south. Reduce your speed to 8 knots or thereabouts and see if you can maintain steerage."

Kingsley acknowledges the instruction and passes the order to the Chief Yeoman, who tells the signal man—"Bunts" in ship's jargon—to hoist the flags for a course and speed alteration. The signal men on the other ships spot the flags snapping in the gale and report the imminent course and speed change. The yardarms of both destroyers are soon flying the same flags, acknowledging that their captains have seen and understood the signal.

Kingsley holds his glasses on *Niagara* and *St Clair*, then shouts "execute." Bunts hauls down the signal flags and *St Croix* immediately alters course to 130 degrees and slows down. The other two ships follow. Their bows turn unsteadily into the wind. The violent rolling eases a bit as the full force of wind and wave comes on to their starboard bows, but the pitching continues. An hour or so after dawn, *St Croix*'s bridge lookouts lose *St Clair* in the mountainous seas, which are now approaching 40 feet in height. With sledgehammer blows, green seas come crashing down onto *St Croix*'s forecastle. She shudders under the attack. Kingsley fears for the safety of his ship and his men. His old destroyer was not designed to absorb this type of punishment. How long would she hold? Which green sea would force her bows under for good, or flood her, or carry away her flimsy superstructure? *St Croix* batters into the sea, *Niagara* not far away. Then *Niagara*, too, disappears.

Taylor must know if the other two destroyers have foundered; he must call for help in searching for survivors, if there are any. No submarine captain can possibly think to mount an attack on such a night. The storm is their greatest danger, not German torpedoes. He tells Kingsley to break radio silence, but *St Croix* cannot broadcast directly to *St Clair* and *Niagara*. Her obsolete radio is not equipped for ship-to-ship communication.

Inside the destroyer, all is in chaos. Men off watch lie fearful in their swaying hammocks. The roaring wind, the water rushing around the hull, and stark fear make sleep almost impossible. The messdecks are awash with sloshing sea water, broken crockery, sodden papers and photographs, and vomit. In the ship's office, the deck is strewn with metal desk drawers and awash with their contents. The adding machine and the typewriter break off their lugs and fall to the deck, sliding across it with each roll. Every sickening lurch brings the sound of something or someone crashing to the deck or against a bulkhead. The hands who have to move about do so a step at a time, a hand-hold at a time, lest they be dashed against bulkheads, hatch covers, or ladders. The ship is rolling so far they must balance themselves with one foot on the deck and the other on a bulkhead. It is virtually impossible to go to the heads. It is almost impossible to do anything normal in the lurching, crashing, corkscrewing destroyer. Religious men pray for their lives. The others try to think of wives, sweethearts, or whores they have known—anything to keep their minds away from the cold, cruel death that rages outside the thin steel shell of the hull.

In the wheel-house the Coxswain fights to hold *St Croix*'s course into the storm. The wind and the waves press relentlessly on her starboard bow. Most of the time he has the wheel almost hard a starboard. But that too is risky because, when the seas fall off momentarily, the ship begins to swing beam on in that direction. Kingsley orders speed reduced to 6 knots, but that is too slow for the helm to keep *St Croix* under control. Just before midnight, Kingsley shouts into the engine-room voice pipe: "Chief, give me revolutions for 3 knots on the starboard screw and 8 knots on the port screw." He can barely hear the acknowledging "Aye, aye, sir."

That seems to work for the moment. *St Croix*'s bows swing back into the wind. She fights to keep her bow towards the storm and to hold enough headway to keep from being pushed beam on into the troughs of the looming seas. The storm builds to full hurricane force. The wind vibrates her rigging and antennas, pushes against her hull, tears at her ventilators, moans loudly around her superstructure. It whips the wave tops horizontally across the seascape. It is impossible to tell where sea and sky divide. Both are white with driven spray. There is no world save *St Croix*. She and her crew are totally at the mercy of this heaving ocean.

Night falls. *St Croix* hangs on to life. The physical damage has been light so far. At 2 a.m. on 8 December a lookout reports a distress rocket off to port. No one else sees it. Nothing can be done, anyway. *St Croix* is in mortal danger. The seas are now 60 feet high and the wind is blowing at more than 80 miles an hour. Suddenly, three green seas in a row slam down on her main deck, buckling the deck-plates of her forecastle. The water collides with brutal power into her lower bridge structure, crumpling the thin steel. It carries away guard-rails, stanchions, and ventilators. It smashes Carley floats and breaks the whaler into kindling wood. It bends voice pipes. It floods into the Petty Officers' mess, the officers' cabins, and the wardroom. The men are ordered to bail. Kingsley tells the First Lieutenant to call the ship's company to don life-belts. The ship begins to fall off once again. Kingsley cannot hold her. He is strangely calm. For a brief instant he accepts his fate. He stares at the raging sea.

Taylor pushes to the engine-room voice pipe: "Chief, this is Captain (D). Stop the starboard engine."

In a moment the starboard engine bridge telegraph rings to "stop." With the port screw turning at almost 90 revolutions per minute, the bow holds.

Taylor shouts to the Chief Yeoman: "Make to COAC, repeat to NSHQ. Hove to at 054 degrees 34 minutes north, 035 degrees 29 minutes west. Sustained damage to bridge structure and forecastle. Request HMCS *Niagara*, HMCS *St Clair* be instructed to break w/t silence and report position, course and speed, damage sustained and whether capable of proceeding to the UK." *St Croix* is now hove to some 300 miles due east of Cape Farewell, but where are her consorts? In the radio room the Morse key taps out the message. It is picked up by the navy's powerful receivers near Halifax and relayed back out to sea. But there is no reply. Radio operators at sea and along the coast listen. Nothing but static comes over their earphones.

Taylor orders Kingsley to work his way east to search for the lost ships, but the low has crossed their track and is moving south; the seas are sweeping east to west. No ship can outrun waves driven by high winds; as *St Croix*'s bows turn east, the seas crash onto her stern. The waves roll up her deck and bury her stem in a cauldron of foam. This pooping and diving will kill the destroyer if her relatively weak stern main deck is crushed and opened to the sea, or if a stern sea drives her deep into the windward slope of a 60-foot wave. It is too dangerous.

Taylor gives up. He orders Kingsley south in search of calmer seas, then windward to St John's.

Far to the west, in Halifax, the Flag Officer of the Royal Navy's 3rd Battle Squadron orders his ships, which are returning to Halifax after escorting a convoy, to search for *St Clair* and *Niagara*. They pass across the planned route of the Canadian destroyers, but find nothing. Have almost three hundred men and two warships disappeared? On 11 December *St Clair* reports her position to the Commander-in-Chief Western Approaches in the United Kingdom. She has made the passage and is steaming for Greenock. *Niagara* calls in the next day. She, too, is heading for Greenock. Far to the west, *St Croix* limps towards St John's, tacking into the still strong wind. In the early hours of 11 December, Kingsley heaves to again, this time about 400 miles from Cape Race. Driven by 60-mile-an-hour winds, the waves batter *St Croix* for fifteen hours. Then the storm abates and, on 13 December, the crippled destroyer noses into the calm waters of St John's harbour. She secures alongside HMS *Ripley*, a British Town Class destroyer, at 9:30 a.m. She is badly damaged. When a warship arrives in port after long, hard days at sea, the libertymen are always in their clean uniforms, waiting to rush ashore as soon as they can. But *St Croix*'s crew is exhausted. Few have snatched more than a few minutes' sleep in the past six days. Most have been sick to the point of debilitation. They sleep.

Taylor leaves the ship in St John's. He must find passage eastward as soon as possible. With the assistance of tugs, Kingsley takes *St Croix* away from her berth on 16 December after minor repairs to her boiler tubes and replenishment of her fuel and fresh-water supplies. They are sailing to Halifax. As the tugs cast off, one of *St Croix*'s hawsers drops in the water astern. Kingsley reacts quickly and immediately orders both engines stopped. The destroyer drifts into the tanker SS *Petrolite*. When the fouled screw is cleared, *St Croix*'s starboard screw-guard rubs up against the same tanker. There is little damage to either ship. Finally, *St Croix* gets under way. Approaching the harbour mouth, the steering gear breaks down. Kingsley guides the ship to sea by using his screws to turn her. At last, they are clear and heading for Halifax. *St Croix* runs into another storm about twelve hours out from St John's. The wind rises as a southeasterly gale batters the destroyer. Her speed is reduced to 10 knots. The gyrocompass and the echo sounder break down; boiler tubes blow out. The Chief Engineer can barely keep a decent head of steam. As the sky begins to clear at sunset on the 17th, even though the destroyer still rises and falls on a heavy swell, she begins to make headway again. At 8:15 a.m. on 18 December *St Croix* ties up alongside HMCS *Prince Henry* at the naval dockyard's No. 4 jetty. Her damage is severe.

St Croix is put in dry dock for the next three months. The Commander-in-Chief of the Royal Navy's Atlantic and West Indies squadron, based at Bermuda, suggests that no more Towns be sent to the United Kingdom during the balance of the winter. He invites the Admiralty to base the Town fleet in Bermuda until the spring. But the destroyers cannot be spared. They continue to escort convoys—and so will *St Croix*, when she is seaworthy again. It is a measure of how desperately the Canadian and British navies need escort vessels that this ancient destroyer is still worth the considerable resources it takes to send her back to sea.

The storm becomes the defining moment in Kingsley's command of *St Croix*. Officers and ratings alike know that it was Taylor who saved them, not their Captain. Stoker Reg Lees even composes a poem that most of the men are soon reciting over beer in the shoreside bars. They dare not recite it aboard ship. Lees calls it, "Why did I ever leave home?"

> Oh, I wish I had listened to mother
> and had never sailed on the sea.
> And if I had never seen the *St Croix*,
> this would never have happened to me.
>
> Oh, we sailed from St John's in Newfoundland
> and headed right out to the sea.
> We thought in ten days we'd be marching
> to the pipes playing "Bonnie Dundee."
>
> We are stranded out here on the ocean.
> We are lost out here on the sea.
> The whole thing's a commotion.
> Oh, why did this happen to me?
>
> Oh, the lookouts can't find any signposts.
> I guess we will just have to roam

with the wind and the waves all around us.
Oh, why did I ever leave home?

Oh, the guys on the bridge are dumbfounded.
They've tried everything that they know.
But with the ocean we still are surrounded,
and the Skipper don't know where to go.

As the months pass during *St Croix*'s extensive refit, Kingsley becomes argumentative and aggressive. Worse, he begins to drink heavily. But the navy is as short of qualified skippers, particularly regular or "pusser" skippers such as Kingsley, as it is of destroyers. Like the old ship he commands, he too must return to sea.

––––––––––

For the first two and a half months of 1941, storms of awesome power lash the Atlantic coast and punish the convoys and their escorts. Though German submarine strength barely increases, the U-boats are sent farther west, to the waters south of Iceland. Allied shipping losses climb from 125,000 tons in January to 325,000 tons in May. Both the Royal Navy and the Royal Canadian Navy struggle to put more ships and men into the battle, but most of the new vessels are corvettes. The news from other war fronts seems to improve, as British and Australian troops strike a telling blow against the Italians in North Africa in early February.

In Halifax the convoys and their escort groups come and go as welders, riveters, fitters, shipwrights, and electricians work their will on *St Croix*. Most of the ratings are sent to the manning depots, where they are assigned to other ships. Some officers are also given new duties. The officers and men who are to stay with the venerable destroyer get leave to visit their families. Kingsley, however, spends most of the three months with the ship, since she is ultimately his responsibility. There is much to be done on her. The storm damage must be repaired, and the steering gear and other vital machinery and equipment must be strengthened. There are also changes and improvements to be made. A list forwarded to Naval Service Headquarters in Ottawa from the Admiralty details 187 different modifications the Town Class vessels need to improve ship handling, crew comfort, and anti-submarine capability. The RCN begins to make some of these changes to *St Croix* during these three months. The remaining mast is shortened and the yardarm lowered. The two rearmost torpedo batteries are removed. So is the forward searchlight platform and searchlight. But there is no time to carry out most of the major modifications that British and even some Canadian Towns are undergoing. When Kingsley takes *St Croix* to sea in mid-March 1941 for equipment trials, and to break in his new crew, his destroyer is little changed from when she was commissioned half a year earlier.

With spring, the weather moderates somewhat, but the war at sea intensifies. With the loss of the *Bismarck* on 27 May, German naval strategy shifts its emphasis from surface vessels to submarines. Admiral Karl Dönitz will shape the second Battle of the Atlantic under the slogan "kill, burn, and destroy." In the Mediterranean, German paratroopers invade and ultimately conquer Crete. When will *St Croix* rejoin the war? She is assigned to local escort duty for convoy HX116, due to leave Halifax on 21 March, but is then scrubbed and replaced by the corvette HMCS *Orillia*. She eventually sails on 10 April 1941 as local escort for TC10, a troop-carrying convoy. She accompanies it as far as the Grand Banks, then returns to Halifax. On her return, she experiences two engine breakdowns. The first occurs when an inexperienced stoker allows the fuel pump to suck air from a near-empty tank; the second, when water contaminates the fuel in a different tank. *St Croix* seems to run out of luck every time she leaves harbour. As a newly promoted Commander, Kingsley chafes for a more modern ship and now begins openly to show his irritation with *St Croix*'s constant mechanical breakdowns.

Each day begins to seem like the day before. *St Croix* spends several hours chasing a false asdic contact on 14 April, but that is the only break in the routine. She and her crew seem destined for this boring fate for the rest of the war while other men and other ships fight on far fields and the deep blue of the mid-ocean. *St Croix*'s war consists of leaving Halifax for the waters near Newfoundland, handing her charges over to the mid-ocean escort, then returning to port to do it all over again. It wouldn't be so bad if Halifax and its people were more receptive to the sailors, but they are not. The town closes up tighter than a drum in the evenings, prices are high, and Haligonians do little to make the navy men feel at home.

The officers and ratings get used to living and sailing aboard *St Croix*; it is not an altogether pleasant experience. The ship is crowded. More men are living aboard her than she was designed for. Hammocks are strung wherever there is space in the messdecks. Between the hammocks and the fold-up bunks the ship came with, the messdecks are overcrowded and impossible to keep orderly. In heavy weather, they are easily flooded. When it is cold outside, a thick dew of condensation forms on the uninsulated bulkheads and ceilings. When the temperature drops, the condensation turns to ice. Mattresses freeze against bulkheads. The Petty Officers' Mess, one deck below the forecastle, is wet almost all the time from condensation and from seawater that leaks from the main deck. In port, the petty officers sleep ashore while their mess and bedding are dried out. Men get sick easily from the constant humidity in the ship.

The crew's head consists of a thin bench over an open trough through which sea water runs. It is almost impossible to use in rough weather. Officers' toilets back up when the valves designed to keep sea water from flooding in malfunction. Seasickness renders many of the men useless at one point or another in almost every voyage. They take refuge where they can, vomiting their guts out, fighting the desire to stay curled up in some corner, needing to get up and on with their duties, often not being physically able to do so. Even in fair weather, with the sun shining, the ship rolls heavily in a beam sea. The safety lines that run fore and aft must be used constantly by crew members lest they be swept overboard.

The stokers have it the worst. The noise from the ventilation fans in the boiler room is overwhelming. The heat is constant. The men work below the waterline and never really know what is going on above them. The boiler rooms are pressurized to prevent flashback and are not easily entered or exited from. If *St Croix* takes a torpedo, these men will probably be the first to die. Yet their job is absolutely vital. The boilers they maintain provide the ship's heat and power and give it its means of moving through the water. Steam pressure must be kept within certain limits, and the mixture of fuel and air maintained in such a way as not to produce black smoke, easily spotted miles away from the conning tower of a patrolling submarine. The engine rooms are not much better, though they are not quite so hot as the boiler rooms. The men tending the turbines keep a constant watch for mechanical breakdown. Are the journals and bearings running hot? Are the turbines performing properly? Are the steampipes transferring steam freely from turbine to turbine? Are the shafts straight and turning freely?

The cooks work hard to turn out decent meals in the inadequately equipped galleys, but after a few days at sea much of the fresh food is gone. Meat is hung in the open air because of the lack of refrigeration. Bread, vegetables, and fruit soon grow mouldy. After a few days at sea, bully beef or canned sausages become regular fare. Breakfast is almost always "red lead and bacon," a concoction of tomato juice and fried bacon. Later in the war, when the United States joins the fight and Canadian destroyers sometimes secure alongside US destroyer tenders, the Canadians are amazed to be served thick grilled steaks, bottled Coca Cola, and fresh ice cream.

Although *St Croix* has bunks (as do all US-built destroyers), the messing arrangements are the same as those aboard other British and Canadian ships. In each mess there is a central table, dishes, cutlery, crockery, and a small store of staples such as jam, ketchup, sugar, coffee, tea, and bread. Sometimes messmen scrounge up a toaster. At mealtimes, the man assigned to fetch the food goes to the galley with a "carry-all" for the food and a "bosh can" for the coffee. The cooks fill the carryall with food enough for the entire mess. That and the coffee are taken back to the mess, where it is divided up and eaten. Men who have just come off watch sleep in their bunks or hammocks (sometimes the hammocks are hung right over the mess table) while the others eat, clean their utensils, and store them in racks and trays. Each man has a small locker for personal gear which he uses as a chair during meals or as a writing desk.

At sea, *St Croix*'s crew maintains a standard cruising watch system. Because a ship must be tended to at all times, the crew is divided into watches. Men on watch carry out their assigned duties in the boiler room, the engine room, the bridge, and elsewhere. The others are "off duty," or, like the cooks, engaged in the same duties at about the same time every day. Canadian naval vessels use a standard three-watch system, each watch being four hours, followed by eight hours off. Two "dog" watches of two hours each are inserted for the ratings between 4 p.m. and 8 p.m. each day. That ensures that they don't have the same watches at the same time every day. As a general rule, each of the four watch-keeping officers stand the same watch every day. The First Lieutenant is always on the bridge between midnight and 4 a.m. The Captain doesn't stand a watch, but can take over from the Officer of the Watch whenever he chooses. Under conditions of an impending attack, usually at dawn or dusk, the regular watch system is suspended and every man will close up to his assigned action station as an ammunition carrier, a gun layer, or a part of the depth-charge crew. After the threat diminishes, a lesser state of readiness—"defence stations"—is ordered and half the ship's company stand down. When even this condition is no longer necessary, "cruising stations" are ordered and the ship returns to the normal three-watch routine.

The constant motion of the ship, the condensation, the water running along the decks in heavy weather, and the noise of the fans, the engines, and the sea deprive men of the basic comforts they take for granted on land. Their clothes and bedding are always damp. They are cold much of the time. They are dirty because there is no fresh water for showers. They have trouble sleeping. They do not eat well. They grow fatigued from hours of scanning the sea for danger, or tending the boilers, or scraping and cleaning and painting in the never-ending fight against rust and corrosion. When *St Croix* escorts convoys at night, their sleep is sometimes interrupted by the alarm bells calling them to action stations. There is an alarming prevalence of tuberculosis on Canadian ships at sea, almost all of which is the result of dampness, fatigue, bad air, and poor food. On the rare days when the sun shines and the air is warm, the weather decks are covered with the bodies of shirtless off-watch men soaking up the rays, breathing the fresh salt air, getting away from the stench of dirty clothing, fuel oil, turpentine, body odour, paint, and wet wool.

St Croix's misadventures continue through the spring of 1941. In the early afternoon of 23 April, the destroyer is proceeding down harbour in Halifax with Kingsley on the bridge. He has ordered revolutions for

14 knots because he doesn't like to manoeuvre in harbour at slower speeds—it is harder to turn quickly if necessary. Ahead, *Reo II*, a small fleet auxiliary vessel, is spotted in the same channel heading directly for *St Croix*. Kingsley orders a blast on the ship's whistle and calls for "starboard 10," but the other vessel keeps coming on. Kingsley orders another 20 degrees of starboard helm and another blast of the whistle, then orders both engines stopped. *Reo II* wakes up, gives two blasts herself, then turns to port. Kingsley calls out "both astern full, hard a port." Three short blasts escape from *St Croix*'s steam whistle. Then the two ships collide. *Reo II* scrapes down *St Croix*'s starboard side, punches a hole in her hull near the tiller flat, and damages the propellor guard.

The inquiry that follows places most of the blame on the captain of the smaller vessel, but Kingsley's superiors are critical of his 14-knot speed in harbour. "This fellow hits something every time he goes out," concludes one. "Seems too bad that two of HMC ships can't get past one another in this harbour," writes another. Kingsley is "lacking in his sense of responsibility," according to Commodore G.C. Jones, Commanding Officer Atlantic Coast. The incident adds to Kingsley's frustrations, and to *St Croix*'s reputation as a hard-luck ship.

By the spring of 1941 the demand for destroyers for the Royal Navy's Home Fleet, the Far East, the Battle of the Atlantic, and other theatres or potential theatres of war has grown to the extent that Britain has too few escort vessels. On 20 May 1941 the Admiralty requests the Royal Canadian Navy to start escorting convoys in the western Atlantic. Thus is born the Newfoundland Escort Force (NEF). The RCN corvettes and destroyers of the NEF are based in St John's, Newfoundland. Their task is to meet eastbound convoys near the Western Ocean Meeting Point (WESTOMP) and escort them to the Mid-Ocean Meeting Point (MOMP), both nothing more than pencil marks on a chart. At MOMP the convoys are handed over to Royal Navy escorts, which guide them to UK waters. The Canadian ships then turn north and steam to Hvalfjordur, the harbour that serves Reykjavik, Iceland. They are refuelled, replenished, and then sent south to meet westbound convoys, which they escort to WESTOMP and hand over to local escorts sailing from Halifax or Sydney.

To accommodate the escorts in Iceland, the Royal Navy sets up a supply base and stations fleet tankers and destroyer tenders in Hvalfjordur, but it is a bad anchorage. The bottom of the harbour is volcanic ash and doesn't afford anchors good holding. The low, barren hills around the harbour offer little protection from North Atlantic gales. There is almost no amusement, recreation, or distraction for the weary sailors. In effect, Iceland has been occupied by the Allies, and the locals do not care to hide their resentment at losing their independence. They are especially protective of their women.

The Canadian escorts assigned to the NEF are painted off-white, with a light-blue and light-green pattern to break up their silhouettes. St Croix stays grey. She continues to ply the waters between Halifax and Newfoundland. Her relatively long range ought to make her a prime candidate for mid-ocean escort, but she is not. Her constant breakdowns and her lack of those modifications necessary for this difficult duty hold her back. Through the spring and summer of 1941, she plods the local convoy tracks. One of her few reliefs from the long and boring days at sea comes on 1 June, when Kingsley is ordered to stop, search, and seize four Vichy French sailing vessels operating out of St Pierre and Miquelon. Ottawa suspects them of being in the pay of the Germans and reporting convoy traffic. St Croix finds one of these ships, the Cancalais, on 3 June. An armed party of one officer and six ratings is put aboard in high seas, despite damage to St Croix's whaler. They force the sullen crew to sail the vessel to St John's. The next day St Croix's crew seizes another Vichy French sailing vessel, the Madiana.

These are weeks of frustration for Kingsley and the crew of St Croix. The summer days are long at these latitudes, and the sun-speckled waters and blue skies are welcome relief from the harsh gales of winter. But each day seems like the day before, and each short night holds promise only of another day like the last. The war is passing St Croix by. To the east, men and warships are fighting the most crucial battle of the war. Some are dying, but they are at least getting a chance to strike a blow at the enemy. St Croix and her crew are dying of boredom in a backwater of the war.

In the more northerly latitudes, it is a cold spring, and ice and fog continue to plague the convoy lanes. On the evening of 16 June St Croix leaves Sydney assigned to escort HX133 to WESTOMP. The convoy runs into heavy fog even as it forms up. St Croix cannot see her charges, but she can hear them over her hydrophones. For four long days she keeps station by sound, briefly sighting the convoy only on the 20th. Her lookouts strain for a sign of the ships, or the fog buoys they stream behind them to keep station in poor visibility. Two vital boiler tubes burst. Kingsley orders *St Croix* about and she carefully feels her way to Halifax through the fog and drifting ice. HX133 steams east to meet its NEF escort, consisting of HMCS *Ottawa* and four Canadian and British corvettes. After nightfall on 23 June, the convoy is attacked by a large wolfpack. The NEF does not come off well; by the time *Ottawa* and her consorts hand their charges over to the Royal Navy, six merchantmen are down.

St Croix is back at sea on 27 June escorting HX135. She is the only escort. It is 4:08 a.m. *St Croix* is passing astern of the convoy, some 400 miles east of Halifax. The watch has just changed. Men are lolling on the decks smoking, playing cards, reading, joking with each other. The Officer of the Watch on the bridge is keeping station with the convoy. Kingsley is in his sea cabin. The lookouts scan the horizon. The asdic repeater pings relentlessly. In the asdic hut, the Higher Submarine Detector (HSD) is listening to the pings through his headphones. He turns the asdic wheel a few degrees to port or starboard after each sound pulse. Below the hull, the asdic head turns through an arc from 45 degrees to starboard to 45 degrees to port as it sends sound waves through the water. Kingsley comes onto the bridge and strikes up a conversation with the Officer of the Watch, but their ears are always tuned to the asdic loudspeaker. Suddenly, they hear a slight echo. A moment later, the asdic operator calls through the voice pipe: "Asdic to bridge, contact bearing red 010. Sir, the contact is showing slight closing Doppler. Range is 700 yards. I think it may be a submarine." The asdic set gives the range and direction of the contact, but it cannot indicate the depth. Kingsley must either guess, or—the preferred practice—order *St Croix's* depth-charges set for different depths.

Kingsley knows there is little risk of a submarine in these waters, but he also knows that his HSD is an especially skilled operator who has been trained in the United Kingdom and who has exercised with Royal Navy submarines. He decides not to take a chance. He leans to the Officer of the Watch: "Sound action stations."

The alarm bells ring through the ship. They bring the sounds of men rushing up and down ladders, of hatches being closed and secured, of gun crews making ready. Everyone dons life-belts and helmets. The

Coxswain takes the wheel. The First Lieutenant reports that the ship is closed up to action stations, then leaves the bridge for the aft wheel-house. He must not stay on the bridge during action stations when an enemy shell might kill both him and the captain at the same time. His action station is always in the aft wheel-house.

Kingsley orders the asdic officer to set charges for 150, 250, and 350 feet and orders revolutions for 15 knots. He tells the Coxswain, "Starboard 10 to 280."

"Ten of starboard wheel on, sir."

And to the Chief Yeoman he says: "Make to commodore. Have gained contact astern of you. Am attacking. Midships."

"Wheel is amidships, sir."

St Croix surges towards the invisible spot just ahead where the submarine lurks.

"Fire on indication."

The asdic officer watches the trace recorder. When it appears that *St Croix* is over the target, he will press the buzzer to tell the depth-charge crew to fire.

St Croix's bow cuts through the water. The ocean is amazingly calm and the sky is blue, streaked with white clouds. Seagulls circle and call. The turbines vibrate below. The pings and echoes get closer together. They merge. The asdic operator reports instantaneous echo. The buzzer sounds. The depth-charge throwers on each side of the after deck-house cough and send their barrel-like loads out into the sea on both sides of the onrushing destroyer. Three depth-charges drop from the stern. *St Croix* moves past. The depth-charges sink. At its pre-set depth, the firing pistol in each depth-charge is activated, sending a spike-shaped firing pin down a short tube to strike the primer. The primer explodes. The explosion sets off the 300-lb main charge. A tremendous pressure wave rushes from the centre of the explosion as the hot gases expand through the incompressible sea water. A submarine hull that is close enough to the blast will be crushed by the water pressure generated by the explosion.

On board *St Croix*, the men on deck watch the sea beyond their stern. They see five explosions in quick succession push great domes above the surface of the ocean. Each dome erupts, sending tons of sea water spurting high into the air. The men in the engine room and boiler

room feel heavy blows reverberating through the hull. The asdic operator reports he has lost contact. Kingsley orders a 180-degree turn at
speed. *St Croix* heels over as she races back to the spot where the contact
was made. The asdic operator reports regained contact. The target is
now moving away. Kingsley orders another pattern of depth-charges
dropped. Contact is lost again, then regained. The asdic operator reports the contact stationary in the water, then it disappears. He
searches, but he cannot regain it. Kingsley orders speed reduced to 8
knots and heads to the spot where contact was lost. Men on deck shout
that they see oil and bubbles, but there is no wreckage. There are no
human remains or body parts. There are no sodden cigarette packs or
shreds of clothing. Kingsley has spent a precious hour on the hunt and
must give it up. *St Croix* rushes to catch up with the unescorted convoy.
The asdic operator is certain he had a submarine in his beam, but the
Admiralty disagrees.

At 10 a.m. on 11 July Kingsley takes *St Croix* to sea once more to rendezvous with a section of convoy HX138. The ships are to meet another
section of this convoy departing from Halifax. The whole convoy is to
take a different route to WESTOMP, steaming through the Cabot Strait
and making for the narrow Strait of Belle Isle, before turning northeast
to meet NEF. *St Croix* is in company with HMCS *Annapolis*, another
Town Class destroyer, and the RCN corvettes *Levis* and *Galt*. *St Croix*
and her consorts join up with their charges and head north, Cape Breton Island out of sight to the west. They encounter thickening patches
of fog. The merchantmen begin to stream their fog buoys. The Officer
of the Watch calls Kingsley to the bridge. On merchantmen and escorts
alike, lookouts stay alert for possible collisions. Fog horns sound eerily
in the gloom. At 4 p.m. the Convoy Commodore signals a reduction in
speed. Kingsley orders the helmsman to move *St Croix* to the flank of
the plodding merchantmen to give them as wide a berth as possible.

They clear the fog bank in the pre-dawn hours of 12 July, but reduce
speed again just after noon when the fog closes in once more. At 8:35
p.m., still enshrouded in fog, the convoy begins a pre-planned course
change to enter Cabot Strait. Suddenly from out of the gloom comes the
unmistakable sound of steel grinding against steel; in two separate collisions five ships, including that of the Commodore, are badly damaged.
The damaged ships leave the convoy and proceed slowly back to Hali-

fax. The rest of the convoy sails through the night and into a fog-shrouded dawn. They meet the Halifax section of the convoy and continue northward. About 250 miles west of the Strait of Belle Isle they run into a large field of icebergs and reduce speed to 6 knots. Fog rolls in again after dark. The ships drift apart in the fog and ice. The convoy becomes disorganized as each master tries to find his way through the dangerous waters. *St Croix* is almost run down by a tanker. The ships survive the night, but at 9 a.m. next day *St Croix* loses power when a main steampipe connecting its intermediate- and low-pressure turbines on its starboard engine collapses. Kingsley orders his ship back to Halifax via Cape Race. On 18 July *St Croix* secures in the naval dockyard. Repairs are made, local leaves are granted, and *St Croix* sails from Sydney on 30 July to escort yet another local convoy. But this time she returns to the welcome news assigning her to St John's and the NEF. On 21 August 1941 she joins Escort Group 21. There is barely time to paint on the white, blue, and green camouflage before EG21 leaves port to meet convoy SC41.

———————

Kingsley leads Escort Group 21 to sea on 26 August. As captain of the group's only destroyer, he is Senior Officer of the Escort (SOE). *St Croix* is accompanied by the RCN corvettes *Pictou* and *Buctouche*. They are to rendezvous with the RN sloop *Ranpura* and three RCN corvettes that have accompanied the convoy from Cape Breton. Corvette HMCS *Galt* has sailed from St John's the day before to locate and shepherd a smaller group of merchantmen to the rendezvous point south of Belle Isle. This is Kingsley's first major responsibility in a war zone. As SOE, he is charged with organizing the convoy's defences. He must ensure that the other warships keep to their stations. He must coordinate the defences if the convoy comes under attack from submarines or long-range German aircraft. He must work with the Convoy Commodore to make sure his charges do not go wandering off in the night, or fog, or bad weather, and, if they do, he must organize the effort to re-form the convoy at sea. He knows he will get little rest until *St Croix* anchors in Hvalfjordur. He will live on the bridge, catch a few winks in his sea cabin, eat stale bully-beef sandwiches, and drink gallons of tea, kye (cocoa), and coffee.

St Croix is sailing into dangerous waters for the very first time. Here the wolfpacks gather. Here they attack convoys without warning. Here men die every night in rending explosions, burn in pools of liquid fire fed by leaking fuel oil, or freeze to death in the cold subarctic waters. Long hours at sea are a strain on mind and body as men wait for the blows to fall. At night they sleep in their life-jackets with their sea boots beside them, never sure that a torpedo is not at that instant speeding its way towards them.

By now, Kingsley has learned to deal with the constant frustration of ice- and fog-bound seas, repeated mechanical breakdown, and the boredom of long watches at sea. Nothing has prepared him for the strain of trying to command an inexperienced escort group in a very dangerous part of the ocean. He is late joining the convoy. There is no sign of *Galt* and her charges. Kingsley must maintain radio silence, so he dispatches *Buctouche* away from the convoy to radio Halifax to radio *Galt* to join up. *Buctouche* does so, but *Galt* does not show up and Kingsley sends *Buctouche* out again. *Pictou* falls behind with engine trouble. On the morning of the 29th, *Pictou*'s engine gives out entirely. Kingsley sends *Buctouche* to stand by her; for several hair-raising hours, *St Croix* is the convoy's sole escort. Just before sunset, *Galt* and her charges show up. The next morning *St Croix*'s steering malfunctions and men are sent to the tiller flat to steer manually. All day the glass falls, swells build from the east, low cloud begins to scud across the seascape, and the seas and wind begin to mount. By dark, the convoy is battered by gale-force winds and the Commodore orders his ships to heave-to. Streaming sea anchors and keeping their bows pointed into the storm, the ships heave and roll in 30-foot waves.

On 1 September the convoy re-forms under the guidance of Kingsley's Escort Group; they are forty-two hours late to the Mid-Ocean Meeting Point. The next day they are joined by the British destroyer *Ramsay*, a welcome addition to the breakdown-plagued Canadian vessels. *Buctouche* and *St Croix* carry out depth-charge attacks on dubious contacts on the 3rd and 5th, but there is no real sign of the enemy. Only one ship is lost from SC41 on this leg of the journey when the straggler *Einvik* is torpedoed 100 miles south of the convoy. She was unable to maintain the convoy's minimum 6-knot speed; there are no survivors. *St Croix*'s fuel supply runs low and, on the afternoon of 5 September,

Kingsley orders course set for Iceland. *St Croix* arrives at her anchorage the next morning.

As mid-ocean escort duty goes, sc41 has been a cakewalk. The mostly untrained Canadian crews sailing inadequately equipped or, in *St Croix's* case, obsolete ships endure bad weather, delays, and irritating breakdowns. Kingsley and his crew are exhausted, and their ship is battered and plagued by constant mechanical troubles. They need a rest and a temporary refit, but they do not get it. sc42 is being slaughtered in the seas southwest of Iceland. On 11 September Kingsley receives his orders: "Being in all respects ready for sea, *St Croix* will sail in company with *Columbia* to reinforce ocean escort sc 41." He and his men and his ship are not "ready," but there is no choice. They clear harbour that night and steam at 20 knots to reinforce the beleaguered convoy. Far to the south, three RCN corvettes led by HMCS *Wetaskiwin* also come racing to sc42's aid. They are led by C. A. "Chummy" Prentice, one of the RCN's few real anti-submarine experts.

On the morning of the 13th the asdic operator reports a contact at a range of 400 yards. It is apparently moving away. It is probably not a submarine so far from the convoy, but there is no point taking chances. Kingsley orders action stations and five depth-charges rumble down into the ocean, but contact is lost and not regained. *St Croix* steams on, joins up with sc41, and takes station ahead of the merchantmen. *Skeena* is SOE. *St Croix* and *Moosejaw*, on the convoy's port beam, settle into the routine zigzag sweep pattern. At 3 p.m. one of the *St Croix's* bridge lookouts thinks he sees something unusual far ahead. The sea is relatively calm, but there are fog patches about. Visibility is about 5 miles. Is there something there at the very limit of his vision? He wipes the lenses and looks again, seeing if that speck is still there. It is.

"Sir, what do you make of that object about 5 miles ahead at green 020?" The Officer of the Watch and the other bridge lookouts train their glasses on the spot. The Officer speaks as he peers through his binoculars: "I think it's a sub." He leans into the voice pipe: "Sir, you'd better get up here. I think we've got a U-boat on the surface."

Kingsley pulls on his duffle coat and sea boots, grabs his binoculars and cap, and scrambles up the ladder to the bridge. "Where is it, Guns?"

"Green 020, sir, looks to be about 5 miles off."

Kingsley has never seen a U-boat running on the surface. He peers at the object for a moment or two. It is barely visible, but he can make out the shape of a conning tower. It is definitely a submarine.

"No doubt about it, Guns. Just sunning himself by the look of it. They must be sleeping over there. Watch him pull the plug as soon as he spots us." He can hardly conceal his excitement. "We've got you, you bastard," he mutters, then turns to the Officer of the Watch. "Sound action stations. Engine room, give me revolutions for 25 knots. Helm, Starboard 15 to 065. Make to *Skeena*, repeat to NAOC, 'Submarine on surface 8 miles ahead of convoy SC42, course 100, speed 8 knots. Am engaging. Give our time and position.' Bunts, run up the flags. Guns, tell the forward gun crew to hold their fire until we're well within range. We don't want to wake him up if he is asleep."

St Croix leaps forward as the alarm bells bring the crew to their action stations, life-belts and helmets on. Two flags shoot up the yardarm, one indicating a submarine sighting, the other that an attack is about to take place. All eyes on the bridge are riveted on the sub. Surely they will be spotted. "Asdic, be ready to sweep green 040 to red 040 when they go under."

Suddenly there is a bit of spray around the distant object. "She's blowing her tank, sir," the asdic operator reports. The submarine quickly disappears.

"Pick him up, asdic," Kingsley needlessly instructs the HSD. The asdic operator turns the wheel through an 80 degree arc. The repeater speaker pings on the bridge as *St Croix* splits the water, charging towards the swirl made by the diving submarine. After twenty minutes the asdic operator shouts, "Contact, sir." Kingsley orders speed reduced to better hear the contact and listen for propeller noises. Then, at 300-yards range, he orders revolutions increased again. The ship leaps forward at 18 knots. Then, "Fire."

Two depth-charges sail away from the ship and four are dropped off the stern, all set at medium depth. The explosions follow quickly, but there is no sign the submarine has been hit. Kingsley orders *St Croix* back across the spot where he believes the submarine to be. He wonders whether it has gone deep or has doubled back. He's there all right, Kingsley thinks, he can't have got far, with his top speed under water barely faster than a walk. The asdic operator reports propeller noises on the hydrophone. The sound beam finds the submarine's hull once again. The echo is distinct on the bridge speaker. The target is moving towards the destroyer. Increase speed. Fire. Six charges again set to medium depth. Again six explosions. Again no wreckage.

"Damn. Where is he?"

The men on the bridge peer momentarily at Kingsley, then at each other. That's not in character, they think. They criss-cross the area. There, a contact. Then, it's gone. "I know he's still here. He couldn't have gotten farther away. Pilot, begin a box-search." Knowing the top underwater speed of a u-boat, the navigator calculates how far the submarine can have got in the hour or so since he dived. *St Croix* starts at the spot where the u-boat went under and searches an expanding square. The fog gets thicker. The convoy is drawing away by the minute. sc42 has already lost sixteen merchantmen and can't be without full escort very much longer. Should they stay with the search for a while more? Or should they leave? In the absence of instructions from *Skeena*, it is Kingsley's choice to make. He wants this u-boat very badly. He wants it for himself and for his crew, and for the months of breakdowns and frustrations and humiliations he and *St Croix* have endured. They will stay a bit longer. Another contact. Can this be it? Six depth-charges rumble down, this time set deep. The six explosions take a little longer to push up their great domes of sea water. Still no wreckage. They continue the search. Again a contact, 800 yards range, appears to be moving towards the destroyer. It must be very deep by now. Speed up to 15 knots. Six more charges, set deep. Six more explosions. Is that wooden wreckage on the surface? The fog has really closed in and it is difficult to see anything. They have been at this hunt for more than two hours. They cannot stay. "Make to Skeena. Possible damage to a u-boat, am rejoining." The Admiralty's conclusion is damning: "The Committee feel that st. croix has little real knowledge of anti-u-boat operations. It is to be noted that the attacks were almost all commenced at point blank range giving the ship minimum chance of setting a correct attacking course."

St Croix stays with sc42 until the convoy reaches UK waters, then parts company and, in consort with *Moose Jaw*, berths at Loch Ewe for fuel

and water. The corvette lands survivors. It is *St Croix*'s first transatlantic
crossing, but there is no time for extended liberty. u-boats are sinking
tons of merchant shipping each night. The war at sea is being lost. So
what that *St Croix* badly needs a boiler cleaning and a full refit, or that
her crew is worn down, exhausted, and low in spirits? She is still afloat
and she carries asdic, depth-charges, and guns. She goes back to sea to
help escort convoy ON17 westward to the mid-Atlantic, then returns to
Iceland. She stays in harbour long enough to refuel, then heads south to
meet ON19A, a small fast convoy bound for Halifax. On 2 October the
Dutch-registry ss *Tuva* is torpedoed. The u-boat escapes unscathed. All
the crew but one make it into the water and *St Croix* is dispatched to
pick up the thirty-one survivors. They are in a heart-rending state. Oil
soaked, freezing, and in shock from the explosion and the cold North
Atlantic, the shivering men are hauled aboard the quarterdeck by eager
crew members. They are handed cigarettes, swaddled in blankets, and
quickly sent below. They crowd into the tiny sick bay and into the already overcrowded messdecks. They are fed sandwiches and given hot
coffee. Space is found for them to bed down. *St Croix*'s crew helps them
clean up and gives them spare clothing. Each man knows that this fate,
or worse, awaits him every moment at sea. They have seen survivors before, of course, but never so close, and never just after a sinking.

In port, Kingsley sees L.W. Murray, Commodore Commanding
Newfoundland Force, and puts his case for a refit. He knows how tight
the escort situation is, but *St Croix*'s evaporator coils are holed, her main
air pumps are defective, sea water is leaking into six of her fuel tanks,
her hull badly needs scraping and painting, and her steering cables need
to be replaced. Murray gives Kingsley one week to fix the most critical
problems; everything else will have to wait. There are too few escorts. *St
Croix* can't be spared. Kingsley is torn between his deeply ingrained
training to make do and his concern about the state of his ship and
crew. He must accept what little Murray offers. It is a generous offer
under the circumstances. *St Croix* sails for Halifax, then to Saint John,
New Brunswick, where she is dry docked on 10 October. The shipyard
workers spend the next five days patching and scraping, painting and
fitting, emptying and cleaning. They concentrate on replacing missing
rivets in the hull and fixing the leaking hull plates. Her bottom is
scraped and painted. Then she goes back to sea with Kingsley as SOE for

eastbound convoy SC50 and westbound convoy ON32. In mid-November the orders arrive for her long-sought refit. She will be dry docked at Saint John again, and Kingsley will be reassigned to command *Skeena*.

On 17 November 1941 Kingsley leaves *St Croix*. He has done the best he can for her and her crew. Sometime in the new year, she will sail with someone else on her bridge. He and this old destroyer have been together for more than a year. They have suffered many trials and few triumphs. But the war and a newer destroyer awaits. Kingsley says his goodbyes and visits the wardroom for a last drink. There is much good-humoured banter about his forsaking an old girl for one much younger. He drains his drink, shakes hands all around, and climbs onto the main deck. He looks *St Croix* over. He thinks for a moment about some of the good times he has had aboard her, but he also remembers the constant feeling of unease at her condition and his inability to trust her to keep functioning at crucial moments. *Skeena* promises to be better. Harry Kingsley doesn't look back.

4

Learning the Deadly Trade: Rudolf Bahr Joins *U69*

I N OCTOBER 1941 Lieutenant Rudolf Bahr once more races across Europe by Admiral U-boats Train. He is headed to the U-boat base at St Nazaire, where the Loire River empties into the Bay of Biscay. Bahr is twenty-five years of age and about to become second-in-command of a crew of nearly fifty men. The prospect of his own command in the not too distant future suddenly dawns on him.

As his train races across the fallow fall fields of the French countryside, Bahr cannot help but think how the world has exploded in a frenzy of dizzying developments since he first set foot on French soil at Brest on 1 June 1940. The Wehrmacht is rapidly closing in on Moscow and Leningrad. Rostov on the Don and Sevastopol in the Crimea are being stormed. The rich oil fields of Maikop, so essential to the navy, are within reach. In North Africa, Field Marshal Erwin Rommel has driven the British out of Tobruk, taken El Alamein, and is headed for the Nile River and the Suez Canal. In the Atlantic, Admiral Dönitz's

U-boats have sent about five hundred merchant ships, for a total of more than 2.5 million tons, to the bottom.

But the costs mount. Three revered "aces" are lost in March 1941. Most disastrously, on 8 March the British destroyer HMS *Wolverine* sinks Günther Prien's *U47*, with which the "Bull of Scapa Flow" in 1939 had penetrated the British Home Fleet's lair and torpedoed the battleship HMS *Royal Oak*. Eight days later, the Royal Navy's HMS *Vanoc* rams Joachim Schepke's *U100*, destroying both Captain and boat. And that same night the British destroyer HMS *Walker* depth charges Otto "the Silent" Kretschmer's *U99*. Kretschmer, the tonnage king with 325,000 tons to his credit, is fished out of the Atlantic and will spend the rest of the war at Camp 30 in Bowmanville, Ontario, from where he will organize an intelligence ring from inside the prison camp.

Such musings are cut short on 9 October 1941 by the sight of *U69* at the anchorage of the 7th U-boat Flotilla in St Nazaire. A large banner with a snorting bull—the most famous submarine insignia, adopted from Prien's *U47*—alerts Bahr that he has reached the flotilla's docks. And he immediately recognizes his new posting, for she proudly displays a row of flags and a laughing cow (*La vâche qui rit*), the symbol of a French milk and cheese advertisement, on her conning tower. Obviously, her skipper has a good sense of humour! Bahr crosses the gangplank and finds Lieutenant-Commander Wilhelm Zahn in his cramped quarters.

"I beg to report for duty, Herr Kapitänleutnant."

"Welcome aboard. We have been expecting you for several days," Zahn warmly replies. "And we are ready to clear port as soon as you have stowed your gear."

In short order, Bahr stores three sets of fatigues, a grey leather suit, a sou'wester, rubber boots, blue underwear, blue sweaters, winter gloves, and his 8 x 60 Zeiss binoculars in the tiny Exec's alcove, separated from the main passageway by only a thin green curtain.

Like the *Prinz Eugen*, *U69* was built by Friedrich Krupp's Germaniawerft at Kiel. But there the similarity ends. Launched in September 1940, the boat was commissioned on 2 November after a series of shakedown cruises. She is part of the Type VIIC class, the largest series of submarines ever produced: of the 1452 craft ordered, 709 were actually built and placed in service. The generic Type VII class is a direct descendant of the UF and UG boats built at the end of the First World War—as modified in the mid-1930s in the Type IA class. Given that the Anglo-German Naval Agreement initially allowed Germany 35 percent of British tonnage, naval leaders in Berlin on 10 January 1935—well before the actual signing of the agreement—had decided to mass produce a class of small submarines, each displacing about 550 tons, to trade off individual unit size for overall quantity (18,500 tons).

The newly designated Type VIIA was a single-hulled craft. The pressure hull was also her outside skin, and all fuel oil was stored inside the pressure hull. Outside ballast tanks gave the boat a bulged appearance. These boats displaced about 800 tons. Their main armament consisted of five 53.3-cm torpedo tubes (one aft and four in the bow), six torpedo reloads, an 8.8-cm deck gun, and a single 2-cm Flak anti-aircraft weapon. Twin-shaft diesels generated just over 2300 horsepower for a best surface speed of 16 knots; electric cells weighing 55 tons permitted a best submerged speed of 8 knots for up to two hours. The diesels needed to recharge the e-cells on average every twenty-four hours, so all U-boats had to run on the surface for extended periods since their exhausts could not be discharged under water. In short, Dönitz's Type VII craft were not true underwater boats in today's sense of the term, but rather submersible torpedo boats.

The initial ten Type VIIA boats were ordered in the spring of 1935. But already the first prototype, *U33*, proved to be underpowered in terms of both horsepower and torpedoes, unwieldy with regard to underwater turning radius, and short on range (4300 nautical miles). Late in 1936, German U-boat designers came up with a number of technical refinements in the Type VIIB successor series. Twin rudders, one behind each screw, offered smaller underwater turning radius and hence greater mobility. The rear torpedo tube was placed between the rudders and inside the pressure hull, thereby allowing a reload. Torpedo storage was enhanced by adding a pair of external storage tubes, one fore and one aft, between the pressure hull and the deck casing, and by storing the stern torpedo reload under the deck plates in the motor room. Higher speed (17 knots) was achieved by adding superchargers to the twin MAN diesels, boosting their power by 20 percent to 2800 horsepower. Last but not least, range was increased to 6300 miles simply by adding fuel tanks. In the process, the Type VIIB class was lengthened by 2 metres; displacement increased by only 17 tons.

The Type VIIC series of *U69*'s design received the last refinement in May 1938. It consisted of a slight increase in length of 60 centimetres— a single full frame section added into the centre of the control room— to house a new active sonar device, the *Such-Gerät*, designed to detect minefields or targets. The cramped conning tower was extended 30 centimetres in length, and the internal fuel tank received a volume increase of 5.4 cubic metres. New small buoyancy tanks on each side of the hull provided greater stability as well as faster dive times because they could be blown and flooded in an emergency. A new oil-filtration system prolonged the life of the diesel lubricating oils, new Junkers diesel-powered compressors reduced the demands on the electrical systems, and a modern knob switch system replaced the First World War vintage electrical knife switches. Crew complement remained at forty-four. Material and labour shortages, however, reduced Dönitz's October 1939 production target from eighteen units per month to fifteen; average building time was set at nine months.

Rudolf Bahr studies his new surroundings carefully. It looks like Hades, he thinks, but soon it will be home. Pipes and ducts, handwheels and instrument gauges at first seem to be unavoidable impediments to movement. Low, round hatches in the bulkheads threaten to decapitate the unwary. Once under way, the air in the steel cigar tube measuring 220 feet in length and 20 feet in diameter—the size of two railway cars—soon reeks of oil, sweat, mould, and urine. Humidity often reaches 100 percent. Leaky batteries sometimes let poisonous chlorine fumes escape. Cheeses stored in the forward torpedo room, and sausages and slabs of smoked ham hanging near the bulkheads, further foul an already odiferous air. There are no skylights and no portholes for ventilation.

U69 is divided roughly into four compartments. Moving from stern to bow, the aft section houses the single aft torpedo tube, the air compressor, and, under the decking, the lone torpedo reload. Two electric motors for submerged running are aligned on the twin shafts that run from the diesels to the screws. Next comes the engine room, the noisy, greasy nether world of the Chief Engineer. It houses the two diesels, sited side by side with a small passageway in between that allows the

Chief and his mates access to the engines' valves and cylinders. Attached to the engine room via a hatchway through a thin bulkhead is a small galley and after accommodation. This area boasts a tiny refrigeration unit, a sink and wash space, a hot plate with two electric burners, a single toilet for forty-four men, four petty officers' bunks, and, beneath the aft deck-plates, half the 50-ton batteries as well as tanks for fuel and for fresh and foul water.

The midships section is reached through a circular hatch that pierces a watertight bulkhead. It contains the mechanical heart of the U-boat, the control room, and consists of a maze of gauges, switches, meters, valves, hand-wheels, pumps, magnetic and gyro compasses, rudder and hydroplane controls, as well as a chart closet and a mess table, which doubles as the engineer's bunk. The compartment, appropriately called *die Zentrale*, is dominated by the two periscopes—the large sky scope and the smaller attack one. Between them are a small hatch and ladder that lead to the tiny conning tower above. No more than 6.5 feet high, the *Turm* houses the equipment used by the Exec to aim the torpedoes or "eels": an attack calculator, a compass repeater, and the attack periscope. Directly above his head is the watertight hatchway that leads to the bridge. This will be Bahr's home on board *U69*.

The forward section is the brain and nerve centre of *U69*. It houses the radio room, listening room, officers' and men's quarters, the skipper's small office, and, beneath the floor plates, the second half of the electrical batteries. It is in this section of the craft that the Enigma cypher machine is stored, signals are coded and decoded, courses are plotted on the secret Atlantic grid charts, hydrophonic readings are taken, and the boat's war log (KTB) is maintained. Last but not least, the submarine's nose contains the "business" end of the U-boat—the forward torpedo room. The inner ends of the four torpedo tubes, arranged in two vertical banks of two, project almost 4 metres into this compartment. Four eels are stored under removable floor plates aft of the torpedo tubes; while on patrol, two torpedoes are customarily suspended from the torpedo hoist on the overhead for quick reloading. Every inch of space has been carefully calculated to store loose gear; every nook and cranny serves a purpose. Watch on, watch off, the men "hot-bunk" the few available bunks and hammocks.

The entire crew, except for the officers, is divided into two divisions: technical staff and seamen. The seamen's division works on three

eight-hour watches: eight hours on, eight hours off, and eight hours for
sundry duties such as eating, kit maintenance, cleaning, and relaxing.
The tower crew, consisting of four lookouts and the Watch Officer,
stands four-hour watches. The machine crew, on the other hand, works
a completely different shift: six hours on, six hours off, repeated every
twelve-hour cycle. During combat, no one rests.

U69 has undergone three weeks of refit and repairs. On 25 October
1941 she eases out of her mooring dock and heads for the arsenal, where
Bahr supervises the loading of the fourteen torpedoes. It is hard and
dangerous work. Each of the 1.5-ton eels has to be stowed into the
tubes, the holders on the upper deck, and the bow and aft compartments. And each torpedo has to be raised from the dock by a heavy
crane and lowered at a steep angle through the loading chute into the
torpedo compartments, where the torpedo mechanic fits the actual
warhead to the eel. Finally, five men manipulate a horizontal set of pul-
leys to slide the primed torpedo into its tube. The eels, miniature submarines in themselves, are of the latest G7E design, electrically powered
and armed with magnetic detonators.

The following day the Chief bunkers 180 tons of diesel fuel as well
as lubricating oils. Next, he supervises the unloading of large glass
containers carefully packed in straw: acid for the electric cells. Thereafter, he undertakes a run-through and trial run. On 27 October the
skipper and Bahr conduct radio drill and trimming practice, followed
by loading the shells for the 8.8-cm deck gun and the 2-cm Flak. A final
sea test reveals damage to the twin diesels which requires twenty-four
hours to repair.

On 28 October *U69* takes on perishable goods under the watchful
eyes of the navigator. Butter, coffee, tea, and whipped cream are locked
up by the skipper for special occasions. Next come eggs, bread, and
fresh vegetables for the galley; potable water for the tanks; and crates of
apples and grapes for the first week of the patrol. Fresh meat is stored in
the small refrigeration unit. Huge, round loaves of bread are stowed in
the forward torpedo compartment and the motor room; slabs of bacon
and ham as well as sausages hang from pipes and bulkheads and overhead in the control room. All supplies are passed by hand down a single,
narrow hatch. The submarine's afterdeck is soon littered with piles of
empty cardboard cartons.

"Let go all lines!" *U69* backs away from her pier in St Nazaire at high water, 2 p.m.* on 30 October 1941. "Starboard engine ahead one-third!" The boat slowly glides away from the pier on electric power. An airforce band plays stirring marches, and a large crowd wishes her good hunting and a safe return. Fifty metres past the harbour locks, Bahr swings *U69* around and gives the orders to start the twin diesels. Black fumes billow from the exhaust and the hull vibrates as the twin screws begin to thrash the waters of the Bay of Biscay. Bahr faintly remembers the blue waters from his cadet days on the *Emden.* "Half ahead both engines!" *U69* is outward bound on her sixth patrol.

As soon as *U69* passes 8 degrees west longitude, Zahn breaks the seal on the orders he has received from Admiral Dönitz. *U69* is to proceed to a position east of the Azores as part of the Störtebecker patrol line (named for a German pirate) to hunt the convoys that ply the Capetown to Gibraltar to England routes. Specifically, German radio intelligence (xB-Dienst) is expecting convoy os11. Feelings of excitement and adventure grip Bahr. Under her previous skipper, Lieutenant-Commander Jost Metzler, *U69* had between February and July 1941 dispatched eleven mostly British vessels of about 50,000 tons. And her new Captain, Zahn, is no slouch either. He is known throughout the submarine force as the man who almost killed Churchill. On 30 October 1939 Zahn, then in *U56*, had torpedoed the British battleship HMS *Nelson* with the Prime Minister on board. But the eels had proved to be duds!

"Alarm [Dive]!" Lieutenant-Commander Zahn's order electrifies the crew. Within seconds the men on watch on the bridge come tumbling down through the main hatch, slide down the aluminum ladder, and crash onto the iron deck-plates of the conning tower. An alarm bell shrieks through the boat. Machinists throw themselves against the handles of the leverage valves to open the ballast tanks to the sea. Air escapes the tanks with a loud roar; sea water races in. *U69* angles down by the bow. Bahr experiences his first patrol dive.

This one, however, is just an exercise. Daily diving practice is mandatory in the Dönitz Volunteer Corps. *U69* conducts test dives three times on 30 October, and four times the next day—in rain squalls and

---

*German war vessels stayed on German time, i.e. one hour ahead of Greenwich Meridian Time.

snow storms. By day, Bahr stands watch on the bridge in four-hour shifts along with a petty officer and two seamen. He quickly discovers that the U-boat's low angle of lookout accords a narrow range of vision. Indeed, the boat needs an extra pair of eyes—aircraft that can scan a wider area of sea—but the submarine service can rely only on a handful of aged four-engine Focke-Wulf 200C Condor anti-shipping aircraft based at Bordeaux. Not for the last time Bahr curses the lack of combined submarine–air reconnaissance in the Atlantic.

By 3 November *U69* has reached her operating zone, grid quadrant BE, 500 miles due west of St Nazaire. Zahn writes in his log: "Now begins the tedious business of searching." The Störtebecker boats—*U552*, *U567*, *U98*, *U96*, *U572*, *U69*, *U373*, *U201*, and *U77*—spend days searching for a sign of smoke on the horizon. Aerial reconnaissance on 4, 5, and 6 November likewise comes up empty. Acting on information from the XB-Dienst, Admiral U-boats moves the patrol line south to quadrant CF, off the coast of Spain.

At 2 p.m. on 9 November all hell breaks loose, as a log entry reveals: "HURRICANE! The needle of the barometer constantly bounces back and forth around 8 millibars." "Flying sheets of water" obscure Zahn's vision. Storm-force winds (10 to 11) from the northwest pound the little craft; mountainous breakers as well as blowing white foam force *U69* to seek safety beneath the waves. When Zahn resurfaces, there is nothing to be seen. "Convoy must have turned away." Headquarters at Kernevel orders the patrol line to proceed northwest at 320° to grid AK, due west of Ireland, in hopes of intercepting a Liverpool-to-Halifax convoy. Six German reconnaissance aircraft on 16 November fail to spot the enemy. Still, Dönitz adds two boats, *U332* and *U402*, to the Störtebecker line.

"Alarm! *Flugzeug*! Dive, dive!" It is 2:10 p.m. on 19 November. The navigator standing the third watch has discovered a glint of metal between the thin, white, puffy clouds dead astern. "*Scheisse!*" cries Zahn, "it's one of ours. The Watch Officer gave the alarm too soon." *U69* breaks off the emergency dive and resurfaces. Nothing in sight. At 11:30 p.m. Kernevel gives up the chase and divides Störtebecker into three new patrol lines: *U69* joins three other boats as Gödecke and is ordered south to attack a suspected United Kingdom–Gibraltar (OG) convoy. Zahn sets course for quadrant BD at 290°. Rain and hail showers dog the boat for the next three days.

Off watch, Bahr climbs into his narrow upper bunk and secures the aluminum guard-rail. A dim light from the control room—the phosphorescent dials of the compasses—as well as a small light over the chart table give the black hull an eerie glow. He sizes up his new charges. Most are mere lads of nineteen or twenty, too young, it seems, to be stalking death beneath the breaking seas of the mid-Atlantic. They will quickly become men of nineteen or twenty. Bahr feels old at twenty-five. Since razors are forbidden in the pressure-cooker atmosphere of the u-boats, the men soon sport thick beards. Water is at a premium, to be used only to brush one's teeth. Occasionally a washbasin with dirty dishwater from the galley is set up in the control room—a luxurious communal "bath" for those on duty. Sea water does not lather up and it leaves a slimy film. Hygiene becomes the subject of low humour among the crew. Neither underwear nor outerwear are ever washed—and only rarely changed. Bahr quickly comes to appreciate why submariners prefer dark "whore's drawers" for their apparel.

Back in the stern, the *Smutje*, or cook, magically produces breakfast, lunch, and dinner on the two hot plates in his tiny galley, all the time dodging the men who rush by him on their way to the diesels and the electric motors. He serves "coffee and cake" around 3:30 p.m. Once the fresh vegetables and fruit, meat, and eggs are gone, a fairly monotonous daily regimen sets in: canned meats, canned vegetables, canned potatoes, and canned ersatz powders. It is at such times that the "Old Man" dips into his private reserves of coffee and cream to boost morale.

The steady rhythm and hum of the electric motors lull Bahr into a semi-sleep. Having experienced his first patrol, he wonders how depth-charges will sound. Will the hull crack? How many will it take to sink the boat? Will death come at 600, at 900, or at 1200 feet? And what will become of *U69* and her crew? Will the enormous pressure of such great depths implode the slender steel tube, or will the boat simply tear into thousands of small pieces, each bound for the ocean floor 3 miles below?

"Proceed to periscope depth!" It is Zahn ordering *U69* up to the surface that shakes Bahr out of his trance. The Captain slowly rotates the periscope 360 degrees and, satisfied that the coast is clear, orders the boat to surface. The hatch is opened and a rush of icy, fresh air rips into the boat. In small groups, the smokers, huddled in their parkas, assemble on the aft deck. At 11 a.m. on 23 November, Admiral u-boats abandons the hunt for the OG convoy and orders *U69* to quadrant AK, the mid-Atlantic southeast of Greenland and southwest of Iceland. "Snow, hail, rain," the war log reads.

The search for prey resumes on the surface. A predictable routine sets in. Four-hour watches for the seamen, six-hour watches for the engine room. Four men and the duty watch officer on the bridge constantly scan the horizon for signs of a convoy or a lone straggler—and the skies for hostile aircraft. That's the "hell above" that has become as much of a curse as the surface screens of destroyers and corvettes that guard the Allied convoys. Bahr marvels at how stable the Type VIIC boats are. They seem unsinkable, no matter how far they pitch to starboard or to port, or rise and fall from bow to stern on the great rollers of the angry Atlantic. The answer lies in their low centre of gravity—augmented by a keel full of iron ingots.

And still the routine continues. The days trudge by in a monotonous rhythm of watches and dog watches, when the men snooze as best they can. The run out to the patrol zones and back in to port is called the "garbage tour," or in German, *Gammelfahrt*. But there is nothing leisurely about ploughing through the grey-green Atlantic swells in November. The men on watch put on extra underwear and sweaters, grey leather suits, duffle coats, and heavy oilskins. Still, they freeze on the bridge. Salt spray solidifies into ice crystals in their beards. Faces are sandpapered a bright red. Eyes become hollow sockets, highlighted by salt-lacquered eyebrows. Binoculars crust over with salt and ice. The extreme cold "welds" rubber boots to the iron deck. Rain, snow, sleet, and hail combine with house-high ocean rollers to make life sheer hell for any watch. One almost looks forward to the daily practice dives that offer a chance to escape the Atlantic's winter wrath.

"Shadow bearing one-six-oh, looks like a merchantman of 5000 tons. Distance 2000 to 2500 metres. Course two-nine-zero!" Once again it is the navigator on the third watch who makes the sighting. It is just after 8 p.m. on 26 November 1941.

"Captain to the bridge!" Zahn is up in a flash and quickly appraises the situation. The smudge on the horizon south-by-southeast might be part of a larger convoy. The sea is in full rage. Wind force 8 to 9. Snow and hail showers to the north, but a half-moon breaking through the clouds to the south. The Old Man orders the navigator below to plot the attack. "Action stations! Right full rudder! Steer three-zero-zero! Both engines full ahead together!" *U69* surges forward as the supercharged twin diesels spring to life.

Zahn has decided to bag his prey—despite heavy seas that prevent him from ascertaining whether the freighter is moving ahead or astern, or has stopped. He can spot the intended target against the black northern horizon only when *U69* rises to the crest of a mountainous breaker. Bahr reaches the platform on the bridge, fastens his powerful binoculars to the target bearing transmitter (TBT), and secures the metal clamp of his safety belt to the superstructure to avoid being swept overboard by the next giant wave that breaks against the bridge. The crew is already at action stations. The torpedo gang is standing by at their tubes. The machinists lovingly tend the diesels.

Zahn turns into the wind. Giant sheets of sea water crash against and then over the conning tower. The tiny craft rises and falls like a cork in rhythm with the 40-foot peaks and valleys of the ocean's broad swells. A scream comes up from the plotting room: "Target speed 8 knots, course two-nine-zero." The designated victim, as far as can be made out from the top of a gigantic breaker, seems to be a loner, an older steamer apparently trying to make Liverpool on her own. For almost two hours, Zahn crashes through the heavy seas in pursuit, determined not to allow his prey to escape. The freighter maintains radio silence, but her zigzag course further extends the length of the pursuit.

After a final sweep of the horizon for hostile aircraft, or "bees," by 10 p.m. Zahn is ready to move in for the kill. Since the freighter seems deep-laden in the heavy seas, the Old Man decides to set torpedo depth at 3 metres rather than 2 as customary. He orders Bahr to get ready to fire a spread of two eels. The excitement of a possible first kill tightens the Lieutenant's every muscle.

"Tubes 1 and 2 ready for surface attack! Open tube doors 1 and 2!" Bahr checks the freighter's course one final time through the Zeiss glasses. The punishing seas seem to abate for a brief moment and the heavy cloud cover breaks ever so slightly. "Target angle left four zero—speed 8—range 800—torpedo depth 3. Stand by!"

The torpedo gang is coiled for action. "Tubes 1 and 2 ready for firing." Time: 10:46 p.m.

"Tube 1: . . . Fire!" Bahr hits the firing button. A jolt.

"Tube 2: . . . Fire!" A second jolt.

"Both torpedoes running!" the radioman routinely reports.

"*Verdammt!*" Both eels fail to hit the target. By the time Zahn and Bahr find the freighter again, the range is down to 400 metres. They cannot believe their good fortune: "Freighter lies fat and ready before our tubes." Time: 11:01 p.m.

"Open tube doors 3 and 4!" Zahn barks out.

"Tube 3: . . . Fire!" Bahr again hits the firing knob.

"Tube 4: . . . Fire!" A fourth jolt.

"*Scheisse!*" The second spread also fails to strike the target. In fact, the freighter had suddenly and unexpectedly veered sharply to port. It is empty! Its thrashing screws are clearly visible in the moonlight as the ship heaves over the top of a breaker. Zahn decides not to waste his last chance, a stern torpedo shot, in the heavy seas. Instead, he orders *U69* to submerge in order to reload the four torpedoes and to await calmer weather.

The watch tumbles down the hatch and slams it shut, just as the Chief dips the nose of the boat under the gurgling breakers. A shower of sea water cascades down the tower into the control room. Bahr peels off his drenched fatigues and underwear and hangs them up to dry in the aft torpedo compartment. Nude, he crawls into his narrow cot. The knuckles of his hands have been beaten into a raw, red pulp by the salt, sleet, and metal. Sleep soon overcomes him.

Zahn brings his boat back to the surface at 2:15 a.m. on 27 November. The freighter is nowhere in sight. For two hours, *U69* plows through the heavy seas at a best speed of 6 knots in search of the target. Tons of sea water crash down the hatch, imperiling the boat's buoyancy. The Old Man orders *U69* beneath the waves and for four hours creeps along in hopes of hearing its screws. In vain. By noon he gives up the search. He is determined next time round to stick with the target come what may, until the heavy seas abate.

The rest of the patrol is just more of the same. Methodical tracking of Allied convoys and loners, stealthy approaches—and empty seas. On 28 November Dönitz informs the Gödecke boats that a westbound convoy has left England and that it should cross the patrol line around 10 a.m. on 29 November. Zahn spots nothing. For four days he criss-crosses the mid-Atlantic in search of the convoy—and spots nothing.

Frustration and disappointment mount. One can read it on the faces of the men. Soiled, unkempt, and bearded, their sunken, hollow eyes scour Zahn's face for signs of relief. None appear.

Somehow the enemy knows exactly where the patrol lines are and directs the convoys around them. And he knows precisely where every grey wolf is and sends his airplanes to destroy them. But how? God damn it, how? Do the thousands of French workers at St Nazaire and Lorient, Brest and La Rochelle get word through to British agents every time a boat leaves its concrete pen? Are there enemy agents on board the hundreds of French fishing boats that ply the Bay of Biscay?

Bahr has even heard hushed conversations about whether the Tommies have cracked the Enigma. Unknown to him, Grand Admiral Erich Raeder in October 1941 expresses doubts, arguing that British air attacks (on eleven out of twenty U-boats whose signals were intercepted the previous month) suggest that the code has been violated. But Admiral Dönitz, the "Great Lion," will have none of it, intimating instead that the codes may have been polluted by treason or espionage. Dönitz repeatedly assures his men that breaking the Enigma-Hydra system lies beyond the Royal Navy's capabilities. When they press him on the issue, he cuts them short: "The possibility of a break is precluded by the constant changes in the key settings." And, he adds ominously, "We will once more investigate further sources of treason."

Dönitz orders naval counter-intelligence to investigate his entire system of radio intelligence. The system begins in a bombproof bunker in the Lorient suburb of Kernevel, where Commander Hans Meckel supervises communications. Notes from Dönitz or his staff are taken by a watch officer to a command transmissions officer for encipherment and transmission. Fifteen to twenty radiomen per shift encipher the messages on an Enigma machine. Only officers prepare the machine's inner settings, which remain in effect for forty-eight hours at a time. All messages receive a date-time number as well as a serial number. And each is checked by another radioman for proper encipherment. U-boats attacking convoys have two special nets: "Diana," named for the goddess of the hunt, and "Hubertus," named for the patron saint of hunters; each has up to six special frequencies of its own. From the bunker, the cryptograms go to the main radio towers in Kernevel, where they are sent out into the ether. They also go to the former French Colonial Office in

Sainte Assise, just southeast of Paris, where a more powerful station repeats the messages every two, six, twelve, and twenty-four hours to give
U-boat skippers every opportunity to hear them.

Captain Ludwig Stummel, "a career signals officer with a glass eye and
a limp," checks the men of the Naval Communications Service and their
known associates. He finds no cause for concern, no hint of treason. His
superior, Vice-Admiral Erhard Maertens, concurs. Still, Dönitz wants
there to be no doubts in his skippers' minds about the Enigma and he
appoints Vice-Admiral Kurt Fricke, Chief of Staff of the Naval War
Command, independently to investigate the security of the Enigma-
Hydra system. Fricke is of one mind with Stummel and Maertens. He
rejects out of hand any idea of "seizure of crypto-material," because the
crews are trained to destroy all equipment if their vessels are boarded
and because all secret materials are in water-soluble ink.

A cautious man, Fricke tightens security measures to restore or to
improve security. All operational orders and grid charts are now to be in
water-soluble ink. All operational orders are to be marked top secret. A
cue word, "Persius," puts new and uncompromised keys into effect.
Dönitz is to address his U-boats not by their numbers but by their Captains' names. The grid diagraphs for the North Atlantic theatre are replaced with substitutes, known only to the U-boat commanders. Next,
Dönitz institutes a system of numerous grid tables, each indicated by a
name and street address—"Gottfried Becker, Blücherplatz 30," for example—with the number providing the key to the disguise. And the
Kriegsmarine issues a new Short Weather Cipher, rendering invalid all
existing ones.

At the very moment that Zahn and Bahr are tracking their freighter
in the mid-Atlantic, Captain Bernhard Rogge lectures the Kriegsmarine
at the Tirpitzufer in Berlin that the sinkings of his auxiliary cruiser *At-
lantis* by the British heavy cruiser HMS *Devonshire* and of the supply ship
Python by the heavy cruiser HMS *Dorsetshire* were not by chance. Rather,
"either treason or cracking of our radio codes played a role in both
cases." The navy brass are incensed at this effrontery and insist that
both sinkings were simply due to "fate."

The Enigma machine, they argue, is secure. After all, it has four different settings. Officers, choosing three of the available eight cipher rotors, make two interior settings every forty-eight hours, allowing 336

different combinations. Moreover, each revolving rotor ring has twenty-six positions, permitting 16,900 posts for three rotors. Then the two outer settings, changed every two days by cipher clerks, have 1547 possible plug connections on the plug board—times twenty-six positions for each rotor, gives another 17,576 possibilities. And when all the factors are multiplied together, Dönitz's brains trust comes up with a theoretical total of sixteen trillion possibilities. "Impossible to crack!"

But Captain Rogge stands his ground. "If our xB-Dienst can break the British naval cypher, then why can't the enemy do the same to ours?"

"Because the British code is much less complicated," comes the reply. "Your worries concerning the German code are irrelevant."

Rogge tries again: "But let us not overlook one thing: what can be mechanically encyphered, surely one day can also be mechanically decyphered."

Admiral Dönitz has heard enough of this. "I must demand that you refrain from entering your suspicions in the official war log. I cannot order you to refrain, but I warn you that to do so will not remain without court-martial implications."

Rogge is beaten. "Your wish is my command." The machine is secure. Period.

But just to be on the safe side, Dönitz adds a fourth active rotor, code named *alpha*, to the left position on the Enigma machine. Commanders can now choose four out of a possible eight rotors for their cipher machines. The mathematical range of possible variations is thus increased from 16,900 to 44,000. The new cipher machine M4, with its "Triton" cipher circuit, which Bahr is one of the first to see at St Nazaire, goes into operation in the Atlantic theatre after 1 February 1942. The boats also receive a new short signal book further to defeat possible decrypting by the Allies. Stummel confidently rules out "a current reading of our messages by the enemy." And Maertens crows: "A current reading of our messages is not possible." Where Allied convoys in the past steered around a U-boat patrol line, it had been due not to their reading German radio traffic but to aerial surveillance, airborne radar, extraordinary direction-finding, or chatterboxes and spies in the French ports.

In the mid-Atlantic, *U69*'s patrol continues. By night, rolling, twisting, and tossing about on the surface, the boat rides the heavy seas in search of prey. By day, submerged to avoid detection from the skies, conditions within the boat become almost unbearable. The stench is disgusting; the humidity oppressive. Moisture condenses on the cold steel pressure hull and runs in rivulets into the bilges. Paper disintegrates; food decays; eggs rot; bread mildews. Everything Bahr touches is wet and slimy.

Reprieve finally comes at 4 p.m. on 3 December via the radio room: "Return at once to base." After thirty-nine days on patrol, *U69* returns to St Nazaire. The crew of the minesweeper sent out to bring her safely through the minefields looks in vain for flags from her conning tower indicating the patrol's "bag." There is no joy in *U69* as she eases up to her berth inside the harbour in the pale moonlight at 4:30 a.m. on 8 December 1941. Rudolf Bahr feels cheated of the months and years of training that had prepared him for this grand mission.

For his lack of success, Zahn is raked over the coals by Captain Eberhard Godt, Dönitz's chief of operations. While conceding that inclement weather dogged the patrol, Godt nevertheless chastises Zahn for having failed to exploit his only chance for a "kill" on 26 November: "Contact was lost due to the lengthy reloading of all four torpedoes while submerged." In future, Godt lectures Zahn, he is to reload only one or two torpedoes, at all times to maintain contact with the target, and to attack at the first sign of calmer weather.

There is to be no furlough, no Christmas in Landsberg. Dönitz needs every available boat for his tonnage war against Allied shipping, and *U69* is in no position to ask for special favours. One-third of her crew is transferred to a new boat just out from Kiel; teenage recruits take their place. More than four weeks of emergency drills, refits, and reprovisioning lie ahead. And a hatch that has let in tons of sea water needs to be resealed.

It is after one of these crash training programs that Bahr learns from a Wehrmacht radio communiqué that Hitler has struck again: on 11 December 1941 the Führer rushes to Berlin from his "wolf's lair" near Rastenburg in East Prussia, and there, over national radio, climaxes a vicious verbal diatribe in the Reichstag against President Franklin D. Roosevelt by declaring war on the United States. It is the Führer's ill-conceived "response" to the Japanese attack on Pearl Harbor, an action by the inscrutable "Aryan" ally, that seems to steal the thunder (and the initiative in the war) from Hitler. But plans for taking the war to the United States are already being hatched out at the Tirpitzufer in Berlin: under Operation Paukenschlag (Drum Beat), Dönitz proposes to send a dozen large Type IX U-boats to raise havoc off America's eastern seaboard from Nantucket to Cape Hatteras and on to Jacksonville; Raeder agrees to dispatch six boats.

The Thousand-Year Reich is now locked in a deadly struggle with Great Britain and its empire, with the Soviet Union, and the United States. Can the American Republic again turn the tide of war in Europe, as it did in 1917? Bahr is wrenched back to reality on 11–12 December, when about forty enemy planes pummel Brest harbour with fifty or sixty heavy bombs.

On 31 December 1941 Admiral Raeder remembers his forces with a special message: "A year of great victories by the Wehrmacht and proud successes by the Kriegsmarine comes to an end. A new one begins. It shall find us tougher, more determined, and more expectant of victory than ever. We will fight on to certain victory in unshakable, loyal obedience to our Führer and in trust in God and in our own strength." Hitler's New Year's message chastises the "plutocratic powers" Britain and the United States for having made common cause with "Jewry and Bolshevism," and promises the final decision in the war "to save our people" in 1942.

The enemy responds with renewed aerial assaults on Brest. On 17 January 1942 forty-five hostile planes drop 213 high explosive and 250 to 290 incendiary bombs on Brest. Admiral Dönitz raises Brest's defences to thirty-four heavy Flak batteries and twenty light, as well as six squadrons of fighter-interceptors. But he is worried about the condition of its defenders: an unhappy mix of overaged reservists and raw recruits, armed with a plethora of captured enemy rifles and immobile artillery. The paper divisions are, in fact, "skeletal units withdrawn from the Eastern Front." Still, Hitler refuses to release either men or guns from Norway or the Baltic.

U69 leaves St Nazaire anew at dawn on 18 January 1942, bound for the target-rich environment of the mid-Atlantic. Course 270°, due west. She weaves her way through the Biscay fishing fleets. The routine sets in: practice dives to 130 metres depth two and three times a day, gun exercises, rigging for silent running, testing the dive planes, and resurfacing. Bahr conducts his regular inspection of the torpedoes. In fact, the bow compartment becomes a floating machine shop every four or five days. It is hazardous, back-breaking, filthy work. One by one, each torpedo, amply coated with grease, is extracted from its tube and then suspended on the loading carriage, where the torpedo gang checks the bearings and axles of its motor, fills all lubrication points with oil or grease, and tests the rudder and hydroplane controls. The eels have a diameter of about 20 inches and carry 800 pounds of high explosives. Each weighs about 3000 pounds and costs 40,000 Reichsmarks. Dönitz has calculated that every U-boat requires precisely 6.6 torpedoes per month. War by slide-rule!

Day after day, Bahr also supervises the obligatory practice dives. He is convinced about the deadly seriousness of the dives. Maintaining balance during the dive is absolutely critical. No one wants to test the pressure hull at 5000 metres! As fuel oil is consumed—especially at high speeds—it has to be replaced in the tanks with sea water. But since the latter has a greater specific gravity than diesel fuel, the compensated changes have to be meticulously calibrated. The consumption of food, the disposal of garbage, the discharge of a torpedo, and even the change in salt content in the ocean water require the Chief to make daily adjustments to balance. "Trimming the boat," it is called. Every detail is duly recorded in the Chief's thick notebook. Nothing—except the spotting of Allied convoys—is left to chance.

The practice dive begins with the alarm being sounded. The watch hurtles down through the hatch and secures its heavy cover. A petty officer and a rating man the hydroplanes. Within seconds, compartment by compartment relays its readiness to dive. A hand signal and a shrill whistle order the diesels to stop. Exhausts and air intakes are shut off. The electric motors begin to hum.

"All clear to dive!" is reported to the control room. The Chief informs Bahr: "Ready to dive!" In reply, Bahr screams: "Flood!" The Chief repeats the order: "Flood!"

Sailors in the control room open the emergency evacuation vents and activate the flood valves. Air thunders up from the tanks as sea water rushes in from below. The hydroplane operators set the foreplane on "Down hard" and the sternplane on "Down." The bow begins to dip. Decks seem to tilt dangerously forward. The boat is silent save for the hissing of the last air escaping from the negative buoyancy tanks.

The Chief undertakes a correction: "Forward up 10, aft up 15." *U69* soon feels stern heavy. The Chief reports to Zahn: "Boat balanced!" The Captain answers: "Close vents!" Hydroplanes and electric engines working in tandem keep the boat on an even keel. A final sounding in the bow and engine compartments reveals that *U69* is perfectly horizontal at 60 feet. "Attention, zero!" is the Chief's final report to the control room. Each torpedo cell has taken on 120 to 160 gallons of water.

Day after day the crew of *U69* goes through each step of the practice dive to ready itself for combat. Then, shortly before noon on 21 January 1942, Zahn spots an oil slick trailing *U69*. "Probably from the fuel line." He determines to take a closer look once the heavy seas abate. But the slick is still there the next day, and on 23 January *U69* completes a test dive by surfacing in her own oil slick. Despite the persisting heavy seas, Zahn orders all slide valves on the upper deck tested, and all hatches on the diving cells and fuel bunkers tightened. He discovers that *U69* has already lost 1 to 2 tons of oil out of each fuel bunker. The oil slick grows and grows, and there is no solution at hand. Just before noon on 23 January, Zahn decides to return to port.

At 7:55 p.m. *U69*'s left rudder jams and for half an hour the boat turns lazy circles to starboard. Insult added to injury! The crew eventually wedges the rudder in the amidships position, and Zahn gingerly sets course (090°) for home. In fog and rain, the boat wallows towards St Nazaire. Submerged running is extremely difficult, owing to the half-empty fuel bunkers. But no enemy "bees" harass Zahn across the Bay of Biscay, and at 1:20 p.m. on 26 January 1942 *U69* passes the safety of the St Nazaire locks.

The patrol is ended almost before it has really begun. Nine days after leaving St Nazaire, the boat is back in port. The minesweeper crew again looks in vain for victory flags. Commander Herbert Sohler, the Flotilla Commandant, does not meet the boat at the pier. Nor do the construction workers from Organization Todt. There is no invitation to visit Admiral Dönitz in Kernevel.

Instead, *U69* is rushed into dry dock. Emergency repairs take five days. Dockyard crews repair the fuel line and replace the seals on the hatches of the buoyancy and fuel tanks. Finally, they replace the main rudder shaft. Thereafter, *U69* undergoes provisioning and refuelling anew. No need to take on new torpedoes. The crew longs for another patrol to erase the bitter aftertaste of the last two. While many of their colleagues are conducting a merry turkey shoot across the Atlantic off the American coast, Zahn and Bahr have nothing to show for nearly three months on patrol.

At 5:30 p.m. on 31 January, *U69* again slips out of the St Nazaire locks, this time bound for the North Atlantic, the ice-choked coasts of Greenland, and then on to New England or Newfoundland. It is Bahr's first return to these waters since 1936 with the *Emden*. German agents have reported that the harbours of St John's and Halifax are teeming with merchant ships, that Canadian railways are congested with trains loaded with food, lumber, and wood pulp, and that every Canadian destroyer and corvette has been pressed into convoy escort service. Munitions and weapons continue to be loaded day and night in Halifax.

Dönitz agrees to dispatch a submarine to Canada to land intelligence agents (Operation Grete) to report on ship traffic from the Great Lakes through the St Lawrence to the Bay of Fundy. One of the agents informs Admiral U-boats of public opposition to conscription in Quebec, and states that Canada is ripe and ready for union—possibly under a revised dominion status—with the United States.

Hopes run cautiously high throughout *U69*. Surely an unguarded American convoy or even a single straggler is bound to pop up on the horizon and fall victim to her. But Zahn is too late. The Americans are beginning to adopt convoy, and British and Canadian destroyers and corvettes jealously and tenaciously guard their charges.

Then, shortly after noon on 6 February, Kernevel alerts *U69* to the expected presence of a convoy of twenty ships in quadrant BE. Zahn searches the broad sweeps of the Atlantic "with *very* good visibility" for thirty-six hours. Again in vain. Bahr is bitterly disappointed and hopelessly frustrated. Is *U69* just an unlucky boat? Has Zahn's string of successes run out?

"Shadow off the right bow! At 340°!"

Zahn is up on the bridge in an instant. It is midnight, 7 February. "Action stations. Flood tubes 2 and 4. Rudder hard to starboard. Course 340°." The shadow is damned close. "Range 350 metres." *U69* lurches to her new course. The Old Man is not about to let this one slip away. He approaches the target, which lies 10 degrees off his port bow. Time: 1:57 a.m.

"Tube 2: . . . Fire!"

"Tube 4: . . . Fire!"

Bahr launches both eels. "*Verdammte Scheisse!*" One torpedo is a surface runner; the other misses the shadow. It is the same story as in 1939: faulty depth keeping and malfunctioning detonator pistol. Admiral U-boats suspects that the eels have been adversely affected by storage during the cold winter in northern Germany.

Zahn takes the target for a cruiser. But within two minutes of firing, the distance between hunter and hunted is down to 150 metres and the Old Man clearly makes out the silhouette of a destroyer across his bow. Course 180°. Almost in motor reaction, Zahn orders another torpedo shot.

"Tube 3: . . . Fire!" Bahr slams the firing knob.

"Miss!"

"Dive, dive! Action stations! Prepare for depth-charges!"

Inexplicably, none come. The tin can harmlessly passes abaft *U69*. Around 4 a.m. Zahn resurfaces and reports the sighting to Kernevel; Admiral U-boats orders *U69* to continue on a course 270°, due west. Another golden opportunity lost!

For nine days *U69* fights her way towards New England in heavy seas and rain showers. At 4:20 p.m. on 15 February, about 500 miles east of Long Island, New York, the watch sights a straggler dead ahead at a speed of 8 knots. She mounts two yellow masts and a single black funnel. "Can it be one of our own vessels?" the log entry reads. After Captain Godt's recent rebuke, there is no choice but to attack. Zahn quickly studies his options and decides on a submerged attack. But the target spots *U69* and begins sharp zigzags. In order not to lose contact, Zahn must stay on the surface. He now favours a surface attack under the cover of darkness.

U69 dogs the shadow throughout the ensuing night, closing the range to 1500 yards by midnight. A new complication sets in: the target has manoeuvred into an operations area reserved for German blockade runners. What to do? Zahn decides not to risk an attack, claiming that low fuel supplies and the danger that this might be a Reich craft militate against sinking. Another opportunity lost?

Kernevel orders Zahn to steer due west, ever closer to the American seaboard. On 18 February the telltale oil slick reappears. Tide and wind reduce top speed to 7 knots. Zahn decides to leave American waters, where air reconnaissance grows daily, and, remembering xB-Dienst's reports of heavy traffic in Canadian waters, heads north for the Grand Banks south of Newfoundland. Dönitz concurs.

U69 sets course for 040°—and promptly steams into rain and hail showers and roaring seas. The u-boat's war log underscores the appalling conditions: "*Heaviest seas imaginable, high seas, heavy breakers, which crash over the top of the tower.*" It would be useless to try an attack under these conditions, Zahn concludes. "Hull is being severely battered, heavy blows, severe vibrations." There is only one escape: *U69* dives for safe cover. For three days, the violent storm rages. Then, in the evening of 21 February, Zahn receives word from another u-boat that five tankers are steaming through grid quadrant CC2490. Quick calibrations reveal it would take forty hours of hard running to reach the area: Zahn decides not to risk this amount of fuel for a "maybe." Obviously, the tankers passed him during the storm two days before.

U69 heads north to a point level with St John's, Newfoundland, and then begins the return leg of the patrol. Late on 23 February, Zahn receives news of a westbound convoy sighted 400 nautical miles east of his position. He decides to engage. By 10:25 a.m. on 24 February the convoy is 25 miles away. The sun is just breaking over the horizon in the east. Zahn decides not to risk an attack in daylight, but to shadow the convoy and to try an underwater approach at twilight. He submerges his boat 15 miles ahead of the convoy and awaits its arrival.

It is a textbook operation. At 7 p.m. *U69* breaks to the surface. "Boat on a collision course with the convoy. Ships' positions precisely charted on the map. Good visibility. Smoke clouds can be seen far away on the horizon." Thirty minutes later the operation comes apart. The convoy separates into several groups of about six ships each. What to do? Zahn establishes contact with *U155* (Lieutenant-Commander Adolf Piening) and they exchange signals by searchlight. *U155* is immediately driven off by an escorting destroyer. Zahn loses contact with the convoy and searches desperately for it on a west-by-southwest course. Again in vain. *U69* spends 25 February with test dives. Late in the afternoon Zahn spots several oil slicks and pursues them—only to lose them in heavy fog by 6:10 p.m. Four hours later Kernevel orders *U69* to break off operations against the convoy. As *U69* charges east for its home base, Zahn laconically records on 26 February that the water temperature has changed from -3 to 13 degrees Celsius in a single day.

On 5 March Zahn gets a final opportunity to engage the enemy. At 9:40 a.m. his radio operator reports fast, twin-screw noises at 270°, and, later, more muffled screw noise at 350°. The Old Man surfaces at once to surprise whatever is up there at first light. But dense fog, steady rain, and choppy seas send him back under the surface. At noon *U69* breaks the surface again. The fog is beginning to lift. At 1:34 p.m. Zahn spies a large passenger liner of 6000 to 8000 tons about 2000 metres dead ahead: "pronounced bow, low funnel, two masts, round bridge." Suddenly, the liner heads straight for *U69*. Zahn orders an emergency dive to remain undetected. He will attempt a submerged attack.

"Flood tubes 2 and 4!"

The target is still bearing down on *U69* bows on at 0°, but Zahn cannot bring the boat to periscope depth immediately. When he finally does, he cannot find the steamer in the heavy ocean swells. Then the periscope lens fogs up. At 1:45 p.m. Zahn surfaces: "Steamer not to be seen." At 2:50 he dives to pick up its screw noises. Nothing. At 3:20 he returns to the surface and races west to get ahead of the liner. Nothing. At 10 p.m. he changes course to southeast. Nothing. At 8 a.m. on 6 March he abandons the search and reports his actions to Kernevel.

Low on fuel but high on torpedoes, *U69* returns to St Nazaire on 17 March 1942. Few of the crew dare step out on the afterdeck for fear of the reproaching glances of the minesweeper crew that guides them safely into port. Again, no flags fly from the conning tower. No band. No flowers. No welcoming "lightning girls"—*Blitzmädchen*, as such "hostesses" are popularly called. Just excuses and explanations to be made. Only the Irish are celebrating this St Patrick's Day.

Thirty-eight gruelling days on patrol without a single kill. Almost in mockery, Rudolf Bahr on 19 March receives his u-boat Badge for having completed two operational patrols. *U69* is scheduled for major refit. Among other things, she is to receive a new fuelling system to allow re-fuelling at sea from the broad-beamed 2300-ton Type XIV boats hastily being converted to 435-ton oil tankers—"milk cows" (*Milchkühe*) in popular parlance. Perhaps raising the time out on patrol from forty-one days to eighty-one with two refuellings will bring *U69* to greener pastures.

Lieutenant-Commander Wilhelm Zahn endures Kernevel's full wrath. This time the after-action report is written not by Godt but by Dönitz: "Although opportunities presented themselves, the Commander once again has had no success. . . . This cannot be attributed solely to lack of luck. The Commander lacks skill and initiative both in general operations and in attacking." Specifically, the Great Lion is incensed that at dawn on 24 February Zahn had chosen merely to shadow the convoy. "Proper tactics would have been to head for the convoy at full speed and to decide on a daylight attack—or at the very least to have kept so close to the enemy as not to lose him, as was the case here." There is no room in the Dönitz Volunteer Corps for timid Kaleus. "The Commander has been relieved of command in order to be more useful at another post." Rudolf Bahr finds little to celebrate on his twenty-sixth birthday on 1 April.

U69 and her Exec say goodbye to St Nazaire for the fourth time in seven months under the boat's third skipper, Lieutenant Ulrich Gräf. Date: 12 April 1942. Destination: grid quadrant DI90, and from there the Caribbean Sea. *U69* is not to join a patrol line but, rather, to conduct individual operations. She is given the code-name "NE" further to confuse would-be Allied trackers.

Under bright sunny skies and a fresh spring breeze, *U69* leaves behind the first cherry blossoms of the year and successfully passes the Bay of Biscay amid the daily buzz of fifty to seventy British "bees." At noon on 17 April, about 500 miles due west of St Nazaire, *U69* is formally introduced to hostile air.

"Alarm! Alarm! Aircraft dead ahead. Bearing one-eight-zero. Distance 5000 to 6000 metres." Gräf is pissed off! "Who the hell would have expected an airplane to emerge through the clouds in this fucking mess?" He is referring to the rain showers and haze that pervade the seas. There is no time to waste. Every second counts. The watch tumbles down the hatch and slams it shut, just as the bow dips under the surface breakers. When *U69* resurfaces half an hour later, there is no sign of the aircraft.

The march west continues. On 18 April a small steamer crosses Gräf's path, but he opts not to pursue since he is still 140 nautical miles away from his daily target goal. The next day Dönitz demands that his boats "absolutely report all recent successful operations" by 20 April—

Hitler's birthday! Apparently, some exorbitant reports flood in to Admiral U-boats, with the result that Dönitz on 20 April is forced to remind his commanders to eschew "fantasy figures" in their reports. "Motto: We are one solid company."

Just before dawn on 22 April Gräf spots another small steamer, but calls off the pursuit when it raises the Spanish colours at first light. *U69* points west relentlessly. Near midnight on 28 April Gräf establishes contact with *U594* and *U572*. All three boats head for a scheduled rendezvous with *U459*, one of the first milk cows placed in service under the command of Lieutenant-Commander Georg Count von Wilamovitz-Moellendorf, nicknamed "wild Moritz" for his antics both on shore and at sea. They are joined by *U558* early on 29 April in quadrant CC72, roughly 300 miles south of the Grand Banks.

At 1:54 a.m. provisioning begins. *U69* takes on fourteen days of supplies in one hour and fifteen minutes, as a rubber dinghy hauls canned meats and vegetables and other non-perishable provisions over from the "cow." After the other boats have likewise been replenished, Gräf and Bahr supervise the intake of diesel fuel and a new supply of fresh water. The operation is tricky—especially at 8 p.m. The milk cow trails a fuel hose kept afloat by inflated rubber bladders from her stern; *U69* slowly comes aft and to the leeward side of *U459*, fetches the fuel hose out of the water, and then connects it to its own fuel tanks. The two boats run at 1.5 knots on a parallel course, connected by a 25-foot-long hawser. Refueling 32 cubic metres of oil takes just over two hours. Too slow! The crew will have to get better at this job.

A few hardy souls avail themselves of the opportunity to wash off more than two weeks' worth of filth by diving into the Atlantic. Although both boats are no longer in the "black pit"—that still safe haven south of Iceland and Greenland and equidistant from Newfoundland and Ireland, beyond the range of Allied land-based planes—no one yet suspects attack from the air in total darkness.

At 10:15 p.m. the two boats part company. The next day Dönitz orders Gräf to set course for grid diagram DO, just east of the Caribbean. *U69* turns to course 232, south-southwest. Gräf intends to reach the operations area via Bermuda. Bahr remembers its sparkling blue waters well.

Around noon on 1 May a small four-master bobs into sight, alone on the broad Atlantic, more than 400 miles east of Norfolk, Virginia, without escort and obviously undeserving of air cover. Gräf studies the vessel with great curiosity and dreamily drifts northward with it.

"Alarm! I am too close!" He opts for a submerged attack; then changes his mind, surfaces, and for fifteen minutes cannot find the schooner. When he finally does, Gräf again submerges, follows in the little ship's wake, and decides to torpedo her. But the schooner appears harmless through the periscope, and at 5:27 p.m. *U69* resurfaces. At a distance of 2000 yards the Second Watch Officer pumps no fewer than sixty-six 8.8-cm shells from the deck-gun as well as sixty rounds from the machine-guns into her at close range as virtual target practice. The vessel, the American barque *James E. Newsome*, disintegrates at 5:28 in grid square CB94. Her crew of nine take to their boats. A modest triumph of 671 tons, to be sure, but a triumph nevertheless. Something to celebrate on the Third Reich's annual Day of Labour.

But Gräf is concerned about the high expenditure of shell. The inexperienced gun crew was constantly plagued by heavy seas, and two men were swept overboard during the action. At least ten shells were lost by the crew owing to the boat's pitching and rolling. The 8.8-cm gun's sights broke with the first salvo—and the little barque had offered a small target. The fifty-four incendiary shells fired proved ineffective, as each time they hit and set fire to the ship's wooden hull the ocean spray doused them just as quickly. A learning experience, indeed.

Gräf sets a course of south-southwest and steams towards the Caribbean through tropical rain squalls. The men begin to enjoy the warmer climes, and swimming becomes a daily treat.

"Alarm! *Flugzeug!*" The navigator standing watch at 8:18 p.m. on 7 May has discovered a glint of metal between the clouds 20 degrees off the left bow. It is a Consolidated PBY-5A flying-boat at 400 metres altitude, range 6000 metres. *U69* dips beneath the waves before the intruder can do any damage. She returns to the surface at 9:18, only to be driven back down at 10:04 by a twin-engine attacker. Obviously, the Americans have shifted some of their air resources to the Caribbean.

U69 reaches her designated war zone in the central Caribbean on 8 May. All ports are brightly lit, as if no one is expecting a German U-boat. Shortly after midnight on 9 May Gräf spots three mastheads in the last remaining light. A submerged attack at 2:30 a.m. fails as the distance between the two vessels is too great. At 3:42 a.m. Gräf fires a spread of two torpedoes at the shadow: one eel breaks the surface just abaft the victim's stern; the other passes its bow harmlessly.

"Distance to target must have been greater than calibrated," punctuates the war log. As Torpedo Officer, Bahr feels the sting of failure. For three hours, *U69* stalks the intended victim. At 6:43 a.m. Gräf orders a final attack with the stern tube. "*Verdammt!*" It is a tube runner! Luckily, *U69* is on the surface and the torpedo gang manages to push the eel out of the tube eight seconds later. Gräf breaks off the chase. Too many torpedoes wasted already. He reports the shadow as a coastal cruiser, type unknown.

Midnight, 10 May. Gräf spies smoke and a mast steaming at 14 knots on the horizon. For more than four hours he gives chase. The first light at 1 a.m. reveals a 7400-ton American Type CI freighter, fully loaded. For two hours Gräf manoeuvres his boat closer. At 3:23 a.m. Bahr fires an eel from tube 2. It, too, breaks the surface short of the target. While Gräf pursues the American for another two and a half hours, Bahr pulls the eels from the torpedo tubes and carefully inspects each one for defects.

At 6:03 a.m. Bahr sends an eel from tube 3 towards the freighter. It, too, misses the target. Gräf is perplexed. "I have no idea why they all fail." In fact, the rate of torpedo failures in the Kriegsmarine surpasses 40 percent in 1942. Gräf breaks off the pursuit because both MAN diesels are overheating and the battery cells of the electric motors, with which he tries to augment diesel power, have run down.

At noon on 11 May Bahr again hauls the eels out of their tubes and inspects them carefully. He even dismantles the warhead on one. "No signs of defect." In the meantime, Gräf sets course east for St Lucia. Just before dawn on 12 May the watch again calls the Old Man to the bridge: "To the skipper. Mast ahead off the starboard bow!" Gräf runs up to the bridge. Bahr already has his Zeiss glasses locked into the TBT and trained on the distant hulk. "Unaccompanied vessel at 090°. Speed 11 knots. Course two-seven-zero. Visibility excellent!" This formality is for the war log. To the control and engine rooms goes the terse command: "Right full rudder, both engines emergency ahead!" The twin diesels roar up to power.

Suddenly, the shadow on the horizon turns away from *U69* and begins to zigzag wildly. "Must have already seen me at 3000 metres." Gräf gives chase and unlimbers his deck-guns. "She's a fat tanker; cannot make out any armament." He orders Bahr to feed a steady stream of information to the conning tower to allow the navigator to plot the best approach for the planned execution. Four pairs of eyes on the bridge, each scanning a different 90-degree arc of the compass, help the Watch Officer on duty search for signs of aircraft. None appear. The control room reports to Gräf: "Sir, the target zigzags around a mean course of 270 degrees. Speed 11 knots."

By 9:02 a.m. *U69* has closed the distance to 400 yards. The Old Man sends *U69* at full speed ahead to close on the steamer. At 9:03 Gräf orders the 8.8-cm deck-gun to open fire with incendiary shells. The second salvo puts the American's deck-gun out of action; the fourth sets fire to its camouflage housing. Red machine-gun fire leaps from the bridge; *U69* replies with her own MGs. The nineteenth incendiary shell sets the tanker on fire. Gräf changes munition and pumps fourteen rounds of explosive shells into her. The target stops dead in the water. Her crew rush to their lifeboats, still in their davits on deck.

Dawn is rapidly bathing the area in bright light, and Gräf quickly decides to submerge and finish the freighter off with torpedoes. "Clear the bridge! Flood and proceed at periscope depth." The alarm screams through the ship. The diesels fall silent. The Chief switches off the ventilators and a nauseating stench of bilge, fuel, food, and sweat permeates the boat. The only audible sound is the steady hum of the electric motors as Gräf makes his final approach under water. You can almost taste the tension in the air.

By now, Bahr is already hunched over the ship's calculator in the conning tower, computing data on the enemy's position and feeding it into the gyro-steering mechanism of his eels right up to the moment of firing. *God*, Bahr prays, *I hope they don't malfunction again!* The Old Man issues final orders from his bicycle seat at the scope in the control room, manoeuvring the boat so that the cripple lies dead ahead of him.

"Prepare tubes 3 and 5 for firing! Flood tubes 3 and 5! Open torpedo doors!" Staccato sentences; not a word wasted.

"Doors opened and tubes 3 and 5 flooded and ready, sir," comes the quick reply from the bow torpedo compartment.

Almost absentmindedly, the Chief chimes in: "Boat balanced."

Gräf yells up the tower to Bahr: "Switch on tubes 3 and 5!" A quick check with the radio room for an exact bearing. "Zero degrees, Herr

Oberleutnant!" A final glance through the scope. "Range approximately 400 metres. To the tower: enemy speed zero knots. Set torpedoes for 2 metres."

Seconds later: "To the tower: enemy angle dead on. One-third speed ahead." The tension is almost unbearable. It is 9:37 a.m. Every eye is strained for a glimpse of the Old Man. And then, suddenly, the anxiety explodes.

"Tube 3: . . . Fire!" Bahr hits the firing knob. A slight jolt.

The radioman confirms the obvious: "Torpedo running!"

A hissing noise from the bow compartment. And an increase in atmospheric pressure as the compressed air that drove the eel out of its tube is expelled into the boat to avoid deadly telltale bubbles rising to the surface.

Gräf nervously counts off the seconds up to 1 minute 5 seconds. *Verdammt!* "Another tube runner; 20 seconds too long." Then a muffled explosion is heard, and Gräf observes a high, black column of fire and smoke leap up the side of the freighter. A direct hit in the engine compartment. The vessel begins to sag down by the stern; concurrently it lists to port. The crew bails out of its lifeboats, many still swinging from their davits, and works feverishly to put out the fires. Gräf already is positioning *U69* to line up her stern tube for the coup de grâce.

"Tube 5: . . . Fire!"

Bahr slams the firing knob down at precisely 10:02 a.m. Thirty seconds later the eel strikes the engine-room bulkheads. "A column of smoke and debris climbs 200 to 250 metres in the air; a column of fire of equal height rises from the smoke pillar. Stern sinks at once; after twenty-two minutes the bow rises vertically in the air and [the ship] sinks."

Gräf lets Bahr have a look through the periscope at the spot where the crippled freighter disappeared. "Many barrels at the site of the sinking, no clues as to her identity, no survivors." Poor bastards! Gräf estimates her at 11,410 tons, half loaded and definitely Victolite Class. He has Bahr look it up in *Lloyd's Maritime Directory*: Imperial Oil tanker, home port Montreal. The Second Watch Officer reports having fired thirty-three shells into the target. "Set course one-three-five."

Lieutenant Gräf then transmits news of the sinking of an 11,410-ton Victolite Class tanker in quadrant ED4726 (13°53' north, 68°20' west) to

Admiral U-boats, now at new quarters in the Avenue Maréchal Maunoury in Paris. In fact, the kill later turns out to be the 6826-ton Norwegian registry tanker *Lise*, plying the Caribbean under contract to the Allies.

Gräf takes *U69* down to 60 feet, out of sight of any aircraft in the area that might have been alerted to the destruction that had just taken place. He allows the crew time to savour the moment. Whatever demon had haunted the boat throughout 1941 has now been dramatically exorcised. The Old Man breaks out the bottle of Napoleon brandy from his private locker and shares a toast with the men in the control room and tower. Christ, it is well past breakfast time, delayed by the hunt and kill; in fact, precisely noon. The last slabs of bacon hit the frying pan; the last smoked ham succumbs to the cook's butcher knife. Even the ersatz coffee tastes good. The canned hash is downright delicious; the rancid Kraut almost palatable. No one complains about the horrendous heat and humidity. *U69* is a happy boat.

That mood turns even more jovial just before midnight when the Second Watch Officer reports: "Mast off the port bow! Bearing zero-nine-five! Speed 12.5 knots! Zigzag course!" Gräf, up on the bridge in a flash, can hardly believe his eyes or his good fortune: another loner without escort. Effortlessly, he allows *U69* to slip beneath the sea just until her decks are awash. The last daylight glows in the west. He waits undetected until the target is within 4500 metres. Bahr once more plots the approach.

"Angle left 80. Distance 4.5. Speed 14 knots. Set torpedo depth at 2.5. Flood all tubes!" The outer doors to the torpedo tubes are opened and the tubes flooded. Gräf decides to fire a single eel; there is no need to waste a salvo on this poor bugger. "Speed half ahead, Chief!" At 3:38 a.m. Gräf turns to Bahr. "Exec, take over and fire."

Bahr's voice trembles as he shouts into the wind: "Tube 2, ready! . . . Fire!"

It is Bahr's first taste of blood. But despite a firing angle of 358°, the eel veers off to port and passes the target far ahead of her bow. Gräf is irate. "Rudder hard aport! Angle left 90. Speed 14 knots. Range 4000. Depth setting 2.5 metres." He is going to fire torpedoes until he finds one that works. "Tube 1: . . . Fire!" This time Bahr plunges the firing knob down. Gräf and his Exec watch the track of the eel in the phosphorescent sea. *Scheisse!* This one passes the target 5 metres behind her stern.

The Old Man is fed up with shoddy eels. He ploughs after the shadow in her wake and orders the deck-gun manned. The target finally spies *U69*, lays down a heavy smoke screen, and moves away astern of the submarine. Her Captain orders his men on deck. At 3:47 a.m. Gräf opens fire at a range of 2000 metres. "Salvos are poorly aimed. Predominantly too long, but since they whiz between her bridge and mast, they thus fulfil their moral effect." A high-explosive shell rips into the target's bridge at the base of the funnel. Her Captain blows off steam. But the vessel, fully laden to the gunwales, refuses to stop in the surging seas. Gräf strafes her upper decks with his machine-guns. By 3:59 a.m. the 8.8-cm deck-gun as well as the machine-guns jam because of broken shell and cartridge cases.

At this very moment, the steamer stops and her crew begins to lower the lifeboats. "Just in time," Gräf records in the war log, "for only the machine pistol is clear for action." The steamer's skipper sends out a report of the action via radio. Incensed by this piece of cheek, Gräf slowly circles his wounded victim. He steams clear of the lifeboats still being hurled into the water by the crew in sheer panic and positions *U69* for a stern torpedo shot. At 4:08 Bahr administers the coup de grâce from tube 5. "Hit astern; dark, high columns of fire and debris. Collapses on itself and sinks within 3 minutes." Bahr once more looks through the scope at the scene of destruction. "Four lifeboats and many floats with about 25 men. Name is unclear: *Black Tern*, 5,032 tons. Black-Diamond Line, New York." Another brief glance at *Lloyd's Maritime Directory* confirms the guesswork: Gräf's third victim is the American steamer *Norlantic*, actual tonnage 2606. She went down in grid square ED7325 (12°30' north, 66°30' west). *U69* fired one eel, eleven incendiary and twenty-two explosive shells, and eighty rounds of machine-gun fire during the action. Another good day's work.

At midnight on 14 May, *U69*'s torpedo gang under Bahr's careful supervision takes advantage of the downtime and the relative cool to reload the four expended torpedoes on the lee side of Blanquilla Island, about 100 miles north of Cumaná, Venezuela. Five hours later, Gräf radioes news of the two kills to Admiral u-boats. He says nothing about the fate of the *Norlantic*'s crew. Dönitz's recent instruction on this matter to all boats is perfectly clear: "For officers only. No survivors are to be taken on board. We have to be hard in this war!"

Apparently, too few Allied seamen are being lost at sea. Dönitz formalizes this practice in his famous "Triton Null" signal of 17 September 1942.

Gräf's orders are to cruise these waters for another week. In the dimming last light of 15 May, he makes out a three-masted tanker in quadrant ED9722. These are dangerous, narrow waters between Margarita Island and Río Caribe in Sucre Province, Venezuela. The target is steering a course of 135°, or southeast, at 12 knots. Gräf's only chance is to pass hard by the Venezuelan coast and to get ahead of the tanker. "With throttles full out I should intercept him just before the entrance" to the Gulf of Paria. He pays no attention to a Venezuelan coast guard cutter that spots him just before midnight.

"Alarm! I must have been spotted by both the coast guard cutter and by shore batteries." It is midnight; poor visibility. Gräf dives at once and heads out to sea towards the tanker. Nothing in sight. At 1:02 a.m. he surfaces and spots the target 5000 metres away, heading for the entrance to the gulf. But searchlights illuminate the U-boat and force it to dive. When U69 resurfaces at 1:38 it has lost the tanker again. For six hours, Gräf patrols up and down off the entrance to the Gulf of Paria, but the enemy manages to slip by him in the dark.

Deeply disappointed, Gräf sets a northern course at 7 a.m. Four hours later he and Bahr chuckle over a signal from Dönitz giving commanders the green light to attack South American ships—save those of Argentina and Chile. Who the hell has time to check national flags or registry papers? And the Brits historically have been perfidious about misusing flags of registry other than their own!

For the next two days U69 chases freighters in the Caribbean. But the story soon becomes monotonous:

16 May	1305 hours:	Alarm! Land-based aircraft.
	1932 hours:	Flying-boat in view.
17 May	1310 hours:	Flying-boat in view.
	1349 hours:	Alarm! Flying-boat approaches.
	1536 hours:	Flying-boat.

It comes almost as a relief when a patrol craft spots U69 east of Grenada in the afternoon of 17 May. It sends three depth-charges Gräf's way; none find their target. The next day *U69* crash dives six times to avoid flying-boats.

At 9:37 a.m. on 20 May Gräf is called to the bridge. "Shadow in sight, right 30°, two tankers, one freighter, one destroyer." The Old Man decides to sneak up on the group from astern the destroyer. But the tin can sights *U69* and forces it to withdraw in a southwesterly direction. At 10:46 a.m. Dönitz ends the operation from Paris by ordering Gräf to proceed at once to Martinique to attack "suspected American naval forces" as well as any French forces (one cruiser, four destroyers), to prevent them from falling into American hands.

For eighteen hours *U69* patrols off Martinique, standing out to sea by day to avoid the blistering heat and humidity. At 6:44 a.m. on 21 May the watch sights a shadow 30° off the starboard bow. Gräf immediately gives chase. The shadow turns away and zigzags. The Old Man decides against using the deck-gun, since the weather is iffy: bright water surface, dark horizon, bright phosphorescence on the sea.

"Prepare to dive! Take her to periscope depth! Action stations!" The crew is alive with excitement. Bahr opens the doors on the bow torpedo tubes and floods the tubes. Twice Gräf approaches the target by dead reckoning, and twice he is off course. At 7:53 he positions *U69* for a third approach and barks out his orders in abbreviated commands: "Bow left 90. Speed 6. Distance 9. Depth 2. Angle 40."

"Tube 1: . . . Fire!"

Bahr bangs the firing knob. Gräf easily tracks the torpedo's bubbles through the scope in the shining sea. His log marks the staccato sequence of events: "Hit amidships. Dark column of smoke and debris with red explosions throughout it. Steamer begins to go down, breaks apart, and sinks" in grid square ED6867, just east of St Lucia. He enters her into the war log as "*Torondoc*, 1,927 tons, fully loaded." This time the target's identity is correct; she is a Canadian steamer. Gräf laconically ends the war log: "At scene of sinking 4 boats and 2 floats."

After lunch on 23 May, Gräf spies another freighter hard off Martinique's west coast. Visibility is superb: estimated range 5.4 miles. The Old Man immediately surges forward to position *U69* between the target and the main harbour of Martinique. The freighter lays down a smokescreen and attempts to radio Fort de France on shore. Displaying neither flag nor markings, the vessel fires two shots from the stern deck-gun at *U69*. Both fall short. Gräf orders *U69* below the surface; the target begins to zigzag, all the while heading for port. "It is an old coal tramp steamer. Empty. 3,500 tons. 8-cm gun manned." Gräf carefully issues final instructions: "Right 95 degrees. Speed 7 knots. Distance 1000 metres. Torpedo 2 metres depth." All is ready in an instant.

"Tube 3: . . . Fire!"

Scheisse! Another miss. At the torpedo's approach, the garbage scow increased speed and changed course. Gräf immediately gives chase, but is driven off at 5:59 p.m. by a land-based aircraft. Time to return to the main task of guarding Martinique's harbour!

On 24 May Admiral u-boats informs Gräf that the French naval forces might surrender to the Americans at Martinique and instructs *U69* to attack all US vessels and any others leaving port. After several renewed attacks from the air, Gräf records with understatement: "I am gaining the impression that aircraft are hunting u-boats!" The very next day at 3:57 p.m. a land-based aircraft barely misses *U69*: "Torpedo detonation. High, white column of water." And on 26 May *U69* crash dives to avoid being strafed by a flying-boat. At 30 metres depth, the boat is rocked by two bombs that explode on either side of her. Close call!

Barely has Gräf recovered from the aerial assault when an unidentified destroyer, covered by a flying-boat, slices into view at 8:35 p.m. Gräf immediately submerges and sets course with the two electric motors to intercept the tin can, but at 9:08 it spots *U69* and bears down on her at full speed. "Quickly into the cellar." The boat crash dives and, at 30 metres depth, is rocked by nine depth-charges (*Wabos*). The lights go off, many of the crew are thrown to the deck-plates, and *U69* vibrates violently from stern to bow. "Rig for silent running." The Chief manages to get the emergency back-up lights on. *U69* creeps along at 120 metres depth. Not a sound but the men's hard breathing.

Wham! Six sharp blows strike the hull. Six more depth-charges. "Take her down to A+60"—140 metres! The hull groans and cracks. Water streams down the steel hull into the bilge. Four more hammer blows; four more *Wabos*. It is the first experience with depth-charges for many of the men—including Rudolf Bahr—and they are frozen in their tracks by the eerie experience. Moreover, *U69* lies five degrees down by the bow. The foreplanes are almost impossible to move. As the KTB records, "The enemy apparently has a superb listening device.

Strange loud, metallic noises on [our] foredeck greatly aid him." Gräf is much relieved: "No asdic."

Suddenly, at 9:45 p.m., the tin can moves off, only to reappear once more off *U69*'s starboard without making contact. As Gräf takes his boat 8 miles off shore, relief spreads throughout *U69*: she has survived her first serious encounter with depth-charges. "Chief, damage reports!" As each compartment reports, Gräf, too, is much relieved: the master gyroscope requires two hours to repair; there is a slight tear in the starboard diesel gravity tank; and there is much glass damage throughout the boat. Repairs take most of the night, and in the first light the Chief inspects the bow and removes the planking and metal sheets that the *Wabos* ripped from the deck. The men welcome the time up on deck to escape the sweltering atmosphere of the hull.

In fact, the cruise under tropical conditions is beginning to take its toll. In the early morning hours of 1 June, Gräf and his Exec calculate that they have spent six of the last nine days submerged off the coast of Martinique. "Water temperatures between 28 and 29 degrees Celsius and boat temperatures between 37 and 42 degrees c." The rigours of repeated dives due to hostile air cover and the monotony of patrolling off a single port have had their effects. "The medical condition of the men, which has been good up to now, suffered especially during the last few days of submerged running in 40-degree heat. Swelling of the outer acoustic ducts (severe deafness, pain), probably caused by drastic temperature changes and air drafts. Sweat eczema."

The monotony of patrol is not eased until shortly before noon on 5 June, when Gräf spies a small abandoned tug and sinks it with seven 8.8-cm explosive shells and twenty rounds of machine-gun fire. He is bitterly disappointed that the MG c/30 jams again; nor does he have enough armour-piercing bullets. Four days later Gräf notifies Admiral U-boats that he is down to twenty days of bare-bones provisions—and that the return leg of the patrol will take nineteen. Dönitz grants permission for *U69* to return to base. Mysteriously, the British Admiralty reports that the 1928-ton Dutch steamer *Poseidon*, en route from New York to Trinidad, has been torpedoed in Gräf's patrol area. Could it be the freighter that Gräf had torpedoed on 11 May and believed he missed?

The Old Man is careful not to include unconfirmed sinkings in his final report to Dönitz: "SANK FOUR. 19,040 [tons]. U69." Overall,

May 1942 has been a record month for the grey wolves: 227 merchant-men destroyed for a total of 967,420 tons. Even Hitler concedes that, in the final analysis, the U-boat campaign might be decisive for the outcome of the war.

During the sixteen-day return trip across the Atlantic, Rudolf Bahr begins the paperwork: shipyard order forms, repair requests, supply lists, fuel requisition forms, furlough papers, and the like. After a harrowing run through the Bay of Biscay, diving repeatedly to avoid British "bees," *U69* makes St Nazaire unscathed at 10:20 a.m. on 25 June 1942. Just before making contact with the escorting minesweeper, several seamen string together four white pennants, each representing a sunken ship, and secure them by a line to the periscope head. Gräf orders his men to fall in in fresh fatigues.

A large crowd of well-wishers lines the quay in the inner harbour. As the slender craft ties up at the pier, a military band strikes up a march. Blue and grey-green uniforms mingle with white. Flowers shower down on the crew. "Lightning girls" from the base hospital are out in full force to greet *U69*. Commander Sohler, chief of the 7th U-boat Flotilla, shouts a hearty welcome, strides across the gangplank, and shakes hands with skipper and crew. Captain Ernst Kellermann, the harbour commander, is also on hand. It makes up for all the sorry homecomings of 1941.

The real festivities, of course, are just beginning. Flotilla headquarters throws a gala reception. Lobster and champagne all around. Then on to a full course of beef and pork, washed down with good German beer. Mail call is followed by the first bath, shave, and haircut in almost ten weeks. The officers don their best double-breasted blues. The ratings, back-pay jingling in their pockets, leave the docks to paint the town red.

St Nazaire can be very generous to a successful crew with money to burn. Admiral Alfred Saalwächter, Naval Commander West, has even put out a book, *Das Land an der Biskaya*, to guide his charges when ashore. Street vendors are only too happy to provide whatever is requested. Cafés and bistros vie with restaurants and fishermen's wharf to feed the still-hungry men. Fresh oysters can be had for 1.50 franc, or 7.5 German Pfennig; in Berlin they are a Mark each! Wine is sold in bulk in 4-litre *jeroboam* or 6-litre *impérial* bottles. Brittany's finest professionals in embroidered blouses and fluffy skirts offer to ease the aches and pains of two months at sea. Bahr takes full advantage of the best that is offered. The finer *établissements* feature gourmet dinners, long wine lists, and exotic long-legged brunettes and redheads as well.

To the victors, the spoils! Bahr has heard too many hushed tales of U-boats mysteriously lost while on patrol to give his actions a second thought. And what, after all, is a young, well-heeled bachelor to do in such a delightful port? The crew is sent in thirds to the seaside resort of Carnac, among others, for a week of R&R; the officers to their "playground" at La Baule. *U69* moves from her arrival pier to a dry dock in a new concrete pen for two months of repairs.

Once his basic needs and desires have been satisfied, Bahr returns to the waiting piles of paperwork. It is well known throughout the service that the Great Lion carefully reads all after-action reports. Bahr types up the formal version of the Old Man's war log (KTB) as well as the Chief's report. *U69* logged 11,099 nautical miles and consumed 158 cubic metres of fuel oil. As Torpedo Officer, Bahr also accounts for each of the twelve eels fired while on patrol and details each of Gräf's attack patterns. Next in line is a formal report on the 139 shells fired from the 8.8-cm deck-gun as well as the 483 machine-gun and 30 machine-pistol rounds. Last but not least, Bahr types out leave papers for the officers and petty officers.

Just as he is blotting the ink on the last drafts on 26 June, Commander Sohler's adjutant stiffly summons Lieutenant Rudolf Bahr to 7th Flotilla Headquarters. Sealed orders await him. Bahr is to report at once to Captain Rudolf Peters, Commander of the 24th Training Flotilla at Memel. Bahr's pulse races as the full impact of the news hits him: command of his own boat, and most likely promotion to Lieutenant-Commander.

Der grosse Löwe is about to put his personal mark on Rudolf Bahr, for he is pleased with the operation. "Well executed first patrol. The tenacity displayed off Martinique during lengthy submerged running deserves special recognition." Dönitz's only critique is that *U69* should not have expended single eels on the freighter sighted on 11 May, but rather have dispatched her at once with a spread.

There is no time to wish old colleagues farewell, for a staff car already stands by to rush Bahr to the central train station—and from

there on to Paris, Berlin, and Königsberg. In fact, Bahr would never see
many of his former colleagues again. After sinking the Canadian ferry
ss *Caribou* bound from Sydney to Port aux Basques on 13 October 1942
with the loss of 136 civilians, *U69*, part of operation Haudegen sent
against ONS165, was rammed on 17 February 1943 by the British destroyer HMS *Viscount* northwest of Newfoundland. The boat's last signal
that day read: "Pursuing the enemy convoy in a heavy storm." All forty-
six hands went down with her.

5

St Croix:
Sub Killer

*S*T CROIX enters dry dock in Saint John, New Brunswick, on 18 November 1941. Over the next few days large numbers of her crew depart. With their sea bags and "micks" slung over their shoulders, they leave for shore duty, to the manning barracks, or to other ships. It is rare for a rating to serve on one warship for more than a year. Most of the officers and petty officers will stay with the old destroyer, but they will live ashore in Saint John or return to homes and families elsewhere in Canada while *St Croix* is put right.

A destroyer in dry dock is a cold, damp place in the winter months in Maritime Canada. Only the most junior and newest of the officer complement, Sub-Lieutenant Dan Dunlop, RCNVR, is forced to endure the cold and the discomfort of living in a ship without power. He is a qualified torpedo officer; he will be responsible for the torpedo and depth-charge crews and for the maintenance and good order of the ship's electrical system.

Lieutenant Cecil J. Smith oversees the refit while waiting the arrival of *St Croix*'s new captain. He has been *St Croix*'s First Lieutenant since April. Tall and with a dark complexion, Smith is a native of Port of Spain, Trinidad. His speech is a peculiar mix of British and Caribbean accents. He served with the Royal Navy from 1918 to 1926 and joined the Royal Canadian Navy in October 1940. It is fortunate that he too is a qualified torpedo officer, since his action station is at damage control on the quarterdeck, not far from the torpedo mounts and the depth-charge throwers. A salesman in peacetime, he is the perfect Number One. He is fastidious, strict, a creature of habit and routine. He has had enough experience at sea to know how to get the best out of his crew. He also possesses a formidable technical knowledge of warships and has dedicated virtually all his spare time aboard *St Croix* to learning about her foibles and peculiarities.

Smith is almost overwhelmed with the magnitude of the job facing him. He must work with civilian contractors and naval technicians and engineers to oversee the repair, replacement, refurbishment, and updating of the vital equipment which gives *St Croix* life and which makes her a warship. First and foremost, *St Croix's* boilers must be thoroughly cleaned. Her fuel tanks and hull must be repaired for leaks, a job that will ultimately prove impossible. All standard equipment, from the officers' toilets to the ship's radios, must be checked and repaired if required. The hull must be scraped and repainted. All corrosion on the superstructure must be hunted down, ground off, and painted over first with primer and then with Western Approaches camouflage colours. All hatches, scuttles, and watertight doors must be checked, and the seals and dogs replaced or repaired.

In addition to the routine maintenance work, Smith receives two lists of alterations and additions to be done to *St Croix* before she is ready to rejoin the Newfoundland Escort Force. The two lists are more than five pages long and include changes necessary for the health and well-being of the crew and for the seaworthiness and fighting ability of the ship. There are almost one hundred required modifications. The two remaining side-by-side after torpedo mounts are to be replaced with a single mount on the centre line. The after 3-inch gun is to be removed and a 12-pounder high-angle gun installed in its place. Each of the three aftermost funnels are to be cut down by 4 feet. The sick bay must be enlarged and more storage space added. There must be sleeping accommodation for an additional seventeen crew members. Any topside equipment that has proved to be unnecessary, such as the second (starboard) motor boat, is to be landed. There is to be improved signalling equipment for ship-to-ship communication. And *St Croix* is finally to get radar.

The new radar set is obsolete even before it arrives dockside. It is the Canadian-designed and -built SWIC radar, similar to the British Type

286. The radar is of the long-wave type, which means it has a very limited range and an even more limited ability to detect small vessels. It cannot pick up a u-boat in a hull-down position—running with the upper deck under water but with the conning tower and bridge above the surface—unless the submarine is practically within hailing distance. It cannot detect a fully surfaced submarine farther than 5 miles. It is plagued with false echoes, especially in a heavy sea. Its yagi antenna, mounted high atop the foremast, must be rotated by hand from inside the radar hut. It is most useful for station keeping while in convoy.

In December 1941 the swic is still the mainstay of the Canadian escort fleet; the British escort fleet is rapidly converting to the centimetric Type 271. Type 271 has much greater range and sensitivity. Its antenna is housed in a large lantern-like structure secured to the lower foremast, above the bridge of a destroyer, frigate, or corvette. The antenna is rotated by electric motor. Type 271 is far less likely to be blinded by bad weather than is the swic. It may be the best anti-submarine radar in the world.

Smith has seen the new British radar. He would give anything to have one of those sets, but he knows it is a forlorn hope. The Royal Canadian Navy always seems to be a generation behind the Royal Navy in adapting new submarine detection technology and anti-submarine warfare (asw) weapons in this war. Every Canadian escort officer knows it. The lag is largely the result of sheer old-fashioned thinking in the rcn's high command both before the war and now. The rn understands the problem, but its new radars, asdics, and asw weapons go to its own ships first. The rcn must make do and fight an increasingly high-technology war at sea with outmoded equipment.

As the snows deepen and the winter storms of late 1941 and early 1942 rake the North Atlantic, the war at sea grows more intense. The German capital ship menace has all but disappeared since the sinking of the *Bismarck*, but Dönitz's submarine fleet grows larger and his wolf-packs now sometimes number thirty or more boats. When their patrol lines are set up, the u-boat lookouts can scan hundreds of miles of ocean at one time.

When a convoy is detected, the undersea raiders gather swiftly to slash and rip at the vitals of the plodding merchantmen. The heavily laden ships sink rapidly. The seamen who manage to crawl free of the sinking ships, or climb out of the oil- and flotsam-choked waters, die quickly in the cold. Those who are left in the water die even faster as the last degrees of heat are drawn out of their living bodies by waters barely above freezing.

All this time *St Croix* lies like a patient in an emergency ward. She rests on large wooden blocks on the floor of the dry dock. Her sides are draped with heavy electrical cable and with air and water hoses. Scaffolds hang along her hull and parts of her superstructure. The square concrete basin reverberates with the sound of riveting, sawing, hammering, and drilling. Air hammers bang away like machine-guns. Cutting torches send showers of sparks to the dockyard floor. Men in dirty coveralls and bowler hats step gingerly around cables and hoses with blueprints and clipboards in their hands. Naval technicians in uniform, carrying briefcases stuffed with confidential drawings visit the dockyard office. In that office Smith keeps track of the work. He and Dunlop spend virtually every day in the coal-heated shack, the heavy condensation freezing on the window-panes. Twice a day Smith dons his duffle coat, crosses the gangway to *St Croix*, and inspects the work. He has received notice that the new captain will be arriving sometime in the second week of January and he is determined that the work be well in hand by then. He knows the new CO will judge his abilities on the basis of how he has managed the ship since being put in temporary command after Kingsley's departure. He knows that the first impression will be very important if his ambition to have a command of his own is soon to be fulfilled.

––––––––––

The man in the dark navy coat standing on the edge of the dry dock is tall and square shouldered. An unlit pipe hangs from the corner of his mouth. His hat is set at a jaunty angle on his large head. He is of fair complexion, with a round, pleasant face over a deeply dimpled chin. He looks down at *St Croix* and frowns slightly. He, too, has seen a list of the modifications that must be completed before she can put to sea. On this cold, blustery, January day he can tell that most of the exterior work is not even close to completion. Where the single torpedo mount is to go there is only a large round hole in the deck forward of the rear deck-house. The funnels still stand at their original full height. The yagi antenna is not yet on the foremast. There is no gun on the rear deck-house. He knows it will be many months before the gates of the dry dock can be opened and *St Croix* reintroduced to her element, the sea.

The officer wears the rank stripes of a Lieutenant-Commander in the Royal Canadian Naval Reserve. He is not a stranger to Town Class destroyers, nor to the *St Croix*. He commanded the Care and Mainte-nance Party at Halifax when the Towns were transferred from the United States Navy more than a year ago. He has spent much of the last few weeks reading every report he can get on the performance of the four-stackers since they have come into RCN and RN service. He has filled himself in on the trials and travails of the *St Croix* and on her repu-tation as a hard-luck ship. He doesn't believe in luck, good or bad, but in hard work and detailed preparation. To that end, he has tutored him-self as best he can for his new command. At sea since the age of seven-teen, he is a complete professional. He is Andrew Hedley Dobson, known as "Dobbie" to his friends and "Hedley" to his wife and family.

Dobson was born 29 July 1901 in Rothbury, Northumberland County, England. The second child of Thomas and Ethel Dobson, his father was a police sergeant. Following the English custom of the day, he was christened Andrew Hedley Dobson as a reminder of the union of the Dobson and Hedley families which had occurred with the mar-riage of his grandparents. Both families were from old Northumberland farming stock. Andrew's mother was loving and doting to her four chil-dren (three sons and daughter Jenny) until Jenny died at the age of three. Ethel never recovered. She died shortly after, and Thomas remar-ried. None of Thomas Dobson's three sons got on with their step-mother. Gordon, the eldest, joined the merchant navy just before the First World War. He was torpedoed, but survived. Andrew Hedley went to sea in 1918, and younger brother Jim sailed for South Africa shortly after the war ended.

Young Dobson was bright, handsome, tall, and well built. He was outwardly retiring, but harboured a strong ambition to succeed. He was not content to tend cargo, clean decks, or coil rope. He wanted to be-come a master. However long his day, and however exhausted he might be at the end of it, he usually crawled into his bed, bunk, or hammock with a flashlight and a book on seamanship or navigation.

Dobson got on well with most people, but he was definite about what he wanted and found it difficult to compromise. Most of his shipmates recognized his quiet determination; those who did not quickly ran afoul of him. When that happened, he could be withering in his criticism. He was always ready for a bit of fun, and he could down a drink and sing a sea shanty with the best of them. But his main goal in life was to establish himself with a solid shipping company, then start a family. He passed the tests for the Foreign Master's Certificate at the tender age of twenty-five, qualifying to take the bridge of a merchantman when necessary. One year later, he went to work as Chief Officer for the Cliffe Steamship Company at Newcastle-on-Tyne.

Dobson's post was an important one, but he wanted a position at sea. In 1927 he left Cliffe and joined the Eastern Telegraph Company. At almost the same time, he was granted a commission as a Sub-Lieutenant in the Royal Naval Reserve. This brought in a few extra pounds a year at a time when he was courting Gertrude, soon to be his wife. They were a handsome couple, very much in love, and they enjoyed the local social life. Things went well until the crash of 1929 ushered in the Great Depression. From one side of the Atlantic to the other, merchant shipping traffic died off as trade ground to a halt. Ships were tied up for years. Seamen, from masters to the most junior deck hands, haunted hiring halls looking for work. Dobson scrambled to make ends meet, but there were few jobs in British ports. In 1932 he and Gertrude celebrated the birth of their first child, daughter Caroline. Dobson grew more determined to provide for his young family. In 1934 he convinced Gertrude that their future lay in Canada. The Dobsons left the United Kingdom forever and settled in Halifax.

The shipping trade was not much better in Canada than in England, but Dobson had more than fifteen years of seagoing experience and not many of his job-seeking rivals had a Foreign Master's Certificate. In the spring of 1935 he hired on as Second Officer of the ss *Nascopie*, the Hudson's Bay Company's northern supply vessel commanded by the venerable Thomas Smellie. A single-stack, coal-burning, steel, ice-breaker type of vessel, *Nascopie* had been built in England and launched in 1912. She had been purchased by the HBC in 1916 and thenceforth followed the melting ice of Davis Strait north every spring to the western coast of Greenland and to Ellesmere, Devon, and Baffin islands in the eastern

Canadian Arctic. She carried passengers, supplies, and even livestock to the company's posts in the far Canadian north. In 1933 her base of operations was shifted to Montreal.

Dobson had never sailed in a ship quite like the *Nascopie*. To begin with, Smellie was a legend in his own time. A robust little man of 5 feet 8 inches height, he stood long watches on the bridge when *Nascopie* was at sea. He knew the coasts of Labrador and the Davis Strait as no man alive, and he knew every quirk of his 300-foot charge. It sometimes seemed to Dobson that Smellie also knew every company factor, Mounted Policeman, missionary, and teacher between the Strait of Belle Isle and Craig Harbour, at the southern tip of Ellesmere Island.

Then there was the ship itself and the seas she sailed. Even in late June, the waters of the Strait of Belle Isle and Davis Strait were infested by growlers and drifting pans of pack ice. The sun never set at these far northern latitudes in the summer, and Dobson was awed by the barren lands north of the tree-line and the hard life of the Inuit who lived there. The job paid well while it lasted, but he was home and looking for more work well before Christmas.

In 1936 Hedley and Gertrude's second child, Tommy, was born. Dobson needed a few more dollars a month to make ends meet and, besides, Germany seemed to be making trouble again. So he joined the Royal Canadian Naval Reserve. The Naval Reserve, or RCNR, was one of two naval reserves intended to provide back-up for the RCN in times of emergency. Modelled after Britain's Royal Naval Reserve, the RCNR was made up of men such as Dobson who were professional seamen. On regular occasions during the winter and for several weeks each summer, they trained alongside the men of the RCN aboard RCN ships. There wasn't much the navy could teach them about seamanship, but they did have lots to learn about the particulars of fighting a war at sea. The other reserve was the Royal Canadian Naval Volunteer Reserve, also fashioned after its Royal Navy predecessor. The RCNVR was made up of rank amateurs, except for the few yachtsmen in its ranks. The regular navy—the RCN—was the "pusser" navy. There, the brass gleamed, the wood was varnished, the officers were immaculate, and seagoing in warships was a business to be taken seriously. As far as the RCN was concerned, the pusser navy was the Real Canadian Navy, like the Royal Navy, while the reserves were for Saturday-night sailors.

The RCNR was glad to have Dobson, with his seagoing background and his quiet self-confidence. After a brief period as a probationary Lieutenant, he was given the rank of Lieutenant RCNR. In the fall of 1937 he hired on as Second Officer aboard the salvage tug *Foundation Franklin* for a short voyage to the north coast of Prince Edward Island, where the steamer ss *Berwindlea* had gone aground in a hurricane. *Berwindlea* was in a bad way. With every surge of the wind-driven ocean, she was grinding her back on the rocks. Green seas washed over her deck every few minutes. If her crew were not soon rescued, they would be dashed to pieces when *Berwindlea* broke up and pitched them into the raging storm. *Franklin*'s captain had a plan: to put a boat and crew on the beach near *Berwindlea* and somehow to rig a lifeline to the stricken freighter. Dobson volunteered to pilot the small boat into the teeth of the raging storm. With him were five other volunteers. Each man would pull an oar.

The 12-foot boat was put over the side. Almost immediately it smashed against *Franklin*'s bulwarks and was badly stove in. Undaunted, Dobson and his men pushed on. The current, the waves, and the howling wind swept them towards the beach 3 miles away. All six men worked the oars with a desperation born of fear and the sure knowledge that death was close. The small boat heaved, pitched, and rolled as the men pulled. They soon neared the beach. They could hear the roar of the surf and see the line of breakers ahead.

Dobson knew that his life and those of the five men with him hung by a thread, but the more numerous lives of the crew of the *Berwindlea* were at stake. He tried to pull through the surf and reach the beach, but there was no hope. The little boat was caught in the treacherous current near shore and spun about. Already stove in, it was almost swamped. He knew they would never make it and their lives would be thrown away in the attempt. He ordered his men to pull away from the beach. The men on *Berwindlea* watched in horror and radioed Dobson's progress to *Franklin*: "Boat being swept into breakers. They are on edge of breakers. They are making big effort to pull clear." Then, five minutes later: "Boat escaped breakers. Impossible for them to land and live. Seas sweeping broadside on beach."

Dobson and his men pulled for their lives. Every muscle strained. The work of staying alive overrode their fear of imminent death. Then, they were clear of the beach and the island. The wind blew them out into the Gulf of St Lawrence, where they were retrieved by the *Franklin*. The sea and the rocks had almost killed them, but Dobson had kept his head. It was a quality the military likes to call "coolness"; others simply call it courage. The crew of the *Berwindlea* were eventually saved by the Japanese freighter *England Maru*, but the stricken ship was torn to pieces in the raging surf.

Dobson returned to *Nascopie* in the spring of 1938 and sailed with her again in the spring of 1939; he hoped to find a permanent position with the company. They thought highly of his leadership qualities and his seamanship, but when Canada went to war in 1939 Dobson was called up almost immediately. He entered active service on 2 October 1939 to command the ex-RCMP vessel *Fleur de Lis*, taken over by the navy at the outbreak of war and assigned to the waters off Nova Scotia as an examination and patrol vessel.

Fleur de Lis was not a warship. Built in 1929, she was an oil-fired vessel of 316 tons displacement. She was just under 165 feet long and about 21 feet wide. Her top speed was a meagre 12 knots. Her complement was six officers and thirty men. She was armed with a single Lewis .303 machine-gun from the First World War period. But even though she wasn't a warship, she was Dobson's first wartime command and he ran her as he would have run a cruiser. On his first day aboard he laid down the law to his officers and petty officers. *Fleur de Lis* was a commissioned vessel in His Majesty's navy and she would be run like one, without exception. He was determined they would understand that unlike other RCNR captains, he would organize his ship the pusser navy way, and not like some tramp steamer.

In some ways *Fleur de Lis* was the perfect first command for Dobson. The ship's normal routine was four or five days at sea followed by as much as a week in port, when he could go home every night if he wanted to be with Gertrude and the children. *Fleur de Lis* and the examination service were the epitome of the boredom of war, however. Each day was pretty much the same as the day before, especially in port. The cooks were called at 5:45 a.m., the Coxswain at 6:45. Then the hands were called at 7:00. They ate, cleaned ship, cleaned themselves, straightened out their messdecks, then did the day's chores. The afternoon was much the same. In the evening, the libertymen went ashore and the ship was secured for the night.

Even the patrols were predictable. Take on fuel, leave harbour, patrol a sector of ocean off the Nova Scotia coast looking for—what? Enemy submarines? Unlikely to see any. Enemy aircraft? Even more unlikely. But at least to check the buoys to make sure they were functioning as they should and had not drifted away. Then steam to the examination ground off the mouth of Halifax harbour and anchor. Check ships going out of Halifax and ships going in. Watch the convoys depart. Ride out a storm. Then, weigh anchor and patrol another area of coastline, maybe in a thick fog or a snowstorm, before returning to Halifax. In mid-April 1940 *Fleur de Lis* met a Royal Navy submarine coming to Halifax to help train Canadian escorts. They guided it in to port. *Fleur de Lis*'s presence ensured that the submarine would not be attacked by friendly aircraft or patrol vessels. It was the only real break from routine in Dobson's brief stint in command. On 21 April 1940 he left *Fleur de Lis* and, with brand new Lieutenant-Commander's stripes on his sleeves, awaited his next assignment. He was due to command an escort vessel, but they were slow coming off the ways in that first year of the war. Besides, he was required to take the Anti-Submarine Commanding Officers Course first, and there were no openings until early 1941. With his family's welfare uppermost in his mind, he applied for temporary demobilization to serve as First Officer aboard *Nascopie* for one more voyage to the eastern North. The navy agreed, and Dobson spent the late spring and summer of 1940 in the North. By late October he was back in uniform overseeing care and maintenance during the transfer of *St Croix* and the other US four-stackers to the RN and the RCN. In early 1941 he took the required escort commanders course and placed near the top of his class. He was then sent to Kingston, Ontario, to oversee the completion of HMCS *Napanee*, a brand new Flower Class corvette, and to become her first skipper.

Napanee's keel had been laid in the Kingston Ship Building Company yards at Kingston on 20 March 1940. She had been completed in just over four months and was launched on 31 August 1940. She was completely typical of her class, 205 feet long and with a displacement of 950 tons and a beam of 33 feet. Her complement was six officers and seventy-nine crew. She was a single-screw vessel driven by a triple expansion engine that gave her a top speed of about 15 knots—not fast enough to catch a U-boat on the surface. Armed at first with a single 4-inch gun on the forecastle and Lewis guns of Great War vintage on her bridge and rear deck-house, she could not outgun a surfaced U-boat any more than she could outrun it. Her short forecastle and stubby lines gave her incredible sea-keeping abilities, but made life miserable for the crew. Her one real advantage as an escort vessel was that she could turn on a dime, even without twin screws. She and her consorts had been designed for coastal patrol and ASW duties, but had been pressed into mid-ocean escort work by the RN and RCN because of the severe shortage of escort destroyers and frigates.

The RN began to make major modifications to its corvettes early in the conflict, changes designed to make them more seaworthy, more stable, and more comfortable for the crews. But although the RCN eventually moved in that direction, such improvements were out of the question in mid-1941 because it needed all the ships it could get to escort convoys. RCN crews lived for days at a time in cold, wet, cramped quarters in ships that tossed and twisted at the first sign of a heavy sea. In a storm, water swept easily into the bowels of a corvette, running through passages and messdecks. With each pitch and roll came the sounds of breaking, falling, and crashing crockery, tools, personal items, and pots and pans. Cooking was all but impossible in heavy weather. If food did leave the galley hot, it was cold when it arrived at the messdeck. This life was debilitating. Lack of sleep, lack of decent food, and the constant need to hold on to something drained men of their energy and even ground some of them into a numbing apathy.

Napanee departed Kingston in a blinding snowstorm on 30 November 1940. She was bound for Montreal, where she was to be commissioned. As she headed into the Morrisburg canal a day and a half later, she grounded hard. Water poured into the ship from holes torn in her hull and through the stern glands. She steamed back to Kingston and was put back into dry dock. Dobson arrived in early April to oversee the repairs and conduct the sea trials, which began in late April. On 12 May she was commissioned in the Port of Montreal, and Dobson took her to the east coast. She sailed as local escort for an HX convoy on 18 June 1940 and was then assigned to the Sydney Force as a local escort.

Few men in the navy knew the waters between Cape Breton and
Davis Strait as well as Dobson. He had sailed them in the *Nascopie*. He
was especially familiar with the Strait of Belle Isle, that treacherous and
narrow body of water that separates Labrador from Newfoundland.
The strait was often fog-bound. Its high tides and strong currents made
for tricky navigation even in the best weather. It was a safe haven for ice
into early summer. The risks to navigation it posed were such that few
ships used the passage in peacetime, except for local traffic, fishing, or
sealing. But in wartime it seemed to afford British-bound convoys a few
hundred more miles of inshore protection before they started the dangerous dash to Greenland and beyond.

Dobson's intimate knowledge of the strait helped save lives in late
September 1941, as convoy SC46 inched its way northeast through the
passage in rain squalls and thick fog. At midday on the 26th, Dobson
and *Napanee* were steaming a course of 080° 10 nautical miles abeam
the Greenly Island fog signal when one of the lookouts spotted a
steamer looming out of the fog and heading in the opposite direction,
towards rocks on the Labrador shore. Dobson ordered *Napanee* about
and revolutions increased. He tried to signal the steamer about the impending danger, but the fog closed in before his signal could be read.
Someone then spotted a second merchantman heading for the rocks
and again Dobson ordered *Napanee* to close the freighter to signal the
danger. This time his signals were read and acknowledged, and the
freighter pulled clear before grounding.

By now the merchantmen were losing direction in the heavy fog. At
8:30 p.m., Dobson received a message from the SOE aboard the *Ottawa*
that an unknown number of ships had gone aground on the north
shore. He ordered *Napanee*'s engine to full ahead, pulled away from
where he thought the convoy was, then headed west to the Labrador
coast. At least five ships had gone aground and one, the *Empire Mallard*,
had already foundered. Dobson tried to get a line aboard *Culebra*, but
the rising seas thwarted the attempt. He radioed Sydney to send a salvage tug and stood off in the dark and the storm to offer the crew what
little comfort he could by way of his presence. It was a long and dangerous night. The little corvette rose and fell heavily as the seas tried to
wash her towards the shore. Dobson stayed on the bridge all night, calling course and speed changes to the quartermaster and engine room to

keep *Napanee*'s stem turned into the storm. It was one thing to heave-to in the mid-Atlantic, another in a narrow strait like Belle Isle.

There was no word from *Culebra*, not even a light. Dobson was exhausted, frustrated, and impatient. He feared men could be dying less than a mile away as he struggled with the storm. He inwardly cursed the fates that had left him and his ship virtually helpless to save them. But he did not let his turmoil show. He knew he was the one man aboard who had no emotional leeway; if his crew thought he was afraid, or nervous, or losing faith, they would, too. His most important job was not navigating, or hunting subs, or guiding his officers in the enforcing of regulations. It was to provide leadership, a point around which the men could rally, a reason for them to say—and believe—"The Old Man'll get us through this, always has, always will."

As dawn lightened the heavy sky, Dobson and others aboard *Napanee* peered anxiously at the shore. There she was. *Culebra* lived yet. Could she be got off the rocks? Dobson nudged *Napanee* closer and signalled *Culebra* his intention to put a line aboard her. *Culebra* answered: "Thanks, but stay clear. Fear we will sink if pulled off. Will await tug." *Napanee* then joined HMCS *Lethbridge* and made for nearby Forteau Bay to take on other survivors, but the heavy seas again rendered the task impossible. In the early afternoon of the 28th, Dobson was ordered to return to Sydney. He was frustrated and disappointed that he could not do more, but his superiors were not. In mid-November Dobson received a signal from the Department of National Defence in Ottawa. It read: "The Department notes with satisfaction a report from N.O.I.C Sydney that 'great credit is due to HMCS *Napanee*,' A/Lieut.-Commander A.H. Dobson, RCNR, for warning a number of ships [of SC46] of the danger into which they were steaming and successfully leading them out of it."

Harry Kingsley had not done a great job with *St Croix*, the officers responsible for postings at Naval Service Headquarters reasoned. Perhaps this man Dobson might do better. So Dobson left *Napanee* at Sydney on 9 December 1941 and returned to Halifax to spend a quiet Christmas with his family. Shortly after the New Year, he is ordered to Saint John, New Brunswick, to take command of *St Croix*.

———

With Dobson's arrival, Smith's heavy burden is lightened. The Captain is now in command. That is good for Smith, but it has no impact on the repair schedule. It is wartime. Skilled shipwrights are in great demand; basic materials are in short supply; and new equipment is even harder to come by. It takes four more long months for the work on the old destroyer to be completed. Slowly the old and no longer useful is cut out and replaced with the newer and better. Each day Dobson checks off another item completed as he inspects the ship. But it is taking too long. Every now and then he drives back to Halifax to stay with his family, but as the days grow longer and warmer and the refit's date of completion nears, there is more and more to be done.

By the end of April, the job is complete: *St Croix* is ready. She is old, but she has taken on a new rakishness with her three after funnels cut down, a fresh coat of paint, and more than sixty modifications, large and small, to her engines and boilers, accommodations, galleys, weapons, and submarine detection gear. On the afternoon of 1 May 1942 the dry dock is flooded and *St Croix* lifts clear of her timber supports. Dobson nudges her into the harbour to begin her overnight run to Halifax. After victualling, fuelling, and taking aboard the last of her new crew, she will go to war again.

By the time Dobson takes *St Croix* to sea in May 1942, the Battle of the Atlantic has entered a new stage. Since mid-1941 the Allies have been able to decode German naval ciphers. This has given them invaluable information on where Dönitz is placing his wolfpack patrol lines and, consequently, the spots the convoys must avoid. The growing number of shore-based high-frequency direction-finding (HF/DF) stations increases the Allied capability to send their merchantmen where the u-boats are not. By the spring of 1942, in fact, a growing number of British escorts have smaller HF/DF sets on board. At least one ship in every British escort group now has the ability to pick up u-boat transmissions while at sea. As more ships are so equipped, it even becomes possible to triangulate a u-boat's position down to a mile or so. That tells the Convoy Commodore and the Escort Commander how near the transmitting u-boat is, and where it is in relation to the convoy. As usual, Canadian ships lag far behind in obtaining the new equipment.

The forces battling the Germans in the North Atlantic have changed as well. When Japan attacked the United States Pacific fleet at Pearl Harbor on the morning of 7 December 1941, the United States declared war on Japan. And even though Germany declared war on the United States four days later, the US Navy had to shift most of its Atlantic destroyer force to the Pacific, where Japanese carrier taskforces were running amok and US warships in good repair were in desperately short supply. This shift of US destroyers to the Pacific added to the tremendous burden already on the Royal Canadian Navy, because, with the exception of a handful of US destroyers and Treasury Class Coast Guard cutters (roughly equivalent to corvettes in size, speed, and armament), few US escorts remained in the Battle of the Atlantic by early 1942.

The US pullout put the onus on the Royal Canadian Navy to fill the gap. The Royal Navy could not possibly do it now that its own destroyers were also battling the Japanese from the Indian Ocean to the waters off Singapore. More underequipped Canadian corvettes and more half-trained crews were thrown into the breach left by the Americans. Even so, there just weren't enough escorts to do the job—and that deficiency prompted a major change in convoy organization.

In February 1942 the Newfoundland Escort Force was abolished and replaced by the Mid-Ocean Escort Force (MOEF). From that point until the end of the war, the escort groups of the Royal Navy and the Royal Canadian Navy (and the single US escort group that remained) shepherded their charges all the way across the North Atlantic. The new convoy scheme worked as follows: fast convoys, still designated HX, left Halifax (New York after mid-September 1942) and slow ones departed Sydney. They were taken to the Western Ocean Meeting Point by the largely Canadian ships of the Western Local Escort Force (WLEF). There, they were handed over to the MOEF, which escorted the convoys to a point just west of Ireland—the Eastern Ocean Meeting Point—where they were handed over to RN local escorts. The MOEF ships then headed for Londonderry, Northern Ireland, for replenishment, resupply, and sometimes a little recreation for their crews. At the same time, the main convoy routes were shifted south, away from Iceland, to shorten the convoy track. This scheme somewhat alleviated the requirement for additional escort vessels—fewer were needed because the distance was shorter—but it also put the main convoy track more squarely into the "black hole"—the area for which there was no air cover.

The new convoy route was shorter, but since the escorts now steamed all of it, they had farther to go. Three of Canada's small fleet of Towns—*Niagara, St Clair*, and *Columbia*—did not have the range and were relegated to the WLEF. That left the RCN with only eight destroyers as the backbone of its mid-ocean escort groups; the six pre-war River Class destroyers and the Towns *St Francis* and *St Croix*. There were four RCN escort groups—C1, C2, C3, and C4—but, unlike most Royal Navy escort groups, their composition was still somewhat a matter of chance. A particular corvette or destroyer could sail with two or even three of these groups in two or three different voyages. That made it difficult for the RCN crews to get used to operating together and working out standard group tactics. The organization of the RCN escort groups, like everything else the RCN tried to accomplish at this point in the war, was severely hampered by shortages of escort vessels and trained crew.

With the entry of the United States into the war, Dönitz shifted his focus to the western Atlantic and the Caribbean. First it was Operation Drumbeat, right along the US eastern seaboard, with Type IX U-boats slaughtering merchant traffic just off the beaches, sometimes using the backdrop of the lights of large cities to help them find their victims. The US Navy thought it could run single vessels to New York, or Halifax, without air cover? Fine. Take advantage of the American arrogance. Then, when the Yanks started to wake up in March and April 1942, Dönitz sent his wolfpacks to the Caribbean to stop the flow of oil from Venezuela to eastern Canada and the US eastern seaboard. The U-boat crews called it their second "Happy Time," with fat tanker targets waiting to burn. There were so few Allied escorts and aircraft about that many of the U-boat captains saved their torpedoes and used gunfire to destroy their victims. As bad as that was to the Allied war effort, it was a stroke of luck for the *St Croix*. When Dobson took his new ship back to war in May 1942, there was only one major wolfpack operating in the North Atlantic.

St Croix arrives at Halifax in the early afternoon of 2 May 1942. The manning and provisioning begins almost immediately. A new draft of ratings is marched smartly onto the jetty under the watchful eye of the petty officers. Then they embark by sections. The stokers go to their mess near the boiler room, the engine room artificers to their mess amidships, the cooks to the galleys. Crates of fruit and vegetables, sides of beef and pork, cans and boxes and bottles are swung inboard by dockside cranes. Most of the Mark VII and Mark X depth-charges are loaded under the quarterdeck, but some are lashed to the deck itself. Ammunition is taken aboard for the remaining 4-inch guns. Some is stored in the ship's magazines, some placed in ready-use lockers near the guns. Smith oversees most of this work while Dobson stays in his day cabin conferring with his officers or working on ship's correspondence with the ship's writer. Smith is staying on as Number One. Dobson is happy to have an experienced man as his executive officer. His Gunnery Officer, Ronald C. Weyman, is new to *St Croix*, but has already served aboard *Niagara* and survived the run to Murmansk. Dobson decides he'll do just fine. The new Subbie, Dan Dunlop, is a mere boy, Dobson decides, and will have to learn the meaning of naval discipline. The doctor, Surgeon-Lieutenant Adelard E. Trottier, will be a welcome addition to the officers' wardroom. He is young and has a good sense of humour. In the friendly noontime banter over pink gins and beer in *St Croix*'s wardroom while she is alongside, he gives better than he gets when he is ribbed about his Quebec accent. But the ribbing is all in fun. The other officers are long-time veterans of *St Croix*. Dobson has made up his mind to show them early on that his ways are not those of Harry Kingsley. Seamen are a superstitious lot; *St Croix* has been dubbed a hard-luck destroyer. Dobson is eager to dispel the rap.

After a short shakedown run as local escort for convoy LC14, Dobson's orders arrive. *St Croix* will proceed to St John's to join Escort Group C1, which will sail sometime on 14 May to rendezvous with convoy HX189. Leaving the cleft in the rock that separates St John's from the heaving North Atlantic, Dobson stays on the bridge for hours feeling the salt spray on his face. It is mostly sunny, but with some clouds and a fresh breeze from the south it is cool on the bridge as the needle-like hull of *St Croix* pushes through the swell at 12 knots. He can easily make out the other vessels of the escort group, strung out on both sides of his ship. The corvettes *Battleford*, *Chambly*, *Chilliwack*, and *Orillia* are pitching heavily in the swell. He remembers what *that* was like. The

River Class destroyer *Assiniboine*, with the Senior Officer of the Escort on board, is much more sedate in her passing. Dobson observes to himself that at least the group is several ships larger than it would have been a year ago. More than anything, he wants to prove the ability of this ship and its crew to be a useful member of the CI team.

A whistle comes through the engine-room voice pipe: "Bridge, we're having some trouble down here; better get the Captain."

Dobson is standing right beside the Officer of the Watch. He leans into the pipe: "Right here, Chief, what seems to be the problem?"

"We're losing oil pressure on the forward pump, could be the pump, could be the old problem of water in the fuel. Anyway, whatever it is, we'll have to reduce speed to about 100 revolutions."

Dobson hesitates for only a second. Again, *St Croix* is to fall mercy to her age. He is bitterly disappointed, but he knows he cannot show it.

"OK, Chief, let me know as soon as you decide what's to be done." Then, to the Officer of the Watch: "Make to *Assiniboine*: 'Having engine problems, reducing to 8 knots, will rejoin shortly, keep the bed warm.'"

But it is a vain hope. Soon, there is another message: "Captain, engine room here. I'm sorry, sir, but we're still not sure what the problem is, exactly. It could be any of a number of things. But whatever it is, sir, I'm afraid we just can't pump fuel from the forward tank."

There is no point continuing. It is a fine bright morning with only a gentle swell, but *St Croix* will not go to war today. Dobson stares ahead, gripping the wooden arms of his high chair: "Chief Yeoman, signal to *Assiniboine*, repeat to FONF St. John's: 'Unable to pump fuel from forward tank. Returning to St. John's NF.' Pilot, plot a course back. We're not far out. I'll be in my sea cabin. Call me when you see something."

It is a bad start for the ship and for Dobson, who is eager to put his command style into action. But it is only a false bad start. Two days later *St Croix* and the Royal Navy Town HMS *Broadway* are ordered to steam to overtake SC84 at a point about 200 miles east of Harbour Grace. The convoy had departed Sydney two days earlier, but eleven vessels had got lost in thick fog and the SOE had detached two corvettes to help with the round-up. SC84 is being escorted by C2; *Broadway* is the senior destroyer of the two and better equipped than *St Croix*, with improved asdic and the new Type 271 radar. She will take over as SOE when the convoy is joined.

The two four-stackers spot the plodding convoy around noon on 19 May. *Broadway* orders *St Croix* to take station on the starboard beam, and the routine work of escorting begins. This is the largest convoy Dobson has ever seen, stretching over miles of ocean with its eight slowly moving columns. The weather is surprisingly good. The seas are moderate and the sky mostly blue by day and black as a coalpit at night, punctured by thousands of stars and crossed by the pale path of the Milky Way. By day, *St Croix* zigzags far ahead and to the south of the convoy; by night she pulls much closer in. The convoy shows no lights at night, but the new SWIC radar allows *St Croix* to track it well enough. By 21 May the convoy has made a steady 400 miles from where *Broadway* and *St Croix* had met it and is some 400 miles south-southeast of Cape Farewell. It is mid-morning.

"Bridge, contact bearing Green 020, range 1500 yards."

Dobson is in his sea cabin resting. He has spent most of the night on the bridge. The Navigating Officer is on watch.

"Is it solid? Is it moving? What are we hearing down there?"

"I dunno, sir. Contact is showing opening Doppler and seems to be moving to the left, but we can't hear screws or anything else that says it's a sub."

The Navigating Officer leans into the Captain's voice pipe: "Captain, bridge. Asdic reports a possible contact at 020, range about 1500 yards. Not sure what it might be."

"OK, pilot, I'll be right up."

Dobson has never had a contact. He's not sure he has one now. But he knows that whatever's down there, he must keep to form: "Make to Broadway: 'Am investigating contact'—give our course and speed."

He raises the ASW officer: "What are you hearing?"

"I'm not sure. There seems to be movement, it's a pretty solid return."

Dobson thinks for a moment. No point in taking chances. "OK, sound action stations. Make to the SOE, 'Am attacking contact.' We'll do a six-charge pattern. Set the throwers at 150 feet and the traps at 100 and 250. That ought to shake things up a bit." To the engine room: "Give me revolutions for 15 knots."

It'll be a high-speed run. *St Croix* turns slightly to starboard as her stem rises and her stern digs in with the speed change. In the asdic hut

Lieutenant Leslie N. Earl, *St Croix*'s ASW officer, peers at the trace recorder while Petty Officer Maurice Biggs, the Higher Submarine Detector (HSD), listens for the returns on the asdic set. The throbbing turbines push *St Croix* across the water. As they approach the contact, the echo returns increase in interval and intensity and the needle scratches more quickly over the moving track chart. At 200 yards, *St Croix* loses contact. They are moving too fast and the contact is too close for it to show up any longer. Earl will push the firing buzzer on estimate alone. He counts down the distance to the contact as *St Croix*'s bows slice through the water. It is 12:31 p.m. He hits the firing buzzer. Aft, Dunlop shouts "Fire." The charges sail off their throwers and roll off the stern. *St Croix* races through the spot where the TNT-filled barrels are sinking to their pre-set depths. Biggs now turns the asdic head aft, hoping to pick up the contact after the explosions, then he takes off his earphones. The sea astern erupts, six times in quick succession, and sends tons of sea water and dead fish skyward. There is no wreckage, no oil, no human remains—nor any further contact. For a few frustrating moments, the asdic set stops functioning. This sometimes happens when the depth-charges go off too close. Dobson stays on the bridge to guide *St Croix* through a box search, but Biggs hears nothing. After an hour, they rejoin the convoy.

St Croix takes part in another fruitless attack two days later. This time the convoy is some 650 miles southwest of Reykjavik when the corvette *Morden* raises a contact in mid-morning. She attacks with a four-charge pattern set at 100 feet, but picks up no real indication of a submarine. Directed by the SOE, *St Croix* and *Brandon*, another corvette, are on the scene only minutes later. *Morden* retires and *Brandon* both listens for submarine sounds and pings with her asdic beam while *St Croix* moves in for two depth-charge attacks.

There is a fresh breeze. The sky is overcast with rain squalls and the waves are growing higher; white caps are beginning to form on their crowns. Dobson orders a shallow setting for the first attack at 12:55 p.m., then a deeper one a half-hour later. But there is no wreckage, just lots of dead fish. Asdic conditions are not very good, and Dobson concludes they are chasing a shoal of fish.

———————

The crossing takes longer than it did in the old NEF, but at the end of the run is Londonderry, a heaven compared with the bleak bays of Iceland. Some of *St Croix*'s officers and crew have been there before, but most have not. By the end of May 1942 this once sleepy northern Ireland port has become a major entrepôt of the war at sea. The Admiralty has been using it as a base for local escort since the outbreak of war. The Americans arrived in June 1941, as the US Navy began to assume more of the responsibility for convoy escort, even though the United States was ostensibly still neutral. All over the harbour, the sights and sounds of a port at war reverberate across the water. Here is a dry dock, with a sloop undergoing a refit. There is a repair yard, where a new radar set and a pair of Oerlikon guns are being added to a RN corvette that has just had its forecastle lengthened. Destroyers, corvettes, frigates, sloops, and other escort vessels, some rust streaked, others dented, others brand new or freshly painted, are secured three and four deep alongside the twenty-one jetties in the harbour.

Coming into Londonderry after a hard crossing of the North Atlantic is balm to a weary sailor's soul. As the escorts enter Lough Foyle—the small bay at the mouth of the River Foyle—the deep green of the Irish countryside engulfs them. Young Edgar Pennefather, secretary to *St Croix*'s Captain, writes home: "The scenery coming up river was lovely after Halifax and Newfyjohn. This certainly is the Emerald Isle. But then, it gets washed off every day." Each mile they sail up river brings them closer to respite and farther from the brutal war at sea. "Everything is terrifically old," Pennefather notes. "Coming up river we saw an old ivy covered castle ruin exactly as illustrated in the best fairy stories. There's a wall around the middle of town which I walked in about half an hour. . . . There are miles and miles of the typical English rows of red brick houses, with a very few, very new, shingle houses."

St Croix is tied up alongside another Town Class destroyer and three corvettes. No sooner is "Finished with engines" rung on the bridge telegraph than the vibration of the turbines stops. Only the ventilation fans can be heard, and the sounds of men stowing away gear and making *St Croix* shipshape after a long crossing. The libertymen prepare for a night on the town. The Officer of the Day is on deck near the brow. The off-duty officers gather in the wardroom. It is traditional that they should do so, drinking gin and beer now that the bar is open again, telling and retelling yarns from their last crossing or from earlier adventures at sea. A few moments after they have gathered, they are in the midst of a song when there is a knock. Dobson sticks his head in: "Mind if I join you chaps for a drink?" It is an unusual request. The Captain rarely fraternizes with his officers.

Smith pushes forward: "Of course sir. What will you have?"

"A small pink gin will do, Number One. You're from the West Indies are you not?"

"Why, yes, sir."

"Do you know the words to 'Waltzing Matilda'? Sort of the unofficial Aussie anthem, I gather. I've always liked it."

Then he begins to sing, slowly at first, almost poignantly, until he finishes the first verse. Then, with glass in one hand and pipe in the other, he picks up the pace, his pipestem marking the beat:

Waltzing Matilda, Waltzing Matilda,
Who'll come a-waltzing Matilda with me?
And he sang as he sat and waited for his billaboil,
Who'll come a-waltzing Matilda with me?

He swallows the last of the gin and slowly puts the drink down. "Thanks so much gentlemen, behave yourselves ashore." And he leaves.

The people—and the girls—of Londonderry welcome them ashore. It is a safe place. The Germans hardly ever bomb it because it is too far away for a concerted air attack. The ratings spend every minute they can in the pubs; the few brothels in this prim Presbyterian town do a roaring business. Dobson and the crew are scheduled for a quick turnaround to escort west-bound convoy ON100, along with the rest of C2, but *St Croix*'s continual mechanical problems thwart the plan. They miss the sailing and spend two more weeks in port waiting for the departure of ON103. This extra time is like a sentence to heaven for the ratings. Dobson's officers are somewhat more subdued in their pursuit of distraction. The food in 'Derry is so bad, and there is so little of it, that they stay close to the harbour much of the time, playing an occasional game of tennis or squash, or a round of golf.

Dobson prefers to be alone. He knows most of his married colleagues honour their vows of fidelity more in the breach than the observance over here, and he does not blame them. But he cannot bring himself to play the game of dashing young naval hero, and he cannot bear the thought of betraying Gertrude, even though she will most likely never find out. When he is not aboard *St Croix*, or attending some meeting or other, he busies himself trying to scrounge a Type 271 radar set, or Oerlikons to replace the two amidships 4-inch guns, or other much-needed equipment. It is frustrating and fruitless. Most of the time he walks in the soft rain, smoking his pipe, stopping at a small pub for an occasional pint of bitter. For a few days, he visits his family in the north of England. When he gets back to St John's, he thinks, he'll try to wangle a short leave to see Gertrude and the children.

The journey back across the North Atlantic escorting ON103 is uneventful. It is just long days at sea, ever vigilant, but battling boredom and ennui just the same. *St Croix* arrives in St John's on the first day of summer, then leaves a week later, still in company with C2, to join SC89. They dock in Londonderry on 10 July. The Convoy Commodore reports to the Admiralty: "The voyage was uneventful and the weather on the whole good." They have a full week to rest. They are due to leave on 18 July to escort ON113 back to the western side of the ocean.

By now, *St Croix*'s officers and crew are getting Dobson's measure. He is far older than most of them and, with his quarter-century before the mast, they find it easy to think of him as "the Old Man." Most of the RCNR officers they have known have had little patience for the myriad rules and regulations contained in the weighty King's Regulations and Admiralty Instructions. But Dobson is far more like a pusser than a Reserve man in that regard, even calling one of his junior officers on the carpet for daring to shave off his beard without his Captain's permission. Dobson more than makes up for his strictness, however, with his almost faultless seamanship and his skill at handling his vessel. The men have no doubt that he knows more about ships and the sea than any of them. And although he is ironhanded when it comes to his officers, he seems much less strict with the ratings, particularly the younger ones, when they face him as defaulters. Like all RN and RCN captains, he keeps very much to himself both at sea and ashore. Most of the ratings never meet him personally, nor expect to. The strict class divisions aboard RN and RCN ships are a matter of tradition and routine, both words that are very important to Andrew Hedley Dobson. But still, his officers and men respect him tremendously. They are well aware of the uneven quality of skippers commanding RCN ships of war, and they think themselves lucky to have a man like Dobson to guide them through the dangers that the deadly seas can throw at them.

At 9 a.m. on 18 July 1942 C2 sails from Londonderry to rendezvous at sea with westbound convoy ON113. A convoy of thirty-three ships in nine columns, ON113 is to steam at 9 knots from UK waters to a point east of Halifax, passing some 600 miles southeast of Cape Farewell. The Commodore is in *Empire Rowan*. The Senior Officer of the Escort is HMS *Burnham*, a well-equipped Royal Navy Town Class destroyer. *Burnham*'s consorts are the RCN corvettes *Brandon*, *Dauphin*, and *Drumheller*, and the RN corvette *Polyanthus*. *St Croix* is due to sail with C2, but cannot on 18 July owing to bugs in her asdic. Dobson is in a cold rage. He had reported problems with the asdic weeks ago, after the depth-charge attacks while escorting SC84, but they had not been fixed properly. For four days, as ON113 steams farther east by the hour, he haunts the Flag Officer's office insisting that the work be done quickly. There are rumours about that HF/DF has picked up a U-boat B-bar transmission ahead of the convoy track. This information only adds to his determination. On 20 July *St Croix* finally sails. Dobson tells the Navigating Officer to plot an intercept course as far west as possible and prays that the engines, fuel pumps, and boilers will hold out as he orders revolutions for 18 knots. It is as fast as he dare go both because of the age of the equipment and the heavy use of fuel at high speed. Although it is normal practice to keep two boilers online at high pressure, one just lit, and the fourth ready to be fired up, Dobson orders the third boiler online just in case. The weather is good to him; as *St Croix* crashes westward, the sky is mainly clear and the seas moderate. Two days out, *St Croix* heaves into sight of the convoy some 700 miles east-southeast of Cape Farewell. *Burnham* welcomes her and assigns her to the port flank of the convoy.

St Croix's first night with ON113 passes without incident. The day dawns bright and clear, with a thin wisp of high stratus. The convoy plods on. *St Croix* and the other escorts are ordered to proceed to maximum visibility from the convoy, and *St Croix*'s Officer of the Watch gives the Quartermaster the appropriate course change. For the rest of the day, *St Croix*'s normal routine continues uninterrupted. This may be the middle of a war zone, but until there is indication of an enemy presence, the food still has to be cooked, the bread baked, the routine maintenance chores performed, and the decks scrubbed and washed. Off-duty men still need time to rest, or play cards, or tell stories. Nothing disturbs the peace of the ship until mid-way through the second dog watch at 7 p.m.

"Captain to the bridge. Captain to the bridge." Dobson is eating his supper alone in his sea cabin. Knife and fork clatter to the plate as he grabs his cap, jacket, and glasses. When he arrives on the bridge, the Chief Yeoman and the Officer of the Watch are waiting.

"Sir, signal from the SOE. Sub on the surface at maximum visibility ahead. He's chasing him at high speed. Wants us to get ready to join him."

"OK, sound action stations." Then, as the alarm bells begin ringing, he calls into the engine-room voice pipe: "Chief, make ready for a good long chase. I want No. 3 boiler and No. 4 fired up. If I call for both ahead full, I'll want at least 300 revolutions."

"Aye, aye, Captain." The Chief is doubtful that the old bucket can hold together at 25 knots or more, but he's got his orders and that's that. He turns from the voice pipe and shouts at his crew over the loud clamour of pumps, turbines, and ventilation fans. "Increase pressure on No. 3 right to the top, and fire up No. 4. The Old Man wants everything we've got. Keep a sharp eye out for breakdowns, especially on them pumps, and watch the bloody bearings and journals."

The alarm bell is still sounding as Smith arrives at Dobson's side: "All divisions report closed up for action stations, sir. I'm going aft."

"Right, Number One. We may be chasing a sub in a moment or so."

The Chief Yeoman hands Dobson a signal.

"We're to join him at top speed. Ring both ahead full, give me 15 degrees of port wheel and steady on to 010."

St Croix surges ahead, stern digging down, screws churning at better than five revolutions every second. Her stem rides high as she carves a long turn to port. The bow wave grows by the second, until the surging water is almost even with the main deck. Even at this speed, it takes

St Croix almost a half hour to close the Escort Commander. The Admiralty radioes *Burnham* that they have picked up a U-boat contact report. Soon an entire wolfpack will be on them. *Burnham* opens fire at the U-boat at maximum range as *St Croix* closes. The U-boat dives. *Burnham* and *St Croix* slow to give their asdic crews a chance to find the submarine. The SOE orders the Convoy Commodore to execute a course change after nightfall, then begins to carry out a sweep, with *St Croix* on her beam. At 8:10 p.m., Dunlop reports to the bridge from his position amidships that he has seen a periscope almost due west at an estimated range of 3000 yards. No one else sees it. Twenty minutes later *Burnham* signals that she will sweep back towards the convoy. It is getting dark and, with the two destroyers way out ahead, there are too few escorts around the convoy. Dobson asks for permission to search a while longer and gets the green light. He must be back by 11 p.m. He orders the Coxswain to hold her course.

It is 9:03. Twilight is darkening the seascape. Someone shouts "U-boat on the surface, bearing Red 20."

Dobson trains his glasses as he barks out orders: "Port ten to 280. Ring both ahead full. Guns, ready on Number 1 gun. Chief Yeoman, make to *Burnham*: 'Am chasing surfaced U-boat, give our course and speed.'" And, into the engine-room voice pipe: "Chief, can you give me 300 revolutions?"

"Captain, we had to let No. 4 die down. I can give you only 270 or so."

"Well, get it on as quickly as you can."

In the boiler room, the Chief slams the cover of the voice pipe and turns to his crew: "They don't fucking well seem to know what they bloody well want up there. Get No. 4 back on line and full pressure on the other three."

St Croix's speed is increasing by the minute. The U-boat is still on the surface and making at least 16 knots, but the destroyer is creeping up.

"Guns. Fire when ready."

"Aye, aye, sir. Number 1 gun, fire as soon as we get within range." The gun is elevated to the maximum to compensate for the deck's backward slant caused by *St Croix*'s speed. Her bow cuts through the sea. The gun coughs. An empty shell-casing falls to the deck, a new shell is rammed home, the breech block is slammed shut, the lanyard is pulled, the gun coughs again. Dobson and the others on the bridge strain through their glasses to see the fall of shot in the waning daylight. They see nothing except the luminescent wake of the still-surfaced submarine and the black plume of its diesel exhaust.

Damned lousy shooting, Dobson thinks. "Cease fire, cease fire. Guns, we can't see to adjust our shot. Let's wait to see what it does."

He trains his glasses on the submarine's wake. He can still follow its every move, even though it is quite dark: "Cox, it's turning to port, come left 010." At 9:42 the U-boat dives.

"Half ahead, let's try to pick it up."

The sound head is lowered and the pinging begins. In the asdic hut, Biggs is listening intently for echoes while Earl watches the trace recorder. Dobson orders: "Fire on estimate, full pattern, medium depth." They will attack as they pass over the submarine's last estimated position, contact or not. A six-charge pattern is laid down. The explosions rumble from beneath the dark surface of the ocean.

"Anything, Mr. Earl?"

"Nothing, sir."

"Continue the sweep. Box search."

Burnham comes up out of the dark, her signal light flashing: "Commencing a box search, twenty minutes a leg. Care to dance?"

"Charmed," flashes back from *St Croix*'s bridge. At 10:20 *Burnham* picks up a contact and flashes it to *St Croix*. Then, Biggs hears an echo. Earl reports the contact, but *St Croix* has come very close to *Burnham* and Dobson orders speed reduced to 10 knots, then 5. *Burnham* signals her intention to make a depth-charge attack, but *St Croix* is too close. Dobson orders "both astern full." In the engine room, the Chief looks at the telegraphs in disbelief: "Jesus, now he wants to go backward. Both astern, increase revolutions to 200."

The wallowing destroyer backs away from her consort, but *Burnham* loses contact as she moves slowly away. Worse, she passes between *St Croix* and the submerged submarine. *St Croix* loses contact. They have botched it badly, and both Captains know it. Both ships return to the convoy, still at action stations. Hundreds of men on thirty-three merchantmen and six escort vessels pass a fitful night waiting.

24 July, 3:35 p.m. There have been no attacks and no contact reports from any of the escorts. The convoy is alert and well aware that it is being shadowed. Just after dawn, Dobson orders "Defence Stations, depth-charge." That releases most of the crew from their action stations, but keeps the depth-charge and asdic men at their posts. As many men as possible must get a chance to eat and rest. He'll change the defence stations crews later so they, too, can rest and get something to eat. Dobson has no doubt that the convoy will be under attack within hours; he wants his men to be ready when that happens. He tries to doze in his sea cabin, but keeps his boots on and covers his face with his cap.

The masthead lookout shouts down to the Watch Officer: "There's two objects on the surface, sir. One's dead ahead, pretty far out. The other's on the starboard beam." They are submarines bearing 295° and 180°.

Dobson goes to action stations. "Make to *Burnham*, repeat to Admiralty: sighted two submarines on the surface; am chasing one bearing 180; the other bears 246 to you. Get that off by light and R/T." He shouts into the engine-room voice pipe: "I need it all, everything you've got." And to the Coxswain: "Starboard 20."

Once again, *St Croix* races across the water. This time, the Chief isn't caught napping. He's kept three boilers fired up and the fourth warm. Within minutes, *St Croix* is speeding after the U-boat, every loose object in the ship banging and rattling as she cuts the wave tops. The engines make the deck-plates and everything else on board vibrate in time with the churning screws.

The Engineering Officer is now standing at the back of the bridge. "What is she doing?" Dobson asks.

"Oh, about 306 revolutions, Captain, but we're working up."

"And how fast is that?"

"Almost 30 knots, sir."

"Well, it's a nice afternoon, Chief, and there's lots of daylight left, so let's keep her at 28 knots."

At 4:38, with *St Croix* now within 6000 yards of the racing U-boat, the submarine dives.

"Reduce speed to 15 knots, lower the oscillator."

Dobson knows they should have had that U-boat last night. It was practically in the bag. He's going to play it very careful this time, very very careful.

They have raced 1500 yards beyond the spot where the U-boat went under.

"Contact, bearing 185. Range, 2400 yards."

"Set charges deep, full pattern, fire on estimate."

Earl watches the trace recorder and Biggs listens intently, but the on-rushing destroyer loses contact at 300 yards. Earl has expected this and counts down the range in his head before hitting the firing button. The depth-charges sail away on both sides and roll off the stern. The sea is churned up by the blasts, but there is no wreckage or oil.

Biggs sweeps to the rear. "Contact, bearing 005. Range, 1000."

"Cox, start bringing her back along our track. Mr Earl, let me know as soon as we lose contact, then wait until we're well past that spot before letting go. I want the same pattern as the last."

Dobson is hoping Earl and Biggs can stay in contact long enough to determine if the U-boat is taking evasive action and, if it is, where it is going. That'll give him time for any last-minute course changes before the depth-charges go into the water. *St Croix* heels over and races for the spot where the contact has been made. Again Earl watches the trace recorder and Biggs listens for the echoes as the asdic beam probes deep for the steel shell of the U-boat. As *St Croix* closes, they lose contact at 500 yards.

"Lost contact, sir. I'll fire on estimate." Earl counts the distance down in his head before hitting the firing buzzer. It is 5:09. Once more two charges sail out from the port and starboard throwers and four drop from the stern. Once more huge domes of sea water erupt in *St Croix*'s wake, then churn skyward. Once more there is no sign of wreckage.

"Well, Mr Earl. Are you sweeping astern?" It is an unnecessary question, and the young lieutenant is embarrassed by it and momentarily filled with resentment.

"Yes, sir." Then, as if to emphasize the needlessness of the question: "Contact, sir, bearing 170. Range, 1000 yards." Biggs has picked up the submarine once again.

Dobson orders the range opened to 2200 yards. Then *St Croix* heels over again. The asdic conditions are perfect and Earl and Biggs are too good to miss, Dobson thinks. What's he doing wrong? Maybe they're dropping the charges too deep.

"Set charges shallow, 100 feet. Fire on estimate when you lose contact." At 100 yards Earl calls out "Contact lost." A few moments later, he hits the firing buzzer. The depth is right. The location is right. The heavy charges sink towards *U90* and explode. The submarine's hull is crushed. In a thunderclap of sea water rushing in to fill the void that was once the submarine's inside, the bubble of life ceases to exist. The torn and twisted hulk begins its drift to the sea floor 2500 fathoms below. Fuel oil, pieces of wood, cigarette packages, cans of food, bits of clothing, and arms, legs, intestines, and pieces of lung and heart drift to the surface as *Burnham* comes up and *St Croix* returns to examine the spreading wreckage.

"Sir, I've lost contact. Breaking up noises," Earl intones.

"Come on out here, Mr Earl, and you'll see why you've lost contact."

The men on the deck have never seen such a sight. There in front of them are the remains of a U-boat and its all-too-human crew. Someone steps gingerly onto the quarterdeck screw-guard as Dobson orders engines stopped for a moment. It's time to collect evidence of the kill. The rating holds a large net attached to a pole. He dips it into the sea and hauls out a white piece of flesh. It is a human shoulder. He scrambles back aboard, dumps it into a bucket, and someone snaps his picture.

ON113's travails do not end with the destruction of *U90*. In fact, they have only just begun. The merchantmen *British Merit* and *Broompark* are torpedoed later that night. The first sinks immediately; the second is taken in tow, but sinks later. On the 26th, *Empire Rainbow* is badly damaged by a single torpedo just before sunrise. She tries to keep up with the convoy, but is torpedoed again later in the day and goes under. One last ship is lost to ON113 when *Pacific Pioneer* is blown out of the water just off the Canadian coast while under escort from the WLEF. The German submariners do not exact a heavier toll only because of inexperienced crews and deteriorating weather.

Dobson is awarded the Distinguished Service Order for the kill. Earl, Biggs, and others also receive commendations. The crew's greatest reward is the news that they will get a good long rest back in Canada before they go out again. Though the RCN has been fighting the Battle of the Atlantic for almost three years, Canada's navy has sunk only its third enemy submarine of the war. No more will *St Croix* be known as a hard-luck destroyer. For now, she is one of the very few sub killers in the entire Canadian fleet.

6

Practising the Deadly Trade: Rudolf Bahr Commands *U305*

E LK ANTLERS and U-boats? Rudolf Bahr barely manages to suppress an urge to laugh out loud as he enters the 24th U-boat Flotilla base at Memel. What quixotic baron, he wonders, persuaded the Tirpitzufer, the naval headquarters in Berlin, to come up with elk antlers for the 24th? Strange choice—even for the exotic eastern Baltic coast. Perhaps a reminder of the days when the Teutonic Knights had briefly but lustily hunted in these wild and isolated East Prussian woods.

Better stifle such thoughts, Bahr—the Great Lion is not a man of romantic sophistry. Nor is Captain Peters. There is hard work to be done and no time to lose. By late summer 1942 Dönitz has an average of twenty-five boats per month coming down the slips, and he is desperate for officers and crews to man them. Moreover, an increasing number of experienced Captains and Executive Officers fail to return from Atlantic patrols. There are rumours in the bar of the officers' club at Memel that the life expectancy of a U-boat is down to four months.

Officers like Bahr with front experience are becoming a rare and precious commodity. Commanders' School instruction has already been cut to the bone to return the skippers to what Dönitz calls "the decisive theatre of the war" as quickly as possible—without totally sacrificing quality.

Lieutenant Bahr stows the gear from his duffle bag in one of the wooden barracks of the 24th Flotilla compound, part of the Agrufront, or Technical Training Group Front. Then he heads straight off to the simulator, a mock-up of the interior of a conning tower built over a large pool that contains scaled versions of Allied freighters, tankers, destroyers, and corvettes. For two weeks Bahr is drilled in the routine: approach, surface attack, submerged attack, crash dives, aim, FIRE! Then, under the watchful gaze of Captain Peters, Bahr and his fellow prospective skippers—mostly young officers recruited from laid-up capital ships, damaged destroyers, and minesweepers, as well as desk jobs—work day and night with the small 250-ton training submarines. They nickname them *Einbäume*, or single tree trunks, because they resemble primitive log canoes. Day after day, in strict alphabetical order, the prospective skippers—"Kaleus"—practise attacks on the target ship, the old Stettin passenger liner *Nordland*. The torpedoes, with dummy warheads, are pre-set to run under the *Nordland* so they can be recovered at the end by special retriever craft. Standard practice is to approach the target "unseen" by day and to fire a fan shot at a range of 700 to 900 yards. Then, while one instructor brings the boat up to the surface and measures the precise distance to target, another on board the *Nordland* reports on the quality of the approach and the shot. The drill is repeated by night, over and over again, until it is almost automatic.

By day, the Flotilla fires eels using compressed gas as the propellant, so as to leave clear wakes for grading purposes; by night, luminous dummy warheads serve the same purpose. The training goes on for four weeks, six days a week. The work is physically demanding but not difficult, especially for Bahr, who learned the deadly trade well from Lieutenant Gräf on *U69*. Rather, it is satisfying.

No one in Danzig even suspects that British cryptanalists at Bletchley Park, having broken the Baltic Sea Thetis key, are active participants in the training program. They carefully record every new boat and skipper sent to Danzig, Memel, or Pillau. They study the officers' every command, habit, and quirk. The Tommies know all their names and the patterns and timing of their radio reports. They document how Bahr approaches a target, at what distance he fires his torpedoes, when and how he reports hits, and how soon he dives after firing. They call it "electronic fingerprinting."

"Graduation" day arrives on 16 August 1942. Captain Peters strides into the bar of the officers' *Kasino* clutching a sheaf of official teletypes from Admiral U-boats. Bahr does not have long to wait. "Oberleutnant Bahr, report to the Flender-Werke at Lübeck. You'll assume command of *U305* as soon as she completes her shakedown cruise." Bahr comes to attention, salutes, and wheels to depart and secure his gear. He is ecstatic. First the *Prinz Eugen*; and now a brand-new boat! But Peters has one more surprise in store. "Oh, and Bahr, get a new stripe for that sleeve. Your name is on the fall promotion list." A double promotion! Captain of a new boat and Kaleu all in one split second. Damn it, this has to be celebrated in style tonight! Drinks are on the Kaleu-to-be.

By now, Bahr knows the train schedules to and from Berlin and Königsberg by heart. There is just time for a quick visit to his always anxious parents at Landsberg, and then he'll be off to Lübeck, that ancient red-bricked Hanseatic fortress on the western Baltic Sea. A beautiful walled city, the place where Thomas Mann had set his Nobel Prize–winning novel *Buddenbrooks*. How well Bahr remembers having admired all those grand Lübeck merchants when they traded in Landsberg once or twice a year. But the war has not passed Lübeck by. As he hails the staff car sent to fetch him once he arrives at the train station, Bahr sees destruction by enemy air fleets all around. A devastating British raid on 28 March 1942, especially, has reduced almost half the city to rubble and ashes. So, he muses, we in the Dönitz Volunteer Corps are not the only ones at the mercy of Allied fliers.

Then reality hits Rudolf Bahr full force: he is truly on his way to the Flender-Werke to take command of *U305*. Two blocks from the shipyard in Lübeck-Siems he orders the car to stop and ducks into a naval supply store. Minutes later, he emerges with a new white cap, the special sign of the U-boat commander. Several Army and SS types passing by are not amused—strictly speaking, the white caps are reserved for the Kriegsmarine's august staff officers (*Stabsoffiziere*). But who is to put national treasures like U-boat skippers on report? And to whom? The Great Lion?

As Bahr approaches the slips of the Flender yards he sees that part of his crew is already assembled. The rest will arrive later in stages. As always with Dönitz, there is no time to lose. Introductions are the immediate order of the day. First to report is Second Lieutenant Johann-Hermann Sander, First Watch Officer. Next comes Second Lieutenant Helmut Bogatsch, Second Watch Officer. Both men were born in 1922; Sander celebrated his twentieth birthday in January, and Bogatsch in July. The Chief Engineer, First Lieutenant Ernst Brenner is older by a year—and experienced. All have been sworn to secrecy since the U-boat is a military secret. Its blueprints are classified as "State Secret" in the civilian sector and as "Secret Documents—To Be Handled by Officers Only!" within the military.

No need for formal speeches, just a word of introduction to set relations straight. "Gentlemen," Bahr snaps, "I run a tight ship. No surprises. No fuck-ups. Then we will get along fine. We have a job to do, so let's do it!"

For the next eight weeks, Bahr and his officers spend every waking hour supervising the completion of *U305*. It is called *Baubelehrung*, building instruction. With a Chief Naval Engineer from Berlin and the naval designers from the Flender-Werke in tow, Bahr, Brenner, Sander, and Bogatsch familiarize themselves with every feature of their new craft. Every weld, every rivet, every bolt is carefully examined. At 200-yards depth, they don't want to discover a shoddy weld. Sander inspects the torpedo compartment and the torpedo calculator, as well as the firing mechanism in the tower; Bogatsch lovingly checks the 8.8-cm deck-gun and the Flak. Brenner climbs daily into the bowels of the boat and examines the engine blocks, mountings, valves, levers, fuel lines, pumps, compressors, superchargers, and electrical wiring. Nothing is left to chance. By mid-September the petty officers and ratings—fifty-one men in all—have arrived. The men sport a white dove band on their caps.

U305 is one of the famous VIIC boats, the largest series of submarines ever produced: 221 feet long and 20 wide, she displaces 769 tons above water and 871 tons below; her draft is 16 feet. Twin MAN 2800-horsepower diesels give her a best surface speed of 17.0 knots; and twin AEG 750-horsepower electric motors provide a best submerged speed of 7.6 knots. Range is a good 9500 miles at 10 knots on the surface; a paltry 80 miles at 4 knots beneath the sea. *U305* is armed with four bow torpedo tubes and one stern 53.3-cm tube as well as a single 8.8-cm bow-deck gun. She can dive to periscope depth in thirty seconds.

On 17 September 1942 the Kriegsmarine formally accepts *U305* from the Flender-Werke and places her in commission that same day. Members of the crew stand at attention in their finest uniforms as the battle flag—black Swastika in a white circle against a black cross on a red background—is raised. Thereafter, Admiral Dönitz assigns *U305* to Commander Eckermann's 8th U-boat Flotilla. *U305* had been ordered on 20 January 1941; her keel laid on 30 August; and she had slipped down the ways on 25 July 1942. Brand new! And Rudolf Bahr is her first commander. It is love at first sight!

The officers and men of *U305* spend 18 and 19 September stowing their personal gear and receiving last-minute operating instructions from Flender engineers. Just before *U305* is scheduled to depart, she acquires two new crew members. Ensign Wolfgang Jacobsen, a gangly teenager, comes aboard as the watch officer candidate. "Christ!" Bahr mutters to himself, "Dönitz is plucking these bloody kids straight from their mother's bosom!" In fact, Admiral U-boats had plucked Jacobsen and 124 other midshipmen from the Naval Air Service School. "I arrived in Kiel one day," Jacobsen later recalls, "joined my boat and we sailed for the Atlantic the next day." Second, Lieutenant Gernot Thiel joins *U305* as an apprentice watch officer to gain a little seasoning. "A veritable floating schoolhouse," Bahr grumbles.

On 20 September *U305* casts off in Lübeck and heads for Kiel, where she secures alongside the Tirpitz Pier later that day. Temporarily assigned to Commander Wilhelm Schulz's 5th U-boat Flotilla, Bahr takes his craft out on shooting patrols from 21 September to 6 October. Assisted by an aimer, a layer, and a loader, Sander unlimbers the 8.8-cm deck-gun, located on the centre line on the foredeck, just fore of the conning tower. It is a vintage First World War quick-firing, medium-calibre naval gun—not to be confused with the Wehrmacht's famous 8.8-cm gun, which serves both as the main armament of the Tiger tanks and as the army's premier anti-tank weapon. Soon, the gun crew can get off fifteen rounds per minute. Not bad! Sander also calibrates the twin 2-cm MGI5I anti-aircraft guns. These are of Luftwaffe design—small, low-muzzle-velocity cannons mounted to the after end of the tower. Peashooters! Good for bagging rabbits! "God damn it," Bahr barks at shore personnel, "where the hell are the 3.7 Army Flak guns that Dönitz ordered back in June 1942 at a special meeting with Wehrmacht commanders?" Stony stares. No answers.

On 7–8 October Bahr takes *U305* to his old haunt of Danzig, headquarters of Eckermann's 8th U-boat Flotilla. It will be home for the next four months. Back to school again. Simulated attacks and crash dives alternate with more testing of the deck-gun and the Flak. A mock Allied convoy in more or less serried columns, with mock destroyers trotting up and down its sides like sheep dogs, is sent into the northern Baltic Sea; *U305* is assigned the task first of tracking it, and then hunting it down. A Luftwaffe squadron flies aerial reconnaissance. "Shit!" This is more air cover than Bahr had ever seen with *U69* in the Bay of Biscay. So, this is where Göring keeps his squadrons on ready alert!

Then, from 11 to 16 October, Sander is front and centre during precombat work-ups and training courses at the torpedo shop at Gotenhafen. The mock assaults with dummy warheads go on day and night. Sander is all right. A little anxious, but experience will overcome that. Bahr makes a mental note to monitor Sander's progress. The work is so intense that Bahr barely has time to celebrate his formal promotion to the rank of *Kapitänleutnant*, or Lieutenant, on 1 October—save for a raucous evening at the Gotenhafen officers' club. Then, for ten days, starting 17 October, *U305* berths at the Technical Assistance Group for Front Boats at Hela to iron out the last remaining bugs in the machinery before heading out on patrol.

Or so Bahr thinks! The engineers at Hela discover low pressure in one of the superchargers and order *U305* to the Holm Shipyard in Danzig for repairs. Poor-quality alloy steel has caused an 8-inch tear in the supercharger of the starboard MAN diesel. Three weeks wasted! Then it is back to Hela and further checks from 1 November to 19 December. Finally, the go-ahead is given to resume at-sea practice. Bahr and the crew of *U305* spend Christmas 1942 in Danzig with Commander Ernst Hashagen's 25th U-boat Flotilla. There is little to cheer about. Rommel's Afrika Korps has been decisively defeated at El Alamein. Far worse, Operation Blue, Hitler's critical push into the Caucasus and to the Volga, has stalled in vicious hand-to-hand fighting at Stalingrad. American supplies continue to get through to Stalin on the northern run to Murmansk, and on the southern route via the Black Sea.

The Great Lion is frantic to get every U-boat he possibly can out into the Atlantic. He exhorts every skipper to "keep but a single goal fixed in your heart and mind: attack, engage, sink!" But he will not tolerate the wanton destruction of Allied seamen in their lifeboats, "not so much on humanitarian grounds as on account of the effect on the morale of our own men." Dönitz rejects anew suggestions that his naval Enigma codes might have been broken. Instead, he assures his staff that all U-boat losses can be "traced to an explicable combination of forces," headed by enemy airborne radar, and confirmed by intercepted British reports of submarines as having been "radio located." He demands from Hitler new torpedoes with proximity fuses designed to "crack" hostile destroyers, and thereby allow the U-boats once again to penetrate into the heart of the convoys. "A proximity fuse will have the great additional advantage that, because a ship sinks so quickly as a result, its crew will not have time to save itself." The Führer promises to have Armaments Minister Albert Speer look into the matter. Dönitz is determined to decide the Battle of the Atlantic in spring 1943.

Bahr is not about to stand in his way. *U305* conducts her final series of shakedown trials early in 1943, and on 18 January begins the march west via Bornholm and Hasle to Kiel, where she arrives four days later. The boat is cleaned and the last tune-up undertaken by the Deutsche-Werke. Provisioning for eight weeks at sea begins on 23 January and lasts for four days. The Chief bunkers 180 tons of diesel fuel. Sander loads his fourteen eels. Bogatsch stores the 250 rounds for the deck-gun. Truck after truck brings mountains of crates and boxes of provisions. Fresh meat for three weeks disappears into the refrigeration unit; into the motor and torpedo rooms goes bread for about as long; and hanging throughout the boat like party lanterns are bacon, hams, and sausages. What seems like tons of canned Kraut comes down the galley hatch. And, finally, something new: a soybean filler called *Bratlingspulver*, designed to "stretch" the food supply. "*Scheisse*! Hope the *Smutje* is a fucking genius!" is the common refrain from men who will expect culinary wonders to be made out of sausage, Kraut, and ersatz powder!

On 30 January 1943, the tenth anniversary of Adolf Hitler's seizure of power, Bahr takes a last stroll on shore and turns in at the officers' *Kasino*. The discussions at the bar are heated, to say the least. The big news from Berlin is that Dönitz has been promoted to the rank of Grand Admiral and appointed Commander-in-Chief of the Kriegsmarine. Raeder and his "big-ship" surface strategy have been swept away—after a vicious hour-long tirade by Hitler about the worthlessness of the capital ships. Admiral Hans-Georg von Friedeburg is the new Admiral U-boats, but the Great Lion will maintain control of his boats, initially from the Avenue Maréchal Maunoury in Paris and later from Berlin-Charlottenburg and Bernau. He is not about to miss the climax of the Battle of the Atlantic! Dönitz's order of the day on 30 January 1943 is crystal clear: "I expect unconditional obedience, unbounded courage, and submission from each and every one of you. Therein lies our honour. Flocked around our Führer, we will not lay down our weapons until victory and peace have been won. Hail to our Führer!"

Less happily, on 2 February Field Marshal Friedrich von Paulus's Sixth Army surrenders at Stalingrad: 150,000 men are dead, 91,000 are off to gulags in Siberia. The resupply of von Paulus's forces had stripped Atlantic Air Command of all but fifteen delapidated Focke-Wulf 200c aircraft! That same day, Dönitz issues another order: "The submarine war has become *the* war at sea. Everything is to be ruthlessly subordinated to it. . . . Every sacrifice must be made for it." On 18 February Propaganda Minister Joseph Goebbels raises the stakes with a strident call for "total war" at the Sportspalast in Berlin. The men in navy blue just laugh: What the hell does Goebbels think they are fighting now? And, most close to home for the men in white caps, word has filtered through that the Western Allies at Casablanca have issued a stirring declaration that "defeat of U-boats remains a first charge on the resources of the United Nations." *U305* and her crew are about to sail into that tempest called the North Atlantic.

Sharp at 8 a.m. on 27 February 1943 Bahr barks out: "Let go all lines! Set course for point red 15!" There is the obligatory military band at dockside, flowers for the crew, and cheers from those left behind. Then a boat from the 19th Minesweeper Flotilla guides *U305* out into the open Baltic Sea. At 10:43 Bahr bids the escort farewell. "Half ahead both engines. Steer three-one-five." Within the hour, *U305* is joined by *U415*, likewise heading out on patrol. Bahr feels a thousand British eyes on either side of the narrow Danish Belts following him and transmitting his

St Croix escorting the British battleship *King George V* off Halifax, March 1941.
[Photo: National Archives of Canada]

View to the stern of *St Croix*. She is rolling heavily and her
depth-charge rails are coated with ice. [Photo: Edgar Pennefather]

(above) *St Croix*'s forward portside No. 2 mess-deck. Bunks are folded up against the bulkhead. Thirty ratings lived in this space. [Photo: Edgar Pennefather]

(left) Three Town Class destroyers just after being turned over to the Royal Canadian Navy from the USN. *Left to right: St Clair, Niagara, Annapolis.* [Photo: National Archives of Canada]

View forward along starboard side of *St Croix* from just behind her aftermost funnel and the starboard whaler. Although it is a sunny day, she is rolling heavily and crew members are using the safety line. [Photo: Edgar Pennefather]

St Croix's after-gun platform and White Ensign. [Photo: Edgar Pennefather]

(left) Harry Kingsley at the time he was captain of the *St Croix*. [Photo: National Archives of Canada]

(below) Forward superstructure of *St Croix* showing storm damage after the aborted December 1940 Atlantic crossing. [Photo: Mrs Mabel McKie]

Harry Kingsley and the other two COS of the RCN Town Class destroyers about to accompany *St Croix* overseas in late November 1940. *Left to right:* Lt-Commander E.L. Armstrong, RCNR; Cdr Harry Kingsley, RCN; Lt-Commander Wallace, RCN; Captain Leonard W. Murray, RCN; Captain Cuthbert Taylor, RCN.
[Photo: Maritime Command Museum, Halifax]

St Croix from forward of the starboard bow. In this photo she still mounts the SWIC radar atop the foremast. [Photo: Maritime Command Museum, Halifax]

Andrew Hedley Dobson, *circa* 1942. [Photo: Dr Tom Dobson]

HMCS *Napanee*. The censor has blocked out her pennant number.
[Photo: Robert Mitchell]

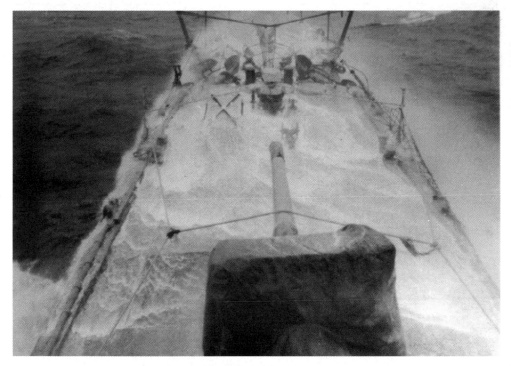

View to the bow of *St Croix* in heavy weather, with her forward
4-inch gun prominent in the picture. [Photo: Edgar Pennefather]

(left) *St Croix* taking on survivors. Photo is towards the stern on the starboard side.
[Photo: Robert Mitchell]

(below) *St Croix* alongside a lifeboat of survivors.
[Photo: William Fisher]

(above) Admiral L.W. Murray, with Dobson looking on, presents an award to Able Bodied Seaman Jim Pullen, the lookout who first spotted *U90*. [Photo: National Archives of Canada]

(left) Bob Hughes, *St Croix* supply assistant, and a bucket of human body parts from *U90*. [Photo: Lorne Hickson]

The last known photo of the *St Croix*'s crew. The man in t[
William Lyon Mackenzie King. William Fisher is

iddle of the second row (with glasses) is Surgeon-Lieutenant
e far right in the second last row. [Photo: William Fisher]

(above) *St Croix* after
her final refit. She has
the 271 radar (housed
in the large lantern-
like structure atop the
bridge and in front of
the foremast) and is
carrying 20-mm
Oerlikon guns on
her midships
superstructure. She
mounts a hedgehog
ahead of her forward
superstructure and
carries an HF/DF
antenna just abaft
the torpedo tubes.
[Photo: Maritime
Command Museum,
Halifax]

(left) William Fisher,
the sole survivor of the
St Croix. [Photo:
William Fisher]

A Very Long-Range (VLR) Liberator. [Photo: National Archives of Canada]

U305 shapes course for the Atlantic, 1943.
[Photo: Horst Bredow, U-Boot-Archiv, Cuxhaven-Altenbruch]

Lieutenant Rudolf
Bahr, *U305*'s first
and only skipper.
[Photo: Horst Bredow,
u-Boot-Archiv, Cuxhaven-
Altenbruch]

Bahr after two
years at sea.
[Photo: Horst Bredow,
u-Boot-Archiv, Cuxhaven-
Altenbruch]

Submarine pens at Brest, France.
[Photo: Horst Bredow, u-Boot-Archiv, Cuxhaven-Altenbruch]

U107 taken from *U69*: a rendezvous at sea.
[Photo: Horst Bredow, u-Boot-Archiv, Cuxhaven-Altenbruch]

Air view of the harbour of Brest [Photo: Horst Bredow, u-Boot-Archiv, Cuxhaven-Altenbruch]

U203 returning from war patrol. [Photo: Horst Bredow, u-Boot-Archiv, Cuxhaven-Altenbruch]

every move to the Admiralty in London. The two boats pass the Norwegian port of Kristiansand, routinely reporting their progress to Admiral U-boats. Little does Bahr know that Bletchley Park is monitoring his reports and that the Royal Navy is plotting his progress in the Submarine Tracking Room.

On 1 March 1943 *U305* and *U415* sail through the Kattegat, with a moderate sea and northwest winds blowing straight at them. The next day they part company off Farsund at the southern tip of Norway. For some on *U305*, it is their first experience with the North Sea. Jacobsen, who had been given no time to pack fatigues, stands watch in his best double-breasted blues. "I was always wet. . . . The first three days I was so sick that I just wanted to dive into the sea and get away from it all." The crew smell fair game and mercilessly haze the Ensign by making him eat "fat bacon on pieces of string."

Meantime, Bahr gives the order to test the new radar detector, the FUMB I (*Funkmessbeobachtunsgerät*) Metox R.600, named after the Paris firm that produces them. Dönitz and his staff have known for some time that the Allies possess shipborne radar, but they are not alarmed. Only in 1942, when Allied aircraft begin to appear in the Atlantic with the British air-to-surface-vessel (ASV) MK I radar, which operates on the 1.4-metre band, does Admiral U-boats become concerned. On 26 August the Great Lion orders immediate installation of the Metox detectors against the new threat from above.

Bahr is not impressed. Operating on the 2.4-metre band, on 2 March his FUMB twice makes contact. Twice it is in error. Bahr and his radioman, Herbert Ballmann, suspect that the Metox is picking up German radars in Norway. But that is not all. There are no antennas that can be installed on Type VIIC boats because they all require drilling a hole for the electrical cables through the pressure hull. The best that can be devised is the so-called Biscay cross—a two-dimensional wooden cross over which two antenna leads are strung to form vertical and horizontal receivers. A member of the duty watch has to rotate the *Biskayakreuz* 90 degrees every five minutes by hand to provide full coverage. At best, the FUMB indicates crude directional location.

But it is a nuisance! When the dive alarm is given, someone has to chuck the cross through the hatch down the tower ladder, and the result often is kindling. Worse yet, the leads from the cross to the radio compartment tend to get caught on the bridge's superstructure, with the result that the hatch cannot be firmly secured. A good number of boats have reported having to resurface to clear the leads. Ballmann also is not pleased with the Metox. "What the fuck are the Telefunken and Siemens engineers doing these days?" he queries Bahr. "Banging their secretaries, maybe, but not doing serious research and development!"

The truth is that under the pressure of war, German research and development can tackle only those projects that are certain to lead to fruition within a single calendar year. Moreover, German engineers in 1942 dismiss centrimetric radar as "utterly unnecessary." They assure Dönitz that the Allies are not one iota ahead of Germany in radar development. Later that year, Telefunken closes down its only centrimetric-radar laboratory at Illberg.

By 3 March 1942 the wind picks up and the sea turns choppy. *U305* is now in that phase of the patrol popularly referred to as the "garbage run," or *Gammelfahrt*: endless days of fighting wind and waves just to get to the designated grid quadrant in the patrol zone. Bahr's war log confirms the *Gammelfahrt*:

3. 3. 43. Dove. Submerged running. Good visibility. 91 sm [sea miles].

4. 3. 43. Surfaced. Proceed to ordered quadrant. Variable visibility. 81 sm.

5. 3. 43. Dove. Submerged running. Cloudy; rain squalls. 123 sm.

6. 3. 43. Surface. Proceed to ordered quadrant. Practice dive. Cloudy; drizzle. 120 sm.

7. 3. 43. Stop to repack jacket of exhaust manifold. Practice dive. Clear skies. 131 sm.

8. 3. 43. Proceed to ordered quadrant. Practice dive. Cloudy; snow showers. 107 sm.

9. 3. 43. Proceed to ordered quadrant. Practice dive. Good visibility. 126 sm.

And so the KTB reads, page after page, day after day. The grid quadrants change ever so slowly: from AN to AF to AE. Apart from the practice dives, there is little to break the monotony. At 8:30 p.m. Z Time on 8 March, Admiral U-boats calls for a weather update; Bahr replies at 4:40 the next morning. Dönitz admonishes his commanders at all times to submit "exhaustive reports" to his headquarters. At 1:45 p.m. on 9 March the Metox makes contact; false alarm again. The crew is bored. Bahr is anxious to reach the patrol line.

Then, at 8 p.m. that same day all hell breaks loose as *U305* enters the North Atlantic through the "Iceland Passage." It is a particularly treacherous body of water, with only 1650 feet of sea over the shallow Iceland-Faeroe Rise. Above sea level, there is a veritable hurricane. The roar of the wind and the sea drowns out all conversation on the bridge. The Atlantic is one gigantic range of breaking waves and white-foam crests. A wave as high as a mountain crashes over the bridge and shatters the Biscay cross against the superstructure. "To hell with the thing!" The westerly gales bring *U305* literally to a standstill. Bahr has had enough. "Prepare to dive! Chief, take her down steady!"

The next morning Bahr tries to run on the surface again. The Biscay cross breaks a second time. It flies down the hatch. The wind is officially measured as force 7—a near gale at 28 to 33 knots. Snow and hail turn each watch into a survival test and cut the men's faces like a razor. A light blinks on the Enigma machine in the radio compartment. Admiral U-boats orders: "Bahr. Head for AK69." More snow. More practice dives.

On 11 March the Great Lion returns to the airwaves: "Bahr. Form new group Stürmer in patrol line on 15 March 2000 Hours. From AK0371 to AL7278, Course 240°, Speed 5 sm." No sooner is *U305* on her new course than Dönitz is on the air again: "Group Stürmer be in new patrol line on 14 March 2000 hours from AK3563 to AL 7215, course 260°, speed 5 sm, intervals 20 sm." Then on 14 March there is still a further course correction: "Groups Dränger and Stürmer starting 15. 3. 0800 hours steer not 260° but 235°." "Damn it, Dönitz! Why not just send our fucking orders and location out over Radio Germany?" Bahr mutters under his breath.

Dönitz has his reasons. His radio intelligence, xB-Dienst, has calculated that Allied convoys run on a ten-day rhythm, four days on the northern route and then four on the southern route across the Atlantic. Radio intercepts—especially from stragglers—provide the xB-Dienst with a good picture of convoy traffic during the first two weeks of March:

3 March SC121, north of Cape Race (Newfoundland)

9 March HX228 at 49°37' north, 39°41' west

11 March ONS169 at 57°00' north, 42°30' west; Commander-in-Chief, US Navy Atlantic intercept

12 March HX229A headed for 56°20' north, 08°30' west

14 March SC122 at 49°00' north, 47°00' west.

Of particular importance for *U305*, the XB-Dienst on 14 March is able to pinpoint SC122 as it intercepts a detailed sailing telegram by Port Director, New York, of 5 March: forty-nine vessels in fourteen columns in a slow convoy. Later that day, radio intelligence intercepts an SOS report of 7 March that eleven freighters have fallen behind the main group. On 15 March the XB-Dienst informs Admiral U-boats that SC122, as of forty-eight hours ago, is steering a course of 73°, rather than 67° as initially reported, and that it currently should be at 49° north, 49° west.

The track is fresh! Dönitz recalls some of the Dränger boats that have been chasing ON170, re-forms them as a new group Raubgraf, and directs them to join Stürmer against SC122 south of Greenland and far west of Ireland. He orders the remaining Dränger boats to concentrate against another convoy just unveiled by XB-Dienst: HX229, south of Greenland and east of Newfoundland. Between the two patrol lines, *U463* is to serve as a tanker and *U119* as a supply boat.

The XB-Dienst informs Dönitz that there are two more convoys in the general vicinity of the Stürmer line: SC121 and HX228. The latter is a fast group out of Halifax. Both convoys are two days earlier than expected. "So there seems to have been another general alteration in the cycle," Dönitz concludes. By now, more than forty Stürmer and Dränger boats "rake" the North Atlantic in search of the convoy. Dönitz's operational orders are clear and to the point: "Night attacks from favourable positions utilizing daylight surface runs to gain position ahead of the convoy." Bahr is beside himself! These useless broadcasts telling U-boat skippers what they already know merely provide more grist to the Allies' decryption mill. The more Dönitz chatters, the better the Allies learn his intentions.

Things are getting interesting! Admiral U-boats directs forty-three Dränger, Raubgraf, and Stürmer U-boats against a suspected ten convoys of 500 ships protected by fifty escorts—most specifically, against

SC122 (forty-nine ships protected by Escort Group B5) and HX229 (thirty-eight ships under Escort Group B2). But Berlin does not seem to appreciate the prevailing near gale with snow and hail showers, nor the sudden appearance of Allied aircraft and destroyers that drive the U-boats into the cellar. SC122, although it covers an area of nearly 11 square miles, easily evades the Raubgraf line undetected. Only two stragglers of just over 10,000 tons fall victim to the Stürmer boats.

Then the winds abate. Well after midnight on 17 March, *U338* makes contact with SC122. In full moonlight, Lieutenant Manfred Kinzel spies about fifty ships in fourteen serried columns. The 2.4 mile perimeter is guarded by three destroyers, one frigate, and five corvettes. Radio intelligence staffers rush into Dönitz's office and report that the Allies for the first time ever have sent an HX convoy out in two parts: HX229 and HX229A.

Admiral U-boats now recognizes that he is attacking two convoys and immediately takes command of the situation. Dönitz orders Stürmer at full speed to form a patrol line across SC122's path; four more boats reach the area in time to be added to the line, for a total of eighteen U-boats. *U338*, having fulfilled its reconnaissance role, is given the green light to join the hunt. At 2:05 a.m., just as HMS *Havelock* picks up *U338* on her radar screen, Kinzel dispatches three freighters (*Kingsbury*, *King Gruffydd*, *Alderamin*) of 17,838 tons; and he cripples a fourth, *Fort Cedar Lake*, later finished off by *U665*.

The Escort Group immediately conducts a "Raspberry," illuminating the inky sea with starshell and parachute flares while charging hard at the perimeter of the convoy, and then making an emergency turn of 180° and heading back out towards the U-boat patrol line. The battle subsides for several hours. At first light the Allied escorts, now augmented by aircraft flying out of Iceland, drive six boats off before they can attack SC122. How did the aircraft find the boats so quickly? Bahr wonders. And in hail and snow at that! In Paris, Dönitz dismisses a suggestion by his staff that the enemy might have airborne centrimetric radar.

While the battle for SC122 rages on, *U305* continues to search for the bulk of the convoy. At 11:38 a.m. on 17 March Dönitz orders *U305* and three of the other northernmost boats in the patrol line, still 10 miles off SC122's port side, to spearhead the attack against the convoy at full

speed. Both sea and wind are moderate; visibility is good. Rudolf Bahr
has no idea that his first patrol has put him into the middle of one of the
largest convoy battles of the Second World War. The most junior skipper in the line, he finds himself in the thick of the action. The three disastrous patrols with *U69* flash through his mind, and he vows to seize
every opportunity to take the fight to the enemy.

At 1:04 p.m. Bahr receives word that *U527* (Lieutenant Herbert
Uhlig) in AK8668 has spotted smoke clouds from "convoy Kinzel," but
that air attacks forced the boat to dive several times. Fifty minutes later
Bahr spies distant clouds of smoke bearing 120° through his Zeiss
glasses. He heads straight for them. It is SC122. Within half an hour he
informs Dönitz: "1420. Enemy in sight. AK9444." *U305* directs two other
boats, *U338* and *U666*, to work their way towards the front of the convoy. The pack is moving in for the kill.

"Alarm! Aircraft bearing three-zero-zero! Dive, dive! Hard left rudder!" Bahr and the four men on the duty watch throw themselves down
the hatch, secure its heavy steel lid, and grab pipes and whatever is
handy as Brenner points the nose down hard at 60 degrees. The men are
already at action stations. The torpedo gang has opened the external torpedo tube doors and flooded the tubes. Not bad: Sander is on his toes!

The plane, which Bahr identifies as a Short Sunderland patrol boat,
had come in at 650 feet from Jacobsen's search sector, but the teenager
had been looking much higher in the sky. Too young and inexperienced! Bahr spied the Sunderland almost at the last possible moment.
He reams out Jacobsen's ass in the control room. "God damn it, you son
of a bitch! You could have gotten us all killed up there! On this boat,
mister, every man bears the responsibility for the entire boat and crew!"
Thereafter, Jacobsen, whenever on watch, is always the first to spot hostile aircraft!

Three hard explosions rock the boat, bombs (*Fliebos*) from the intruder up above. They lift *U305* by her stern. Dishes and gear fly through
the boat. Brenner reads off the depth gauge: "Thirty metres, Herr
Kaleu!" The lights flicker and then go off. The steel hull groans in agony.
Deck-plates jump. Lamps rattle. Flakes of paint come down from the
deck-head. Brenner throws the electric relays of the auxiliary system and
light is restored. He rigs the boat for silent running. For half an hour
U305 clings to the security of 80 metres of water above her bridge. The

worst thing is that the crash dive has broken off contact with sc122. Submerged, *U305* is both "deaf" and "blind."

At 3:02 p.m. Bahr orders the boat to the surface. The ventilators are activated to pump fresh air into the hull.

"Alarm! Aircraft at one-five-zero! Dive! Hard a port!" It is 3:21 p.m.

Where the hell did that one come from? Bahr wonders. And how did he know precisely where we would surface? The men anxiously await the bombs. None come. Sweat pours from an anxious crew. Shit luck!

At 3:59 *U305* surfaces again. The smoke clouds have disappeared. Ballmann reports from the radio compartment that the Enigma board has lit up like a Christmas tree. Twelve u-boats—*U89, U91, U435, U468, U530, U600, U616, U638, U653, U664, U665,* and *U758*—have all dropped out of the hunt owing to fuel shortage, damage from depth-charges and bombs, or lack of torpedoes. The two patrol lines are down to about thirty boats.

"Alarm! *Flugzeug* bearing one-one-zero! Dive. Hard a starboard!"

At 4:48 p.m. Brenner again plunges the boat down as hard as he dares. Again, he rigs the boat for silent running. No noises except for the silent hum of the e-motors on slow ahead. Again, no bombs. This time Bahr stays in the cellar for the better part of an hour. There is no sense going up again. The enemy somehow seems to anticipate his every move.

In fact, both attacks out of the skies have not been by Sunderlands at all, but by American-built Consolidated (Convair) vlr (very long-range) b-24j Liberator heavy bombers from the Royal Air Force 120 Squadron operating off the "aircraft carrier" Iceland. In order to extend their range to 2600 nautical miles, the raf has removed the armour from these planes and self-sealing from the fuel tanks. It has also added a minimum armament of acoustic homing torpedoes and 1500 pounds of depth-charges to make them true submarine hunter-killer craft. The four-engine Liberators have a version of the British asv mk i radar on board. It was these "eyes" that tracked *U305* for two hours from above at a range of 10 miles. These new long-range b-24s—of which Britain receives 3000 and Canada 1200 in 1943—have eliminated the 600-mile-wide "black pit" or "Greenland Air Gap" by late spring 1943. There is no place left for the u-boats to hide on the surface.

Moreover, and unbeknown to Bahr, Flight-Sergeant "Smokey" Stoves from the Liberator has alerted the convoy's screen to the whereabouts of *U305*. At various times throughout the afternoon of that St Patrick's Day, the British destroyer HMS *Havelock* and the frigate HMS *Swale*, as well as the American destroyer USS *Upshur*, have all left the convoy in search of *U305*. No luck. The confusion of about fifty ships and thirty U-boats in a relatively small area has caused too much electronic shadowing to allow accurate pinpointing. In addition, HMS *Havelock* has lost her asdic.

Still, the Allies keep the U-boats under surveillance. The "secret sensor" that the Germans are unaware of is shipborne "Huff Duff," or high-frequency direction-finding. Allied HF/DF equipment requires a large birdcage antenna on the masthead of escorts, one easily spotted by friend and foe alike. "Dr. Arnulf Clodius," a marine researcher from Caiscas near Lisbon, is a welcome guest at the posh Hotel Reina Christina in Algeciras. He mingles with local Spanish fishermen and often accompanies them on their outings. In fact, Arnulf Clodius is a secret agent from Admiral Wilhelm Canaris's Abwehr. He takes pictures of Allied warships plying the Strait of Gibraltar and sends the film to Lisbon for developing. The German laboratory there detects strange-looking "mattresses" on the latest photos of Allied warships and immediately sends the pictures on to Berlin for analysis. But Admiral Canaris's photo experts are concerned that Clodius might be exposed by unauthorized personnel recognizing the background in his pictures, and they employ an expert to retouch the photos by erasing all background. In the latest pictures, the rock of Gibraltar is clearly visible—behind a large antenna on a warship. Thus, the laboratory erases rock and antenna alike! HF/DF remains secure from the Germans.

In Paris, Dönitz is aware that the Allies can pick up his radio signals. Again, he is not alarmed. First off, there are too many of them during any given week—500 by 1943—for instantaneous decryption and exploitation. Second, the U-boats are under strict orders to keep their messages short; no more than thirty seconds at most. Third, the messages are in the "unbreakable" Triton Enigma code. The enemy would have to capture "one of our boats," something that the Grand Admiral considers "unlikely." And fourth, German scientists assure the navy that the accuracy of DF—a factor of distance to the source—is limited to a few miles. In fact, Huff Duff has an effective range of about 25 nautical miles.

Once more, Dönitz searches for other reasons for the frequent and accurate detection of his U-boats. Espionage? Perhaps. He orders Vice-Admiral Erhard Maertens's Naval Communications Service to investigate possible leaks and to take "*radical* measures" to eliminate them. Yet another Allied secret device? Perhaps. As early as 9 March, two boats on patrol in the Atlantic reported being tracked by a "red searchlight" aboard an escort destroyer. Dönitz at once gives high priority to research into the development of an infra-red detection system that will allow the U-boats to illuminate targets at night. In all likelihood, the commanders had probably spotted British aircraft Leigh Lights, which, cabled into the ASV IV radar, illuminate submarines on the surface at night; they may have a reddish tinge due to either clouds or smoke.

Rudolf Bahr has heard of this "Jules Verne" world of electronic cat-and-mouse games, but he has not given it much thought. Who has time in the thick of a convoy battle to consult these electronic gadgets? Hell, by the time one "homes" in on a target, the enemy probably will have had time to move in for the kill! Sci-fi stuff! Techno-thriller for schoolboys!

In the "real" world of the Battle of the Atlantic, Bahr at 5:56 p.m. comes up to periscope depth in grid quadrant AK9452 for a fourth time that 17 March. But he is leery about surfacing for fear of yet another air attack. One hell of a first patrol, he muses. Radio traffic from Admiral U-boats has confirmed that *U305* is in the middle of one of the biggest convoy battles ever, and more than 1400 miles south of the Denmark Strait in the middle of the bloody Atlantic. But he is not about to cut and run. Like a terrier, he clings tenaciously to SC122 for the rest of the afternoon. *U305* is one of only two boats to remain in the middle of the convoy. At 3:08 p.m. Bahr reports his last sighting of the convoy in AK9442, heading east.

"Alarm! Frigate in sight! East. Speed about 8 knots." It is 5:58 p.m. This is getting to be a pain in the ass! Down to periscope depth. A quick peek. The frigate's stack dips completely out of sight in the troughs of the gargantuan breakers; then it rises almost to the sky on the return crest. Incredibly, HMS *Swale* fails to spot *U305* at a distance of only

1100 yards—despite reports of the submarine's whereabouts from the corvette HMS *Pimpernel* and the destroyer HMS *Havelock*. Bahr cannot believe his luck. He surmises that the frigate must have returned to screen the convoy.

Back on the surface, Bahr is relieved to see that the aircraft has not returned. "Full speed ahead both engines! Chief, let's see what she can do!" The two MAN diesels roar up to power. *U305* runs at 16 knots, full out, to get around the front of SC122. Bahr maintains contact.

6:42 p.m.: Smoke on the horizon.

7:19 p.m.: Radio signal to base: "From Bahr. Several smoke clouds in quadrant 9462." Bahr sights a friendly U-boat—probably *U527*—half an hour later.

8:36 p.m.: Bahr again reports to Dönitz. "Convoy AK9541. Eastern course."

9:13 p.m.: Again to Dönitz: "Convoy in AK9542. Course 80°. Speed 8 knots." The Great Lion admires the rookie: this is the kind of dash and spirit that the Volunteer Corps needs!

Bahr's dogged perseverance pays off shortly before midnight. Position: 52°55' north, 29°18' west. Visibility: good at 6 miles with a bright moon peeking through gaps in the clouds. Sea and wind are moderate, but rising. Around 11 p.m. Bahr dictates the following for the war log: "Darkness has set in. I am directly in front of the convoy. Bright night with good visibility. Wind has picked up. In other words, advantageous conditions to attack, even if only at great distances." Clear, precise, realistic!

At 10:32 p.m. Bahr radios Admiral U-boats: "Convoy in AK9524. Course 60°. Speed 8 knots." *U305* lies 7 miles ahead of SC122 and waits. Bahr, on course 130°, intends to enter the convoy between two escorts off his starboard side and then aim for the freighter on the point, the *Empire Moon*. A textbook operation.

Around 10:45, Bahr adds a fresh entry into the KTB: "I approach the convoy at slow speed. I can make out two destroyers in this good light, presumably scouting screen standing in front of the convoy. I pass right between them at a distance of 2000 metres from each. Ahead another destroyer. I turn to attack approach." *U305* is on collision course with a huge convoy in AK9529. It is time for steady nerves and clear thinking.

"Alarm! Open torpedo doors 1 to 4. Flood torpedo tubes!"

First Watch Officer Sander from the bridge feeds final information via the calculator to the torpedoes. Bahr keep a sharp eye on the two escorts, HMS *Swale* and HMS *Pimpernel*. There is no reaction yet!

"Tubes 1 to 4 ready, Herr Kaleu!"

The torpedo gang will do! Ballmann in the radio compartment picks up noises from one or two destroyers, their propellers thrashing the water at high speed. Too late to worry now! Bahr trains his cross hairs on four fat, overlapping freighters off the right bow, steaming east at 8 knots. No sense being modest!

Distance: 1550 yards. Bahr orders the eels set for a depth of 10 feet and tells Sander to stay sharp and to be quick. All of a sudden, HMS *Pimpernel* leaps towards *U305* at high speed. Her Huff Duff operators have finally detected *U305* on their screen. "Shit!"

11:09 p.m.: "Tube 1: . . . FIRE!" Sander slams the firing knob. A jolt. "Tube 3: . . . FIRE!" Another jolt.

There is no time to follow the torpedoes or to see whether they find their targets.

11:10 p.m.: "Tube 2: . . . FIRE!" Again, Sander hits the knob. A jolt. "Tube 4: . . . FIRE!" Another jolt.

"*Verdammt!*" The eel in number 4 remains stuck in the tube. Some son of a bitch in the torpedo gang must not have set it properly! There will be hell to pay for this once the action is over!

At 11:11 p.m. Bahr orders *U305* to safety at 500 feet. As the boat descends, there are sharp pinging noises against the hull. Asdic! It sounds like the Tommies are all standing on her deck and banging away with ball peen hammers! Then there is the noise that every U-boat skipper longs to hear: "3 torpedo detonations can be heard in the boat. First after 3 minutes 47 seconds; second after 3 minutes 58 seconds; third after 5 minutes 7 seconds." The crew of *U305* hears boilers exploding under water and feels as though there are pieces of the wreckage floating down all around them. Bahr surmises that he has hit three freighters in the convoy's second column. Countless warships criss-cross overhead. None detects and attacks him.

In fact, the freighters hit are in the fifth and sixth columns of the now ten-column convoy. Both are British. Sander had overestimated the convoy's speed at 8 knots, hence the eels missed their designated targets, passed their sterns, and continued to run, 3 miles in all, until stopped by other cold steel hulls. The first ship struck is No. 92, ss *Port Auckland*, an 8789-ton refrigerated ship of the Port Line, London. She is on her way to Belfast from Brisbane with 7000 tons produce, 1000 tons general cargo, and mail. The G7E hits her starboard in the engine room. The second vessel torpedoed is No. 84, the smaller 4256-ton cargo ship ss *Zouave*, skippered by Captain W.H. Cambridge, en route from Pepel to Tees with 7100 tons of iron ore. The *Zouave* slips beneath the waves within five minutes of being hit, taking thirteen of her crew of forty-three with her. Raw irony: Captain Cambridge's son, Sub-Lieutenant John Cambridge, had gone down with the *Hood* when she was sunk by the *Bismarck* in May 1941; Rudolf Bahr had watched the action from the *Prinz Eugen*. The third detonation that Ballmann hears most likely is a depth-charge from HMS *Pimpernel*.

Bahr stays submerged for almost two hours after firing his fan shot at SC122. Then, just after midnight on 18 March, he decides to come up to survey the scene. "Surfaced. Nothing to be seen of the convoy. A lightly burning freighter lies dead in the water at a distance of 9000 metres. Hit in the engine room. Nearby a destroyer slowly cruising up and down." The former is the crippled *Port Auckland*. Smoke and fire columns billow out of her. Lifeboats hang bow down in their davits. Bahr decides to put the ship out of its misery. He has a single torpedo remaining in the stern tube. At 12:41 a.m.: "*Coup de grâce* from tube 5. . . . Hit amidships. Short bright explosion. Then a 200-metre-high thin, black smoke cloud. All the while, a destroyer has been criss-crossing the scene at high speed."

The "destroyer" is the British corvette HMS *Godetia* under Lieutenant M.A.F. Larose. She picked up radar contact with *U305* at 3000 yards and immediately gave chase at almost 16 knots. But *U305*, on full throttle, is about a knot faster on the surface. Larose orders the 4-inch gun to open fire, but before it can do so, Bahr dives. Since HMS *Godetia*'s asdic is out of commission, there is not much that Larose can do. Just for good measure, he drops a single depth-charge to let the U-boat know that it is not yet out of harm's way.

Bahr records the moment: "Destroyer searches; drops a detonator; but no depth-charges." The Old Man hooks the *Gruppenhorchgerät*, or hydrophone array, to the boat's loudspeakers so that the crew can share the success. At 2:35 a.m. Bahr writes in the KTB: "Continuing, bursting, breaking noises. In between a muzzled detonation; probably boiler explosion. Noises can be heard well throughout the boat. Nothing more can be heard after 8 minutes."

The entire action from start to finish has taken about three hours. The Allies have lost two ships with 15,000 tons of cargo and 129 bags of mail. But the Great Lion will not be pleased 100 percent: only twenty-one Allied seamen died in the action; the rest were fished out of the Atlantic by the escorts. For the next three hours, Bahr remains submerged, running blindly in the presumed direction of the convoy with both e-motors on one-third. Several times, Ballmann picks up the faint sound of destroyers overhead, but there is no attack on the boat.

U305 surfaces at 4:35 a.m. in a blinding snow storm. Within minutes, Bahr is on the blower to Admiral U-boats: "Last contact with convoy in AK9529, course 60°, speed 8–9 knots. 4 columns, 3 destroyers in front." Bahr has but one thought: "After the convoy!"

8:15 a.m.: Entry into the KTB. "Alarm! Have surfaced smack-dab in front of a destroyer, which suddenly appears right in front of me at a distance of 1.2 nautical miles. Has not seen me." Down into the cellar with all due speed! "Chief, forward planes 15; rear 10!"

Half an hour later, Bahr brings *U305* back up to the surface. The weather is still miserable. "Poor visibility, snow and hail showers." Life in the North Atlantic! But the weather neither deters nor inhibits the enemy.

9:15 a.m.: "Dived at approach of destroyer, 50°, 800–1000 metres."

9:48 a.m.: "Surfaced."

9:58 a.m.: "Dived, destroyer 60°, 1000 metres off."

11:30 a.m.: "Surfaced. . . . 1 destroyer in sight."

11:50 a.m.: "Dived at approach of aircraft."

Airborne and seaborne ASV MK 1 radar, combined with Huff Duff, have given the Allies the edge in the Battle of the Atlantic. Dränger and Stürmer boats manage to dispatch just two stragglers from convoys SC122 and HX229 on the morning of 19 March.

At 1:55 p.m. Bahr informs Admiral U-boats about the previous day's action. "AL7175. 2 freighters, 1 destroyer suspected crippled. . . . 2300 hours 3 hits on convoy. No observations due to enemy action. Sunk one cripple class 'Port Adelaide' with coup de grâce. 8+2 eels, 78cbm oil. 1000 millibars. Snow showers. Variable visibility. Bahr."

It is one of those radio signals that thrills the men and women at Bletchley Park as well as at the Admiralty's Submarine Tracking Room. Since December 1942 they have been slowly unravelling the Triton riddle; in March 1943 they are reading it fast enough to be operationally useful. The results are stunning, as Bahr quickly discovers.

2:22 p.m.: "Aircraft 070°, est. 6000 metres."

2:45 p.m.: "Aircraft 110°, est. 6000."

2:53 p.m.: "100° Destroyer. . . ."

2:59 p.m.: "Aircraft, direction 100°, est. 4500 metres. Dived. Aircraft did not attack me but steered the destroyer in my direction; circles all about the boat."

3:47 p.m.: "Detonation."

3:49 p.m.: "Detonation."

Bahr brings the boat to the surface at 5 p.m. to pump some badly needed air into her, but by 6:08 p.m. aircraft force him into the cellar again. He records five bombs from VLR Liberators and three depth-charges from destroyers in *U305*'s war log that afternoon.

The men in *U305* are exhausted from the constant crash dives. There is no time to prepare a proper meal: mildewy bread and soggy sausage is the best the cook can do. Heat, humidity, sweat, and urine foul the boat. The single functional toilet is useless at depths greater than 80 feet because of the immense outside water pressure. Flush, and the Atlantic rushes in uninvited! Bahr orders buckets put out for the crew's relief.

At midnight, Bahr returns to the surface. The watch cracks the hatch and cold, clear air rushes into the cesspool called *U305*. The war log registers the general feeling of relief. "Due to the many dives and the short periods that the boat is above water, the air supply and the batteries are nearly exhausted." Under a bright Atlantic moon, the crew of *U305* for almost four hours charge her e-cells, ventilate the hull, and drain the bilge. The smokers come topside to the "conservatory" on the after deck in groups of three and four.

The next day, 19 March, is one of frustration and disappointment. Clear skies allow Allied aircraft based on Iceland to patrol grid AL almost continuously, which translates into more and more crash dives for the U-boats. Only three stragglers from the two convoys are torpedoed. Shortly after noon, the water jackets of *U305*'s twin exhaust manifolds begin to leak badly and the boat takes on 6 tons of water. Manually operated bilge pumps work round the clock. The same old problem as before: substandard packing—Made in Germany!

For hours, Bahr searches in vain for SC122 and HX229. At midnight on 20 March he stops the boat and repacks the twin exhaust manifolds. Allied air continues to dominate the battle. A Sunderland from RAF 201st Squadron finds and destroys *U384*.

The battle for convoys SC122 and HX229 is winding down. At 2:17 a.m. the boats receive formal notification from Admiral U-boats to break the action off after a final search at dawn for stragglers. Then, in North German dialect (*Platt*), further to deter possible hostile listeners, Dönitz orders Dränger and Stürmer boats to head south "in great leaps" and to look for loners. He also wants precise reports on location, provisions, fuel, weather, and battle results from all boats. More ammunition for Bletchley Park! At 4 a.m. Bahr radioes: "Am breaking off operation."

The greatest convoy battle of the Second World War is over. March has been the best month ever for the nearly 250 U-boats in service, as they sink 108 Allied ships totaling 627,377 tons. Put differently, while the "grey wolves" sank 129 tons of shipping per boat in January, by March that figure skyrocketed to 230 tons per day. The battles for SC122 and HX229 had pitted forty-three U-boats against 130 freighters and tankers protected by a screen of thirty destroyers and corvettes. The Allies lost twenty-one ships (thirteen out of HX229, eight out of SC122) of 140,842 tons; the Third Reich one U-boat of just over 700 tons. The Great Lion is ecstatic: "This is the greatest success ever achieved in a single convoy battle and is all the more creditable in that nearly half the U-boats involved scored at least one hit."

The patrol has also been a stunning success for Bahr. Although he has destroyed "only" two freighters of roughly 13,000 tons, his actions in dogging SC122 have come to Dönitz's attention. Bahr survived three attacks by destroyers and almost constant harassment by Liberators from Iceland. After each crash dive, he searched, sniffed, and probed until he re-established contact with the convoy. On each occasion, he reported its location, with the result that at least five other boats were able to close in on SC122. By any stretch of the imagination, a stellar performance by a "green" crew and a Kaleu out on his first patrol.

But this is not the time to celebrate. Not yet! The Great Lion in Paris is still hungry for fresh meat. The xB-Dienst has uncovered a new convoy, SC123, to the south. Bahr's Enigma board lights up on 20 March:

3:37 p.m.: "Bahr . . . Proceed from AK4428 to 7998 on 25.3. 0800 hours as patrol line Seewolf."

5:44 p.m.: "Bahr . . . Proceed from AK4179 to BD1348 as Group Seewolf 25.3. Northeast convoy expected starting 25.3."

For five days, Bahr and fifteen fellow skippers of the Seewolf patrol line cruise grid quadrant AK south of Greenland in search of the convoy. Has it passed the line? Did it sail earlier than expected? Pack-ice barriers with drift ice dog the patrol. The xB-Dienst intercepts an American U-boat report detailing the precise location of a second patrol line, Seeteufel. But how? There have been no contacts with enemy aircraft. No U-boats have made radio contact with hostile vessels. It must be "pure conjecture on the part of the enemy." Where else but on the direct convoy route Halifax–Liverpool southwest of Greenland would one expect the U-boats to be?

Then, at 9:56 a.m. on 25 March, Admiral U-boats radioes the news that all skippers have been yearning for: "Convoy in direction northeast is expected today." In the early hours of 26 March, *U564* (Lieutenant Hans Fiedler) makes contact, but misinforms the group that SC123 is *westward* bound. The dolt! Dönitz at once instructs Seewolf to deploy to the southwest; then, realizing Fiedler's error, to reposition 150 miles north towards Iceland. Only two boats from the patrol line make contact, and immediately are driven off by aircraft. Two others, *U469* and *U169*, are destroyed from the air.

In fact, the Seewolf and Seeteufel boats have met a new foe: 6th Support Group, built around the escort carrier USS *Bogue* (CVE 9), commanded by Captain Giles E. Short, and three or four flush-deck destroyer escorts (DEs). The *Bogue*, 13,390 tons fully loaded, mounts a flight-deck on a converted merchant hull, carries around one thousand officers and men, and can launch up to twenty-eight aircraft. "First Bletchley Park, then airborne and seaborne radar," Bahr thinks out loud, "and now hunter-killer groups featuring mobile floating airfields! The Atlantic is no longer a level playing field. And yet, naval intelligence in Berlin informs us that the escort carriers will be used only in naval operations, and not with convoys!" The U-boats are like caged animals desperately trying to fight back. Bahr once again is the advance scout riding point.

He does not disappoint. At 2:03 p.m. on 27 March, *U305* sights a new convoy, HX230. Bahr is on the radio in a flash: "1418. Enemy in sight. AJ3837." At 2:56 p.m. he passes along additional vital information: visibility is low at 5 to 8 nautical miles, and two destroyers seem to be screening the convoy. In truth, Bahr has stumbled into a hornet's nest: HX230 consists of forty-five freighters and the eight warships of Escort Group B3; six additional escorts are on the way to assist the convoy. By 4:04 p.m. Bahr is able to report that it is a slow-moving convoy, 8 knots, tops.

Once again, Dönitz is impressed by the young Kaleu's terrier-like ability to snap at the heels of the enemy. At 4:25 p.m. he issues new orders to twenty-two boats: "Operate against east-bound convoy at greatest speed." For the next two hours, *U305* dutifully performs its prescribed role as watchdog over the convoy. Bahr is anxious to close in for the kill, but Dönitz wants all twenty-three boats in action, not just a lone gunslinger.

At 6:52 p.m. there is an incoming radio signal. "To Bahr. Attack permitted only when another boat reports contact." At 8 p.m. Bahr laconically enters into his war log: "I am standing in front of the convoy." But there is not even a fleeting thought of disobeying Dönitz. Bahr does not want his career to end.

Only a few isolated U-boats establish contact with HX230, and only one, *U610*, scores a kill: a single freighter of 7156 tons. By 10 p.m. rain showers and darkness end the pursuit. Shortly after midnight, a despondent Bahr radioes: "Have lost contact."

"Alarm! Destroyer at 800–1000 metres! Course 090°." *Verdammt!* Where the hell did he come from? "Hard a starboard! Half ahead port engine!" Bahr tries to make a run for it. But there is no escaping this seasoned hunter. Starshell and flares illuminate the dark sea. Bahr undertakes another hard turn to starboard to let the destroyer pass his stern. No dice. The tin can also makes a hard parallel turn. Range: 220 yards! "Apparently, he has seen my wake!" Bahr is almost eye to eye with the destroyer's skipper, the two vessels are so close to each other!

"Alarm! Alarm! Action stations! Clear the bridge! Down one-seventy metres—and fast! Depth-charges on the way!" Commands fly through the ship. By the time Bahr's feet hit the deck of the control room, the red alarm light is already flashing. Air gurgles out of the ballast tanks;

sea water rushes in. Within what seems like seconds, one violent explosion follows another. Sledgehammer blows. Ten in succession. Bahr counts them carefully. The boat is pitch dark. Men tumble onto the deck-plates. Hams and sausages fly from their hooks and roll along the filthy deck, rendering movement almost impossible. Some of the young lips move in silent prayer. A few men cross themselves. No one wants to end his first patrol this way!

"Rig for silent running! Port engine six zero revolutions; starboard seven zero!" The Chief miraculously manages to get the auxiliary lights back on. There is no need to put on the hydrophone headsets in the radio compartment, since the men can clearly hear the tin can's screws and pistons directly overhead. Asdic pings bounce off the hull in staccato beat. All eyes are on the needle of the depth-gauge and urge it on: 100 metres, 125, 135, 145. More detonations. "The bastard!"

Brenner finally reports: "Boat steady!" The pounding from above ends just as suddenly as it had started. Relief. A few silent tears. Ballmann from the radio compartment whispers: "Destroyer noise growing weaker!" Bahr orders a check of the boat. The report is encouraging: no major damage beyond the lights. He records in the war log: "I suspect that I ran into the convoy from behind, and that I came across its starboard destroyer." Damned close call!

For the next two days, the Atlantic takes centre stage from submarines and tin cans. Rain, snow, hail, and sleet alternate. Wind force 9, a strong gale, makes cruising on the surface impossible: there are high waves, dense streaks of foam, and crests of waves beginning to topple, tumble, and roll over. When Bahr tries to surface, he soon regrets challenging Neptune. "In the span of a few minutes 8 tons of sea water enter the boat. Visibility 500 metres." Back down into the cellar. March 30 brings more of the same, mainly hail showers.

An unusual spring hurricane from the southwest ends all hope of further action. The convoy disperses into small groups and individual ships and steams off to the east. At 11:25 a.m. Admiral u-boats concedes that the situation is hopeless. "Break off operation against convoy." Bahr radioes in his agreement and informs Dönitz that he is down to 20 tons of diesel fuel. Shortly before midnight, Admiral u-boats instructs *U305* that it will arrange refuelling at sea from *U463* (Commander Leo Wolfbauer). The rest of the Seewolf boats are ordered to get ahead of the convoy "at all costs" in order to "intercept individual ships when the weather improves." Somewhere in the North Atlantic, more than a thousand miles south of the Denmark Strait, Rudolf Bahr acknowledges his twenty-seventh birthday with Kraut, soggy salami, and pasty soybean-filler. He feels old; the average age of U-boat commanders is just twenty-three. Admiral U-boats laconically records in his war diary: "The operation against the HX convoy lasted for 4 days from 27–30.3.43. covering 650 miles, 28 boats were detailed against the convoy." The balance sheet is negative: one freighter of 7156 tons destroyed and two U-boats lost.

At 4 p.m. on 5 April 1943, Bahr manoeuvres *U305* alongside the "milk cow." Wolfbauer sends up the welcome flag signal, Romeo Papa Charlie (Request the pleasure of your company); Bahr at once replies, Whiskey Mike Papa (With much pleasure), and heads over to *U463* for some libations and news. Bahr begins to unwind. In the meantime, the Chief supervises the transfer of 13 cubic metres of diesel. A surgeon comes over from *U463* to see to a few cuts and bruises from the nasty crash dive on 28 March. *U305*'s war log reflects the relaxed mood. "The sea has become calm. There is only a slow, westward surge. Hence, no problems refuelling." Later that night Bahr informs Admiral U-boats: "Have begun march home."

The return *Gammelfahrt* begins. The war log each day for the next week simply records: 160 nautical miles, 190, 158, 140, 140. The passage through the treacherous Bay of Biscay is uneventful. At 6:20 a.m. a minesweeper takes *U305*, with its two pennants proudly flying from the periscope head, under its protection. The watch on the bridge spies the first green patches of grass and the white houses of Brittany with their red tile roofs. The powerful Zeiss glasses reveal the year's first lilacs and magnolias in bloom. The sound man reports the Atlantic shelf beneath them rising in 200-yard terraces. Bahr orders the Chief to cut the diesels as soon as the boat reaches the lighthouses—one at each end of the two long arms of the harbour mole—and to switch on the e-motors. At precisely 10:15 a.m. on 12 April 1943 Rudolf Bahr personally makes the last entry into the KTB by hand: "Have run into Brest." And then he signs the log.

News of the successful patrol long ago reached Brest. *U305* is accorded a hero's welcome. The docks are awash in flags of the 1st (or

Weddigen) U-boat Flotilla, named in honour of the German ace of the First World War, Lieutenant Otto Weddigen: a U-boat steaming through a large, bold *U*. An army band plays stirring marches at the pier, where a navy honour guard stands at attention. The army's base commander has come to the dock, as have the *Blitzmädchen* with their flowers. There are uniforms galore: white and blue, green and grey. Some Wehrmacht veterans are on leave from the Eastern Front, poor buggers. Even a few dock workers—French as well as German—have come to catch a glimpse of one of the returning heroes. The seamen are already gathering on the deck. First bowline and spring, then sternline and spring are made fast.

Bahr barks down to the control room: "Boat secured! Ring off main engines! Reception on deck!" Lieutenant Sander crackles back: "First division ready for inspection!" Chief Brenner reports: "Engine crews and technicians standing by for inspection!" "Shit!" Bahr muses, "what formality for this garbage scow!" But better not upset naval etiquette! "Attention! Eyes right!"

Lieutenant Bahr throws a snappy salute in the direction of the chief of the 1st U-boat Flotilla, Commander Werner Winter. The latter crosses the gangway onto the deck of *U305*. "Choose your words carefully," Bahr reminds himself. Winter had not been at all amused last fall when Commander Reinhard "Teddy" Suhren, returning from a three-month patrol, had shouted from the bridge of *U564*: "Are the Nazis still at the helm?" Word of that got back to Dönitz! Bahr takes the simple route: "Respectfully report *U305* back from its war patrol!" Salute. Handshake. Congratulations.

Winter insists on providing lunch at the officers' club, followed by good German beer and tales of the harrowing patrol. The Flotilla Chief then springs a surprise on the officers: "Gentlemen! I have arranged for some R&R at our special retreat inland. I think you will find it quite satisfactory! I will supply the place, the food, the drinks, the band. You provide your own horizontal refreshment!" "The pompous ass," Bahr mutters under his breath. So this is his contribution to the war effort!

But Bahr quickly loses his rough edge as he arrives, freshly showered and shaven, at the flotilla's country resort, a lavish seventeenth-century castle in the rolling hills of the Bretagne. The Châteauneuf is an architectural jewel, complete with sunken marble bathtubs, a venerable library, and woods filled with pheasants for willing sportsmen. *Carpe diem*. Inside the castle, the band plays, the wine flows, and never-ending waves of food roll in on silver platters. Then, shortly after midnight, the couples begin to drift upstairs one by one. Bahr has selected a petite, raven-haired French nurse. She leads him to one of the rooms, where the drapery is fine velvet and the sheets pure silk—and where she quickly erases the pain and suffering of the last patrol.

The next day it is back to reality. Bahr supervises the workmen as they strip *U305*'s decks of all moving parts and move her into one of the mammoth bombproof concrete pens for refitting and repairs. Then comes the tedious task of typing up the KTB as well as the obligatory report to Admiral U-boats. Chart after chart for the entire patrol; for each approach to target; for each torpedo fired. Bahr lets the Chief do his own report, and Sander the painstaking statistical compilations of torpedo angles, depths, estimated speeds, runs, and deviations. A British bombing raid in broad daylight on 14 April reminds Bahr how vulnerable the Dönitz Volunteer Corps is to hostile air. A second raid forty-eight hours later again drives the message home.

Bahr takes his lunches at the See Kommandant, a fine German restaurant that features oysters and sauternes, lobster and champagne dinners. Occasionally, he manages to slip back to the Châteauneuf and into its silks. But most nights he ends up at the Casino Bar in town. There, Madame personally meets every paying customer with a kiss, the piano player attempts everything from the stirring "Tiger Rag" to the suggestive "J'attendrais le jour et la nuit," the waiters serve escargots and shrimp with Médoc, the champagne flows until dawn, and the lovelies are both willing and talented.

Reality again sets in—from a quite unexpected source. Bahr is summoned to Paris for 15 April to report directly to the Commander-in-Chief, Kriegsmarine, and Admiral U-boats. It is a whirlwind tour. The Great Lion, who is about to move his headquarters to Berlin-Charlottenburg, meets Bahr and his officers—along with those from other boats—in the plaza in front of the Préfecture. A band plays and an army of high officers and officials look sufficiently impressed. The Grand Admiral then shakes hands with each man and pins an Iron Cross 1st Class on Bahr, and 2nd Class on Sander and Bogatsch. Finally, he directs a few clipped remarks their way along the lines of "attack, engage, destroy!" Bahr later recalls only how gaunt Dönitz looked. After one hell of a night at the U-boaters' special bar in Paris, the Sheherezade, it is back to Brest. Mission accomplished.

Back at his home base, Bahr finally has time to tour Brest. It is not quite as dour and shabby as he had remembered it to be from his first visit in June 1941. Vastly expanded during the reign of Louis XIV by Jean-Baptiste Colbert and fortified by the great Sébastian de Vauban, Brest had become a thriving naval and mercantile port by the nineteenth century. Its 14-mile-long roadstead, the Rade de Brest, is fed by the waters of the River Penfeld and protected from the sea by the Quélern Peninsula; ships reach the ocean through a gap in the peninsula called the Goulet Passage. Two features dominate the harbour: the great Recouvrance swing bridge over the Penfeld in the east and the two long moles (*jetée est* and *jetée sud*) in the west. The French Port de Guerre had been the first U-boat base, but then it was relocated to more spacious grounds some distance to the west.

The submarine pens are most impressive—and are still being expanded. Bahr enters the U-boat compound through a massive tower gate inscribed with the bold slogan "Through Struggle to Victory." He can't help but wonder which careerist bureaucrat lifted the "struggle" theme from the Führer's *Mein Kampf.* Each pen houses two submarines—three in a pinch. Each is protected against the now constant British air raids by a concrete roof that ranges from 14 to 20 feet in thickness. And each reeks of oil, seaweed, tar, exhaust fumes, smoke, and piss. Ah well, there is always the Casino Bar!

And there is always work to be done. Bahr and Brenner go down to the U-boat pens every morning to supervise repairs and refitting. Sander works feverishly with the torpedo division in Brest to get to the root of the problem with the eel that had failed to clear tube 4. A sanitation gang washes down the inside of the boat, while painters scrape rust off the outside and repaint the hull and the superstructure. Bahr takes part in the celebrations for the Führer's birthday, 20 April, and caps the day off with champagne and lobster, by now his favourite respite, at the See Kommandant—and by a raucous evening at the Casino Bar.

In the afternoons, Bahr is back in school. First, there is a torpedo update. Torpedo failures—every submariner's nightmare—have been on the rise again. In response, the Torpedo Directorate has developed a new pistol detonator for the torpedoes, the PI2. It draws its power directly from the larger batteries of the G7E rather than from its own.

More important, the Torpedo Directorate confirms that *U435* deployed a new torpedo in the March convoy battles that shows great promise. The FAT—colloquially called *Flächenabsuchender Torpedo*, or surface-searching torpedo—is unique in that it follows a back-and-forth "ladder" course. It tracks its victims until it hits one! Useful, Bahr thinks. After an initial straight run of anywhere from 550 yards to 7.5 miles, the FAT begins a series of alternating turns, each 330 yards in diameter. The parallel legs of the straight rungs of the ladder can be preset either short (1300 yards) or long (2200 yards). Speed ranges between 5 and 7 knots. Dönitz optimistically gauges its success rate at 75 percent.

Bahr, along with other skippers, is taught how to fire the FAT and how to avoid being hit by one. Five to fifteen minutes before firing a FAT, a U-boat has to issue a special "FAT Warning" on the medium-wave band alerting other boats to stay clear of the area for thirty minutes. There's no honour in being sunk by one's own FAT boomerang!

Second, Bahr gets an update on the latest developments in the world of electronic radar. The old FUMO 29 (also called GEMA after its manufacturer) that Rudolf had been trained on in Memel has proved to be unsatisfactory. And now Dönitz and his staff express fears that the GEMA sets give off radiation, allowing Allied radar detectors to home in on the U-boats. Research has begun into a new radar detector, eventually called FUMO 61, based on the Luftwaffe's FUG 200 "owl," or *Hohentwiel*, nightfighter radar. The thought of adding yet another electronic device—and possibly another one designed to radiate—does not sit well with the young Kaleus.

Third, the Kriegsmarine has plunged into radar detection with a vengeance. In February, while *U305* was out on its first patrol, an RAF Stirling had been shot down over Rotterdam. The wreckage had included a black box labeled "Experimental 6," a prototype of a new air-to-surface-vessel radar, the MK III, operating at 9.7 cm. It proves to be both effective and undetectable by the German Metox sets, which are calibrated down only to 20 cm.

"So, this is how the Tommies always know our whereabouts," Bahr grumbles, "but our bloody Metox and that assinine Biscay cross have no idea where they are!" Incredibly, the German scientists and naval electronics experts who test the ASV MK III against Metox arrive at disastrous conclusions. Instead of immediately developing a German equivalent to the MK III, these experts conclude that since the Metox receivers are prone to overheating, enemy radar must be picking up this radiation to home in on the U-boats. There, in their studied opinion, lies the reason for the rash of U-boats being destroyed from the air. Within months, an irate Dönitz orders every Metox set removed from the U-boats.

Fourth, Bahr attends briefings on the new "secret weapons" that are being designed to win the Battle of the Atlantic. *U551* has already been detached to Wernher von Braun's rocketry base at Peenemünde on the Baltic Sea and there experiments with firing 30-cm *Wurfköpfer Sprengraketen* from a rack of six rockets installed on its after deckcasing. There are also promising tests on *U441*, with 8.6-cm line-carrying rockets designed to "snare" an airplane in mid-flight, as well as with high-explosive rockets. Other shops are working on developing an infra-red detection system that will allow U-boats to "illuminate" hostile craft at night with a red searchlight.

Above all, German scientists labour hard and long to protect the U-boats against enemy radar. With the help of the Buna-Werke at Merseburg, scientists at Heidelberg struggle to perfect a synthetic rubber coating called a *Tarnmatte*, or camouflage mat, that can "absorb" British airborne H2S radar. Experiments with coating *U67* with 4mm-thick synthetic rubber (Oppanol) panels end in failure; any reduction in enemy sonar detection due to these panels is offset by the sound produced by the panels peeling off as the boat moves through the water. Another experiment consists of releasing containers of calcium-hydrate (CaH_2) into the sea on first contact by enemy asdic; the chemical reaction produces calcium-hydroxide, a gaseous white product that should give off the same sonar impulses as a U-boat's hull. And against suspected Allied "infra-red observation," Grand Admiral Dönitz demands development of "infra-red fog"—chemical substances which can be put out by a U-boat, and which will produce "infra-red rays by heat development."

Finally, Bahr is alerted to more modest anti-radar decoys being built. A system code-named "Aphrodite" is designed to create false radar echoes. Thirteen-foot-long aluminum foil strips or dipoles are tied to a 200-foot-long wire that connects a large hydrogen-filled balloon to a sheet anchor. Crews inflate the balloon on deck and then simply throw anchor, string, aluminum strips, and balloon overboard. The decoys, which Hitler approved in June, should be operational by September.

Further down the production line are Thetis buoys that will feature a 16-foot-long wooden pole with a series of four thin metal dipoles designed to deflect ASV radar; a rectangular cork floatation device; and a 16-foot-long steel tube. As with Aphrodite, the crew of a U-boat will have to assemble the device on deck—wooden rod into one side of the cork float, metal tube into the other as a submerged counterweight—and then hurl it into the Bay of Biscay. Although Hitler orders Thetis in June 1943, production difficulties delay it until January 1944.

Each evening Bahr returns to his bachelor officers' quarters with a headache from all this scientific mumbo jumbo. The simple, chivalrous world of a submarine commander playing a game of cat and mouse with a destroyer commander has been turned into one of move and countermove by hordes of white-smocked laboratory scientists playing at death with black boxes, cathode-ray tubes, primitive computers (bombes), rotors, dipoles, and wires.

Last but not least, the Great Lion provides his Kaleus with some psychological support. While conceding that the enemy is "several lengths ahead of us by virtue of his radar location" in his attempt "to rob the submarine of her most valuable characteristic (stealth)," Admiral U-boats nevertheless promises succour in the form of "new weapons and gear." Above all, "character" will determine the Battle of the Atlantic. "I expect you to continue your determined struggle with the enemy and by pitting your ingenuity, ability, and toughness against his tricks and technical developments, finally to finish him off." Early in May, Bahr receives an order requiring submariners to file a testament along with an inventory of their belongings. That, indeed, is a down-to-earth approach to war!

From 8 to 11 May 1943, *U305* undergoes the by-now routine drill of fuelling, stowing ammunition, loading torpedoes, taking on provisions, testing the radio equipment, and conducting a final shakedown cruise. At 7:30 a.m. on 12 May 1943 she casts off from her berth and, under the watchful gaze of a minesweeper, heads west into the Bay of Biscay. Twice the next day she has to crash dive to avoid hostile aircraft. The skies above the bay daily drone with the sounds of sixty to seventy British planes.

"Where the hell are the long-promised reconnaissance craft, Herr Göring?" Bahr is pissed off. He is not alone. Dönitz constantly screams for air support and derides the Luftwaffe's modified medium bomber, the JU 88C, as being "too slow, [with] unsuitable armament, [and] water-cooled engines sensitive to gunfire." Nor is Admiral U-boats impressed by Luftwaffe promises to develop an effective long-range reconnaissance plane—by the year 1946!

As *U305* passes 8 degrees west longitude on 14 May, Rudolf rips the seal off his patrol orders in his cabin. *U305*, along with twenty-one other boats, is to form patrol line Mosel in the North Atlantic. The XB-Dienst has uncovered another target, HX239. The hunt for the coveted Knight's Cross is on.

In fact, HX239 is a fast convoy out of Halifax with forty-four merchant ships; it left New York on 13 May. The next day Escort Group B3, consisting of two destroyers, one frigate, two corvettes, and three Free French naval craft, takes the convoy under protection. Dönitz's XB-Dienst discovers the convoy's speed, position, and course that same day from an intercepted Allied radio transmission. Admiral U-boats unleashes his grey wolves: "Northeast bound convoy is expected from 2000 today."

But Bahr has knots in his stomach. Something is terribly wrong! Every day, and sometimes several times a day, Ballmann calls him to the Enigma machine to share an urgent message. It is a litany of woe:

5 May: "Destroyer. Attacked. Sinking. *U638*."
        "Attacked by destroyers. Depth charges. Leave boat. *U531*."
6 May: "Attacked by corvette. Sinking. *U438*."
        "Aircraft. Bombs. Rammed by destroyer. Sinking. *U125*."
7 May: "Air attack. Sinking 47N 05W. *U663*."
11 May: "Attacked by aircraft. Sinking. *U528*."

Countless boats simply do not return Dönitz's repeated requests to report. Where are they? Is there a black hole, a "Bermuda triangle" out there somewhere?

Still, the Enigma board lights up like a Christmas tree:

"Attacked by aircraft. Sinking. *U89*."
"Depth-charges by three destroyers. Sinking. *U186*."
"Bombed by aircraft. Sinking. *U463*."
"Have lost contact. Attacked by aircraft. *U640*."
"Attacked by destroyer. Sinking. *U128*."
"Destroyers. Aircraft. Unable to dive. *U528*."
"Attacked by aircraft. Sinking. *U646*."

"Turn that fucking machine off!" Bahr cannot take more of this chorus. It is debilitating for the crew's morale. He orders songs played over the boat's loudspeaker system. Life is no paradise on *U305*, either. The boat's septic war-log entries give but a small clue to the havoc that the enemy is wreaking in the Bay of Biscay:

13 May: "Surfaced. Dived under. 1 Detonation. 1 Detonation."
14 May: "Surfaced. FUMB makes contact. Dived. Submerged. Aircraft. . . . Dived. Surfaced. FUMB makes contact. Dived. Surfaced. FUMB noise. Dived. Surfaced. Dived."

The crew is exhausted from the crash dives. Nerves are frayed. Patrol is as bad as U-boat school, Bahr decides.

It gets even worse. At 1:16 p.m. on 15 May, with *U305* lying 35 miles ahead of convoy HX239, the duty watch at the last possible moment spies an ancient Armstrong-Whitworth Whitley bomber diving out of the clouds at them.

"*Flugzeug*! Aircraft dead astern! Alarm!" There is no time to go into the cellar.

"Hard a port! Engines full speed ahead! Every ounce, Chief! Pour the piss to her!"

Bahr shouts an entry for the war log: "I turn away hard, engage the Flak." It is like firing a peashooter at a grizzly! "Aircraft opens fire and drops four bombs during low-level approach (30 m)." The plane swoops over *U305*'s bridge so low that the watch feels the heat of its engines and exhausts.

But the crazy son of a bitch is not done yet! Bahr records: "Shoots from the tail section guns while flying away. Alarm!" The hail of small cannon fire has damaged the foreplanes. *U305* refuses to dive! Her stern sinks beneath her. "Every man forward!" As many of the crew of fifty as can be spared rush towards the bow to help push the nose down. No use. The hydroplanes won't budge. The needle of the depth-gauge refuses to move off 9.5 metres.

"Full speed astern!" It is the last hope: both engines jump into full reverse. The crew rushes back through the boat towards the stern torpedo compartment. Finally! Not elegant, but effective: *U305* slowly slips beneath the waves over her sternplanes. "Damage report!" As usual, only the fickle electrical system is down. The Whitley does not return.

The next day, 16 May, Bahr personally takes the watch after lunch. He wants to see what the hell is going on up above. The usually reliable Metox had not reported the intruder. Now it is going bananas! "Both diesels half ahead. Steer three-zero-zero. Ventilate." But this is going to be anything but a routine cruise on the surface. Bahr wants to see what is agitating the bloody Metox receiver. "Action stations! Man the Flak! Set a zigzag course!" Might as well make it as difficult as possible for the fly-boys. But none come into view. After seventy minutes, Bahr concludes that the Metox receiver is *kaputt*.

Later that evening Bahr orders a crash dive to test the boat for leaks; there are none. Next he tests three torpedo tubes suspected of leaking. Sander fires an unarmed torpedo from tube 4. No leaks. Next from tube 1. Again, no leaks. Then from tube 3. *Verdammte Scheisse*! Three won't fire. The torpedo's batteries are damaged. Bahr surfaces and the torpedo gang spends three hours reloading tubes 4 and 1 and checking the other eels for damaged cells. On 17 May the Enigma spits out a message for Ensign Jacobsen. "Heartiest congratulations on your promotion." There, Bahr muses, is a vital piece of operational information!

By now *U305* is well into the North Atlantic. Admiral U-boats at 10 a.m. on 19 May orders Bahr to proceed to grid square AJ63. Three hours later he gives final orders for the new operation: "Form as patrol line Mosel. Bahr . . . On 21.5. at 2000 hours in patrol line from AJ6417 to AK7592." No one on the German side has any inkling that the Bletchley Park computer bombes will decrypt this order by 2:43 p.m. on 20 May, and that Submarine Tracking Room in London is poised to direct HX239 around the Mosel line.

But the XB-Dienst has not been inactive either. Around 7 p.m. on 20 May it intercepts part of the Allied order for HX239 to alter course, and

Admiral U-boats immediately redeploys Mosel towards the southeast in hopes of outfoxing the Brits. At 7:28 p.m. Bahr's Enigma board again lights up: "'Mosel' in new configuration. Bahr. . . . Tomorrow 2000 hours in patrol line from AJ6417 to AK7559. Maintain radio silence." Hell's bells! Has it finally dawned on the Great Lion that somebody out there just might be reading his god-damned radio traffic?

Not a chance! At 11:32 the next morning, the Enigma board lights up again. "Goup Mosel. . . . Today 2000 hours deploy in new patrol line." At 6:55 p.m. Ballmann is hard at work again in the radio compartment: "Group Mosel to course 110 degrees at once. Top speed." And just over an hour later: "Group Mosel. . . . On 22 May 0800 hours patrol line proceed from AK7375 via 8748 to BD2117." Those buggers in Berlin-Charlottenburg might just as well let Goebbels broadcast the stuff over the open airwaves!

The cause for all the radio traffic is that on 21 May the XB-Dienst also learns of another convoy: ON184, comprising thirty-nine freighters protected by Escort Group CI as well as the 6th Support Group with the escort carrier USS *Bogue*, is slowly steaming towards the Mosel line from the east. Hence, Dönitz's constant electronic chatter.

Bahr's fears are soon realized. At 9:24 a.m. on 22 May, standing in AK8748 as ordered by Admiral U-boats, *U305*'s Metox receiver finally goes off at 1.67 metres on the band. Bahr records in the war log: "Aircraft in view, 170 degrees, course west-northwest, about 6000–7000 m. Cannot recognize type. Dived under to remain out of view and not betray the patrol line. 4–5 detonations, far off."

By 9:40 a.m. *U305* is back on the surface. *Gott im Himmel*! Bahr cannot believe his eyes: south-southeast steams what appears to be a convoy, ON184. This is XB-Dienst's fast westbound convoy of thirty-nine merchant ships, about to meet HX239. Unbeknown to Bahr, Grumman TBF Avenger torpedo-bombers from the escort carrier USS *Bogue* as well as the destroyers USS *Osmond Ingram* and HMCS *St Laurent* the night before had chased off three U-boats. Bahr adjusts the 8 x 60 Zeiss binoculars: "Masthead and trail of smoke in sight 170 degrees. . . . Pursue with flank speed." He knows full well from his first tour what Dönitz expects: report, maintain contact, and only then ATTACK!

At noon on 22 May, *U305* surfaces in grid square AK8749 to investigate a faint radio signal that Ballmann has picked up. The sparker once again is right on the money: "Masthead in sight 120 degrees." Low clouds, variable visibility, light sea. Bahr immediately shouts instructions down to the radio-room to pass on to Admiral U-boats: "Destroyer AK8784." First part of the mission accomplished. Now, to find the rest of the convoy. "I surge ahead to close with the convoy I suspect lies behind" the tin can. Bahr has no idea that radio operators from the hunter-killer group have intercepted and decrypted his signal to Admiral U-boats.

"*Achtung*! Action stations! Man the Flak guns!" Once again, no Metox warning. No radar impulses. No time to dive. Bahr screams down to the control room: "Aircraft 190 degrees. Single-engine land craft attacking! About 5000 m. Closing rapidly." The intruder appeared out of the clouds from nowhere. And what the hell is a small, single-engine craft doing out here in the middle of the bloody Atlantic?

Bahr wheels *U305* hard to port just as Bogatsch's Flak opens fire. The plane, actually a Grumman F4F Wildcat fighter from the USS *Bogue*, is piloted by Ensign Stewart E. Doty. At 10:00 a.m. it swoops down over the U-boat at 60 feet and drops four MK 17 depth-bombs. Three missiles fall 45 to 55 yards off to the left, but the fourth *Fliebo* takes an errant course and splashes into the ocean forward of *U305*'s conning tower. The pilot sees the submarine lurch sideways, a bluish oil slick trailing her stern. A few minutes later the U-boat is bow up in the water at a sharp angle. Ensign Doty is beside himself with joy and radioes the *Bogue*: "I got the son-of-a-bitch. He's straight up and down."

Not quite! But a fierce blow rocks the boat. Valves blow. Deck-plates jump. Steel ribs moan. Bulkheads creak. A few rivets pop. Bolts bend. The inside of *U305* is cast in darkness. A constant stream of water soon fills the bilge—and rises.

"Shit!" It's Brenner. The Chief reports that sea water is pouring in through the galley hatch—even though it was made "depth-charge proof" only two weeks ago in Brest. The diesels cut off. Bahr snaps the Zeiss glasses upward: the Wildcat is slowly heading off. He orders the watch off the bridge, and Bogatsch's Flak crew to leave their popguns and get down below—ASAP.

"Alarm! Take her down Chief! Fast! As far as you dare! Brace for depth-charges!" Brenner had already sprung into action: "Blow tanks 5, 4, 3, and 2!" Bahr orders the e-motors one-third ahead slow. The men are in a state of shock, stiff from stress and fear. It is a little after noon. This time it is another Avenger torpedo-bomber, also from the USS *Bogue*, that drops four depth-bombs from 125 feet. With the leak in her side, *U305* cannot dive beyond 200 feet. There is no time for damage assessment, for Ballmann reports the thrashing of destroyer blades getting louder.

Verdammt! "Chief, we have no choice but to go down to 500 feet. Will she hold?" Brenner merely shrugs his shoulders. These kind of situations are never written up in the manuals.

Once more, Ballmann reports propeller noises. A tin can above criss-crosses *U305*'s position several times. Bahr awaits a crescendo of *Wabos*, or depth-charges. None come. The noise of the screws grows more faint. "What's he up to? Is he simply playing dead to lure me to the surface?" Bahr plunges down the dark passageway to the radio compartment. Ballmann reports low noises on the band between 100 and 150 degrees—as well as another, more steady noise at 135 degrees. Unbeknown to Rudolf, one of the tin cans cruising above is the Canadian destroyer HMCS *St Croix*.

In the meantime, Brenner and his technical division have had time to undertake damage assessment. It is much worse than Bahr has expected. Apart from water still pouring in through the galley hatch, the Chief has a long list of damages. He troubles the Old Man only with the most critical items: "Section 11J leaking. Battery 11 several cells leaking. Diesel fuel and battery acid in the bilge." The poisonous fumes already are spreading throughout the boat. There is not a moment to lose. Almost in prayer, Bahr orders the Chief to take her up slowly.

At 3:15 p.m. *U305* breaks the surface. There are no hostile vessels on the sea. The nightmare has lasted two hours. First things first. To Admiral U-boats: "1301 hours grid square AK8781 bombed by single-engine land machine. Am dropping out of line to repair damages." Bahr scans the horizon. No sign of enemy aircraft. But the sea has picked up significantly. Three minutes later he spies a destroyer, course east-northeast, rising and falling up to its bridge and stack in the breakers. Nothing to do but run for it. Bahr sets a course due north as fast as Brenner can make *U305* go.

"Alarm! Aircraft! 180 degrees!"

Shit! Not again! Bahr ruefully yells out an entry for the KTB: "Same conditions as before. Aircraft came out of the low clouds 0 degrees. 30

to 40 sec. later the bombs already drop. No FUMB radar impulses!" And just as in the attack on 15 May, this bold bastard also strafes *U305* with his machine-guns! Or are they MGS? Seems like heavier artillery. More like small air-to-surface "rocket projektors." Can't be! Bahr orders evasive action—"Hard left rudder! Steer two-five zero"—but *U305* responds only slowly. Brenner has just blown all tanks, and the boat rides the heavy seas like a cork.

The Avenger's four *Fliebos* hit the water just off *U305*'s bow. "Extremely violent vibrations." By now the crew is accustomed to the ensuing darkness, rattling deck-plates, groaning ribs, and inevitable asdic pings of hostile destroyers closing in to finish them off. Thank God, no new ruptures of the hull or superstructure. Bahr orders the crippled boat into the cellar one more time. Brenner to Bahr: "Herr Kaleu, the front hydroplanes are stuck!" Again! Once more, Bahr has no choice but to rely solely on the stern planes. Ever so gently, the Chief takes the boat down stern first to 265 feet and levels her there.

Bahr orders another damage report. It is sobering. Twelve of the sixty cells in the forward battery room are either discharged or are leaking acid. Diesel from Fuel Oil Tank 2 just behind the forward torpedo compartment has spilled over into Battery Room 2. The war log records: "So, section IIJ has been ruptured." Both compressors in the forward torpedo compartment have been ripped from their foundations. Bahr's only choice is to creep along submerged and hope for the best.

"Two torpedo detonations. Continuous detonations; sometimes four in rapid succession, sometimes one at a time." The enemy is throwing everything it has in its arsenal at *U305*: torpedoes launched from airplanes, depth-bombs, depth-charges, and "hedgehogs." The *Igl*, as the Germans call that infernal machine, is a naval adaptation of the army's spigot mortar, which can hurl two dozen bombs with about 700 pounds of high explosives 200 yards straight over the bow and blanket any area in which a submarine is suspected. The hedgehogs are not pre-set for a certain depth, but have an electric impact trigger. It is murderous fire. Bahr cannot help but marvel at how well the engineers and workers at Flender-Werfte in Lübeck put *U305* together.

A third damage report. It is the worst by far. All bow torpedo tubes are inoperable. "Tube 3 is bent; torpedo cannot be extracted. Tube 1, outer door cannot be opened. Tubes 2 and 4: outer doors cannot be fully opened. Tube 5: o.k. Inside flanges on Tubes 1 and 2 no longer watertight." The all-wave radio is down, as is the Metox. The sparkers manage to repair the direction-finder and the 200-watt transmitter. Bahr has no knowledge that the enemy is experimenting with a new killer weapon: modified Fairey Swordfish torpedo-bombers armed with air-to-surface rockets.

At midnight, Bahr takes *U305* up to the surface. By now the men are short of breath, their eyes hollow and red, and they reek of sweat, diesel, and urine. The bilge is filled with a noxious and potentially deadly combination of fuel oil, battery acid, and sea water. As every submariner knows only too well, hydrochloric acid and sea water produce chlorine gas.

The duty watch throws the tower hatch wide open and fresh, cold, clean air surges into the tower and control rooms. The diesels roar up to power. Ventilators whir. The men come up in small groups to catch fresh air. While blowing air out of the tanks, Brenner discovers that Ballast Tank 5 in the bow has cracked. To trim the boat, the Chief partially floods Ballast Tank 1 in the stern. Finally, Brenner blows out the buoyancy tank and rigs it as a makeshift diving tank.

Meanwhile, the electrical gang has been working with jumper cables to bypass the twelve damaged cells. No go. Only more bad news: the other fifty cells have by now also been polluted with diesel fuel. The entire inside of the boat reeks like a chemical laboratory. With a grim sense of humour and irony, Ballmann reports from the radio compartment around 2 a.m. on 23 May that Admiral U-boats has issued an all-points bulletin to the Mosel group: "Bahr reports 1300 hours 1 destroyer in AK8784." *U305* had sent the report in at noon the previous day! The Tommies have probably gotten word of it to ON184 more quickly!

In fact, chaos and confusion reign at Headquarters, Admiral U-boats, at the Steinplatz in Berlin-Charlottenburg. The xB-Dienst had remained ignorant of ON184 and its escorts until late on 21 May, and hence the Mosel boats were running "blind" into the proverbial buzz saw. Their confused and confusing reports pertain to two escort carriers, one escorting each of the two convoys: Task Group 92.3 consisting of the uss *Bogue* and five American destroyers; and Escort Group 4 composed of HMS *Archer* and four escort warships. In panic, Dönitz orders his U-boats: "Halt! Stop in area reached."

Bahr hardly needs this admonition to "halt." *U305* has already run into the buzz saw. Having received the Chief's damage reports, Bahr next orders a practice dive to see what his boat is still capable of doing. Limited to juice from only half her batteries, *U305*'s electric motors propel the boat very slowly beneath the waves. No crash dives, from now on, that's for sure. Then the accursed foreplanes refuse to budge from upward position 7, where they had been secured while on the surface to prevent the heavy swell from suddenly forcing the boat into an unplanned dive. What next?

The fate of boat and the crew weigh heavily on Bahr. *U305* has lost half her battery power; all bow torpedo tubes are out of commission; the galley hatch continues to leak; one ballast tank is cracked; two compressors have torn loose from their foundations; the Metox is down; and now the foreplanes are stuck. The boat is in 16,000 feet of water, almost 1500 miles due south of Greenland, and most of her remaining diesel fuel is in the bilge rather than in the oil tanks. Wryly for the war log, Bahr writes: "Due to the damages, I decide to break off operations."

SOS Bahr to Admiral U-boats: "1521 hours bombed in AK8757. Heavy damage. Clear for diving but not for action. Am returning. Request Metox. Bahr." Ten hours later, Berlin responds that Bahr's supply boat, *U459*, commanded by his old friend Wilamowitz-Moellendorff, will rendezvous with him at 10 a.m. on 25 May in BD65. Along the way, Bahr links up with *U231* (Lieutenant Wolfgang Wenzel), also in need of resupply. Like *U305*, *U231* had been savagely bombed by carrier-based planes after dawn on 12 May. Her main and long-wave radio senders are out, and Bahr can now confirm her survival.

At 1:36 p.m. on 25 May, *U305* finds the "milk cow." Bahr hastily takes on fuel, provisions, spare parts, and a new Metox. He transfers a seaman badly wounded during the Avenger bomb attack to *U459*, which has a surgeon aboard. He also receives the news that the Great Lion's son Peter died on 20 May 1943 when *U954* was attacked by a B-24J Liberator while stalking convoy SC130. Dönitz's terse comment in his war diary reveals no emotion: "The loss of *U954* in the vicinity of the convoy is taken as certain."

Then it is home to Brest. But the Tommies are not quite through with Bahr and *U305*! The KTB bears witness to the saga in its usual laconical style:

26.5.	1600 hours	5 Detonations.
	1617 hours	6 Detonations.
	1643 hours	8 Detonations.
	1700 hours	10 Detonations.

Forty-eight hours out of Brest, after having dived three times to avoid being seen by hostile submarines, there is a final indignity from above:

30.5.	1851 hours.	Aircraft, northerly course. 15,000 metres.
	1856 hours.	Second aircraft. 10,000 metres. Dive.
	2000 hours.	Through periscope: a Sunderland, course roughly southeast.
	2033 hours.	Aircraft at 170 degrees. East, ca. 10,000 m.
	2100 hours.	Alarm!

Mercifully, still another sighting on 31 May, detected by the new Metox, turns out to be a friendly Ju 88c. Shit! Finally air cover—less than a day out of Brest! With the assistance of two escort vessels, Bahr gingerly guides *U305* straight into one of the submarine pens in Brest. Time: 7 p.m. Date: 1 June 1943. It has been exactly two years to the day since Bahr first ran into Brest on board the *Prinz Eugen*.

7

Bolero

ANDREW HEDLEY DOBSON, the company of HMCS *St Croix*, the men of the Allied navies and merchant navies, and the crews of Dönitz's grey wolves are all dancers in the great ballet that is Operation Bolero. Bolero is the Allied build-up of men and machines of war in the United Kingdom that must precede any cross-channel attack into occupied Europe. Bolero is named after a Spanish folk dance of the late eighteenth century immortalized by French composer Maurice Ravel in a ballet first performed in 1928.

Bolero sweeps the dancers forward with deepening tempo and growing power until it explodes in a final crescendo of orgiasmic climax. And so it is with the war at sea. By the summer of 1942 the tempo of this ballet increases daily: more merchantmen and escort vessels are launched in the shipyards of the United States, Canada, and the United Kingdom; more U-boats are put to sea from France's German-occupied Brittany ports. Allies and U-boat men alike are caught up in the growing frenzy of the dance, but for very different reasons. The Allies struggle to keep the ballet going and the dancers whirling ever faster to the swelling strain. The Germans fight to stop the music; if they cannot, the score will become the requiem of their "thousand-year Reich."

It is not for lowly destroyer captains and mere officers of escort vessels, or even humbler lower-deck men, to discern the shape of the war at sea as viewed from the lofty heights of Allied war councils. If they could, however, they would see a distinct change of pattern in the first half of 1942.

The change begins with the dramatic breakthrough of the German battleships *Gneisenau* and *Scharnhorst* from Brest to Germany through the
English Channel itself in mid-February. The German navy executes the
daring channel dash in broad daylight under the very noses of the British
in response to Hitler's demand that these two capital ships be called
home. In Brest they are the constant targets of Allied bombers, Hitler
reasons, and will sooner or later be destroyed. Better to risk death, or sal-
vation, in one dramatic stroke than die slowly in a far-away French port.

Hitler's order cuts a Gordian knot of indecision and uncertainty in
the high councils of the German navy. From the outbreak of war until
the end of 1941, Grand Admiral Erich Raeder has insisted that his capital ships—battleships, battle-cruisers, pocket battleships, heavy and
light cruisers—will play the dominant role in the war against Allied
commerce. Massive German resources go to the construction and manning of giant warships such as *Bismarck* and *Tirpitz*. Much less is de-
voted to U-boat construction. The sinking of *Bismarck* in May 1941
sounds the death knell of Raeder's dream; the withdrawal of *Gneisenau*
and *Scharnhorst* from Brest gives it the last rites. The priority now is on
U-boats; the steel and the men will go to the undersea force, while the
remnants of the surface fleet languish. In June 1942 fifteen new U-boats
are launched. In July, thirty-two. In August, thirty-one. In September,
thirty-two. In all, Dönitz's flotilla increases by 238 boats in 1942.

By the summer of 1942 Dönitz's North Atlantic fleet contains close
to two hundred operational U-boats; his wolfpacks comprise twenty to
thirty boats and his patrol lines stretch for hundreds of miles. To make
matters worse for the Allies, the Germans change their coding machines
in early 1942; for almost a year the Admiralty cannot read Dönitz's mail,
while the German naval intelligence service xB-Dienst continues to
crack Royal Navy codes. Allied merchant tonnage losses skyrocket from
fewer than 500,000 tons a month at the beginning of 1942 to more than
1.5 million tons a month by mid-year. The great oceanic ballet slows,
but it does not stop.

St Croix is an old ship. She is regularly plagued with water in her fuel
tanks, breakdowns in her steering gear, and hundreds of other minor

ailments. But the RCN is hard pressed to provide destroyers for its escort groups, so she and *St Francis*, the two original long-legged Town Class destroyers, stay on the North Atlantic run. Dobson is now an experienced escort commander as far as the RCN is concerned. He has had almost fourteen months at sea in command of *Napanee* and *St Croix* and has killed a U-boat. Virtually all his officers and most of his crew are also veterans. *St Croix* is assigned to escort group C1, due to accompany SC94 to UK waters; at the last moment she is diverted to anti-submarine exercises in Conception Bay. She misses the convoy and is then attached to C4.

C1 meets convoy SC94 east of Newfoundland with its one destroyer—*Assiniboine*—and six corvettes on 2 August. The weather is terrible, with heavy fog and rain grounding the RCAF's shore-based aircraft. The U-boats move in for the kill, and the battle begins 5 August and lasts until nightfall on the 8th. Eleven of the thirty-six ships starting the journey are sunk, with the loss of only two U-boats: *U210*, rammed by HMCS *Assiniboine*, and *U379*, rammed by the RN corvette *Dianthus*. *Assiniboine* is so badly damaged that she will be out of action until early 1943.

Dobson and his ship narrowly escape the slaughter of SC94. They and C4 are assigned, instead, to SC96, and Dobson is appointed Senior Officer of the Escort (SOE). At this stage of the war, convoy escort in the western Atlantic is still controlled and coordinated by the United States Navy. The four Canadian and one American escort groups sailing from St John's are designated as sub-units of the US Navy's Task Group 24. C4's official designation is Task Unit 24.1.14.

The appointment as SOE is a new and much more arduous task for Dobson. As Senior Officer, he must work with the Convoy Commodore in protecting the convoy. He not only commands his own vessel but also the other ships of C4—the River Class destroyer *Ottawa*, the RCN corvettes *Amherst*, *Arvida*, *Pictou*, and *Sherbrooke*, and the RN corvette *Celandine*, which is the only one of C4's ships equipped with the Type 271 radar. Dobson will be the primary link between the escort group and senior naval authorities in Canada, the United States, and the United Kingdom. He will be the sole maker of command decisions on deploying the escorts by day and by night, and on fighting them when the convoy is under attack. He must keep a picture of the convoy in his head at all times and know where his ships are at every minute, so he can direct them the moment danger arises. When his convoy sails beyond the range of land-based aircraft, into the black pit where u-boats hunt and ships die violently in the night, he alone will bear the responsibility for the safe passage of his charges. He will get even less sleep than the meagre moments he was able to snatch in his sea cabin when he was responsible for one ship alone. If his charges are attacked, his body and mind will be stretched to the breaking point, and possibly beyond.

Men at war know that chance plays a key role in their fate. sc94 is a slaughter. The very next slow convoy—sc95—is escorted eastward by A3, the only United States Navy Escort Group still involved in the Battle of the Atlantic. Three u-boats attack; on 16 August the Swedish freighter *Suecia* straggles from the convoy and is beset by a surfaced submarine 500 miles west of Ireland. The submarine commander gives passengers and crew thirty minutes to abandon ship, then sinks his victim by gunfire. There are three open lifeboats. They drift apart as day follows day without rescue. A violent storm passes through the area and two of the boats founder. On 23 August sc96 is plodding eastward, with *St Croix* zigzagging in the van, when a lookout spots the lifeboat in late morning. Dobson manoeuvres *St Croix* alongside. Nineteen men and one woman are picked up 300 miles from the Irish coast. The *Suecia*'s Third Mate had steered the lifeboat for three straight days without sleeping.

By the luck of the draw, sc96 dodges the wolfpacks completely. On 25 August it reaches UK waters and splits up, allowing *St Croix* to speed ahead to Londonderry to land the survivors. Dobson remains untried as Senior Officer in a convoy battle.

On Friday, 4 September, convoy ONI27 leaves Liverpool with thirty-four ships, most in ballast, bound for the east coast of Canada. For the first two days the convoy heads west into gale-force winds and pounding seas. On the 5th, *St Croix* leads C4 out of Loch Foyle and steams for a rendezvous with ONI27. By nightfall on the 5th the junction is made and Dobson places his escorts in position around the convoy. Convoy Commodore E.O. Cochrane, RNR, aboard M/v *Athelduchess*, shapes course for Newfoundland, steering 262°. On the 6th the weather clears and the RAF's Coastal Command sends a Sunderland to orbit the convoy. *Celandine* reports trouble with her radar, which is working only intermittently. That could be a problem, Dobson thinks, but maybe it won't be needed. For the next four days, all is peaceful. It is warm, with mostly blue skies and high white clouds during the day; the Milky Way glows through the middle of the sky at night. The merchantmen move westward in nine stately columns, to the centre of the Atlantic, to the limits of Allied air support, and into the black pit beyond.

———————

Dönitz's wolfpacks are not permanent formations; they form and dissolve on his orders. Group Vorwärts, with thirteen boats, comes together in late August to sweep southeastward across the sea lanes from Cape Farewell to Ireland. The boats have a brief encounter with SC97, scatter, then re-form with reinforcements from Group Stier on the very day ON127 leaves Liverpool. Reading the RN's codes, Dönitz knows about the convoy's departure. The southernmost boat of Vorwärts spots ON127 at twilight on the 9th, but the convoy is too far away to catch before nightfall. Dönitz orders the group to move at high speed to the south and west, to catch the convoy the following day.

Just before noon on 10 September, shore HF/DF stations intercept a U-boat transmission; the origin is plotted at some 68 miles astern of the convoy. A signal flashes to Dobson in the early afternoon, but since the convoy is well past the submarine, there is no need to take special precautions. ON127 steams on, her escorts deployed with St Croix zigzagging in the van and the others doing the same on both beams and astern at maximum visible distance. It is a standard deployment of escorts for daylight defence. Course is 241°, convoy speed is 6 knots. The sky has become overcast with high cloud, but it is clear to the horizon and there is only a moderate swell. Throughout the little escort fleet, men on watch peer at their radar screens, listen to their asdic headsets, and sweep the horizon with their binoculars. Below, others sleep, wash their clothes, play cards, read, shoot the breeze, or snack on fresh bread and jam. Ahead of the convoy, U96 runs silently at periscope depth until St Croix is just in view, then goes deep until the screw noises pass over. Then, U96 comes back to periscope depth to make one last check on the fat targets looming ahead. Three torpedoes are fired; at 2:35 p.m., they thunder into the sides of Elizabeth van Belgie, second ship in ON127's port column, and F.J. Wolfe and Svene in the second and third columns.

The dull thuds of the explosions reach *St Croix*'s bridge just ahead of the radio-telephone (R/T) message. Signals Officer Lieutenant Jack Isard is the Officer of the Watch. He hits the action stations alarm button and summons Dobson to the bridge. Dobson has heard the explosions and is already on his way. First Lieutenant Smith reports the ship closed up to action stations, then makes his way aft to the damage control position near the after steering controls.

"Coxswain, Port 15 to 080. Ring on full ahead, both." Dobson swings *St Croix* back to the convoy at high speed. He thinks only two ships have been hit.

"Make to Admiralty, repeat to NSHQ, COAC, FONF, and Commander Task Group 24: 'Convoy attacked 2 ships torpedoed.' Give our position." He pauses for only a second or two. "Make to *Ottawa* and *Celandine*: 'Sweep back along convoy track,' and tell *Sherbrooke* to stand by for survivors."

St Croix closes the convoy quickly, then steams down its columns towards its stern. The asdic repeater pings constantly on her bridge; the black flag signifying a hunting escort snaps at her yardarm. At 5:19 p.m. Lieutenant Leslie N. Earl, the ASW officer, reports a doubtful contact 800 yards ahead. Dobson orders Sub-Lieutenant Dan Dunlop to prepare a six-charge pattern set to 100 feet. The Mark VII depth-charges hit the water and sink. Their explosions blow tons of sea water skyward, but there is no sign of wreckage and the contact disappears. Dobson tells *Ottawa* to sweep far to the rear and orders *Sherbrooke* to sink the crippled *F.J. Wolfe*. He is certain the convoy has passed over the U-boat and that the German will surface and shadow it as soon as he thinks he is clear. In the meantime, he doesn't want to leave the *F.J. Wolfe* afloat. She still carries secret convoy papers and code-books, beside being a danger to navigation. He orders *Sherbrooke* to sink her at the first opportunity, then takes *St Croix* over to the port side of the convoy to assess the damage. With *Ottawa* astern and *Sherbrooke* still picking up survivors and detailed to sink the *F.J. Wolfe*, he has only three corvettes for close escort.

At 2:56 p.m. *Arvida* picks up a contact and lays down a ten-charge pattern. There is no apparent result. Dobson orders *St Croix* back to the van of the convoy, stays at action stations, and resumes zigzagging and sweeping ahead. It is 5:13 p.m. local time. The overcast has cleared and visibility has increased to 10 miles:

"Contact. Range 1000, bearing 180."

The submarine, if it is one, is 1000 yards ahead of the centre column and directly astern. With *St Croix* about 2500 yards ahead of the convoy, there will be only seconds to spare in which to come about and make a proper attack run.

"Hard a port. Come to 180. Give me a ten-charge pattern set shallow. Signal the commodore 'contact dead ahead of you. Am attacking.'" Dobson shouts into the engine-room voice pipe: "Give me revolutions for 15 knots."

St Croix heels over as the Coxswain spins the wheel to port. Slowly she starts to come around. The convoy is progressing at half *St Croix's* speed; Dobson can see he will be in among the merchantmen in less than a minute. It will be a close thing. *St Croix's* stem seems to move ever so slowly. Then, finally, she is heading back down the convoy track. The Commodore's ship is a bare 1000 yards ahead, and the two ships are closing at a combined speed of more than 20 knots.

"Where's that contact now?"

"Range 500 yards, sir, we're going to lose it any second."

The screw noises of the convoy's remaining thirty-one ships will shortly mask the noise of the submarine, while the sea churning beneath those screws will break up the probing asdic beam.

Dobson shakes his head. Damn, he thinks, we're not going to make it. There's no room left.

"Cox, steer between columns 5 and 6. Torps, secure from depth-charges. We'll try to pick him up astern."

St Croix again passes back through the convoy, her asdic probing in vain. Suddenly, there is a tremendous explosion off to the left; a column of oily black smoke and sea water rises against the starboard side of the tanker *Empire Oil*. She is badly damaged. Four minutes later, she is struck again on the port side. She will have to be abandoned. Dobson quickly assesses his chances of turning out of the lane and over to the starboard side of the convoy without colliding with one of the oncoming ships. It's too risky. They'll have to go through the convoy until they've reached the rear, then turn back.

As soon as *St Croix* clears the last row of the convoy, Dobson orders her around and back up to the front of the convoy between columns 4 and 5. Suddenly, there is a contact ahead. Dunlop fires a shallow pattern. Nothing. Reload quickly. It is evening and at this far northern latitude the sun is already moving to the horizon. Contact again. Range 600 yards. Bearing 140°. A ten-charge pattern is fired set to 150 feet. Again nothing.

Dobson's thoughts scream inside his brain. Damn, damn, damn. They're all around. How many of them are there? They're right inside our screen. How the hell did they get inside us? What do I do? What do I do? For the first time since the start of the war, Dobson feels the stab of fear in his guts. He is not afraid for himself, but for all the ships and men around him. There is no one to turn to for answers. The fate of the convoy rests on him. He has never been in such a situation before. The questions race through his mind. How do I re-establish a defensive perimeter? Should we stop to rescue survivors? Should we sweep astern? Should we change course? If we do, should we do it now or wait for nightfall? How do I shake these bastards? How? The small boy that is inside every man wants to cringe in the corner of the bridge. Let someone else sort it out! I've had enough of this damned war! But he does not lose control. He has duties and responsibilities. He has always taken care of his family, his ships, and his crews. He will not let his men down. None of the officers standing with him sense the turmoil inside him. He must not let them see. He cannot be afraid or uncertain. He is their ultimate source of strength.

He goes back to basics; the tactics are tried and true. A submerged U-boat can move only at walking speed. Keep those bastards down now, and the convoy will roll over them. Sweep astern and keep them down. Make them stay down until dark and lose them in the night, perhaps with a course change or even some decoy tactic, such as sending one of the corvettes off to the north to fire starshell. Dobson orders *St Croix* astern to join *Ottawa* in sweeping back along the convoy track. He orders *Celandine* to join him. Asdic conditions deteriorate at nightfall and suddenly there are contacts galore, but all quickly fade. They are shoals of fish, or whales, or thermal layers created by the cooling surface water at night. None are for real. Dobson stays astern of the convoy to hunt and keeps *Ottawa* with him. They have the speed to get back fast if they need to, but the corvettes do not. A signal flashes to *Celandine*: Rejoin the convoy, now some 10 miles distant. *Celandine* turns westward and increases speed to 12 knots. But she soon gains a contact and stays to hunt it. Dobson orders her to break off. She must return to the convoy and take charge of its defence. Again she heads westward, but too late to help the freighters *Marit II* and *Fjordaas*. The first is torpedoed at 8:25 p.m. and the second an hour and ten minutes later. They stay afloat, for now.

At 11:55 p.m., *St Croix*'s radar obtains a contact at 1.25 miles, bearing 140°. Dobson orders the Coxswain to double back quickly. Suddenly, the lookout in *St Croix*'s crow's-nest spots the luminescent wake of a surfaced submarine off *St Croix*'s port beam. It is moving in the opposite direction. *St Croix* heels over again, but the U-boat dives. Five depth-charges splash into the sea and explode at 100 feet. They send up great towers of sea water. But the submarine escapes and eludes the destroyer's probing asdic beam.

Dobson closes the convoy; day one of the battle of ONI27 is over. Three ships have been sunk, one abandoned, and two more badly damaged. The U-boats have escaped without damage. Worse, much of the destruction took place in broad daylight! Dobson orders his consorts into night formation. *St Croix* is in the van, *Ottawa* at the stern. One corvette is off each bow of the convoy and one off each quarter. Dobson keeps *St Croix* at action stations until dawn. *Sherbrooke* is now some 25 miles back. With great difficulty she has sunk the *F.J. Wolfe* with gunfire. In his fatigue, Dobson has become obsessed with tidying up after the Germans. There'll be no hulks left behind his convoy, no wrecks for the Germans to board and loot at their leisure. He is grimly determined to bury his own—men and ships—and to carry on.

C4 was on the defensive from the very start of the battle. The U-boats caught the convoy by surprise and set the pace of the action all afternoon and into the night. But now, Dobson's uncertainty and hesitation are gone. He has no choice but to fight and, if he must fight, he will struggle to do so on his own terms. He is determined to wrest back the initiative. The word is passed by R/T. Any contact, radar or asdic, must be attacked immediately and with a full measure of force. The U-boats must not be allowed to gather, or reposition themselves, unmolested. His orders are followed to the letter. At 1:25 on the morning of the 11th, *Arvida* drops a ten-charge pattern. Minutes later, *Amherst* does the

same. A half-hour passes. *Ottawa* detects a U-boat coming in from the
port quarter and attacks. Two hours later, *Celandine* spots a surfaced U-
boat and opens fire. The submarine crash dives and the corvette drops a
ten-charge pattern set shallow. The aggressive tactics appear to work.
No ships are torpedoed. At dawn, Dobson lets up a little and secures
from action stations. The crew must get some rest and a hot meal. He
leaves the bridge to sleep in his own sea cabin. He is exhausted. As he
drifts off, the events of the last eighteen hours replay themselves in his
head. The Germans will be back, he thinks. What will I do then?

It is 11 September; 4 p.m. The day has passed quickly, with but a single incident, when *Ottawa* attacks a doubtful contact in mid-afternoon.
Dobson is on the bridge. Lieutenant John Isard, the Signals Officer, is
standing watch. It has been three hours since a signal was received from
the Admiralty reporting radio transmissions from three submarines in
close proximity to the convoy track.

"Mr Isard. I've no doubt they're organizing for an attack after nightfall. If they come in as they did yesterday, they'll move in from ahead.
Let's see if we can catch them before they do."

"Aye, aye, sir."

Isard orders revolutions for 12 knots, and *St Croix* slowly moves
ahead to maximum visibility distance, some 5 miles ahead of the convoy. Then she resumes her zigzag search pattern. Eyes scan the seascape.
Ears listen to the ping of the asdic repeater. There is a moderate sea running, and the horizon is obscured by haze. The lookout in the crow's-
nest is the first to spot the surfaced U-boat just emerging from the haze:

"Sir, U-boat on the surface. Bearing 340°. Range 5000 yards."

Isard and Dobson peer through their glasses. There it is, coming
right at them. Is he asleep? Dobson wonders. That arrogant bastard!
He'll dive any second. I must close the range quickly.

"Action stations, Mr Isard." The alarm bell begins ringing. "Ring on
full ahead, both. Cox, starboard 15 to 340. Engine room, give me 300
revolutions as quickly as you can. Guns, get ready on number 1 gun."

Dobson can feel *St Croix* picking up momentum almost immediately. He can feel the increasing vibrations from her ancient turbines.
Ahead, he can still see the U-boat.

He picks up the sound-powered telephone. "Mr Dunlop, make
ready for a full ten-charge pattern, set shallow."

Now he sees the tell-tale sign of the U-boat blowing its tanks. "He's going under Mr Earl. Sweep Red 40 to Green 40 as we come off way. Half ahead, both. Speed 12 knots. Get busy Mr Earl." *St Croix* slows to give the asdic a chance to work.

"Sir, contact bearing 010, range 1000 yards."

The German is going deep, fast, with full left rudder.

"Starboard ten to 020. Fire on indication, Mr Earl."

"Lost contact."

"Where is he, Mr Earl? He's got to be down there somewhere."

"He's just gone, sir. Nothing. No echoes, no noise."

Bloody hell. Bloody fucking hell. We had that bastard cold. He wants to shout, to turn to Earl and berate him. He controls himself. He must maintain control.

"Pilot, plot courses for a box search. Mr Earl, let me know when you've got something"—as if Earl needs to be told to report a contact! Suddenly all the weariness sweeps over him again. It seemed so easy the first time. Almost by the book. Chase a surfaced U-boat, force it down, pin it down, then kill it. This time nothing seems to work as it should.

"Sir, report from *Ottawa*, Number 11 has been torpedoed. Hit on the port side, sir."

The *Hindanger*. And here we are out in front, with *Sherbrooke* still who knows where. Christ!

"Secure from search. Shape course for the convoy."

"Message from *Ottawa*, sir, the convoy's altering course to port for the next five hours."

Good move, Dobson thinks. Maybe that'll throw the bastards off. He has left *Ottawa*'s captain, Lieutenant-Commander C.A. Rutherford, in charge as acting Senior Officer.

Night is falling again and the action will surely pick up now.

It does. The dark of the night is rent by the explosions of torpedoes, the glare of white distress rockets, the illuminations of starshell. Ships sink and men die in the pitiless ocean. At 11:10 p.m. *U211* penetrates the screen and torpedoes *Empire Moonbeam* and *Hektoria*. At 1:27 a.m., *Daghild* is torpedoed. *Celandine* manages to blow a U-boat to the surface in one depth-charge attack, but fails to destroy it. Still obsessed with burying his own, Dobson orders *Amherst* to sink *Hindanger* and further denudes the convoy of defences. All night the escorts attack. But

Celandine's Type 271 radar set, the only decent set in the escort group, breaks down. For the most part, c4 is now blind beyond a mile or so.

At dawn, *St Croix* secures from action stations. Exhausted, hungry men wolf down their red lead and bacon and hot bread, then collapse into bunks and hammocks. But there is no rest for Dobson, at least not yet. Four more ships have gone down during the night and the convoy is still at least a day away from Newfoundland air cover. Dobson knows he has made mistakes: *Sherbrooke* is still far astern of the convoy, and now *Amherst*, too, is lagging back. Worse, *St Croix* and *Ottawa* are running out of fuel. Is help available from St John's? Should he try to get reinforcements so that *St Croix* and *Ottawa* can leave the convoy and refuel? He radioes St John's. Like a glass of cold water in his face, the answer comes back quickly: "No escorts available to relieve prior arrival WESTOMP. Make every effort to fuel from appropriate vessel in company if necessary."

There it is, then. Not unexpected. Make the best of it, Dobson, you've got no choice. It's war, you know. This isn't some game of Canadian football where you can bring in fresh men from the side when you've stubbed your bloody toe. Dobson flashes the message to *Ottawa*. They'll refuel now from one of the remaining tankers. Afterwards, c4 will go into a defensive stance. One of those goal-line stands, as the Canadian footballers call it. He never did understand that "American" game!

It is a beautiful day. High fluffy cloud, a fresh breeze to produce just enough wave motion to rock the ship, and no haze on the horizon. Visibility must be at least 10 miles. Dobson deploys his four available escorts in a line across the front of the convoy, with *St Croix* on the starboard wing, *Ottawa* on the port, and the two corvettes in the centre. He is gambling that the u-boats will continue to try to penetrate his screen from the front. There is no dearth of u-boats this day. *Arvida* spots a surfaced submarine in mid-morning and makes a six-charge attack. In the afternoon *Arvida* makes another attack, as does *Celandine* and *St Croix*. The submarines do not penetrate the screen. There are no sinkings. Though *St Croix* and the other escorts go to action stations throughout the day, there is still time for rest and attending to the normal chores of cleaning and maintenance. In the meantime, every hour brings them closer to the airfields at Gander and Argentia and to the Catalinas that will help them bring their charges home.

By noon on the 12th, there are still twenty-three ships in company: the American freighter *Liberty Glo* is missing; the *Laurits Swenson* and the *Heranger*, two fast Norwegian merchantmen, have decided that their speed is a better safeguard of their security than the convoy and have steamed on ahead. A Panamanian, *Stonestreet*, has dropped astern because of engine trouble. She is belching smoke. No one gives her much of a chance. The other ships missing from the original complement have gone down.

There are no more U-boat attacks, not even sightings, on the 13th. *Sherbrooke* and *Amherst* rejoin, and Dobson deploys his escorts according to the book. At 2:50 p.m. a lone Catalina shows up from Newfoundland. They are through the black hole. They will be safe now. The long and deadly ordeal is over. Dobson spends the afternoon resting in his sea cabin. Tonight, HMS *Witch* and HMCS *Annapolis* will join the convoy, further shoring up their defences. Three-quarters of an hour before midnight, *Witch* reports that she and *Annapolis* are now close by. Her Captain asks Dobson to please remain Senior Officer until the morning. Dobson agrees.

Smith is on the bridge ready to take the first watch of the new day. The Chief Yeoman hands Dobson a message. It is from *Ottawa*, 5 miles ahead of the convoy and investigating two radar contacts. Dobson signals Rutherford aboard *Ottawa* that the contacts are probably *Witch* and *Annapolis* and to disregard them. Then he goes back to his sea cabin and, for the first time since leaving Londonderry, begins to take his sea boots off before he lies down on his cot. Rutherford reads Dobson's message and decides not to order his ship to action stations.

The voice pipe whistles almost as his head hits the pillow: "Captain to the bridge."

Dobson pulls on his sea boots and slips on his cap and jacket. He goes quickly to the bridge. Smith's face is grim as he hands over a message from *Witch*: "Believe *Ottawa* Torpedoed."

"Sir, two white rockets ahead."

They all look up. A bursting display of white pyrotechnics marks the spot of the stricken destroyer.

Dobson is quiet as he gives his orders: "Action stations, Mr Smith. Ring on full ahead both. Starboard 10 to 280."

They stare ahead into the dark as St Croix's bow parts the sea and throws back a luminescent wake. Then they spot their wounded consort. She has lost way, but is on an even keel. Rutherford has ordered Ottawa's engines stopped while he assesses the damage. There is much of it, and heavy casualties, since most of the ship's company were in their messdecks when the torpedo struck. St Croix sweeps up to Ottawa's starboard side, slows, and begins to move closer. As she pulls abeam of Ottawa's bow, a massive explosion tears a huge gap in Ottawa's side, just behind St Croix. St Croix pulls ahead and turns back down Ottawa's port side. Dobson stares silently at the doomed ship. She has broken in two and is sinking rapidly. Men are trapped in the lower asdic compartment and in the boiler room. There are screams in the voice pipes. Men dive over the sides. There is a loud rush of steam and escaping air as bow and stern point skyward, then plunge to the bottom. On the surface, shattered bits of wood, cork, Carley float, and empty life-vests bob to the surface. A few flares still burn. Drifting corpses are covered with thick fuel oil. A few survivors thrash about. Dobson orders Celandine to pick them up and Arvida to screen her. He raises the Commodore on his R/T and orders an immediate course change. Then he orders half ahead, both, to begin a search for Ottawa's killer. The crew throw life-jackets and floats into the huddle of survivors as St Croix begins to pick up speed. This is no place for a lone destroyer.

Most of Ottawa's company are lost, including Rutherford, last seen handing his life-jacket to another man; 114 RCN officers and men are dead, and the agony of ON127 is still not over. One more vessel is torpedoed later that night. St Croix attacks a contact, but without success, and then what is left of ON127 is passed to the control of Witch and the other escorts of the WLEF at daylight on the 14th. C4 heads for St John's. The next afternoon Dobson secures his destroyer alongside Harvey's No. 3 wharf in St John's harbour. St Croix has covered 2811.7 miles since leaving Londonderry and has but 3 tons of fuel and two depth-charges left. It has been an exhausting voyage, hard on body and mind alike, and with less than happy results. Seven merchantmen and a precious Canadian destroyer have been lost.

The assessments that Dobson's superiors make of his performance are mixed. Captain H.T. Grant of the RCN, Captain (D) Newfoundland, thinks Dobson "handled the situation well throughout" and used sound tactics, considering the weakness of his defence and his lack of effective radar. US Navy Admiral R.M. Brainard, Commander of Task Group 24, believes that Dobson's aggressiveness served the convoy well: "While losses were heavy, they might have been heavier without such positive action in counter-attacks." The Royal Navy is not so kind. One officer in the Admiralty considers the defence to have been "a complete muddle." The official evaluation is gentler, but still damning: "It is considered there was an unnecessary waste of effort in sinking damaged ships. . . . It is the enemy's purpose to sink our tonnage. On no account should the convoy escort be weakened and the enemy's task completed by escorts being detached to sink our own ships in North Atlantic waters."

––––––––––––

Despite the RN's evaluation of Dobson's performance, he remains Senior Officer of C4. The River Class destroyer *Restigouche*—known as "Rustyguts" to all in the navy—replaces *Ottawa*. They depart St John's for another run eastward late on 22 September to meet convoy SC101. The junction is made the next morning and the course is shaped for Ireland. They steam through dense fog, and three ships get lost. When the sky clears for a bit on the 24th, two stragglers from convoy HX208 join them. They push on. On the afternoon of the 27th, the convoy is forced to heave to some 300 miles southeast of Cape Farewell as a massive storm with gale-force winds sweeps out of the northwest. They endure the storm for seventeen hours before they head eastward again. Two ships are missing. Three days later *Sherbrooke* intercepts German-language radio transmissions while standing by a straggler 20 miles astern of the convoy, but this time the luck of the draw is with them. There are no submarine attacks, not even a contact. On the morning of 4 October *St Croix* anchors at Moville to refuel before heading up-river to Londonderry. They have a week for rest, recreation, victualling, and munitioning before they start back with convoy ON137. Escort crews can now normally anticipate a week in port at either end before putting to sea again. It is not enough time, really, for men who have been in this fight since early in the war and who have endured the war in all its horror. But the pace of Operation Bolero is picking up; unknown to those who man the escorts, the United States and Britain will shortly mount Operation Torch—a landing in North Africa to begin the campaign to wrest the southern shore of the Mediterranean from the Axis.

On the morning of 11 October 1942, c4 heads to sea to rendezvous with ON137 off Oversay. The three sections of ON137 effect junction well before noon and course is shaped for the east coast of Canada. The weather report is showing the beginnings of a major depression in mid-Atlantic, with tight isobars and increasing winds. By dawn on the 13th the ships are riding heavy swells that indicate a storm to the northwest. At their average speed of 11 knots, there is no chance to pass ahead of it. The swell increases and the sky darkens as they pound westward. There is no sunset, just a grey twilight atop a sea beginning to heave up waves of 10 to 20 feet. The wind whistles through the rigging. The ships begin to plunge into the deepening wave troughs. A mixture of rain and snow beats at their superstructures. By dawn they are in the teeth of a mid-Atlantic hurricane. The convoy heaves to, trying desperately to keep way on. They are some 300 miles south of Iceland.

The Admiralty signals Dobson that they and two other storm-bound convoys are to change to a more southerly course. Dobson is happy to oblige, but refuses a request to detach two corvettes to search for *Stornest*, a freighter torpedoed somewhere to the south. The corvettes will not survive, he tells his superiors. By morning the weather moderates as the storm passes on. The convoy begins to sort itself out and to head in its newly assigned direction. One ship is missing. Dobson sends *Arvida* and *Sherbrooke* to look for *Stornest*, but the search is cancelled by the Commander-in-Chief Western Approaches. The convoy steams towards Greenland waters.

On the morning of 16 October, Dobson reads the dreaded message from the Admiralty: "IMMEDIATE SUBMARINE WARNING. U/Boat has made a first sighting report on 7640 kilocycles at 0840z of a convoy or important unit probably ON 137 or SC 104." But which convoy is it? There is nothing to do but take maximum precautions. *Restigouche* has a HF/DF set aboard, but *Celandine* is still the only c4 ship with Type 271 radar. They will have to be especially alert. Now they enter a fog bank. The merchantmen stream their fog buoys, and the escorts keep station with their otherwise quite useless SWIC or newer SW2C radars. Dobson tells *Celandine* to move out ahead and sweep in a circle around the convoy. Any submarines trying to get close on the surface should be detected by her radar.

It's maddening. They may be out there, but where? We can't see them and these damned radars of ours are worthless, Dobson thinks.

"Captain, message from the Commodore. He says he has picked up the sound of an underwater explosion and has seen a torpedo track on his starboard quarter."

He must be dreaming. In any case, no one's been torpedoed. There's only one option, anyway, and that's to push on.

"Thank you, Chief Yeoman. Keep me apprised of any further developments."

"Sir, message from *Celandine*. She's attacked a contact 3 miles ahead. Says she's dropped a full pattern at 50 feet and saw a periscope in the middle of it."

"Sound action stations."

The Commodore may have been seeing ghosts, but not *Celandine*. They're here, all right, Dobson thinks, but I've got to be cautious. There's still too much fog around to see surfaced subs. We can't conduct any sort of an offence. This is no time to send the escorts chasing off. He's never been prepared to admit he made any serious mistakes with ON 127, and yet . . .

"Contact, sir. Range 600 yards, bearing 340." One of the bridge lookouts yells: "Wake, sir, just off the port bow."

They must be very careful. *Celandine* is off in that direction, somewhere in the fog.

"Torps, make ready to drop two charges at 100 feet. That should shake them up, if they're down there."

The two explosions bring up tons of sea water, but no sign of U-boat wreckage.

"Sir, signal from *Celandine*. She wants permission to sweep astern."

Dobson agrees. Within a few minutes *Celandine* draws near *Amherst*, which has just fired a ten-charge pattern over a firm contact. *Amherst* detects no result and begins to swing round for another run. *Celandine* comes up and drops a pattern of her own. Again nothing. The water is thick with oil, but from what? As night begins to fall, *Celandine* rejoins the convoy.

The attacks have come from u-boats attached to Group Wotan, with twelve boats, and Group Panther, with fifteen. But the storms and the fog play havoc with the wolfpacks' efforts to track and pin the convoy. By noon on the 17th the seas are showing signs of another storm. By nightfall, convoy and hunters alike are in the midst of a full gale. Winds of 60 to 80 miles an hour toss the ships about on waves that reach 30 feet in height. The foam is whipped off the wavetops and breaks into spray. The men pass the night holding on, or puking their guts out, or praying, as the roar of the wind, the pounding of the waves, and the corkscrew motion of the little vessels remind them of the fate that awaits them should they or their ships falter. One ship—the US freighter *Angelina*—does falter. She straggles, drifts away, and is torpedoed at 3:31 p.m. There are only nine survivors to be picked up by the convoy's rescue ship HMS *Bury*.

Angelina is the only victim. The u-boats cannot track ON137 any farther in this latest storm. They leave to hunt other prey. But *St Croix* is now running dangerously low on fuel. Since the seas continue to run high on the 19th, Dobson decides to head south to Ponta Delgada in the Portuguese Azores to refuel. It is closer than St John's. Perhaps he might even be able to rejoin ON137 before it reaches its destination.

The seas moderate as *St Croix* heads southward and the air temperature increases almost by the hour. The men doff their sweaters and sit topside to soak up the warm sunshine as *St Croix* nears the subtropical island group. Portugal is neutral, so they will not be allowed to stay long—just long enough to put 380 tons of fuel into her tanks and as much fresh fruit and vegetables and other goodies as they can get aboard in a night. By nightfall on the 20th they can see the lights of the little fishing port. They tie up before midnight, and the fuelling and victualling begins. Pineapples, tomatoes, bananas, chickens, and wine for the wardroom are quickly purchased from dockside vendors and loaded. Only members of the victualling party are allowed ashore. The perfume-like smells of flowers and fruit that waft from shore and the soft subtropical night fill many of the men with longing—for wives or sweethearts, or any woman who can make the war go away for a while.

But there is no time. They leave the next morning; the convoy is now too far ahead and they must steam straight for St John's.

St Croix is overdue for a refit. After they make St John's they proceed via Halifax for Saint John, New Brunswick, where the ship's boilers will be cleaned, her hull scraped and painted, and other essential repairs made. They arrive on 11 November and leave on 18 December. They shape course for St John's, but an equipment breakdown forces them to make for Halifax. They arrive early on the morning of Saturday, 19 December. The stores are decorated for Christmas and there is snow on the ground; Dobson has not seen Gertrude or the children for seven months.

Saturday night: the dancers applaud and await the next number from Jimmy Ames's Mellow Nova Scotians. Hedley and Gertrude are in the ballroom of the Nova Scotian Hotel in Halifax. Since the start of the war, Saturday night has been dinner and dance night at the venerable old hotel, but the Dobsons have had little chance to go. He ought not to be here now, except for the breakdown in *St Croix*'s boiler room. He called home from quayside just before 6 a.m., waking Gertrude with the news that he would be in town for at least a day or so. It couldn't be more than that because the Flag Officer Newfoundland Force was already complaining loudly about *St Croix*'s unavailability. Gertrude wonders if, maybe, that breakdown . . . but never mind. He's here, that's all that matters, and they will have some unexpected time together.

The orchestra begins playing "Stardust." It does an acceptable rendition of the song made famous by the Artie Shaw orchestra. Hedley and Gertrude have loved the tune since the time they first heard it. They dance. Most of the men on the dance floor are in uniform, particularly in the navy blue of the Royal Navy or the Royal Canadian Navy. Like Dobson, they hold their partners close as they sway to the melody. He smells Gertrude's perfume and feels her body pressing against him. He guides Getrude slowly around the floor. He tries to lose himself in the melancholy tune. Her head nestles on his shoulder and he closes his eyes. He sees *Ottawa*, broken in half, sinking rapidly before his eyes. He hears the shouts of her crew, the screams of men scalded by steam, rent by explosion, or trapped below decks as the sea rushes in. He is alone with these horrors. He cannot share them with anyone, not even her. No one can understand who has not been there. He hears the song end and walks Gertrude back to the table. She wants to talk about plans. The war seems to be going well. The Allies are ashore in North Africa, and an entire German army is trapped at Stalingrad. He has not seen her for a very long time, but he has changed since then. He is tired of the war. He can feel no enthusiasm for such talk; there is too much war left. Soon, they go home. The night will be too short as it is, and he must be at the dockyard early in the morning.

St Croix leaves St John's on the morning of 11 January 1943. She has been switched back to escort group C1 for the foreseeable future. The Senior Officer is Lieutenant-Commander L. Johnston, RN, aboard HMS *Vansittart*, one of the venerable but still very effective V & W Class destroyers built at the end of the First World War. *Vansittart* and another RN destroyer, *Chesterfield*, have been attached to C1 for this trip only. Dobson is puzzled by this, but dismisses it as just another mystery of the war that he will never be given to understand. A day out of St John's, the escort effects a rendezvous with HX222 and proceeds to UK waters. Dönitz tries to intercept the convoy, sending Group Jaguar against it, but bad weather and sunspot interference with German radio traffic foils a coordinated attack. Only one ship is sunk, and the escort reaches Londonderry on 22 January 1943.

In Londonderry Dobson discovers the answer to the mystery of why the two RN destroyers had joined C1 for the crossing. The Royal Navy has decided that the Royal Canadian Navy is falling down on the job. Most of the RCN's mid-ocean escorts are being pulled off the North Atlantic run for intensive training in the United Kingdom and to have better ASW gear installed. *St Croix* is no exception, even with one U-boat to her credit. *Vansittart* and *Chesterfield* had been the Canadians' back-up; the Admiralty hadn't trusted C1 to get the job of escorting HX222 done on its own!

The Admiralty's thinking grew out of such disastrous convoy fights as that for ONI27 and for SC107, a calamitous battle that the RCN had fought at the beginning of November. The straw had broken with the fight for ONS154, a westbound convoy escorted out of Londonderry by C1 in late December. The escort had consisted of River Class destroyer *St Laurent* and five RCN corvettes. All had the new Type 271 radar, but their radar operators were unfamiliar with their equipment. The convoy had been spotted by the twelve-boat Group Spitz on 26 December just after entering the black pit. The battle began in heavy weather when *U356* passed through the convoy, sinking three ships and badly damaging a fourth. *St Laurent* attacked the submarine with gunfire and depth-charges and sank it with all hands (though this feat was not confirmed until after the war). Then the Germans lost contact with the convoy, and only one ship was destroyed until the morning of 28 December. That day, the u-boats attacked again. By the end of the battle, nine merchantmen and the destroyer HMS *Fidelity* had gone down.

Some weeks before ONS154, the Admiralty had started pressuring British Prime Minister Winston Churchill to convince the Canadians to shift their navy from the North Atlantic battle to the UK–Gibraltar run. That run could be made under cover of shore-based aircraft and could provide good operational practice for the RCN's crews. The UK–Gibraltar convoy run had become especially important since the November Torch landings. The Admiralty pointed out that the vast majority of ships being lost in the Atlantic were escorted by Canadian vessels. But then, the slower convoys that the RCN always escorted presented the Germans with the easiest targets. After ONS154, however, the RCN could no longer resist the pressure. On 9 January 1943 the government in Ottawa acceded to the British request. *St Croix* and her consorts were heading for the famed Pillars of Hercules.

By the beginning of 1943, Allied shipyards were building merchant vessels faster than the u-boats could sink them, although losses in men and cargoes remained very high. In December 1942 the Allies lost more than 300,000 tons of shipping to u-boats. Stockpiles of almost everything in the United Kingdom were shrinking rapidly. There were barely more than 300,000 tons of non-military oil reserves, enough for only three months of rationed usage, though the Royal Navy still possessed a reserve of about 1 million tons. Dönitz's fleet now consisted of some 390 submarines, with more than 200 of them operational at any one time. That gave him the ability to sustain between sixty and seventy u-boats on patrol. Shipping losses dropped in January 1943 when massive storms whipped across the North Atlantic, pounding hunted and hunter alike, but the slaughter of merchantmen picked up when the weather eased.

On 14 January 1943 Churchill and Roosevelt met at Casablanca to discuss war strategy. One of the topics covered was the war at sea; the conclusion the two leaders reached was that the defeat of the U-boat menace must have top priority before an invasion of the continent could be mounted. In fact, Allied losses thus far meant that a once-planned 1943 cross-channel invasion had to be postponed for at least a year. Both men knew that Josef Stalin would be furious about the news, but there was little choice. There were simply not enough bottoms at sea, or coming off the ways, both to feed Britain and to bring Bolero to a successful conclusion.

During her Londonderry layover, *St Croix*'s two ancient 4-inch guns on her port and starboard beams are replaced with two modern 20-mm Oerlikons. These can be used against surfaced submarines or aircraft. Additional .50 machine-guns are also mounted to beef up her ability to defend against air attack. Half her crew gets immediate long liberty, the rest attend to the cleaning, painting, and repairs that are always necessary. Then the roles are reversed. When all have had sufficient time ashore, their training begins on simulators. They are drilled in depth-charge attacks, anti-aircraft defence, gunnery, and boarding. *St Croix* then sails for HMS *Western Isles*, the Royal Navy's anti-submarine training base at Tobermory, Scotland. For six days *St Croix* and CI undergo a rigorous training regimen under the watchful eye of Commodore G. Stephenson, known to all his students as "the Terror of Tobermory." He is a legend in his own time, as he inspires and terrorizes escort captains and their crews to do their very best. With the aid of a Royal Navy submarine, the crew practise ASW techniques and all the other offensive and defensive functions escorts are expected to perform. They end their training with a night firing exercise, then head back to Londonderry for their first run to Gibraltar.

Just after midnight on the last day of February 1943, *St Croix* sails from her Moville anchorage to rendezvous with the steamer *Houston City*, which she will accompany to a junction with convoy KMS10 bound for Bone, Algeria. At Gibraltar, CI will leave the convoy, put into port for a day of hurried refuelling and revictualling, then accompany another convoy back to the United Kingdom. Since the Canadians are still "on trial" as far as the Royal Navy goes, CI is given a new temporary Senior Officer: HMS *Burwell*, herself a Town Class destroyer.

On Monday morning, *St Croix* and *Houston City* join KMS10 off the west coast of Ireland. The convoy is to sail almost due south until it is half way down the Portuguese coast, then head southeast towards Gibraltar. Each day, just after dawn, Coastal Command aircraft join the convoy, first sweeping ahead for surfaced U-boats, then orbiting until afternoon. The convoy route will bring the ships well within the range of German shore-based aircraft, but that is a risk cancelled out by the RAF's ability to provide almost constant air cover from either the United Kingdom or Gibraltar.

As the convoy steams south, it leaves the cold of an early North Atlantic March behind. Not only is the air warmer at these latitudes but there are far fewer of the vicious mid-winter storms that so often batter the ships on the run from St John's to Londonderry and back. Each night they see new and unfamiliar stars appear on the southern horizon; each day brings warmer weather and strange new sea birds. For four days, the journey is almost like a tropical cruise. Off-duty men work on their tans or stare out over the placid Atlantic as the convoy works its way south. On the morning of 3 March the corvette *Fort York* attacks a contact ahead of the convoy, then loses it. No one else picks it up. Perhaps it is nothing. Perhaps they will slip by the Bay of Biscay and the Portuguese coast undetected.

It is 10:40 a.m. on 4 March. The convoy is 150 miles to the west of Vigo, Spain. It is a beautiful day at sea. There is high broken cloud, the winds are light, and the sea is sky-blue with a light chop. Visibility is 11 miles. The nine columns of the convoy are heading almost due south at 11 knots. Lieutenant Paul S. Major, RCNVR, is *St Croix*'s new Torpedo Officer. It is his watch. He is looking out over the calm sea trying to detect the horizon through the subtropical heat haze. Suddenly, he hears a faint drone of aircraft engines off to the west. It is not the familiar sound of the RAF Catalinas' two Pratt and Whitneys. Major checks on the position of the RAF aircraft. He makes out one of the Cats about 5 miles astern. He turns to see the other, orbiting to the south of the convoy. He turns to the west. Through his glasses he can make out two dots approaching from 270°. He makes their height out at about 15,000 feet.

"Captain to the bridge."

"What is it, Mr Major."

"Enemy aircraft, sir. Bearing 270, height 15,000."

Dobson rushes to the bridge. Major points to the oncoming aircraft. "I think they're Condors."

Dobson peers through his glasses at the growing specks.

"I think so, too, Mr Major. Sound action stations, make to *Burwell* 'two Focke-Wulfs, bearing 270, 15,000 feet.'"

Burwell has already spotted the German bombers. They are four-engine Focke-Wulf Condors. These bombers have a normal operating range of 2200 miles and are used both to spot and track Allied convoys and to bomb them. Churchill calls them "the scourge of the Atlantic."

"Air-raid warning. Guns, alert your crews."

Eyes look skyward. Men shield their eyes from the sun and point at the enemy bombers. The gun crews swing their weapons around and elevate the muzzles to the sky.

"On my order, commence firing."

The two bombers are now close in. They start to cross the convoy from west to east. *Burwell* opens fire. So does *Shediac*. Lieutenant Ronald C. Weyman, RCNVR, *St Croix*'s Gunnery Officer, orders his crews to open up a moment later. The anti-aircraft guns on the merchantmen join in.

The cacophony of pom-poms from the corvettes, high-angle 12 pounders and Oerlikons from the destroyers, and .303- and .50-calibre machine-guns from all the ships is deafening. Flak bursts dot the sky over the convoy. The bombers drone on, too high to be reached. The bombs drop, tiny bundles of death growing larger with every second. A column of sea water rises beside the fourth ship in the second column, but she is not hit. None of the bombs strike home. The Focke-Wulfs swing around to the north. The convoy ceases firing. One of the bombers makes a pass at one of the Catalinas, and the distant rattle of machine-gun fire can be heard as the Cat ducks into a cloud. Dobson orders *St Croix* to put about, hoping to lure this attacker back into the convoy's range. But the Luftwaffe is through for the day, and the convoy secures from action stations.

As the bombers disappear towards the horizon, Dobson orders the Officer of the Watch to return to the convoy, now some 8 miles away.

About 2500 yards ahead of them is *Shediac*, flying her black flag. She signals that she has a contact and is running short of depth-charges. From the time the bombers flew off until now, she has made five runs on this and a previous contact. She asks for assistance. Dobson acknowledges and calls for both ahead, full, to close the corvette as quickly as possible. At 2:15 p.m., *Shediac* drops eight more depth-charges, set deep. From somewhere below, large air bubbles rise to the surface of the sea. At 2:20 she attacks again with six more depth-charges, also set deep. Another burst of air bubbles rises to the surface, along with a gush of diesel oil. *Shediac*'s asdic operator hears the sound of a submarine blowing its tanks. *Shediac* reports this information to *St Croix*, and all the guns of the two ships train on the spot where they think the u-boat may break the surface.

Lieutenant John D. Devlin, RCNVR, *St Croix*'s ASW officer, has just joined the ship's company. He hasn't the long experience of the now departed Lieutenant Earl, but he is eager to show his stuff. It is 2:25 p.m. He hears the echo of the asdic and sees the contact on the trace recorder at the same time:

"Contact, sir. 500 yards. Astern of *Shediac*. It's pretty solid, sir."

"Fire on indication, Mr Devlin."

Devlin watches the trace recorder, then pushes the firing button. Six Mark 7 depth-charges go down, two off the beam throwers, four off the stern. The sea broils up in *St Croix*'s wake. There is neither wreckage nor fuel oil.

"Sweep astern, Mr Devlin."

"Aye, aye, sir. Contact. Bearing 160, range 400. Firing on indication." Dobson orders hard a starboard and *St Croix* heels over in a sharp turn. We ought to come out right over it, Dobson thinks. Then, almost immediately, Devlin hits the firing button. Six more depth-charges go into the sea, followed by six more explosions below.

"Lost contact, sir."

"Carry out an observant," Dobson orders. They will search for wreckage and human remains. He is positive they and *Shediac* have bagged a u-boat, but they find only traces of diesel oil and more air bubbles. They don't know it, but they have run into Group Robbe, designated to attack convoys bound for the Strait of Gibraltar.

At 3:10 p.m., *St Croix* and *Shediac* head back to the convoy, rejoining two hours and forty minutes later. In time, the Admiralty will assess the attack reports of the two escorts and conclude that the Canadian warships have "probably slightly damaged" a German submarine. In fact, *St Croix* and *Shediac* have destroyed *U87* homeward bound after taking part in an attack against convoy UCI south of the Azores.

Twilight comes on. Dobson looks at the sky. It is going to be a fine evening. He calls for a cup of coffee and settles into his chair, lighting his pipe. The bosun pipes "cooks to the galley," then "hands to supper." The smell of food wafts up from below. It will be lamb tonight. He looks at his wristwatch, for he's getting hungry. Young Mr Page, the subbie, is due on watch in a few minutes. He's just getting the hang of it. Dobson decides to wait a bit before he eats so he can observe how Page is doing. Page is trying to get his watch-keeping certificate by the time they return to the United Kingdom.

"Sir, message from *Burwell*. Aircraft approaching from the west." It is 7:10 p.m. Three more Focke-Wulf 200s are coming at the convoy with the evening sun at their tails. Dobson spots them almost immediately. They are somewhat lower than the pair that attacked them earlier in the morning.

St Croix goes to action stations, and so does the rest of the convoy. The bombers circle the ships, then attack one of the stragglers just to the rear of the starboard wing column. Three columns of water rise near the ship, one ahead, one on each side, as the convoy's guns open up. The bombers are too high. Neither side draws blood, and the bombers head almost due east as the convoy secures from action stations. Two more German bombers show up the next day, but they do not attack and stay well out of range.

On 6 March, at 12:02 p.m., *St Croix* detects a nearby U-boat transmission and heads off to the west in company with *Napanee*, Dobson's old command. They run for close to an hour but find nothing, and return to the convoy at 1:45 p.m., taking station some 2000 yards ahead of it. At 2:18 p.m. the third ship in the first column, *Fort Pascoyac*, is torpedoed. A minute later the fifth ship in the fifth column, *Fort Battle River*, is also torpedoed. The first merchantman is only slightly damaged and able to proceed. The second takes water in the stern and begins to settle. Between 2:20 and 3:03 p.m., *St Croix* makes three depth-charge attacks without results. The water astern of the convoy has been stirred up by the passing of the merchantmen, and asdic conditions deteriorate by the minute as more depth-charges go down. *Shediac* too hunts astern, but gains no results. There are no more attacks from enemy aircraft or submarines. Late on the afternoon of Sunday, 7 March, *Burwell* and *St Croix*, low on fuel, leave the convoy and steam ahead to Gibraltar. *St Croix* secures at berth 27 at 8:50 p.m.

———————

The day after *St Croix* departs Londonderry for Gibraltar, one of the most important gatherings of the Second World War opens in Washington. It is the Atlantic Convoy Conference bringing together representatives of the United States Navy, the Royal Navy, and the Royal Canadian Navy to discuss the current state of the Battle of the Atlantic. The conference opens on a discordant note. US Admiral Ernest J. King, unable to commit large numbers of destroyers to the North Atlantic battle, threatens to pull the USN out of the fight. The Canadians, on the other hand, demand full command responsibility for naval and convoy operations in the northwest Atlantic. They are, after all, bearing a much greater load than is the small US contingent. In the end, the conference recommends that US control over the western part of the North Atlantic be lifted, that the USN take general responsibility for southern convoy routes, and that the Canadians assume control of a new war zone dubbed Canadian North West Atlantic Command. Canadian Rear-Admiral L.W. Murray is named Commander-in-Chief of this new Command area. Royal Navy control is extended westward past the middle of the Atlantic. Murray thereby becomes the only Canadian to command an Allied theatre of war in the Second World War.

But that is not all the conference does. It also decides on a concerted drive to rid the North Atlantic of the u-boat menace. The British have determined that the size of a convoy seems to have no bearing on the number of ships it loses. It is the size of the escort that matters. There will, therefore, be larger but fewer convoys. This new system will allow the Canadians and British to enlarge their escort groups from an average of six to nine escorts per group. There will also be more escort groups, more support groups, and more escort carriers, such as USS *Bogue*. The Royal Canadian Air Force is finally allotted enough VLR Liberators to fly air cover over the western Atlantic from Newfoundland. The air gap will be closed.

As if to underscore the importance and necessity of the decisions made at this conference, convoys SC122 and HX229 depart New York on 5 March and 8 March, respectively, just as the conference breaks up. The two convoys are escorted to the Western Ocean Meeting Point (WESTOMP) mainly by Canadian ships, then handed over to two RN groups, B4 and B5. Alerted by deciphered British radio transmissions, Dönitz concentrates four wolfpacks with a total of forty-four U-boats in the path of the two convoys. The battle begins on the night of 16/17 March; when it ends on 19 March, twenty-one merchantmen have been sunk and not one U-boat has been destroyed.

The slaughter of these combined convoys is the last of its kind. The US support group built around the USS *Bogue* and four new British support groups (one with escort carrier HMS *Biter*), backed by end-to-end air cover by the RCAF and RAF, begins to take a heavy toll of U-boats. The aircraft from these carriers bring the war to the U-boats as do the new dedicated sub-killing ships such as the US destroyer escorts and the British River Class frigates. The support groups are especially effective in destroying the U-boat supply system that Dönitz has built since the start of the war. Milk cow after milk cow is tracked down and sunk. Of ten operating in the spring of 1943, only two are still afloat by the end of the summer. The U-boats must cut their war patrols short.

The Canadians, too, acquire new escort vessels in mid-1943. First comes a second generation of six River Class destroyers, ex-RN vessels. In June the RCN also begins to take delivery of its first seventy River Class frigates, virtually all of which are built in Canada. The arrival of these new ships allows the RCN to form its first all-Canadian support group in June.

Gibraltar is the main British base in the western Mediterranean. Neither Dobson nor any of his crew has been there before. It is an eerie place, blacked out every night, with the lights of Algeciras twinkling across the bay. British and American warships, from large fleet carriers to cruisers to destroyers, are secured at berths or anchored to mooring buoys in the harbour. Escort groups come and go as patrol vessels ply the waters of the Strait of Gibraltar to detect U-boats trying to slip into the Mediterranean from the Atlantic. The port is crowded with service-men, refugees, and Spanish shipyard workers. The bars teem with sailors. Dobson wants to spend a few hours hiking up the side of the Rock, but the paths are closed for security reasons. Besides, there is al-most no time. CI sails on the afternoon of 8 March to accompany con-voy KMS9 to the United Kingdom. Dobson is Senior Officer again.

The passage takes five days. On Friday afternoon, 12 March, a lone Focke-Wulf shadows the convoy for some hours before dropping a few bombs, which hit nothing. The following day the corvette *Prescott* sights a surfaced submarine and rushes to the attack. Dobson assigns *Napanee* to her aid and orders the convoy to make two emergency turns to port to throw the attackers off. *Napanee* and *Prescott* search for the submarine until the early morning hours of Sunday, 14 March, when they return to the convoy. Another German bomber begins to track the convoy the next morning, but does not attack. *St Croix* and most of CI leave KMS9 late on Sunday afternoon and anchor off Moville; *Napanee* and *Baddeck*, another Canadian corvette, stay with the convoy a while longer.

St Croix's sentence to the Gibraltar run has expired. Most of the RCN escort groups begin to return to the North Atlantic, and she is no excep-tion. Battling frequent breakdowns of steering gear and other vital equipment, she joins *St Laurent* in Iceland in early April to escort ONS2 to the east coast of Canada. She is plagued with equipment failure and arrives late. She is assigned to sweep far ahead of the convoy, where she spots an open lifeboat and picks up the survivors of *Ingerfire*, a straggler from ONS1 sunk only hours earlier. *St Croix* makes two more crossings with CI in April and May, escorting SC127 and ON184.

The Allied offensive against the wolfpacks that was portended by the Atlantic Convoy Conference peaks in May 1943; forty-seven U-boats are destroyed in that month alone. For the most part, the Royal Canadian Navy does not share in the mass killing. It has neither the offensive power nor the up-to-date equipment to match the Royal Navy and the United States Navy. Instead, it continues to carry out its close escort missions, though with a great deal more skill than before.

In early May convoy HX237 is met off the coast of Newfoundland by Escort Group C2, consisting of three RCN corvettes, two RN corvettes, and one RN destroyer. An RN support group built around the escort car-rier HMS *Biter* sweeps far ahead of the convoy and enables it to break

through a u-boat patrol line set up by Group Löwenherz. The RCN
corvette *Drumheller* combines with an RCAF Sunderland of 423 Squadron
flying out of Castle Archdale, Northern Ireland, and the RN destroyer
Lagan to sink *U753* on 13 May. The convoy loses no ships. The tide has
clearly turned.

St Croix plays no role in the spring offensive. She has not had a refit
in six months and her aging equipment needs rest and repair. When her
generators cease functioning at the start of June, she returns to Halifax.
It is an unusually warm spring on the Canadian east coast. Dobson
spends as much time as he can with Gertrude and the children. The
warm air, the flowers in bloom, and the budding trees add to the feeling
of optimism. It is an open secret that the Battle of the Atlantic is going
well. In fact, the news is good from almost all the war fronts. Dobson
has always taken the sea as he has found it. He has no expectations from
wind and wave. It is the life he has chosen. War has made that life
more complicated and certainly deadlier, but the sea remains as it always was, immutable in all its moods. In the meantime, the beat of
Bolero intensifies.

8

Deadly Encounter: *U305* and *St Croix*

RUDOLF BAHR'S near-catastrophic second patrol represents the U-boat experience in microcosm. May 1943 is a disaster. German submarines go down at the rate of more than one a day. To be precise, Admiral Dönitz calculates that 31 of the 120 U-boats operating in the Atlantic are destroyed in the first three weeks of May. A 26 percent reduction in force in twenty-one days! On 24 May Admiral U-boats draws the obvious but drastic consequences and calls off the Battle of the North Atlantic; he instructs his boats to go to less dangerous waters southwest of the Azores to operate against convoys running between the United States and Gibraltar. "Losses in May have reached an impossible level."

The Commander-in-Chief of the German navy harbours no illusions about the slaughter that has just taken place in the Atlantic and the Bay of Biscay. Quick work by his staff fine-tunes the rough statistics. Whereas 148 boats, 148 captains, and 6356 men were lost in the first forty months of the war, 112 boats with 112 captains and 5534 men are destroyed from January to June 1943. Put differently, whereas before March 1943 the u-boats had destroyed 100,000 tons of Allied shipping for every boat lost, that ratio after March is down to 10,000 tons for every u-boat. Six out of every ten boats lost are because of air attacks. And among those officers and ratings whose ships are attacked and incapacitated on the surface, only one in ten survives. "The overall situation in the u-boat war," Dönitz later concedes, "was bitterly serious and tense." How long, Dönitz queries himself, can he justify this carnage?

But what to do? British and American strategic bombers continue to run their murderous missions over German cities day and night. Between 24 and 27 July, Hamburg is turned into a blazing inferno by Operation Gomorrah. Cinders—which Dönitz first suspects to be evidence of "bacteriological warfare"—fall as far away as Kiel on the Baltic Sea. Allied freighters, and especially the American mass-produced Liberty ships, run vital supplies to the Soviet Union without interruption. And American forces and their equipment land in Britain with impunity. It is only a matter of time, Dönitz lectures his staff, before these forces will assault Fortress Europe. It is the duty of the Kriegsmarine—and that means the u-boats—to repel the invasion. The grey wolves must continue to stalk their prey, even if there is "no longer any chance of major success."

Grand Admiral Dönitz is adamant that the fight must continue. "We have succumbed to a technical problem," he lectures his staff, "but we shall find a solution." Bahr's very life depends on that! Dönitz reminds his men that they, and they alone, are keeping Allied forces tied up in the Atlantic, B-24s and Lancasters away from German towns, and the Red Tide out of civilized Europe. The outcome of the global war now hangs on the Battle of the Atlantic. And that, in turn, depends entirely on the u-boats. Every officer and every seaman needs to keep before him but one word: *Tonnagekrieg*. Sink more ships than the enemy can build, and you will win the war. It is a simple matter of double-entry accounting. "Find, engage, destroy!"

Dönitz is certain that his "cubs" are fully with him. "Deportment of commanders and crews is unbendingly firm and full of fight." To the few who might be wavering, he offers stirring rhetoric, appealing to their "spiritual tenacity," their "spiritual force," and their "spiritual bearing." He demands iron discipline. "Be strong! Do not falter! The foe, too, is weary!" In mid-June 1943 Dönitz lectures his skippers to remember the old military and naval adage: "Better to perish with honour than to strike the colours."

And he falls back on the "heroic" example of his Führer for inspiration. Dönitz's ringing decree of September 1943, "On Combatting Smear Campaigns and Petty Complaints," is quintessential Nazi fare. He rails against "those who openly transmit their own miserable attitudes to their comrades" and threatens them with "summary courtsmartial." He demands that the Führer's "National-Socialist Weltanschauung," this "precious unity," be defended "with rigour, patience, and steadfastness, through our struggle, our work, and our silence." In short, he orders his 30,000 submariners to persevere unto death. "Faith in the Führer is a German officer's first and foremost duty." And he promises new weapons that will snatch victory from the jaws of defeat at the eleventh hour. Rudolf Bahr and *U305* will be among the first to receive them.

As required, Bahr turns in his after-action report and then heads straight for the Casino Bar. Unsuccessful Kaleus are not invited to the Châteauneuf! But Madame is as gracious as ever. The Beaujolais and champagne flow in rivers, the shrimp and snails are passed around generously, and the piano hammers out the same old tunes. The lovelies are just as lovely and just as accommodating as before. But somehow things have changed. There had been no boisterous reception at the pier when *U305* limped into port on 1 June: only a few fellow skippers and one or two *Blitzmädchen* from the hospital. The streets are now darkened at night. Hostile bombers, it seems, drone overhead almost constantly. The heavy Flak can be heard from as far away as Quessant. Many of the U-boat pens are empty, a sure sign that the tide has turned in the Battle of the Atlantic. And so many highly decorated aces, with their Knight's Crosses adorned with oak leaves and swords and diamonds, have disappeared. In their place have come an army of former schoolboys and Hitler Youth. Children marching off to war!

A week later, Bahr receives the official reaction of the Operations Division, Admiral U-boats, to his after-action report. After conceding in a single sentence that his boat had been severely pounded from the air, it concludes: "Opportunities for success were not accorded the commander; nothing more to be added." The son of a bitch! Easy for the staffers in their crisp double-breasted navy blues, enduring the rigours of war in their châteaux and Sheherezades, to write sarcastic fitness reports. To hell with them! Time to visit the family at Landsberg. It has been more than a year since Bahr has seen them. The rest of the crew also go on furlough.

While officers and ratings are on leave, *U305* is laid up for more than two months in dry dock at Brest. She is a beaten boat. Battalions of engineers, welders, machinists, riveters, mechanics, and electricians work on her day and night. The damaged cells in Battery 2 are ripped out and replaced. The galley hatch is refitted and made watertight—again! The troublesome foreplanes are repaired. New foundations are installed for the two compressors. The cracked ballast tank receives new panels. The naval engineers at Brest rip her bow off and painstakingly reconstruct the four torpedo tubes and their outer doors.

And then work begins to instal the new gear. First off, *U305* receives a second Flak platform called the *Wintergarten* to house a new Flak defence suite known as Turm 4: a pair of twin 2-cm anti-aircraft guns called *Flakvierlinge*. On 30 June Dönitz decrees that no boat would put out to sea without these quadruple cannons. High time: ten of the seventeen boats that try to navigate the Bay of Biscay late in July 1943 are destroyed. Dönitz issues precise instructions to his commanders: "In case of doubt, stay up top and shoot." Although the new Flak can spew out 240 rounds per minute, it has an effective range of only 3000 feet, hardly sufficient to prevent an F4F Wildcat or a TBF Avenger from dropping its lethal loads. The promised 3.7-cm guns are still not ready.

Second, Dönitz's electronic wizards have been busy in the laboratories coming up with a better FuMB, one that can detect Allied ASV Mk III radar. They are aided in this development by photocopies of the Canadian SCR 602 radar obtained by German agents. The researchers develop the *Hagenuk*, so named after its manufacturer. Technically, the new FuMB 9, rushed to the front in August 1943, is a frequency scanner, or *Wellenanzeiger* (*Wanz*), that features automatic frequency search on the entire range twenty-four times a second. *U305* is one of the first boats to receive the *Wanz* GI—as well as a new, round dipole (*Runddipol*) permanent antenna. To make sure that his skippers do not get into a defensive frame of mind, Dönitz cautions them that *Hagenuk* should not "affect the tactics of boats near the convoy" or persuade boats "to submerge if the enemy is not in sight." U-boat commanders quickly discover not only that the *Hagenuk* does not cover the 9.7-cm wavelength of the ASV MK III radar but also that it radiates. No sooner installed, Dönitz will order it removed from boats early in November 1943.

Most important, *U305* is one of the first boats to get the new "top secret" G7ES torpedoes. For months now, the Torpedo Directorate has been testing a new "destroyer cracker" at Gotenhafen. Experienced commanders such as Lieutenant Bahr, from experienced boats such as *U305*, are brought to Gotenhafen for three days to be briefed on the new weapon, officially classified as T5. At 24 knots, it is 4 knots faster than any torpedo in Dönitz's arsenal. It has the new Pi4 non-contact and impact pistol and a highly sensitive acoustic homing device.

Bahr has to postpone his visit to Landsberg and instead heads for Gotenhafen. There, at the Torpedo Directorate, he is taken into a hall where a T5 model is mounted on a pivot and told to stand 3 feet away from its nose and rattle his keys. The damned thing actually turns towards him! An acoustic torpedo at last. It is capable of picking up the propeller noises of a hostile destroyer running at 15 knots at a range of 350 yards.

Bahr is assured that the "wren" (*Zaunkönig*)—which the Allies call a "gnat" (German Naval Acoustic Torpedo)—will "revolutionize" the U-boat war. Captain Ulrich Thilo, head of the Torpedo Training School, takes Bahr out into the Baltic Sea on a high-speed motorboat at night to witness a hands-on demonstration. Peering over the rail at the grey waters of Danzig Bay, Bahr spots a greenish, iridescent eel in the water. The motorboat begins evasive action. It turns hard to port; the eel follows. It veers to starboard; the eel follows. It zigzags; the eel follows. Whether it slows or accelerates, the boat cannot shake the pursuer. Finally, the wren ducks under the target just as it has been pre-set to do. But then the bloody thing turns around and comes at the motorboat a second time! Again, it ducks under the target. And again, it turns in a circle and comes at Bahr a third time. These "ladder" patterns continue until its batteries are exhausted. A FAT with an acoustic homing device: it's a marvel!

Bahr is also instructed to fire the T5 only when submerged and running on the electric motors, because the wren is supersensitive to any noise, regardless of origin. Thereafter, he is instructed to dive immediately so that his own boat will not fall prey to an errant T5. Moreover, the Kaleus are cautioned that the torpedo has a short arming range of only 450 yards—designed precisely to "crack" tin cans bearing down hard on U-boats. Reacting to Dönitz's incessant pleas, Albert Speer, Minister of Armaments and Ammunition, has rushed eighty of the new eels to twenty front boats, including *U305*.

On completion of the torpedo training course, Bahr heads for Landsberg for the first time in almost two years. The war has turned ugly for Germany. At every major train station, he is confronted by massive destruction of the inner cores of the cities. The American President has accurately described the Führer's Fortress Europe as one without a roof! Bahr's trains are frequently delayed because of air raids, and often rerouted on to makeshift lines because of the random destruction of bridges and tracks. While on leave, Bahr hears the news that on 24 July the Duce, Benito Mussolini, has been removed from power by the Fascist Grand Council. Will Italy again become the diplomatic whore of Europe, as in July 1914?

Landsberg, at least, has been spared the devastation from above. So far! There are still eggs and butter, cheese and milk to be had from local farmers. The first fruits are ripening on the trees and the fields of grain and beets are verdant, a good sign that his parents will survive the coming winter. There is even *Schnaps* at Bahr's favourite Kneipe by the banks of the Warthe River.

Still, Bahr's thoughts remain out at sea. How are the Allies able to pinpoint his whereabouts with such precision? No matter where or when *U305* surfaced on its last patrol, it was met by an intruder from the sky—one that immediately brought destroyers in his trail. The customary shower of *Fliebos* and *Wabos* at all times is followed by rockets and torpedoes launched from aircraft, and hedgehogs fired off the bows of tin cans. Asdic pings dog the boats on every patrol. And some kind of undetectable sensor—is it infra-red detection as Dönitz claims?—alerts the enemy to the whereabouts of each and every boat during every minute of the patrol.

Are the Tommies picking up and reading the Enigma's Triton, as some skippers insist? Dönitz vigorously defends the inviolability of his system. In fact, German naval intelligence does not undertake a thorough investigation into U-boat radio communication security. But, just to be on the safe side, by July 1943 Admiral U-boats equips all naval

Enigma machines with a new M4 cipher. It features a second "Greek" rotor called *beta* that is put into service by a given code-word. The possible combinations of Enigma-Triton-*beta* codes are in the trillions. Dönitz confidently records in his war diary that the possibility of the Allies "having cracked our ciphers has been cancelled out by an immediate change of cipher settings." Surely no human brain can break such a system? Dönitz dismisses as "improbable" an agent's report from the United States that the US Navy is reading German submarine codes in the summer of 1943.

Moreover, Admiral U-boats introduces new code-names for future operations and a new numbering code for the navy's Atlantic grid chart. And he now has available 400 U-boats, or 25 percent more than he demanded in his great treatise of 1939. Of the boats available, 182 operate in the Atlantic.

But there are problems to surmount as well. The Tommies have changed their naval cipher, thereby putting the XB-Dienst out of service for the rest of 1943. Even at the height of its ability to read the British Combined Naval Cypher No. 3 in March 1943, for example, while the XB-Dienst managed to decipher 175 radio messages, only ten were cracked in time to be operationally useful. Now, at best, radio intelligence can only estimate that Halifax to Liverpool convoys run in a ten-day cycle, New York to Gibraltar in a fourteen-day cycle, and England to Gibraltar in a fifteen-day cycle. Dönitz is under no illusions: "My greatest problem is to find enemy convoys at all."

Dönitz is so confident that the new M4 machine and the T5 wrens will tip the balance in the Atlantic in his favour that he abandons operations against the Gibraltar route—where Focke-Wulf 200C Condors afford at least a modicum of aerial reconnaissance—and on 23 August orders a return to the North Atlantic, "the decisive area." And, given that Allied shipborne radar has a range of at best 6 miles—asdic of only 1500 yards—there is every chance that U-boat captains, who can spot convoys at ranges of up to 12 miles with the naked eye, will be able to run at them hard on the surface and then close in for the kill. It all looks good on the staff planning boards in Berlin!

Officers and crew of *U305* return to Brest by 24 July 1943 and at once familiarize themselves with their rebuilt and newly fitted boat. They also notice that Brest's air defences have been beefed up by two new Flak batteries and that the concrete U-boat pens are being increased to fifty-one. Six days later, Bahr hears that disaster has struck the "milk cows" out in the Atlantic:

"Attacked. Bombs. Sinking at 64N 10W. *U504*."

"Attacked by aircraft. Sinking 46N 10W. *U641*."

"Aircraft. Bombs. Sinking 46N 10W. *U462*."

Treason! That is the only explanation for losing three U-tankers in the same quadrant! Admiral U-boats orders another investigation by the Naval Communications Service.

On 3 August the 9th U-boat Flotilla at Brest, like all the others, receives a terse but clear message from Admiral Dönitz: "All U-boats. Shut off Metox at once. Enemy is capable of intercepting." Dönitz follows this instruction up with a decree that only officers—and not their crews—are to know about *Hagenuk* and *Zaunkönig*. Everything depends on surprise. No leaks will be tolerated. Bahr briefs First Watch Officer Sander on the *Zaunkönig*; Lieutenant Bogatsch practises daily with the new twin double-barrel 2-cm Flak mounted on the new *Wintergarten*; Radioman Ballmann memorizes the manuals for the new *Hagenuk*; and Chief Brenner checks and rechecks the new mounts for the compressors, the new torpedo tubes, their new flanges, and the new galley hatch. In short, the new boat!

There is so much gear to master that Bahr is given a Third Watch Officer, Second Lieutenant Gerhard Dohrmann. Lieutenant! Christ almighty! The kid is all of nineteen years of age. Wonder from what Hitler Youth camp they snatched him? Never mind, on to business. *U305* was supposed to have been out on patrol by the end of July, but installation of the *Hagenuk* and delivery of the T5s has delayed her departure for nearly two weeks.

On 15 August 1943 Admiral U-boats issues a general instruction to his captains for the renewal of the Battle of the Atlantic. The summer has been another disaster: while the Germans sink only one merchant ship along the Gibraltar route, they lose fifteen U-boats, including eight tankers, to the American hunter-killer groups. Obviously, new operational orders are called for. Dönitz reminds his commanders not to forget well-worn tactics. "In the last analysis, the object always remains getting to the heart of the convoy; indeed, if at all possible, as always, undetected." Tonnage sunk is all that counts. The object is to hit the enemy unseen and by surprise. "Basic Principle: attack hostile air and naval units only if there is no other way to get to the freighters." *Tonnagekrieg*.

Dönitz then breaks the principles of submarine warfare down into three major components:

1 / **Approach**. Surprise is the key. The *Gammelfahrt* will dull the senses. Boredom will rob spotters, radiomen, and technical personnel of their sharpness. Remember that "enemy escorts at sea and in the air" are stretched so thin due to "Allied Mediterranean operations" that the convoys will have "only the absolutely essential number of escort vessels." Hit fast, hit hard, hit the first night. The u-boats must approach a convoy like "an attacking animal in every struggle in nature." The Kaleus must first "sniff" out their prey; then pounce! *Tonnagekrieg*.

2 / **Attack**. Once a convoy has been attacked and hence put on alert, there is no need to panic! Of course, the merchant mariners will clamour for destroyers and aircraft. But "on average it will take at least a day until new forces arrive on the scene." There is plenty of time to do major damage. Find a place ahead of the convoy, remain at periscope depth, then attack! *Tonnagekrieg*.

3 / **Hostile escorts and aircraft**. Dönitz concedes that the third phase of the operation will be "the last and the most difficult." The object at this stage is to "decimate the escorts" and thereby "loosen up" the convoy's protective screen. Gunning down a destroyer and a corvette or two will have two salutary effects. First, it will open the convoy's "belt protection" and allow the grey wolves to enter its inner sanctum. And, second, it will exert "considerable moral effect on the enemy." Crews of destroyers and corvettes that survive such attacks will not only operate more prudently next time but will also spread word of the new danger on the deadly seas. No longer will their skippers regard escort duty as a "hunting sport"!

Expect enemy attacks by day or night, as aircraft will direct the escorts to U-boats sighted from above. Expect the tin cans to come at you head on at "course zero." This allows the best possible torpedo shot with the T5s. "Make sure that you remain visible long enough for the destroyer to get a good fix, so that he can run right at you." Then dive to periscope depth, and at full speed run right at the tin can. Aerial spotters will expect you to do the opposite—to run away! Then steam in a circle, return to the spot where the hostile last saw you, approach on electric power only, and "crack the destroyer" wide open; "no problem" with the new T5s. "Basic Principle: Every destroyer sunk means relief for the attacking U-boats in attaining their goal—attack upon the freighters." *Tonnagekrieg.*

The same principles apply at night. Enemy air forces will be grounded owing to fear of mid-air collisions in the darkness. And they cannot operate off carriers by night. Moreover, enemy radar sensors have a range of only 1000 to 1600 yards. Stay on the surface during a night attack, as this will allow you to get a second shot off at the tin can—if need be. The ideal is to get yourself in a position where you can simultaneously fire a fan shot from the bow at the convoy and a T5 wren from the stern tube at a destroyer.

Do not be alarmed by the danger from above. First of all, the enemy's Sunderland and Catalina flying boats are slow and cumbersome. Second, his four-engine attack bombers (Boeing B-17F, Short Stirling, Handley Page Halifax II, Avro Lancaster, Consolidated B-24 Liberator), while faster than the flying boats, are nowhere near as fast or as dangerous as the British Bristol Beaufighters in the Bay of Biscay. Third, carrier-based planes (Avengers and Wildcats) pose little threat; returning captains have described them to Dönitz as "tired cranes." Finally, the planes can carry but few bombs and their pilots will be conservative, as they naturally want to return to base.

Attack is the best antidote. "When there is doubt as to whether to dive, it is better to remain surfaced and ward off attacks." The enemy will approach in a steep glide, drop four to six bombs, and simultaneously blaze away with his guns. "Fire is to be opened continuously from all Flak guns." Standard practice is to "proceed with both diesels full speed ahead" and to "keep the aircraft right astern so as to present a narrow silhouette and be able to use all the Flak guns." Above all, proceed at all times "with courage and tenacity."

Dönitz instructs his Kaleus not to bunch together in groups of ten at a time. Rather, they are to disperse to make it more difficult for the enemy to find them. The day of the wolfpack is gone. "Our goal is a simultaneous battle all around the convoy in order to loosen up his entire security system." Groups of two or three boats are best, as they will attract six or eight destroyers. The more the merrier. "Basic Principle: The attack must develop concentrically from all sides. Therefore, form no groups larger than 2 boats—at most 3."

With regard to electronic traffic, Admiral U-boats urges his commanders to send only the bare-bones details over short-wave and long-wave radio. Be positive! "Do not report too much unhappy news in order not to influence the other boats, for every radio signal somehow manages to wander through all the boat's compartments." Obviously, Dönitz is not concerned about possible British intercepts and decrypts. Quite the opposite. "If need be, send out matters of which the ordinary soldier needs to know nothing by *Offizier* cipher."

Last but not least, another lecture on "spirit." U-boat commanders are enjoined to act in "cold blood" and to fire "lightning fast." Fire first; look later. The fewer questions asked, the better. This new offensive against the convoys will "demand more commitment, courage, and tactical virtuosity than was the case in the past." Germany's desperate plight and the captains' ready acceptance of "iron necessity" will see to it that the job gets done.

"Fucking shit!" Bahr cannot believe what he is being told. Since when is the enemy short on escorts? And since when do opponents arrive "at least a day" after an attack on a convoy? Bahr has witnessed no "prudent" behaviour or slacking "morale" on the part of escort captains. And since when is enemy air down at night? Has Dönitz never heard of Leigh Lights? And since when are Avengers and Wildcats "tired cranes"? Has the Grand Admiral, who prides himself on reading every U-boat war log, not read *U305*'s report on its encounters with the USS *Bogue*'s aircraft? There is no word in the general instruction about the lethal hunter-killer groups. Or about ASV Mk III airborne and seaborne radar!

And just how are the commanders in the heat of a convoy *Schlacht* supposed to position themselves just textbook perfect so as to be able simultaneously to "crack" a tin can from the stern tube and three or four freighters from the bow tubes?! My God, has the Great Lion been away from the front so long? Is he burned out after three years of this constant struggle? Or has Hitler's perverted Nietzschean obsession with the "will to win" fully corroded him?

But there is precious time to be made up! Sander loads the twelve torpedoes methodically according to Dönitz's instructions: four T5s, four G7a FATs, and four T3s, including two with FAT pattern-running ability; and two of the wrens to be in Tubes 2 and 5, ready to fire at a moment's notice. Diesel fuel, lubricating oils, provisions, ammunition for the new Flak, and spare parts are bunkered and stowed between 17 and 19 August. The *Hagenuk* comes on board and is built in on the 20th; it is tested at sea the next day. There follows a quick shakedown cruise, a final testing of the new gear, and then hasty farewells.

At 4:30 p.m. on 23 August 1943 Bahr takes *U305* out on her third patrol. Admiral U-boats that very day radioes his commanders a farewell message, reminding them yet again that he expects each and every one to "resume the struggle under new circumstances with the old toughness and decisiveness." *Jawohl*!

Dönitz might have been less sanguine about the new patrols had he known what was transpiring at Bletchley Park. The brain trust of the Code and Cipher School is hard at work cracking the new M4 *beta* rotor. It gets a huge break: Dönitz does not change his short-signal code-book. Within days of the changeover to the M4 and the *beta* rotor, Bletchley Park is able to decrypt the latest Triton code and to send the information on to the Submarine Tracking Room (STR) in London as well as to its American counterpart, OP-20G, in Washington, DC. Decryption takes anywhere between a few hours and eleven days.

Another piece of luck—combined with good detective work. Commander Rodger Winn at the STR finds a reference in an Enigma intercept to a British sighting report, and immediately deduces that the xB-Dienst has broken the Royal Navy's Combined Naval Cypher No. 3. Commander Kenneth A. Knowles of the US Navy on 28 May discovers the same break of communications security by the xB-Dienst. The new Naval Cypher No. 5 goes into effect starting 10 June 1943. Even when xb-Dienst breaks that cipher weeks later, it takes it so long to decrypt messages that the information by then is operationally useless.

As Bahr feared from the start, the Allies marshal immense armadas of ships and planes to meet the new u-boat threat. The British continue their doctrine of close escort, augmented by an occasional carrier but mainly by three squadrons of forty-five American vlr Liberators equipped with the British asv mk iii radar flying out of Iceland and Northern Ireland. The Royal Canadian Air Force adds a fourth squadron of Liberators based at Gander, Newfoundland. The Greenland Air Gap is a bad memory from the past. Four British and five Canadian escort groups of twenty-four destroyers, five frigates, and fifty-four corvettes, all with asv mk iii shipborne radar—except the Canadians, half of which still have their unreliable, short-range, but Canadian swic or the newer sw2c radar—patrol the northern routes. In the Bay of Biscay, long-range Bristol Beaufighters and de Havilland Mosquito fighters chase Göring's ju 88 heavy fighters and Heinkel 177 Greifs from the skies.

New are the six deadly American hunter-killer groups, each with an escort carrier and three destroyer escorts, dedicated asw ships akin to the rn's River Class frigates. Although British intelligence officers are concerned that using the decrypts of Dönitz's radio transmissions to target u-boats for sinking might tip off the Germans to the fact that the Enigma-Triton codes have been broken, the Americans have no such concerns. Their hunter-killer groups—really, task groups—send out planes to search for u-boats sighted by Huff Duff in advance of the convoy's arrival; more and more, the u-boats have to fight it out with the hunter-killer groups far removed from their real targets, the convoys.

The Americans have developed a lethal routine: the surface group forces a u-boat to go into the cellar; precisely at the moment that it is diving, its most vulnerable position, carrier-based planes swoop down from the skies and attack the "grey whale" with machine-guns, rockets, depth-bombs—and with the new mk 24 acoustic torpedoes, the Fido or "Wandering Annie." Both aerial attack and crash dive take forty seconds—an eternity for the Kaleus! Bahr remembers the uss *Bogue* and its pesky Wildcats and Avengers all too well from the last patrol! On 24 August he tests the repairs done to *U305* by ordering a deep dive to 400 feet. *Scheisse!* The *Hagenuk*'s flange is not watertight; nor is the main rudder shaft; nor is the Resten ventilator. Too late now! The *Gammelfahrt* continues through the Bay of Biscay. Ballmann reports minor "detonations" from the radio compartment on 25, 26, and 27 August—nothing serious. But shortly after noon on 27 August, Chief Engineer Brenner reports gas in Battery Room 2—the same battery that was put out of commission on the last patrol. *Verdammt!* This patrol is starting off right where the last one ended! But Brenner is Johnny-on-the-spot. He evacuates all forward compartments and inspects the battery cell by cell. The culprit: the leaking Resten ventilator has allowed a small amount of sea water to seep into one or two of the e-cells. Chlorine gas levels are sufficiently low to allow the forward compartments to be re-occupied. When Bahr receives orders on 29 August from Admiral U-boats to head for grid quadrant BD60, he is confident the repairs will hold. His orders are to conserve fuel if at all possible, to maintain radio silence, and to await further orders. Once in the area, *U305* remains submerged by day and surfaces only twice each night for two hours at a time to reload the batteries and to ventilate the boat.

———————

St Croix leaves St John's on 5 August 1943, red and white stripes painted on her funnels. She is now a part of the RCN's C5 Escort Group, known far and wide as the "barber-pole brigade." It is the newest of the RCN's escort groups, but it is made up largely of veterans of the long war at sea. HMCS *Ottawa II*, successor to the destroyer whose death throes *St Croix* has so recently witnessed, is Senior Officer of the Escort. C5 escorts HX250 eastward in one of the least eventful passages of the war. As the SOE records: "This convoy has been one of the dullest the group has had. There was no sign of the enemy, nor even a non sub contact to attack. Once the fog had vanished, life was altogether too peaceful."

They expected it, of course. Dönitz's withdrawal from the Atlantic had been apparent to even the lowliest rating for some weeks. There had been almost no U-boat attacks, and fewer sinkings. Was the war in the Atlantic finally over? Had Allied naval and air power prevailed over the grey wolves? Dobson spends many peaceful hours on the bridge trying to understand how the Admiralty's reports on submarine activity can be so damnably accurate. And a lucky thing too, he thinks. It is a gentle cruise and he finds much time to relax in his sea cabin and read his back issues of the Hudson's Bay Company magazine, *The Beaver*, which were in his mail after the last re-fit. With his war record and his service aboard *Nascopie*, he thinks he will surely be a top contender for a permanent position with the HBC when this damned war is finished. Better keep up on company matters.

It is barely a month since *St Croix* emerged freshly scraped and painted from the shipyard at Halifax. Once again her equipment has been updated, but she is still behind the latest generation of British and American ASW technology. In Halifax, her obsolete SWIC radar was dismantled and replaced with a Canadian-built version of the British Type 271. She now has a high-frequency direction-finding set and antenna installed. Her torpedo launchers have been modified to fire MK X depth-charges and her forecastle holds the famed RN hedgehog. But she still carries the older asdic.

The crossing takes only six days; C5 steams slowly into the entrance to the Foyle on 11 August, where, with two ships on each side of the harbour tanker anchored off Morvil, the group refuels. Then, with the compulsory pilots embarked, they proceed up-river to 'Derry, securing to the designated jetty, where the mail is waiting. There is also a message from Commodore (D) Western Approaches, Commodore George Simpson, RN, that *St Croix* is hereby detached from C5 and assigned to a new Canadian support group, EG9. EG9 will consist of the RCN Towns *St Croix* and *St Francis*, the RCN corvettes *Chambly*, *Morden*, and *Sackville*, and the RN River Class frigate *Itchen*, whose captain, Commander C.E. Bridgeman, RNR, will be the group's Senior Officer. On 9 September *Itchen* leads the little flotilla down the Foyle to nearby Larne Bay in the Irish Sea, where the group will learn how an escort group operates.

Dobson and the other captains of EG9 have to learn a new way of practising an old trade. Their mission is no longer defensive; they have to learn how to fight their ships as submarine hunter-killers. They have to learn to work as a team in detecting U-boats and tracking them while leading their consorts to the attack. They learn tactics pioneered by the great Johnny Walker—Captain Frederick John Walker, RN—who has become the master of U-boat killers. Captain of the sloop HMS *Stork* and SOE of the 36th Escort Group in the early part of the war, and now SOE of the 2nd Escort Group and captain of the sloop HMS *Starling*, Walker has taught his escort commanders to approach their contacts slowly, in what has become known as a creeping attack. They set their depth-charges deep and are guided to the target by a consort standing off to the side which keeps the U-boat in its asdic beam. Walker also insists on a hunt to the death, no matter how long it takes. That had been impossible in the early days of the war when a prolonged attack on a submarine by one or two out of five or six escorts guarding a convoy left the merchantmen unprotected. It is more than possible now, and it is becoming increasingly common for Allied escorts to stay on the hunt for long hours at a stretch, and sometimes for more than a day. Whenever *Starling* leaves harbour at the head of her escort group, her loudspeakers play "A Hunting We Will Go." Walker will die of a heart attack at the end of July 1944. During the course of the war, the two vessels he commands account for twenty destroyed U-boats, the most by any sub hunter on any ocean.

Dobson and the crew of *St Croix* throw themselves into their training with great enthusiasm. They are already veterans in this sub-killing business, but they have long experienced the deep frustrations of convoy escort: forcing submarines under, but then being called back to a convoy; picking up survivors of merchantmen and consorts, and not being able to wreak immediate vengeance; seeing ships blown up in the night without even gaining a contact. Now *they* will be the hunters, using new weapons and tactics, and backed by Allied airpower, to carry the war to the enemy. Now it will be the U-boats who will cower in the night.

From Larne Bay EG9 steams to Plymouth, their new base. They are to take part in a new Allied offensive designed to sweep the Bay of Biscay of Dönitz's scourge. Londonderry was for defenders; Plymouth is for hunters. They will depart on 15 September. Dobson is well pleased with his officers, most of whom are new, and he welcomes each aboard personally. They come to his cabin for a short interview. He tells them that although *St Croix* is old, she has done, and will continue to do, yeoman service in this war as long as her crew doesn't let her down.

Dobson's new First Lieutenant, Acting Lieutenant-Commander Percival Francis M. DeFreitas, is forty-three and the oldest man in the wardroom. An RCNR officer like Dobson, he had been born in the United Kingdom but was living in the British West Indies when the war broke out. He knows he is unlikely to get a command at this stage of the war, when so many younger men have gained watch-keeping and executive experience, but he is determined to do his part to help his new captain run a taut ship. *St Croix*'s Navigating Officer, Lieutenant Robert Timothy Noel Porter, joined the ship the previous July. He is regular navy and, at twenty-three, young for such heavy responsibility. Dobson thinks he is one of the best pilots he has ever worked with.

There are four officers aboard who are qualified torpedo and depth-charge specialists: Acting Lieutenant-Commander Paul Simon Major, RCNVR, thirty-one; Lieutenant George Buckman Wright, RCNVR, thirty-three; Lieutenant Charles Alexander Ross, RCNVR, twenty-seven; and Sub-Lieutenant William Leonard Page, RCNVR, twenty-one, the youngest officer aboard, who originally joined the navy as an Able Bodied Seaman. Ross is the only new man among them. Major will run the depth-charge crew during action stations. Lieutenant John Fraser Gallagher, RCNVR, twenty-seven, is the ASW officer. Lieutenant (E) Derrik Ridge, RCNVR, twenty-eight, is the engineering officer responsible for the engines and boilers. For this mission, there will be a celebrity of sorts aboard: Surgeon-Lieutenant William Lyon Mackenzie King, thirty, is the nephew and namesake of Canada's Prime Minister.

Itchen leads EG9 out of Plymouth at 4 p.m. on 15 September 1943. It is a beautiful sunny day. The harbour is calm, but as the ships reach open ocean they begin to rise and fall on a heavy swell. The wind picks up. Following *Itchen* in line astern are the RN sloop HMS *Crane*, a last-minute substitute for *St Francis*, then *St Croix*, *Chambly*, *Sackville*, and *Morden*. At first, they steam west, but next day *Itchen* receives a signal that EG9 is being detached to Commander-in-Chief Western Approaches to act as a support group for North Atlantic convoys; six hours after that, she is told to steer 330° to rendezvous with the inbound convoy HX256, which is 500 miles west of Ireland. HMS *Crane* is ordered to leave the group to join Johnny Walker's hunter-killers in the Bay of Biscay. Dobson is disappointed. The excitement of the impending Biscay hunt fades rapidly. Once again *St Croix* is destined to spend long days in the North Atlantic watching and waiting for submarines that do not come any longer.

At dawn on the 17th, EG9 sights HX256; as per standard operating procedure, Bridgeman places his group at the disposal of the Senior Officer of the Escort. The next twenty-four hours pass slowly as the large collection of freighters and tankers steams towards the United Kingdom. The men on *St Croix* spot ships they have seen before on their many crossings. This time the merchantmen seem more loaded than usual. Every square foot of deck space is filled with lashed and covered tanks, trucks, armoured cars, disassembled aircraft and, most important, landing craft. The off-duty men lean over *St Croix's* railings, cigarettes in hand, and speculate about an invasion of Hitler's Fortress Europe. Some of them remember the early days of the war when convoys half this size were escorted by one lonely destroyer and three or four corvettes. From their vantage on the flank of the convoy, they can easily see five other escorts; they know there are at least that many out of sight ahead, astern, and on the other side of the convoy.

Just before midnight, *Itchen* receives a signal from the Commander-in-Chief Western Approaches: "If HX-256 not threatened, leave at dawn 19th September and proceed to support ONS-18 estimated course and speed at 0800A 19th 056°15' north, 026°55' west." ONS18 is making 6.5 knots westward, and signals intelligence indicates a large gathering of U-boats ahead. *Itchen's* signal lamp flashes the orders to the rest of EG9. On the bridge of *St Croix*, DeFreitas is just getting ready to take the first watch when the Chief Yeoman hands him the message. He calls Dobson in his sea cabin: "Sir, message from *Itchen*. The group is to leave the convoy at dawn and rendezvous with ONS 18."

"Where is ONS18, Number One?"

"Sir, Pilot reckons we'll be about 150 miles south of them by morning."

"OK, Number One. Make the course and speed change. Make sure the Officers of the Watch are informed. We'll keep a close eye on *Itchen* at first light."

Dobson calculates that at these northern latitudes at this time of year, dawn will probably come around 6 a.m.

At precisely midnight on 7–8 September, Berlin orders *U305* to BD9146, there at dawn on 10 September to refuel and to receive provisions from *U460* (Lieutenant "Hein" Schnoor). The two boats rendezvous one day later than planned, and *U305* takes on provisions for ten days as well as 30 cubic metres of diesel fuel. Dönitz orders radio silence so as to assure the greatest possible surprise for the Allies. But by the 13th, Bletchley Park decrypts the order of 7–8 September. Bahr's position is broadcast to every Allied air and sea unit from Ireland to Newfoundland.

At midnight on 15–16 September Dönitz reveals his final deployments: "Form Group 'Leuthen.'" In named order on 20 Sept. 2000 hours in patrol line." The "prongs" of Leuthen's "rake" are to be 10 miles apart. The line is to consist of twenty boats—*U275, U422, U341, U260, U386, U731, U238, U270, U645, U402, U584, U229, U666, U641, U952, U378, U758, U377, U603*, and, in the middle of the line, *U305*. All are equipped with the *Zaunkönig* torpedo.

Nice touch, Herr Grossadmiral! As a fellow Prussian, Bahr appreciates the operation being named after Frederick the Great's smashing victory of December 1757. Although the xB-Dienst is still not able to crack Naval Cypher No. 5, it guesses correctly by "dead reckoning" that a westbound group, which it labels Convoy 43, has just left England bound for America. Almost concurrently, the xB-Dienst learns from an agent in Madrid that a convoy of forty-five ships is about to leave Halifax bound for Murmansk via Reykjavik. Acting on this information, Dönitz sites Leuthen directly in the path of HX256, ONS18, and ON202. There is no substitute for luck.

Throughout this period, the Great Lion, obviously nervous about his first venture into the mid-Atlantic since May, has peppered his boats with countless messages reminding them how to make best use of the new weapons. As a result, Bletchley Park decripts a series of new terms: *Hagenuk, Aphrodite*, and, above all, *Zaunkönig*. Commander Winn at the STR now is certain that something big is up! He equates Dönitz's return to the central Atlantic to "the last dying struggle of a caged tiger."

Winn's premonitions are confirmed almost immediately. By 9:43 a.m. of the 18th, the Royal Navy's Operational Intelligence Centre has received Bletchley Park's deciphered orders from Dönitz to the Leuthen patrol line. The next day a Royal Canadian Air Force 10th Squadron Liberator out of Reykjavik en route to Newfoundland, and shadowing ONS18, sights and destroys *U341* about 160 miles west of the convoy. Indisputable visible proof: the u-boats are back in the central Atlantic. And by the morning of 20 September, Bletchley Park manages to decrypt Dönitz's detailed general instruction of 15 August. In short, the

Allies now know Leuthen's precise position, the numbers of the boats, the names of their commanders, Dönitz's tactical instructions to the grey wolves, and the fact that they carry secret new weapons. Electronic "fingerprinting" at its finest!

German radio intelligence, on the other hand, simply knows that numerous convoys are out there, somewhere in the vast Atlantic. The xB-Dienst picks up a major leap in Allied radio traffic in the eastern mid-Atlantic on 18 and 19 September. This communication reaches a record high of sixteen radio messages on 20 September; most of the signals are to Canadian receivers, including Naval Service Headquarters, Ottawa. Even more disturbing, the xB-Dienst discovers that during the week of 20 to 26 September 1943, forty Allied signals pinpoint the location of a U-boat. Of these, twenty-one boats are located in the eastern and eleven in the western North Atlantic. The grey wolves, in contrast, continue to hunt convoys blind, or by dead reckoning, as Admiral U-boats charitably calls it.

Shortly before midnight on 19/20 September, *U402* (Commander Siegfried von Forstner) sights convoy ONS18 and reports the information to Admiral U-boats. The moment of battle has arrived.

"Alarm!" Rudolf Bahr spots an aircraft with Leigh Lights approaching at 12:48 a.m. on 20 September—within minutes of *U402*'s sighting of ONS18. But Bahr has no idea that another convoy, the forty-one merchant ships of ON202, lies just ahead of him. Two minutes later, the boat next to him, *U270*, commanded by Lieutenant Paul-Friedrich Otto, spies several dark shadows to the north. Otto reports his sighting to Dönitz at 1:55 a.m.—and it is immediately picked up by Huff Duff on Escort Group C3, under Commander P.W. Burnett, consisting of the destroyers HMS *Icarus* and HMCS *Gatineau* as well as the Flower Class corvettes HMCS *Drumheller*, HMCS *Kamloops*, and HMS *Polyanthus*. The latter sends the newest arrival to the group, the Royal Navy frigate HMS *Lagan*, to investigate. It finds *U270* at 2:44 a.m. Fifteen minutes later, Otto draws first blood: his wren blows HMS *Lagan*'s stern off at a range of 3000 yards. A triumphant inauguration for the T5!

Admiral U-boats now orders Leuthen to concentrate against ON202. "All possible boats are to get at the convoy during the coming night. The danger from aerial location decreased by weather conditions." *U238* torpedoes two Liberty ships of 7000 tons each—*Theodore Wright Weld* and *Frederick Douglass*. But wrens fired by *U645* and *U402* fail to find their targets, the escorts HMCS *Gatineau* and HMS *Polyanthus*. It turns out that the *Zaunkönig's* Pi4 pistols are so sensitive that turbulence created by the wakes of destroyers sets the eels off.

Admiral Sir Max Horton, Commander-in-Chief Western Approaches, a submarine veteran of the First World War in which he commanded E9, has witnessed enough carnage for one night. He orders ONS18 and ON202, as well as Escort Group C3 and Escort Group B3 (the Royal Navy destroyers HMS *Keppel* and HMS *Escapade* and Royal Navy corvettes HMS *Narcissus* and HMS *Orchis*), to join up. The merchant aircraft carrier HMS *Empire MacAlpine* is already in the area. He hopes EG9 will be able to reach the position of the two convoys by daybreak on the 20th.

———————

At dawn on 19 September 1943 the signal light on *Itchen's* bridge begins to flash out its messages to the ships of EG9: "Execute course change on my signal; form up on me and steer 310 in line astern." The signal flag is hauled up on the yardarm. Signal flags go up on the yardarms of the other ships of EG9 as they prepare for the course change; all eyes are fixed on *Itchen*. At 6:45 a.m., the flags snap down and the escorts heel over and pull away from the convoy. They head just a few degrees west of north at 12 knots, with *Itchen* in the lead. At 3:50 p.m. *Itchen* receives a radio message from HMS *Keppel*, Senior Officer of B3—the close escort for ONS18—warning that EG9 is being tracked by the Germans and suggesting that *Itchen* and her consorts approach the convoy by an evasive route. Bridgeman orders the group to change course to 040. They steam ahead into nightfall. Aboard *St Croix*, Dobson warns his officers to take extra care, but he does not call the ship to action stations. There will be a long night ahead and he does not want to upset the ship's routine until he is forced to. He doubles the watches, tells Gallagher to pay close attention to the asdic, and checks the radar hut to make sure that the set is working properly.

To the northwest of the onrushing EG9, the RN destroyer *Escapade*, one of the escorts on the starboard beam of ONS18, detects two U-boats moving in to attack. She reports the encounter, then drops a full pattern on one, and starts a depth-charge and hedgehog attack on the other.

Suddenly, there is a massive explosion of blue flame on her forecastle. Somehow *Escapade*'s hedgehogs have exploded just as they leave their spigots. The deck and part of the forecastle are mangled and twenty-one crew members are killed. She is out of the hunt and turns for home.

EG9 steams on. A half-hour before midnight on 19 September, still forty-two miles on the port quarter of ONS18, *Chambly* reports a radar contact. *Itchen* joins her in an attack, and Bridgeman orders *St Croix*, *Morden*, and *Sackville* to continue on. As dawn breaks, *St. Croix*'s crow's-nest lookout spots *Escapade* heading east. Dobson orders the quarter-master to close. He calls up *Escapade*'s captain on the short-range radio-telephone to ask if there is any help they can render. She is a terrible sight to behold as they come near. Deck-plates are stove in. Beams and railings and bits of her forward gunshield jut up at odd angles or hang over the side. The ship's forecastle is black and pitted. All the glass on the forward part of the superstructure is missing. Smoke wafts up from a massive hole in the deck. There is nothing *St Croix* can do, thank you, *Escapade*'s skipper tells Dobson. There are mutterings of "Jesus Christ" and "Holy shit" as they pass slowly along *Escapade*'s length. Dobson orders speed increased as they pull away. Soon *St Croix* spots the convoy and takes up a position on its outer screen. *Itchen* and *Chambly* join shortly after. *Itchen* has had a long night, mounting an unsuccessful depth-charge and hedgehog attack on a just-submerged submarine at 1:42 a.m.

At 9:45 a.m. on 20 September, five VLR B-24s of the RAF 120 Squadron from Iceland are over the two convoys. Aircraft x120 makes the first positive sighting of a grey wolf 15 miles north of ON202. Fifteen minutes later Admiral U-boats radioes: "Convoy AK3931. Course west." *U731* (Lieutenant Werner Techand) has reported the contact. "Damn it," Bahr curses, "I established contact with the convoy last night, unknowingly." It is the first time that Bahr has blown a tracking assignment.

At about noon on the 20th, the laborious process of joining the two convoys begins. *Gatineau*, Senior Officer of C2 guarding ON202, has received a garbled message about the junction from the Commander-in-Chief Western Approaches. He knows they are to join ONS18, but he isn't exactly certain where the other convoy is, nor what course to steer to reach it quickly. Instead of continuing on course—the actual order—the convoy begins to cut to the south, paralleling ON202. It is hours before the confusion can be sorted out. The captain of *Keppel* will later write:

> The junction was not a success . . . the Senior Officer of c.2 Group (GATINEAU) had received the order affecting the junction and the new route in a very garbled state and it had been passed to the [Convoy] Commodore completely omitting one position in the route . . . This mistake had the most far-reaching results . . . the two Convoys gyrated majestically round the ocean, never appearing to get much closer and watched appreciatively by a growing swarm of u-boats.

The task of joining ONS18 and ON202 is further complicated at 4:29 p.m. when *Keppel* picks up a contact and a lookout spots a periscope 5 yards from her starboard beam. *Keppel* turns sharply to drop her ready pattern of depth-charges. The contact is right under her, too close for hedgehog. The submarine eludes her. Then she makes three more depth-charge runs while holding contact. Still no luck. She signals *St Croix*, *Itchen*, and HMS *Narcissus* from B3 to continue the hunt; she must rejoin the convoy to help shepherd the ships together. By nightfall, the two convoys begin to merge, but the ONS18 ships are still too far astern. They will have to wait for morning before they can fix things up. There are eighty-eight merchant vessels guarded by seventeen escorts, a rescue ship, and the *Empire MacAlpine*. *Keppel* is Senior Officer of the lot. The combined convoy is one of the largest of the war.

At 4:13 p.m., *U338*, commanded by Bahr's old comrade Kinzel, prematurely gives the agreed short signal, "Am remaining surfaced for Flak defence." Immediately, half a dozen boats charge the enemy cavalry style as they attempt to break through both VLR Liberator cover and escort screen to get inside ON202. Most of the Leuthen boats do not receive the short signal and dive to escape air and escort attacks. Kinzel's intent is in the best spirit of Dönitz's general instruction. Forty ships in ten serried columns: Who could resist the temptation? Dönitz urges the u-boats on: "Remain surfaced and proceed to convoy at full speed." But the outcome is disastrous: an acoustic Mark 24 or Fido torpedo from a B-24 Liberator destroys *U338*; other Liberators force *U731* to crash dive to 500 feet; and depth-charges from two escorts drive off *U386*.

The Great Lion is not pleased with the course of the battle. Too few boats bear the brunt of the fighting. "All the boats should have remained on the surface as ordered." The combined Flak of twenty boats would have driven off hostile air and allowed the U-boats to "loosen" the screen and get down to the real business of sinking the freighters.

Bahr is frustrated. He's in the midst of the battle, but *U305* just can't get a precise fix on any target. At 2:12 p.m. Dönitz signals the obvious: "Can expect westbound convoy to pass boats starting today. In case it is sighted, operate against immediately at full speed." Bahr searches the ocean for ON202. He knows these waters 1000 miles due south of the Denmark Strait from previous patrols. But nothing heaves into view.

"Captain to the bridge! Alarm! Aircraft approaching. 1720 hours, west by northwest at 1200 metres."

Bahr springs into action. "Emergency! Dive! Dive! Chief, level off at 100 metres!"

U305 quickly plunges beneath the surface. "Has not seen me," Bahr sighs, as no *Fliebos* crash around his boat. At 5:45 p.m. he resurfaces.

"Rear planes 15; front 5!"

Bahr rushes to the bridge. "Freighter at 2500 metres. I approach. Soon discover a destroyer screening the freighter."

Ballmann notifies Admiral U-boats at 7:22 p.m.: "1 Destroyer, 1 freighter. Quadrant AKO259. *U305*."

Bahr follows the smoke clouds on the horizon, hoping to get a good shot in later that evening under cover of darkness.

Then all hell breaks loose. "Aircraft at 250° attacking out of the eastern sun. Range 5000."

Damn it, the spotters must be asleep! Sons-a-bitches! Bahr is all over them.

"Clear the MG! Hard a port! Open up with the Flak!" The twin 2-cm guns on the port side fire eighty rounds at the intruder. "Detect no effect." But the bloody new *Flakvierling* on the new *Wintergarten* does not get off a single shot! Too cumbersome. The Liberator, on the other hand, has no such problem. Its cannons emit a lethal stream of fire, and its pilot releases four depth-bombs. They fall to the starboard side. "Without particular effect." Close call!

"Contacts bearing dead ahead! 010°. Getting louder!" Ballmann has picked up a tin can's screws. "Radar impulses increasing sharply!" The sparker is almost beside himself with anxiety. "Impulses amplitude four!"

"Periscope depth!" Bahr barks out. "Switch to e-motors, Chief!" Asdic pings bounce off U305's hull like a thousand small hammer blows. The sound of destroyer blades is audible throughout the boat. Bahr slowly rotates the periscope 360 degrees. "Destroyer (Churchill Class) in sight. Bearing zero degrees. Range 6–8000."

"On periscope depth, Chief! Action stations! All tubes ready for action!"

The torpedo gang shifts into high gear. "All tubes flooded and ready for action, Herr Kaleu!"

Normally, Bahr would order a fan shot from the bow tubes. Not now! It is time to test the new "destroyer cracker." At 9:33 p.m.: "Correction: Distance 1500 metres. Estimated speed 12 knots. Angle left 060 degrees. Depth 4 metres."

"Tube 2: Ready . . . FIRE!"

With a jolt, Sander sends the eel on its deadly way. Time: 9:51 p.m. Date: 20 September 1943.

"Alarm! Emergency dive! Prepare for depth-charges! Battle stations! Level off at one-sixty!"

Bahr anxiously watches the second hand of his watch as it slowly—agonizingly slowly—sweeps over the dial. One minute. Two minutes. Two minutes ten seconds. Two minutes twenty. Two thirty.

"Torpedo detonation!"

———————

The Liberator circles the spot where U305 disappears, then turns towards the convoy, easily visible about half way to the horizon. The crew has been in the air for nearly eleven hours and fuel is running low, but they must pass word of their contact on to the escort before they turn back. They descend to 500 feet. The co-pilot sees two destroyers apparently attacking a contact, and a third that has just turned away.

"There." The co-pilot shouts over the noise of the engines and points down and to the right. The pilot pushes his yoke forward and banks the

Liberator into a tight circle over the destroyer. The navigator makes his way back to the waste gunner's position, leans out the opening, and flashes his signal light at the destroyer: "Have depth charged submarine 15 miles astern. Can you follow me?"

St Croix has just turned away from Narcissus and Itchen when the Liberator begins to circle and flash its message. On the bridge the ship's Gunnery Officer on this trip, Lieutenant George B. Wright, is the Officer of the Watch. Dobson is standing by his elbow; he holds his glasses on the bomber and, reading its signal, calls out: "Guns, make to Itchen: 'Permission to check contact 15 miles astern of you.'" Wright passes the instructions to the Chief Yeoman, who then bangs out the message on St Croix's signal light.

"Sir, Itchen says to proceed," the Yeoman tells Wright.

"Right. Signal the Lib that we'll follow him."

The Chief Yeoman takes the smaller signal light, holds it in the crook of his arm, aims it at the Liberator, and conveys Wright's reply.

Wright leans to the voice pipe: "Chief, give me 250 revolutions. Cox, starboard 15 to 045. Keep that plane in sight."

In the boiler room, stokers rush to flash the two after boilers. In their haste, they mess up the fuel-air mix. Up top, black smoke begins to boil out of the two after funnels. Dobson steps forward and flips up the lid on the engine-room voice pipe:

"Now look here, Chief. We didn't ask for a bloody smoke screen, did we?"

"Sorry, sir, we're working on it. It'll be clear in a minute."

The voice-pipe lid slams shut. The destroyer works up to speed as the Liberator grows ever distant. Dobson has his glasses on the aircraft, but takes them down every few seconds to check their base course. He watches Wright intently as Wright gives speed and course changes. If there is a submarine there, he'll immediately assume command.

"Cox, port 5 to 040," Wright orders.

The old destroyer slowly builds a head of steam and races eastward into the darkening sky. Dobson decides to take over.

"Mr Gallagher, lower that dome as soon as we reduce speed. Sweep ahead from red 40 to green 40. Mr Major, I want a full pattern set shallow. If that bastard's still afloat, he'll be back at periscope depth by the time we get there. Chief, what's our speed?"

"We should be doing 24 knots, sir." They had refuelled earlier in the day. There's plenty left for hours of high speed run now if they need it.

Ahead of them the bomber is circling in the twilight. It drops a smokefloat and a flare.

"Chief, when we ring half ahead, we'll reduce to revolutions for 15 knots. Mr Gallagher, Torps, get ready."

"Ring half ahead. One hundred fifty revolutions. Port 10 to begin zigzag."

St Croix loses way fast; Dobson holds on to the bridge dodger. The dome is lowered and the asdic repeater begins to ping on the bridge. Gallagher shouts, "Contact dead ahead, range 1200 yards."

Dobson reaches out to steady himself as the ship starts to heel over, going into its turn. He is about to tell the Coxswain to hold course when he is suddenly thrown back against his chair, then against the pelorus. The ship rolls violently beneath him. The roar of the explosion sweeps over him. Its jolt is overpowering. His cap flies off. Everything loose on the bridge is flying through the air. An intense pain stabs at his side. All is bedlam. He scrambles to his feet and tries to shake off the effect of the blast. Then, a split second later, a second explosion tears through *St Croix*'s stern as a depth-charge explodes. *St Croix* begins to list to port. Men on the quarter-deck are hurled into the air or smashed against the after deck-house and the depth-charge rails. Some are blown into the water, others crash down onto the deck. Miraculously, there are only five or six dead, but many are wounded and more are knocked senseless. Some of the men on the exposed upper deck scramble to the well-deck. Stoker William Fisher, twenty-three, can make out Dobson peering aft. Dobson looks very worried.

Dobson picks up the bridge telephone and rings the power crank: "Give me a damage report, Number One."

DeFreitas has already surveyed the scene of the blast. Parts of the rear port quarter are a mess and the port depth-charge rail is hanging into the water, but the engine room and boilers are intact. Mackenzie King and the sick-bay attendant are bandaging the wounded.

"We've taken a hit near the port propellor and we're taking on water. I think we can stay afloat, though. There's five dead that I know of. I don't know how many other casualties we've got."

"He's bound to try to hit us again, Number One. Get as many of the injured as possible into the whaler and the motor boat. Then cut the Carley floats loose and tie them to the boats." If *St Croix* is going to go down, Dobson reasons, we ought to get as many men as possible in the boats and on the floats. Hell, he thinks, we may even get her going again if she'll float, and if that bloody U-boat doesn't come back! Where is *Itchen* anyway? There she is! We well might save the old girl yet.

"Chief, can we get moving?"

"The boys are shaken up plenty, sir, and a few things've come loose, but there's been no serious damage. Yes, I think so, sir."

"OK, then. Let me know as soon as possible. Guns, fire starshell to mark our position."

As *U305* sinks fast, Bahr hears one deep muffled bang and one light sharp crack. Then, a series of extremely loud detonations. "Probably several *Wabos* exploding all at the same time," he records in the war log, "then one or two isolated detonations."

Ballmann peeks out from the radio compartment: "Herr Kaleu, screw noises have disappeared."

"Up to periscope depth!" Bahr slowly swings the scope on its axis. "Dusk has set in." There she is! "Destroyer lies dead in its tracks, listing slightly to port, smoke pouring out of her. The after mast lies tilted towards the stern."

Bahr surmises that the tin can has received a hit just abaft the bridge. Ant-like figures crawl all over her broken decks. Her motor boat and whaler swing wildly from their davits. Smoke pours out of two of her four funnels. Starshell illuminates the grisly scene. She'll hound no more U-boats, he muses gleefully.

"An aircraft circles above the destroyer," Bahr notes casually in the KTB. He decides at once to finish the crippled destroyer off. "Sir! Propeller screws at two-eight-zero!" *Verdammt*! A second tin can has come to assist the cripple. "Course east! Range 6000 metres! Exec, time to finish her off!"

Sander feeds the final data into the calculator in the tower: "Angle zero degrees. Distance 1000 metres. Depth 4 metres!" Then he screams: "Flood Tube 3."

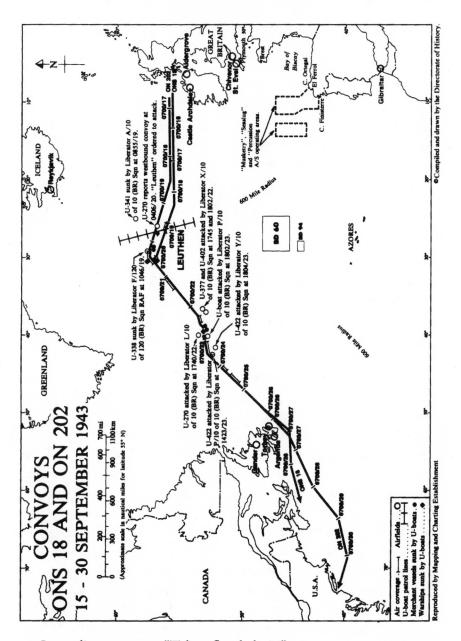

CONVOYS
ONS 18 AND ON 202
15 – 30 SEPTEMBER 1943

©Compiled and drawn by the Directorate of History.

Reproduced by Mapping and Charting Establishment

Immediate response: "Tube 3 flooded, sir!"

"Tube 3: Ready . . . FIRE!" Another jolt rocks the boat.

"*Coup de grâce* out of Tube 3," Bahr records in the war log. Time: 10:44 p.m. The standard T3 torpedo runs straight and true. "After 1 minute 02 seconds hit abaft the bridge. High, red, fiery mushroom.

Heavy smoke pours out of her," Bahr records. "Then cannot see the aftership any longer."

The second torpedo strikes *St Croix* just as *Itchen* is coming in sight. It is the killing blow, especially for the stokers and engine-room artificers. As the sea pours into the engine and boiler rooms, those not killed outright scramble up the ladders, undog the hatches, and pour onto the main deck. Some of the men are badly scalded from escaping steam. Others have had limbs crushed in the blast. For most, however, there is no time to get clear.

Dobson knows there is no hope anymore. "Abandon ship. Get a message off, quickly." The radio-telephone is dead. The signalman hits the keys to the Morse set, rapidly tapping out "Torpedoed, abandoning ship." There is no time for anything else, no time even to flash a visual signal to *Itchen*. Everyone who can dives over the side and makes for the boats and Carley floats already in the water. As the broken ship heels over, Dobson doffs his coat, kicks off his sea boots, tears off his binoculars, and dives in. For a moment he shivers uncontrollably in the cold water. Then he begins to swim through the thick fuel oil and the debris. "I've got to get away from the suction," he thinks, got to get to a boat. With powerful strokes, he splashes towards the whaler. He hears the loud moaning of air rushing out of the rapidly sinking ship and turns to watch her bows slip beneath the sea.

"Destroyer bearing down fast at one-eight-zero!" Christ, Bahr wonders, just how many tin cans are up there? What was that the Great Lion told us about Allied escorts being stretched to their limits?

He again spins the periscope full circle. "Looks like a Jervis or Hunter Class vessel." He decides to run a circle pattern as per general instruction from Dönitz, and then to try a stern shot. Maybe Dönitz is right about firing from both ends when in the middle of a convoy! Visibility: poor. "It is already downright dark."

"Flood Tube 5!" Time to test another destroyer cracker.

"Tube 5 flooded, sir!"

Sander furiously enters final corrections into the torpedo calculator. *U305* quietly positions herself for the shot on electric power. Quadrant: AKO218. Time: 10:53 p.m. Bahr takes a last look through the scope over his stern post.

"Distance 1000 metres. Left bow! Angle one-four-three. Depth 4 metres. Tube 5: Ready . . . FIRE!" The usual jolt.

Scheisse! The bloody wren is a tube-runner! It sticks half-way out of Tube 5! The tin can is wheeling around and bearing down hard on *U305*. Her skipper must finally have picked the U-boat up with his radar or his Huff Duff. He is at full throttle. "I can see foam streaming from her stern." Bahr's situation is critical: "Cannot go into the cellar because the torpedo is half way out of the tube." Only the outer torpedo doors can withstand the tremendous atmospheric pressures at 500 feet depth. Bahr sweats blood at the periscope. The tin can is now at 500 yards! It is the Royal Navy frigate HMS *Itchen*. She is set to ram *U305*.

"Herr Kaleu! The eel has fallen out of the tube!" Good news from the stern torpedo gang.

"Destroyer: angle 70 to 80 degrees."

There is not a second to lose before *U305* is sliced open like a sardine can. "Chief! Flood all tanks! Fast! Down hard!"

The plane operators throw their weight against the handles of the hydroplanes. *U305* noses down sharply at 60 degrees. Whatever is not tied, nailed, or bolted down hurtles through the compartments. Hams and sausages fly off their hooks.

"After 57 sec. torpedo detonations; not *Wabos*," the war log reads. Obviously, an aircraft as well as the tin can above. What did Dönitz say about those Liberators based on Iceland? Not as fast as the British Beaufighters in the Bay of Biscay! Shit! The Great Lion should be out here now!

"Sir! Picking up strong sounds at 020° and 145° on the band!"

Bahr turns towards the radio compartment. "Detect sinking noises." A second tin can in the bag! Good old Ballmann. He can hear a dolphin at 3 miles! Bahr decides to go deep and head away from the mêlée above. No sense in surfacing—only to tangle with that Liberator! And the torpedoes have to be reloaded, anyway.

The torpedo slashes towards *Itchen*, but a cavitation caused by the frigate's roiling wake attracts the missile away from the stern. It explodes 30 feet from the screws. Bridgeman decides it's too dangerous to stay. He radioes *Keppel* that *St Croix* has been torpedoed, that he must leave the scene, but that he'll return for the survivors in the morning.

Bahr's torpedoing of the *St Croix* and the latter's starshell barrage suddenly re-energize the entire patrol line. *U270*, *U260*, *U952*, and *U641* all "march to the sound of the guns" in the best Prussian tradition. Dönitz spurs them on: "The sinking of five destroyers is a great success. Get into contact by daylight today. . . . Make the most of any further chances against destroyers by day so as to have the enemy ripe for the main blow against the bulk of the convoy itself by night."

U260, on arriving at the scene of battle, fires a T5 at the escort corvette HMS *Narcissus*; it fails to find the target and the U-boat has to go into the cellar, where it is pounded by depth-charges. *U229*, already in the area, gets a T5 off against the Royal Navy destroyer HMS *Icarus*, but it too fails to find its target. HMS *Icarus* collides with the Canadian corvette HMCS *Drumheller* as it veers to escape the wren. So much for the "Royal Collision Navy," as some arrogant Brits dub the RCN.

Almost unnoticed in the chaos, the Royal Navy corvette HMS *Polyanthus* has been lying in the debris left behind by the *St Croix* and fishing survivors out of the water. Almost unnoticed. An hour after midnight Lieutenant Oskar Curio of *U952* spots the vessel. The corvette abandons her rescue mission and beams her sonar on to *U952*. Curio looses a *Zaunkönig* at *Polyanthus*. The torpedo streaks for the corvette's stern. *Polyanthus*'s rudder is hard a port as the torpedo rushes towards her. Instead of striking the corvette's stern, the T5 crashes in through her thin sides and explodes just feet away from her magazine. The corvette is literally torn to pieces and sinks almost immediately; *Itchen* eventually picks up only one survivor. Later that night *U229*, *U641*, *U270*, *U377*, and *U584* all fire wrens that either fail to home in on their target or detonate in the wakes of enemy destroyers and corvettes. Bloody sensitive birds!

"Asdic impulses!" *U305*, at a depth of 500 feet, at midnight on 20–21 September makes out the sounds of three destroyers searching for her. The Old Man can hear the whir of propeller blades as the hunters crisscross above. Either they are inexperienced or they are anxious to get back to the convoy: "Very inaccurate *Wabos*," the war log reads. Inaccurate, but good: "No duds." The depth-charges continue on and off until the last detonation at 5:02 a.m.

With the help of the men on the whaler, Dobson pulls himself up and makes his way to the tiller of the crowded boat. It is filled with injured men covered in thick fuel oil. The motor boat is nearby. Both boats are towing Carley floats filled with cold and exhausted men. Dobson tries to keep their spirits up by leading a sing song. Every now and then they fire off a flare. To the west they can see flashes and hear the whump of explosions as the convoy battle draws farther away, leaving them behind. Dobson tells his crew that someone will be back at dawn, that they've only got to hang on until then. The whaler is half awash from leaks and overcrowding. Every now and then the sea washes over the struggling survivors. Dobson holds onto the tiller and calls across to the motor boat to stay close. It is important that no one drift away. When morning comes, someone will be back to find them. A larger group of survivors will be easier to spot. The men break out the emergency rations stored in the boats and pass out biscuits, chocolate, and water. They share the few remaining cigarettes. The weakest of the men slip away from the Carley floats, their lifeless bodies swept away by the swell. Towards morning, some of the men on the nearest float ask to be taken into the overcrowded whaler. Dobson tells them to wait a bit longer and that he'll give up his seat if no one comes soon. He too is cold and wet and tired, and the sharp pain in his back makes it difficult for him to sit. But he knows the welfare of his crew comes first. The loss of his ship and so many of his crew has left an emptiness inside him. Over and over he questions his decision to try to get the ship going. It was that decision which doomed so many stokers and engine-room artificers. He thinks of Gertrude, Caroline, and Tommy, especially of that sunny day when they were last together. Mostly, he is glad just to be alive at this moment.

Dawn breaks over a cold and empty sea. The convoy is far to the west. The anxious eyes of the little flotilla of survivors scan the horizon. Then, they spot *Itchen*. They yell. They wave. They set off the last of their flares and burn the last smudge pot. *Itchen* is still steering to the north, away from them. Someone tears up his cap and tries to burn it, but it's too wet. They tie a rag to an oar, light it, and hold it up. The rag falls into the sea. They tie another rag to the oar and wave it back and forth.

"She's seen us!" *Itchen* alters course and flashes her signal lamp. It seems like hours before she is alongside, lowering her scrambling nets, pulling them aboard, wrapping them in blankets, giving them rum and hot tea, and hustling them below, out of the cold morning air. *Itchen's* crew does it quickly; a stopped ship is a sitting duck. Dobson is the last to leave the whaler. He searches for his officers. DeFreitas, Wright, Gallagher, and Mackenzie King are missing. So is young Page. No one remembers seeing them in the boats. He is told that seventy-six ratings have been pulled aboard; sixty-six men are missing. He is exhausted and cold to the bone. His back hurts badly. He is hustled to Bridgeman's day cabin and his wet clothes are stripped away. Then he is wrapped in a thick blanket, given a tumbler of rum, and made to lie down in Bridgeman's bed. He falls into a deep sleep almost immediately.

Bahr surfaces at 6:30 a.m. Time to put Admiral U-boats in the picture: "2109 bombed without effect in quadrant 0218. Thereafter T5 hit astern ships on approaching destroyer. 2244 hours coup de grâce for destroyer and further T5 hit on second destroyer. Bahr." He is certain he has also bagged HMS *Itchen*. Admiral Dönitz in Berlin is ecstatic: "15 *Zaunkönige* shot at destroyers; 6 sunk and 3 others probably sunk." Germany has regained the initiative "in at least one theatre of the war." Dönitz issues a glowing Wehrmacht radio communiqué, informing Germans that the Battle of the Atlantic has been rejoined!

But heavy fog envelops the mid-Atlantic battle area in the early morning hours of 21 September. Visibility falls to 200 yards. Dönitz, anxious to get at the freighters now that nearly ten destroyers have been reported "cracked," urges his commanders on. "The distant escort girdle can be penetrated by U-boats in the fog, so that when the fog lifts, they can all be in close proximity to the main body of the convoy." Obviously, Admiral U-boats remains convinced that the boats can fight off hostile air with their quadruple Flak while surfaced, pick off destroyers by day, and then dispatch the main convoy by night.

The thick fog makes a mockery of his theoretical planning at the Steinplatz. "Operation against the convoy in the mid-Atlantic was inhibited by fog throughout the entire day. At least 12 u-boats stood near the enemy in heavy fog." Most reluctantly, Dönitz postpones the "mass attack" on ON202 to later that evening, weather permitting. A quick check reveals that seventeen boats, in fact, are still nipping at the convoy's heels.

"Alarm! Searchlight at 100°. Clear the bridge! Crew to action stations! Stand by for depth-charges!" It is 8:12 a.m. aboard *U305*. Those bloody Liberators and their radar-guided Leigh Lights! Brenner takes her down to 500 feet. The log reads: "4 detonations far off, not meant for me." Bahr surfaces at 9:38 a.m. and spies Forstner's *U402*. After a brief conference, the two captains agree to search for the convoys west-southwest; *U305* at 250° and *U402* at 260°. By noon, the fog makes searching an impossibility. HMS *Keppel* depth charges and then rams *U229* in the soup; "a most satisfactory episode," in the words of Commander M.J. Evans.

In Berlin, Admiral u-boats concludes that the Leuthen boats are too far to the east to gain contact with the convoys. At 3:27 p.m. he orders them to steer a westerly course at 9 knots. The object now is to maintain contact with the convoy: "So that when visibility improves, all boats are on to it and the attack on the main body can be carried out during the coming night."

Tonnagekrieg. Hour after hour, *U305* plunges through the fog in search of ON202 and ONS18, but in vain. Over and over, Ballmann shakes his head in answer to Bahr's queries about getting a fix on the enemy. The hydrophones pick up nothing, and the u-boats have no radar. Bahr gives up the chase and submerges at 2:51 a.m. on 22 September.

At 4:14 a.m. Bahr decides to go up for a look. "Chief! Blow all tanks! Action stations! Clear the MG!" The boat breaks the surface and the Old Man rushes to the bridge in search of the convoy. But ON202 and ONS18 are still nowhere to be seen. For two hours, while Brenner and his technical division charge the batteries, pump the bilge, and ventilate the boat, Bahr cruises on the surfaces in quadrant AK4579.

Finally, at 6:05 a.m. he makes a sighting. "At 200 degrees freighter in sight, very close." But the freighter veers off and Bahr loses contact "due to very heavy fog." He must re-establish contact. "Full speed ahead both engines!" The MAN diesels roar into action. After a brief glimpse, the shadow in the distance disappears again. Bahr cannot make out whether it is a straggler or part of a convoy.

In desperation, he orders *U305* back down beneath the surface. "The hydrophone box is extremely unreliable and indicates only a single contact at 305°." Back up on top, he sets course for 305 degrees. "Nothing in sight; fog has lifted somewhat." It is 6:35 a.m. Two minutes later Bahr makes out a low profile 70° off the starboard stern, at 500 yards distance. What can be lurking in that soup? The shadow turns to 60°, sets a white toplight, and then turns to 40°. At a distance of 400 yards the pesky little bugger fires his bow gun. "Shot passes close by the tower"!

"Alarm! Hard to starboard! Both emergency ahead! Dive!" As *U305* starts to nose down to 10 metres, the shadow fires a second shot and passes close by the stern of the rapidly descending U-boat. Bahr goes down to 300 feet. He can distinctly hear the pistons of the intruder passing overhead. "Throws 15 *Wabos*. Set too shallow. Asdic!" Then, at last, there are "no propeller sounds." Bahr later learns that he had been astern the convoy and that the flea up above was the anti-submarine trawler HMS *Northern Foam*. Christ, what indignity! One night you "crack" two destroyers; the next you're almost bagged by a bloody fish boat!

U305 breaks the surface at 10:30 a.m. and reports on the previous action. "Ran upon freighter 0640 in fog. Quadrant AK4579. Artillery fire, *Wabos*, Asdic. *Hagenuk* and sonar completely down." Later, back at Brest composing the official war log, Bahr is pleased with his original choice of words: much, much better than telling *der grosse Löwe* that he almost got sandbagged by a fisherman!

By noon, the seas are getting rougher, but visibility extends more than a mile. Bahr sets a southwesterly course (230°) at 8 to 9 knots, in hopes of running up the side of the convoy and positioning himself ahead of it for a fresh attack—when the damned fog lifts. "Position unclear; for days no fix by sun or star sightings; have seen sun and moon only once. I consider operating according to sighting reports from other boats useless since their sightings probably are no better than mine."

By now, the battle for ONS18 and ON202 has lost all direction and shape. The combined convoys are scattered over an area of 30 square miles. Even in the fog, Dönitz ruminates, they should be easy prey for the grey wolves! At 3:20 p.m. the soup begins to lift. Commander Evans has brought the two convoys up one behind the other on a 7-mile-long narrow front—"a very grave mistake," in his own words—thereby offering the Leuthen boats a target-rich environment.

U666 manages to penetrate the joined convoy's van—a most unusual tactic—and immediately draws the attention of several warships, including *Morden* and *Itchen*. In the ensuing chaos in total darkness, several warships almost collide. *Morden* attacks *U666* with depth-charges. Then, at 11:59 p.m. *Itchen* illuminates the u-boat with a searchlight at a range of less than 400 yards, and opens fire with her 20-mm Oerlikon guns. *Morden* joins *Itchen*'s fire. Lieutenant Herbert Engel quickly squeezes off two T5 eels. One explodes in HMCS *Morden*'s wake. The other streaks for *Itchen*.

Itchen's crew are as accommodating as they can be to the survivors aboard their ship in the midst of a battle. The lone man from *Polyanthus* and the eighty-one men from *St Croix* are cleaned up and fed. The few seriously wounded are bedded down wherever there is space. By nightfall on the 20th, Dobson and the rest of his crew slowly come alive. With little to do, they congregate on the upper deck to follow the convoy battle and pitch in to help wherever they can. Bonds of friendship begin to form with the *Itchen*'s crew. The men from the *St Croix* ache for their lost ship and missing shipmates, but they are also relieved to be alive. They have survived their worst nightmare. As the convoy plods westward under fire, their thoughts turn to home, leave, and families, or a carousing liberty.

Itchen is in the thick of the fight all that day and into the next. It is a desperate battle; on the 22nd the escorts report u-boat contacts almost by the hour. Just after midnight, *Chambly* attacks a u-boat 5 miles ahead of the starboard wing column. A little more than an hour later, HM ships *Renoncule* and *Roselys* depth charge a u-boat off the convoy's port quarter. *Northern Foam* attacks a u-boat astern of the convoy at 4:35. *Keppel* rams a u-boat 15 miles astern at 6:20. As dawn breaks, RCAF Liberators arrive from Newfoundland. Two of them make three attacks; one 45 miles ahead of the convoy, the other two 20 miles off the port quarter.

Itchen attacks a contact at 9:30 p.m. and gains a radar contact on another submarine two hours later. Then, just before midnight, her lookouts spot a U-boat on the surface. Bridgeman brings *Itchen* to action stations and orders his Officer of the Watch to steer straight for it.

As *Itchen* picks up speed, her forward gun crew ram a shell home and prepare to fire. Bill Fisher is standing by the funnel, holding the railing and looking forward into the darkness as *Itchen* heels over in a tight turn. Suddenly, *Itchen's* searchlight stabs through the darkness. He spots a U-boat in the bright white beam. It is about 300 yards ahead, cutting across *Itchen's* bow. The forward gun fires, but the shell lands short. The gun crew opens the breech and begins to slide another shell home. At that very instant *U666's* torpedo hits aft and explodes. Within nanoseconds, the hot gases and the shredding metal produced by the torpedo explosion touch off the explosives stored in *Itchen's* magazine. The shock wave from the blast expands through the thin bulkheads of the ship. There is a wrenching explosion. Fisher is thrown 30 feet into the air and comes crashing down on a gun deck. He can hear the roar of the sea rushing into *Itchen's* hull and the screaming of trapped and wounded men. The deck is slanting rapidly and the ship is wrenched by secondary explosions. There is a loud rush of steam and escaping air. She'll be under in seconds. Where is his shipmate, Stoker Rod McKenzie? He was there just an instant ago. Fisher calls out, but there is no answer. He dives over the side. As he hits the water, there is another explosion just under the surface. A depth-charge has gone off as the stern begins its long plunge to the ocean floor. Fisher is sucked under and almost crushed by the water pressure, but he struggles to reach the surface. He comes up coughing and choking on the thick fuel oil that covers the sea near the sinking wreck. He plunges ahead, trying to escape the vortex as *Itchen* goes down. He looks back and sees the frigate's screws disappear beneath the sea. Around him shocked survivors are clinging to bits of wreckage, trying to clear their heads, trying to wipe the stinging oil from their eyes. The convoy is coming up behind them. They will be shredded by the churning screws of more than six dozen merchantmen if they cannot get out of the way.

The first ship to come up is the American freighter *James Smith*. Her gun crew have been firing at what they think is a submarine running on the surface when *Itchen* explodes just ahead of them. Within moments, their ship is passing through men struggling in the water. Sailors throw lighted life-rings into the sea. Someone leans over the side and yells "Are you Americans?" There is no answer. The sailors aboard *James Smith* conclude that the survivors are from a sunken U-boat. The *James Smith* passes on. Some of *Itchen's* crew are sucked into her screws.

Fisher swims for his life, struggling to get his duffle coat and shoes off. The sea is rough. He cannot see very far, but spots a man holding onto a board and swims over. It is very cold and he is starting to cramp up. After about an hour, the other man slips away. Fisher bobs up and down in the wakes of the passing ships. There are many bodies floating on the water. For a while, starshells illuminate the scene, then they stop. Fisher makes out a small flare burning not far away and yells over to ask what the other man is holding onto. It is a float, the other man yells back. Fisher struggles over and finds a survivor clinging to two life-rings. He slips one on. It is unbearably cold. He begins to slip into and out of consciousness. It is three hours since *Itchen* went down. There is almost no one left of her crew, or of the crew of the *St Croix*. The lone survivor of *Polyanthus* is also dead.

At 3 a.m., 21 September 1943, Stoker William Fisher, born in Victoria, British Columbia, bobs up and down in the middle of the North Atlantic dying from cold, exposure, and shock. He can dimly make out a light somewhere ahead of him. He thinks it is the light of heaven and that he is drawing closer. He remembers prayers taught to him when he was a boy. He thinks about his mother. He is at peace with himself as he waits to die. He knows there is a place he will go to where he will be warm and where there will be light. A rope hits him in the face and he hears voices: "Grab the rope, grab it." The rope is thrown again, and this time he manages to hold on. Someone pulls him to the gunwale of a motor launch. He is grabbed by his hair and his sweater, and hauled aboard. He is hustled up the side of the Polish freighter *Wisla*, which also picks up Able Bodied Seaman Flood and Petty Officer Clark, the only other survivors of HMS *Itchen*.

As Fisher struggles to stay alive in the cold water of the North Atlantic, the convoy battle goes on. At 2:20 on the morning of 23 September,

U238 fires a FAT fan shot at the starboard outer column of ONS18 and ON202. Contact! Three freighters of 15,872 tons—*Skjelbred, Oregon Express*, and *Fort Jemseg*—slip beneath the sea. Admiral U-boats is after the jugular: "Everything depends on boats getting to grips tonight." Bahr and *U305* stay in the fight. At 7:18 on the evening of the 22nd he spies an oil slick and smells smoke to the south. "Course: 190 degrees. After it!" By 8:21 p.m. the fog at last begins to lift. At 8:48 p.m. the duty watch spies a freighter on the misty horizon at 160 degrees and a distance of 8 nautical miles. Contact at last! He radioes Admiral U-boats: "1 freighter. Quadrant AJ9638. *U305*."

In fact, the freighter is close to 10 miles distant and *U305*, in Bahr's words, is "silhouetted bright and clear against the setting sun in the northwest sector" of the convoy. "Must get out of the light so as not to be seen at dusk," Bahr notes in the KTB. According to dead reckoning by the navigator, Senior Helmsman Friedrich Migge, *U305* should be ahead of the convoy.

Shortly before midnight, Bahr dives to get a hydrophone bearing. Nothing. At 12:07 a.m. on 23 September he records: "One detonation, perhaps from a torpedo." Bahr's feelings are mixed. "Hopefully another boat has at least managed to crack my freighter," but he half wishes that it will still be there when he surfaces again. Four unexplained detonations follow. At 12:25 a.m. Bahr orders *U305* back up to resume the search for the elusive convoy. For three days now both hunter and hunted have ploughed eastward towards the fog belt of the Grand Banks of Newfoundland—waters that Bahr plied in the *Emden* in 1935. Seems like another life ago!

"Alarm! Aircraft in sight! 300°. Distance 6000 metres. Elevation 1000 metres." So much for Dönitz's claim that hostile air will be down at night! Bahr sees the bright Leigh Lights in the black sky. "I anticipate the attack. But nothing happens." Instead, the Canadian VLR B-24 Liberator from Newfoundland flies over the convoy—and reports sighting another U-boat, possibly *U641* or *U422*. The P/10 has missed its chance to avenge the *St Croix*!

U305, along with *U641*, continues to search for the convoy towards south-southwest. Nothing. At 3:10 a.m. Bahr dives to let Ballmann pick up a hydrophone bearing. Nothing. At 3:48 a.m. Bahr takes his boat back up to the surface. In the distance he can see the sky lit up by starshell. An inviting environment! But then he suddenly remembers a radio message from *U641* (Lieutenant Horst Rendtel) at 10:11 a.m. on the 21st that his submarine had almost been suckered into precisely such a starshell trap by a hunter-killer group! At 4:22 a.m. Bahr notifies Admiral U-boats of his suspicions: "0158 hours starshell [quadrant] 9621. Starshell 0301 [quadrant] 9375. Am in 9621. No hydrophone contact. Suspect hunter group. That's all. Bahr." Bahr takes *U305* down again.

His hunch proves to be wrong: the starshell at 3:48 a.m. was, in fact, over ON202. For the second time in two days, Bahr's "nose" for convoys has failed him.

But Bahr has not lost his terrier-like determination to bring the enemy to bay. *U305* crashes through the Atlantic swells in search of the convoy. Admiral U-boats loves this kind of spirit. "Make full use of all chances to attack that offer." Wailing squalls and flying spray drench the watch on *U305*'s bridge. The west-southwest wind whips in their faces and the fog returns. The Old Man seems obsessed with finding the enemy. Most of the crew is quite satisfied with having "cracked" two tin cans!

Not Bahr. He drives his boat and his crew on. At 8:57 a.m. he spies starshell at 300 degrees. He is not going to let that "ruse" deter him a second time. "At them! I consider this to be the last chance to get off a final shot—even if it is the suspected hunter group." Nothing will deter him. An aircraft appears on the horizon. "Clear the MG!" The aircraft— another Canadian Liberator—veers off and follows *U305* on a parallel course. Visibility is again becoming impaired. Another aircraft; again it veers off. Bahr radioes its position to Admiral U-boats.

At 10:39 a.m. spotters on *U305* report two shadows on the northwest horizon at a distance of 9 nautical miles. Again, Bahr radioes the sighting to Admiral U-boats, and then adds that he intends to get a hydrophone bearing. Neither radiogram is confirmed by Admiral U-boats. Where the hell are those bastards in Berlin? At the Komische Oper? Bahr sets course at 310 degrees in pursuit of the two shadows. By 12:15 p.m. he is close enough to see that it is not ON202, as he had hoped, but "two freighters" steaming at 10 or 11 knots. Another message to Admiral U-boats. Again, no reply.

Scheisse! These are not two freighters! Dead ahead of *U305* lies "a corvette at zero degrees"! Bahr repeats the tactic that bagged him the *St Croix*. He takes *U305* through a circle pattern to position himself for a T5 shot from the stern tube, all the while letting the corvette close the distance to 5 miles.

"Alarm! Dive! Chief, take her down to periscope depth! Crew to action stations! Sparker, draw me a bearing!" Ballmann cannot establish contact in any direction. Damned *Hagenuk*! The useless toy! Almost panic-stricken, Bahr orders: "Both e-motors, full speed ahead!" He heads straight for where the corvette ought to be. "Nothing to be seen." The sea is empty. *U305*'s war log for the operation against ON202 ends at 4:15 p.m. on a discouraging note: "Am pursuing the two freighters without hope of success." The two "freighters" later turn out to have been the British rescue ship *Rathlin* and the Free French escort corvette FFS-*Renoncule*.

At 5 p.m. on 23 September Ballmann calls Bahr down to the radio compartment for a message in the top-secret *Offizier* cipher. It is from Admiral U-boats: "Break off operation against convoy. Fall off eastward." It is over! Bahr orders *U305* on an easterly course, away from Newfoundland.

Grand Admiral Dönitz has been following the radio traffic from Leuthen closely. He is most encouraged by what he has heard. Reports from the front indicate that from the twenty-five wrens fired, twelve destroyers have been reported sunk and three, "probably sunk." Nine merchantmen of 46,500 tons have also been claimed destroyed, with another two of 16,000 tons damaged. Twelve of the twenty Leuthen boats have had a hand in the destruction. German losses are reported at two U-boats. In fact, only three escorts have gone down, *St Croix*, *Polyanthus*, and *Itchen*. And now that the secret of the wren is out, both the RCN and the RN rush to provide noise-making gear that their escorts can trail behind them to attract the deadly missiles. Dönitz's estimate of the merchant shipping losses is closer to the mark. ONS18 and ON202 have between them lost six ships grossing some 36,000 tons.

Der grosse Löwe is concerned that "the demands made on the boats' crews have reached their limits." Further operations will only "lead to losses of boats, since their capacity for operations is exhausted." After all, the commanders and their crews have been at action stations continuously now for three days and three nights. Dönitz notes in his war diary that *U305* at 12:09 p.m., and again two hours later, sent in the last reports on ON202.

Now that the adrenaline is ebbing, Bahr is glad the three-day mêlée is over. Time for a reprieve. The crew needs it. He strolls through the boat to take the measure of his men. A boyish grin spreads across his face. What a sorry, though comical sight they are! Most are still in their sweat- and grease-stained dark underwear. Many are in socks or knit slippers, with bilge oil, urine, and chlorine brine lapping at their ankles. Their eyes are hollow and reddish, with dark circles under them. Their hair is unkempt; their skin grimy. Precisely one month's worth of beard, stubble, and peach fuzz cover their faces. And they are so young! A children's crusade, Bahr muses, just like the one that Peter the Hermit led to the Holy Land as part of the First Crusade! His Chief Engineer at twenty-two is the grand old man of the boat. His Exec has just reached twenty-one! And his Third Watch Officer just turned the odometer to nineteen! "Christ sake," Bahr reproaches himself, "look at yourself first! All of twenty-seven. And I wonder how I look to them? Probably just as ragged and exhausted!" The men simply smile at Bahr's slightly curled lips and admiring glances.

"Damn it, but I am proud of them!" Seventy-two hours straight suspended between killing and being killed! Bahr slowly strolls from compartment to compartment, shaking hands and talking to his crew. Most of them have not eaten anything except a soggy sandwich while passing by the galley. Stale water has been their only drink. "*Smutje*, break out whatever is left in your refrigerated unit and feed the men! Spare no expense! Ha!" For the three officers of the watch, the engineer, and that national treasure, Funker Ballmann, Bahr opens his private locker and dispenses cognac from a bottle of 1936 Remy Martin VSOP and Swiss Suchard chocolates. God, they have earned it! Bagged two tin cans!

For almost a week, *U305* cruises the Atlantic awaiting orders from Admiral U-boats. Brenner and the technical division turn to their usual tasks: charge the batteries, empty the urine buckets, ventilate the hull, pump out the bilge, and check the twin MAN diesels and e-motors. Sander carefully examines every T5, T3, and FAT left on board. He wants no more tube-runners! Bogatsch is on deck oiling the quadruple and twin 2-cm Flak and checking why the *Flakvierlinge* never got a shot off during the battle. The Old Man was pissed off, to say the least! The crew comes up on deck in small groups to ventilate their lungs. The smokers come up to do the opposite. Bahr lies in his bunk half asleep, dreaming of Avengers and Wildcats, of Liberators and Leigh Lights, of escort carriers and hunter-killer groups.

In Berlin-Charlottenburg, Admiral U-boats and his brains trust undertake an exhaustive "Final Survey of Convoy 43." They quickly conclude that the psychological aspect of the operation alone has made it a major success. Dönitz's men are back in the central Atlantic! They have taken the fight to the enemy once more. The Grand Admiral records in his war diary: "For the first time in months a U-boat group was again sent out to operate against a convoy in the North Atlantic." The "new weapons" made the difference: *Zaunkönig, Hagenuk,* and quadruple and twin Flak. The weather—dense fog—was "very decisive," for it alone prevented the level of destruction that Dönitz had desired. Seven destroyers "cracked" the first day; five the next. Thereafter, the Leuthen boats should have been able to decimate ON202 "without difficulty." Instead, they dispatched "only" six freighters of 36,442 tons.

The lessons learned are straightforward. First, "it is essential that as many boats as possible of the patrol line are always hard against the convoy, so that the convoy escort—aircraft and warships—is split as much as possible and so that the few boats hard against the convoy do not bear the brunt of the fighting alone." No more "cavalry" charges, however chivalrous, by just a handful of boats—like *U338* on the first day of the operation. Second, Leuthen's "aggressive action against the escort forces" translated directly into fewer depth-charges and, hence, fewer losses. The loss of two boats, Dönitz concludes, "bears no relation to the losses by the enemy." He places the latter officially at twelve destroyers, frigates, and corvettes as "definites" and three as "probables"—by any standard, "a very satisfactory result, which might have been considerably better if the weather had been favourable."

Finally, Admiral U-boats singles out the *Zaunkönig* for special praise. Of the twenty-four firings reported, "13 hits were made with certainty and 3 probably (54%)." Only one—on *U305*—was a tube-runner. "The firings were made for the most part from position 0 at distances of around 3000 metres." In other words, there had been no need to give the T5s such a short (450 yards) arming range; Dönitz orders immediate "adjustment" to 900 yards. "It is a disadvantage for the boats that they are forced [by the short arming range] to dive after firing." They must be kept on the surface to maintain continuous action. All boats in the west are to be outfitted with the wrens. Production levels are to be raised from 60 to 160 per month.

Across the English Channel, Submarine Tracking Room comes up with radically different figures. Whereas the U-boat commanders, lacking visual confirmation, report hits strictly according to detonations registered while submerged, STR is able to tally actual damage on the surface. It arrives at a hit ratio for the *Zaunkönige* of just under 25 percent: two rather than ten hits by following shots, two by direct shots, and one *coup de grâce* on a freighter. Above all, London calculates from ON202's after-action reports that nine torpedoes (not three as conceded by Dönitz) had exploded at the end of their run; four (and not two) prematurely; and three in the intended victim's wake. Three had been duds.

For Admiral U-boats, however, there is but one thing to do: exploit Leuthen's success at once. German Abwehr agents in Portugal report from diplomatic sources that sixteen troop transports are scheduled to leave Charleston and Savannah, and another ten, Philadelphia, for Liverpool on 30 September. In addition, the xB-Dienst has just decrypted a four-day-old signal from a straggler out of a new fast, westbound convoy, ON203.

This might be just the ticket, Dönitz muses! Since in the past, operations against westbound convoys were always followed "by subsequent operations against eastbound HX or SC" convoys, "it can be assumed that the enemy now also presumed a U-boat disposition on the W to E convoy route about in the area of BC20." Why not, then, cross the Tommies up and deploy the boats against another ON or ONS group westbound for America? The xB-Dienst decrypt could not have come at a better time! Dönitz orders his eleven boats cleared for action to remain in the central Atlantic, and to await the arrival of eight fresh boats from home waters and from western France.

On 25 September 1943 Admiral U-boats forms the available nineteen boats into the new patrol line Rossbach—again, named after one of the great Prussian king's victories, this one over the French in November 1763. And the Great Lion does not forget his trusty "terrier," Rudolf Bahr. At 1:25 a.m. that day Bahr receives the following from Admiral u-boats: "'Bahr' will join Group 'Rossbach' and will extend the reconnaissance patrol by one position to the south." *U305* arrives in her ordered quadrant, AK6781, at 4 a.m. on 27 September, well ahead of schedule. Bahr is back in his customary game preserve: 1000 miles due south of the Denmark Strait.

But he fails to see ON203. His war log for 26, 27, 28, and 29 September has a crushing monotony: dived, surfaced, dived to get a hydrophone bearing, surfaced, dived, surfaced, dived to get a bearing! Nothing in sight. No contact made. Admiral u-boats grudgingly recognizes that the adversary has directed the convoy to pass Rossbach to the north. But how did he know where the patrol line was? Espionage? Among Dönitz's own staff?

In truth, Bletchley Park decodes Dönitz's Rossbach order of 24 September within twenty-four hours. Undaunted, Dönitz at 10:12 p.m. on 29 September instructs the Rossbach line to steam east-northeast at 6 knots to a position just southwest of Iceland. The xB-Dienst has intercepted another signal from a straggler and concludes that a pair of westbound convoys, ON204 and ONS19, will cross Rossbach's path by 1 October. At 10:54 p.m. on 29 September Admiral u-boats directs his patrol line to spread out at intervals of 15 nautical miles and to "rake" the area. "Starting 1. 10. are expecting slow southwest convoy. Maintain radio silence except for tactical reports. If possible, remain undetected." The boats deploy in an extended line 270 miles long.

By 10:42 a.m. the next day, Bahr is certain that the convoy is approaching Rossbach. "Dived at approach of aircraft 200° at 6000 metres on parallel course." And again at 2:12 p.m.: "Dived at approach of 2 aircraft (land based) at 070°, distance 6 to 7000 metres." *U305* is forced to proceed submerged. ONS19 and ON204 successfully detour north around Rossbach. Luck? Some sort of new secret sensor? Perhaps infra-red?

This time the security of the Rossbach line is breached first by aircraft. On 30 September two planes, one a North American B-25 Mitchell and the other a Lockheed Hudson, overfly the patrol line. It is time to move Rossbach. Shortly after midnight, as 30 September gives way to 1 October, Dönitz repositions his line further northeast once more; xB-Dienst has gotten wind of yet another convoy, HX258. Nothing! HX258 also goes around the Rossbach boats, this time to the south.

Damn it! It is as if the Allies have access to Admiral U-boat's messages. Or is it his staff?

Dönitz moves Rossbach towards the north yet again, bringing the patrol line to within 200 miles of Allied air bases at Iceland. The Allies quickly seize the main chance. Hostile air cover continuously forces the U-boats to stay submerged, where they are "deaf" and "blind." Then *U448* and *U402*, and later *U160*, *U275*, and *U952*, fight off fierce assaults by five US Navy B-34 Ventura medium-range bombers and ten RAF A-29 Hudson patrol bombers. A twin-engine Ventura from 128th US Navy Squadron sinks *U336*; a Hudson from 269th RAF Squadron destroys *U389* with rockets. And Royal Air Force VLR B-24 Liberators damage two other U-boats.

"Alarm! Action stations! Aircraft at 160°. Clear the MG." What Bahr identifies as a "Halifax" long-range bomber dives out of the clouds at 6000 feet. "Aircraft is apparently just as surprised as I am." The pilot blazes away "wildly" at *U305* with all guns, while Bahr's boat likewise pops away with the twin and quadruple 2-cm Flak. Neither one does any damage. "No bombs." The "Halifax"—in fact, another Ventura of 128th US Navy Squadron in Iceland—veers off and does not attempt a second pass over *U305*.

At 8:44 p.m. on 1 October, Admiral U-boats relocates his patrol line for the fourth time in three days: "Redeploy by 2 October 0800 hours 60 nautical miles to the north." They are ever closer to Iceland and Greenland, but there is nothing in sight that night—or on the 2nd, either. Bahr meets up with *U448* (Lieutenant Helmut Dauter), but they also have not seen anything. At 8 p.m. on 2 October Dönitz undertakes the fifth relocation for Rossbach: "Move patrol line another 50 nautical miles 350°. Starting midnight 3 October course 350°, speed 7 knots, until in new position." Dönitz is expecting still another westbound convoy. He learns from a Reuter communiqué that the Canadian destroyer HMCS *St Croix* was one of the three or four tin cans acknowledged by the Royal Navy as recently destroyed.

Bahr points *U305* almost due north. Again, he sees nothing. The only entry in the KTB for 3 October: "Set clocks back one hour."

At the southern end of the patrol line, the situation is not nearly as calm. *U666* endures depth-charges for a good part of the day; hostile Hudsons and Venturas continue to harass the line. By now, Admiral

U-boats is frantic. At 10:20 a.m. on 4 October he orders a sixth change in course: "At 1000 hours course 090°. Speed 8 knots." Bahr dutifully wheels *U305* around and heads dead east. The other end of the Rossbach line over the next several days is severely pounded from the air: Venturas and Liberators from RAF 120th Squadron on Iceland damage *U731* and *U641*. There is still no sight of a convoy.

By 6:33 p.m. on 4 October, Admiral U-boats acknowledges the obvious: "Expected west-bound convoy apparently passed our patrol line yesterday evening." But Dönitz is determined, if nothing else. He orders a seventh deployment: "Today 2100 hours proceed course 195° about 150 nautical miles. Proceed so that enemy cannot detect."

Bahr orders the navigator to abandon the easterly course and to steer south-southwest. By now, the Rossbach group is like a gigantic looping FAT torpedo, snaking "ladders" through the North Atlantic in a desperate search for a convoy—any convoy. Dönitz has now received fresh intelligence from the xB-Dienst that a slow eastbound convoy, SC143, will approach the sixteen remaining Rossbach boats by 7 October. He instructs the patrol line: "Intention is to catch east-bound convoy roughly in AK80 and 90 and to provision boats low on fuel in this area."

Bahr runs on the surface throughout that night. His position is about 420 miles east of Cape Farewell off the tip of Greenland, at the southern exit of the Denmark Strait. At 8 a.m. on 5 October he takes stock of his situation. *U305* is now forty-three days out of Brest. "My fuel oil (55 cbm) probably does not suffice for the coming convoy operation and the trek home thereafter."

A thorough check of *U305* confirms her battered state. Ballmann reports that the *Hagenuk* is dead. Moreover, the GHG (*Gruppenhorchgerät*) passive sonar array is also down. Perhaps the two-dozen circular sound-receiving diaphragms mounted around the forward planes, Ballmann suggests, have been damaged. Just then, one of the planesmen reports that neither foreplane will respond to his touch. *Verdammt*! Just as on the last patrol. Once more *U305* can dive only with her stern planes. And as if all that is not enough, Brenner discovers during his routine inspection that fifteen cells of that troublesome Battery 2 are leaking—again!

So that "Halifax" did some damage on 1 October after all! That explains why the GHG did not pick up anything; the diaphragm sensors are shot to hell! There is no use trying to refuel at sea because the boat can neither crash dive nor get a hydrophone bearing. Without those functions, she is useless. Rossbach will have to proceed against SC143 without *U305*. Bahr radioes Dönitz at 9:46 a.m. on 5 October 1943: "Beg permission to return after catching east-bound convoy. In addition to previously reported damages, foreplanes completely useless. Battery 2 limited. . . . Bahr." Seven hours later Admiral U-boats responds simply: "To Bahr: Concur."

Other boats are even lower on fuel. At 1:24 p.m. on 6 October, Berlin orders Bahr to rendezvous in four days with Lieutenant Techand's *U731* in quadrant BD3335 to pump 10 cubic metres of diesel into the failing tanks. But before the rendezvous can take place, *U731* later that afternoon of 6 October makes contact with what it believes to be a convoy. Could ON204 still be in the area? Or is this the expected SC143? At 8:10 p.m. Dönitz sends out an all-points radio bulletin: "In event of convoy, all boats operate against it at full speed." At 10 p.m. *U758* (Lieutenant Helmut Manseck) reports a destroyer in AK6196. Twenty minutes later, *U731* is back on the airwaves: "1 destroyer AK6258."

It must be SC143—Dönitz is convinced of it. A large German flying boat, a BV 222 Viking, reports a convoy of thirty-nine freighters screened by an escort carrier and nine escort craft. At 11:15 p.m. Admiral U-boats instructs the Rossbach patrol line: "All boats operate at full speed according to 'Manseck' sighting. There is not much room to the east." Bahr has no choice but to give it one last try. He orders Brenner to gear the diesels up to *Zweimal* AK—double full speed, an unofficial command reserved for emergencies such as this! Bahr is willing to trade off an exponential rise in fuel consumption for one last crack at the convoy. "I decide to operate against the destroyer sighted since I can then intercept the convoy where it is expected at dawn." For the next eleven hours, *U305* slices through the rising seas off the coast of Greenland in search of SC143.

It is a labour of Sisyphus. Not a single Rossbach boat establishes contact with the convoy. SC143 has also slipped around the patrol line. Not even the sighting of the convoy by the Luftwaffe BV 222 is picked up by the U-boats. Dönitz is crestfallen. "The convoy operation by group Rossbach is to be gauged a failure due to the loss of 5 boats." In

fact, Admiral u-boats lost six boats—against enemy losses of one destroyer and one freighter!

At 10 a.m. on 8 October Bahr calls it quits. He enters his reasons
into the KTB for the benefit of that staff officer with Operations Division in Berlin who likes to critique the Kaleus. "Am breaking off operation against convoy for the following reasons: 1) For two hours now I
am at the intersection point with the convoy . . . no contact, not even an
aircraft. 2) In event adversary has headed north, no hope of getting
ahead of him in this strong wind. 3) Not a single report of a sighting
that would indicate the convoy." It is time to head home.

At 1:50 p.m. on 10 October Bahr spies *U731* and forty minutes later
attempts the tricky transfer of fuel oil. Heavy north-northwest swells
combine with gusting west-southwest winds to frustrate all efforts
at refuelling. The Atlantic is a furious cyclone of froth and foam as
wind and surge do battle. Bahr attempts to tie up next to *U731* with
standard hawsers; they "snap repeatedly." He then tries to lash the two
boats together with his emergency fire hoses, with the same results.
"There are no other hawsers on board." Bahr and Techand eventually
agree to renew the operation next day at 9 a.m. "We hope for better
weather."

No such luck. A force 7 near-gale that had started on 8 October still
blows on the morning of 11 October and visibility is decreasing rapidly.
Furthermore, *U731* is not at the agreed-upon rendezvous point. At 11:20
a.m. Techand radioes to call off the attempt; given the weather, Bahr
agrees within three minutes. The two skippers decide to head home in
tandem, submerged, and to await further instructions from Dönitz. At
6:25 p.m. Admiral u-boats orders *U731* to take on fuel from another boat
and releases *U305* to set course for France.

The *Gammelfahrt* begins again. Day after day of running submerged
by day and on the surface at night. Dive and run for thirteen hours
submerged. Surface and charge batteries, ventilate, and pump the bilge.
Then repeat the cycle—again and again. At 8:24 p.m. on 13 October
Admiral u-boats confirms that *U305* is to put into Brest. Finally, at 11:56
p.m. on 22 October 1943, *U305* eases up to her berth in Brest.

There is a small but enthusiastic welcome: a military band, several
"lightning girls" with flowers, a few skippers of other boats, Harbour
Commander Captain Erwin Kaehlert, and even some curious dock

workers. After all, Bahr proudly flies two red flags from his periscope head, one for each of the two destroyers that he reported "cracked"! But Bahr notices that the great submarine pens are unusually empty—and pockmarked with bomb craters. The Tommies have been busy from the air!

"Boat moored! Ring off main engines! Reception on deck!" Exec Sander is ready: "First division standing by for inspection!" Chief Brenner has turned out his technical division: "Engine crew standing by for inspection!"

The Commandant, First U-boat Flotilla, strides on deck and congratulates Lieutenant Bahr on the two tin cans. Bahr salutes: "Respectfully report *U305* back from patrol!" He sports a full beard and proudly wears his white cap. A broad smile spreads across his face. There is a warm reception at the officers' club, followed by roast pork, potato dumplings, and Beck's beer. Then it is off to shower, shave, and release the tension of almost two months out on patrol. This time Commander Winter cannot deny Bahr the pleasures of the Châteauneuf!

———

At the naval hospital in Halifax, Leading Stoker Donald Bullock lies in bed recovering from a knee operation. He had slipped while climbing down the ladder to *St Croix*'s boiler-room pressure lock just before she left Halifax for the last time. Nurses come to his bedside holding a newspaper with the headline "St Croix Torpedoed and Sunk." He is shocked. Who survived? Which of his shipmates were saved? The paper has no answers. As days pass, the nurses bring him more details. Finally, one suggests that he call home to assure his family that he is all right. He suddenly realizes they will not know he was not aboard. He calls on a payphone wheeled into his ward. His sweetheart is at his mother's house in Montreal. They are both worried sick and awaiting word of his fate. Two weeks later his mother meets him at Central Station. She hugs him very tightly.

At her home in Halifax, Gertrude Dobson tears open the envelope in her hand and looks at the simple printed letterhead. It reads "Commodore (D), Western Approaches, 6 College Avenue, Londonderry." On it is a short hand-written note. It is dated 9 October 1943:

Dear Mrs Dobson,

I write to send you my deep sympathy in your great loss and with my message send those of all this Command who had worked so long with your husband and his fine ship's company.

As you will know the whole story, you will realize that he was killed in battle against the enemy he had hunted and fought for so long. I had met him here frequently in the last 5 months and learned to know and admire his cheerful quiet and determined character.

Yours very Sincerely,
George Simpson,
Commodore, RN.

9

U305

LIEUTENANT Rudolf Bahr returns from the Châteauneuf refreshed, if not relaxed. Arriving at his temporary quarters at the École Navale, he finds the official evaluation of his third patrol by Dönitz's "God of Operations," Rear-Admiral Eberhard Godt, already waiting. No sarcasm or arrogant condescension this time. "The Commander fought energetically and tenaciously against the Leuthen convoy, and successfully used every opportunity to shoot. Especially valuable is the first eyewitness account of the effectiveness of a T5. Confirmed Successes: 2 destroyers sunk." Now, that's better!

U305 is once again in dry dock—this time for a month and a half. The shipyard instals new gears for the troublesome foreplanes, new diaphragms for the GHG, and new cells for Battery 2. A new radar detector, FUMB 7 or *Naxos*, is to be used in conjunction with a new *Hagenuk* or *Wanze* set. The *Naxos* provides coverage of the high-frequency end of the spectrum between 8-cm and 12-cm wavelengths—the very band in which the enemy's 9.7-cm ASV MK III radar operates. And, finally, there is the new 3.7-cm Flak. This one is no peashooter: it has twice the effective range (2.5 km) and twice the weight of shot (0.73 kg) of the old 2-cm Flak. *U305* is one of only eighteen boats fitted with the 3.7-cm gun. Last but not least, rust is scraped off her hull and superstructure, and both get a new coat of navy grey. *U305* had looked like a garbage scow coming in. The crew is given three weeks furlough—generous, but deserving, after three strenuous patrols in less than one year.

Many of the men are convinced that the Old Man is a superb mariner, tactician, and officer, and that he leads a charmed life. They regard him as a sort of "life insurance policy." They have heard the rumours in the bars that the average life of a boat and her crew is down to ninety days. They have seen the empty submarine pens in Brest. They have witnessed the steady stream of teenagers reporting for duty with the Dönitz Volunteer Corps. But they have now been with Bahr and *U305* since September 1942, and on patrol for eight months, since February 1943. And what patrols!

Bahr is also slated for a furlough. As he heads back to Landsberg on the Admiral U-boats Train along the now all-too-familiar route via Paris, Cologne, Frankfurt, and Berlin, he decides to follow up on a dark suspicion. In Berlin-Charlottenburg he stops in at the Steinplatz: Headquarters, Admiral U-boats. After some bureaucratic obfuscation— after all, the documents he seeks are stamped *Geheim*, or "secret"—he is allowed to see excerpts of the radio traffic (*Funkkladde*) for *U305*. The more Bahr flips through the pages, the more unsettled he becomes.

First patrol: *Funkkladde* for 27 February 1943 to 10 April 1943. Forty-two days. Fifty-one radio messages to and from *U305*. More than one per day. Multiply the total times roughly thirty Raubgraf and Seewolf boats and the grand total is about 1500 messages.

Second patrol: *Funkkladde* for 17 to 30 May 1943. Thirteen days. Twenty-three radiograms. Almost two per day. The total is impossible to estimate, since *U305* had to return to port prematurely.

Third patrol: *Funkkladde* for 29 August to 13 October 1943. Forty-five days. Thirty-seven radio broadcasts to and from *U305*. Just less than one per day. Multiply the total times roughly thirty Leuthen and Rossbach boats and the grand total is about 1100 messages.

These are excerpted pages only, and just for two patrols! How many messages would there be if those for all the U-boat Flotillas, the Training Division, the boats in the Black Sea, the Mediterranean Sea, the Baltic Sea, the Indian Ocean, the Pacific, and the Barents Sea were totalled?

As his train rolls across the reddish-brown fall foliage of the Mark Brandenburg, Bahr cannot get his mind off this immense radio traffic. Although most of the messages he read were brief, some were ten to twenty lines long in the *Funkkladde*. Since the xB-Dienst is picking up a good bit of British radio traffic, is there not a chance that the other side is doing the same? Bahr remembers that a fellow captain, Heinrich Schonder of *U77*, had earlier expressed similar fears "that the Limeys have penetrated the Enigma M key." And Bahr recalls a book he had read at Flensburg-Mürwik as a cadet: Hector C. Bywater, *Strange Intelligence: Memoirs of Naval Secret Service* (1931). In it, Bywater had warned of the dangers attached to frequent and routine radio broadcasts in time of war. Unknown to Bahr, Commander Otto Kretschmer had tried—in vain—to draw Dönitz's attention to the book two years earlier.

Since most of the messages in the *Funkkladde* repeat over and over again only a very few standard code words—quadrant, speed, convoy, course, weather, date, time—might not the Tommies be able to piece together the cadence and rhythm of repeated messages, even if not the precise M4 Triton *beta* settings? Might this explain the fact that every single convoy hunted on the last Rossbach patrol—ON203, ONS19, HX258, ON204—managed to detour around the U-boats with impunity? Surely, Dönitz and his bright staffers can read their own *Funkkladden*! After all, by 1943 they average 2563 radio messages per day!

In Landsberg, Bahr finally has time to catch up on what has transpired in the war while he was out on patrol. The Western Allies, having landed at Sicily back in July, crossed over to the mainland in September. Marshal Pietro Badoglia, the Duce's anointed Duke of Addis Ababa, concluded an armistice on 3 September. Just like July 1914! Well, Bahr laughs with a calculated gallows' humour, we won't miss their "navy" too much! But the Italian tragi-comedy is overshadowed by developments on the Eastern Front. The Red Army's counterstroke at Kursk by late September has driven the Germans behind the Dnieper River. Seventeen Panzer armies—all that the Third Reich had left—were badly battered, if not annihilated.

The good people of Landsberg want to know the latest about the Battle of the Atlantic. Bahr stalls them with generalities, then with stories of individual confrontations on the deadly seas, and finally with his "cracking" two destroyers—one an exotic species from far-off Canada. He chooses not to tell old friends and neighbours about Liberators, Avengers, Wildcats, and hunter-killer groups, hedgehogs, *Wabos*, and *Fliebos*. Nor does he say that the enemy has destroyed almost 380 U-boats in 1943 alone, or that discussions at the officers' Kasino in Brest revolve around not if, but only when and where, the Western Allies will land in the spring of 1944.

At his mother's request, Bahr agrees to sit for a formal photographic portrait. He compares the end product with a photo he had taken while he was on *U69*. It jolts him. The full head of hair has receded on both sides of his head. The once sparkling eyes are dreamy, almost sad. The Lieutenant's cocky grin is gone. Bahr has aged significantly in the two years between the pictures.

Sleep eludes Bahr. He lies awake night after night, struggling to find an answer to what went wrong between the euphoria of Leuthen and the despair of Rossbach. And just what do those *Funkkladden* that he studied in Berlin indicate? Over and over, his mind replays the desperate Triton ciphers that Ballmann had brought him throughout September and October:

"Attacked by destroyer 57 N 24 W. Sinking. *U844*."

"Attacked by aircraft. Sinking. *U94*."

"Attacked by destroyer. Sinking. *U631*."

Why does only one out of every seven boats return? Where are the "aces" he used to idolize? And how did the Allies manage to find and sink all five "milk cows" between June and August 1943? And four more by October? Above all, where is the Great Lion? Does he not know that his men are being slaughtered like lambs out in the Atlantic?

Conditions have become critical even in a rural backwater like Landsberg. While there is sufficient food available—if you know how to barter with the greedy farmers—medical supplies, coal, gas, oil, and machinery parts are getting as scarce as hens' teeth. The little city on the Warthe has escaped aerial bombardment, but all around it Bahr sees bridges, roads, and railway tracks shattered by the never-ending death that rains down from the skies. Just as in the North Atlantic! Do the Brandenburger see the same Lancasters and Liberators?

Landsberg is too depressing, too confining. There are too many questioning looks from friends—and even from family. One evening as Bahr is sitting at the local Kneipe with a beer and a Korn, he unfolds and glances at an illustrated poem that *U305*'s technical division presented to him at the Casino Bar after the last patrol. Entitled "Such a Little Squirrel," it depicts their provisioning at sea by *U460* (Lieutenant Schnoor) on 11 September. *U305* is shown as a little squirrel pleading "Please,

please, fine things," as "Hein" Schnoor gladly hands over a sumptuous sausage. Nostalgia wells up inside Rudolf as he reads the poem:

Such a little squirrel sometimes has it tough.
It runs and hunts and bites and chews,
but slowly the stomach has it rough,
even if it's Rudi Bahr's canoe.
Then comes as savior big and pretty
Engineer Schnoor—Engineer 460,
and gives the little guy power and juice.
Schnoor, once again you did that smooth.
A thousand thanks and may you go far,
once again to you—Engineer Bahr.

It is signed by Chief Brenner on behalf of his division, Second Watch Officer Bogatsch, Third Watch Officer Dohrmann, and Staff Surgeon Dr Günter Loytved. The latter has just been assigned to *U305* for her next patrol because Dönitz's order to engage attacking aircraft with the quadruple Flak has led to a sharp rise in serious injuries on the U-boats. Bahr countersigned the "document" in good fun. First Watch Officer Sander—poor bugger—had been sent off to yet another electronics course.

Not Goethe, not Schiller, that's for sure. With its forced rhyme, it is plebeian, hokey, corny. But God, I love it! Bahr muses. Straight from the heart. The submarine world is the only one he knows anymore. Family, neighbours, friends, former teachers, and school chums have all become strangers. The Dönitz Volunteer Corps, with all its warts and wrinkles, is home. Period.

When Bahr returns to Brest, he finds that it, too, has changed. Madame and the Casino Bar have become distant, the discourse forced. The food at the See Kommandant has taken a turn for the worse: from champagne and lobster to vin ordinaire and bouillabaisse. Flak rises over city and naval base each night. The Allies bomb the submarine pens with 12,000-lb "Tallboys" almost every week. The Maquis conduct acts of sabotage seemingly with impunity. And British Intelligence has eyes and ears in every café, bistro, and établissement. Still, Brest is home. *U305*'s next patrol is scheduled for early December.

Admiral U-boats has shifted the centre of gravity and changed the tactics in the U-boat campaign once more. His boats suffered a stinging defeat on the North America–Great Britain convoy routes in the autumn of 1943. Twenty boats were lost between 15 September and 7 November; concurrently, the grey wolves destroyed but eight merchant ships and four Allied warships, including HMCS *St Croix*. The American hunter-killer groups have sunk nine of Dönitz's ten U-tankers, necessitating shorter German patrols. Allied aircraft based especially in Iceland and Newfoundland have battered the wolfpacks to the point where concentration translates only into greater losses. "The enemy," Dönitz notes in his war diary, "has all the trump cards in his hands." Hostile aircraft even bomb Dönitz's headquarters at the Tirpitzufer in Berlin, forcing him into makeshift facilities code-named the "Koralle" at Bernau, northeast of the capital. Finally, while Allied commanders gain combat experience with every passing day, the U-boats lose experienced officers and men at an alarming rate. "No special news to report" has become the standard entry in Dönitz's KTB for the submarine war.

Most ominous of all, the U-boats have been stripped of their primary weapon: invisibility. The Allies pinpoint and attack them with deadly precision—in fog, ice, snow, rain, and hail, by day as well as by night, above the surface as well as below. Are they using unknown wavelengths from ship and air radar? Are the German short-wave transmitters revealing the whereabouts of the U-boat? Is sabotage at play? Vice-Admiral Maertens's Naval Communications Service yet again fails to turn up any clues. The slaughter on the deadly sea continues.

———————

For a second time, Admiral U-boats draws the unavoidable conclusions and abandons the central Atlantic. "Under the present circumstances it is pointless to send the U-boats out to fight." But what to do? Allow the Allies to land men and equipment in England unchallenged? Never! "The submarine war must go on"—even if it is only as a "defensive war" to keep the Allies "from the shores of Europe."

Dönitz is under no illusions. "Finding the enemy has always been the main problem, even at the best of times." Theoretically, every U-boat commander should be able to scan up to 8 nautical miles of sea from his bridge. Thus, by placing the individual boats of a patrol line 15 miles apart, not even a straggler ought to be able to pass a line. Realistically, however, visibility is often restricted to several hundred yards by fog, clouds, rain, snow, hail—and by the mountainous Atlantic seas. There is just too much surface to cover. Each quadrant on the grid chart—AK, for example—extends 900 kilometres, or 486 nautical miles, on each side! Dönitz needs effective radar or extended air reconnaissance; he has neither.

Still, Admiral U-boats sends his forces out again—and once more to the south to raid the convoy routes between Gibraltar and Great Britain. The Type VIIC boats coming out of Brest and Lorient, La Rochelle and St Nazaire will not need to be refuelled at sea. Agents in Portugal and Spain can supply good intelligence on Allied convoy movements in and out of Gibraltar. And the Gibraltar–Great Britain routes are well within the range of Luftwaffe planes based in western France. Perhaps for the first time in the war, Dönitz will be able to coordinate air and sea forces in the Battle of the Atlantic.

Accordingly, *U305* is not to return to her old haunts south of the Denmark Strait. Rather, Admiral U-boats orders her to the waters south of the Bay of Biscay (AL74), off the coast of Portugal, in hopes of intercepting the Gibraltar convoys bound for Britain. If need be, *U305* can follow the convoy route up north. But there will be no more turkey shoots of U-boats in the central Atlantic.

The Great Lion remains concerned that his commanders have settled into a defensive frame of mind with their new *Naxos* radar detectors and T5 destroyer crackers. The tally for November is disastrous: a single merchantman sunk, at the cost of ten U-boats! Thus, Dönitz fills the air waves with new exhortations:

"Take advantage of any chances to attack offered."

"Something must be sunk out of this convoy tonight. At 'em."

"Bring honour to your name."

"Go after 'em at top speed."

"You have only tonight left, so put all you have into it."

Rhetoric in place of radar!

But not even redirecting the U-boats to the Gibraltar–Great Britain run brings success. In the first month of the new campaign, twenty U-boats and about thirty aircraft manage to sink only two ships and to damage two others—at the cost of ten u-boats. Intelligence remains spotty at best, inaccurate or nonexistent at worst. The two or three daily reconnaissance flights by the Luftwaffe are too few and too far between to provide continuous and exact aerial reconnaissance. Beacon signals from aircraft all too often cannot be picked up by the u-boats. Out of frustration, the Luftwaffe transfers its twin-engine HE 177 Greif heavy bombers to the Mediterranean in November 1943.

Throughout the first week of December, Bahr and his officers super-vise the work of getting U305 ready for patrol. The men know their tasks and work like a well-oiled machine. It is the same old rhythm: Brenner takes on 180 tons of diesel and lubricating oils; Sander loads the twelve eels, including four T5s; Bogatsch, assisted by Dohrmann, hauls ammu-nition aboard for the twin 2-cm machine-guns as well as the 3.7-cm Flak; and Migge carefully stows the customary mountains of sausages, eggs, bread, milk, cheese, fruit, vegetables, soy-bean filler, and canned meats and Kraut. Dr Loytved searches for his medical ward. Christ! What did they promise him in medical school? The Nazi Party cruise-ship *Wilhelm Gustloff*?

On 7 December Bahr is called to Commander Heinrich Lehmann-Willenbrock's 9th Flotilla Headquarters for a last-minute briefing. Ac-cording to the reports of captains just returning from patrols, the Allies have come up with a devious device to defeat the *Zaunkönig*. More and more T5 torpedoes—perhaps as many as three out of every four—are exploding harmlessly in the wakes of escort vessels. This should not be happening, for the Torpedo Directorate has adjusted the Pi4 pistol to be less sensitive to turbulence. It can mean only one thing: enemy warships must be deploying some kind of an acoustic device to lure the wren away from the ships' propellers. But what can possibly make more noise than that? One u-boat on 1 December reported that it had heard what sounded like an "industrial symphony" combining a "heavy rattle, singing, heavy humming, and cracking like an overloaded spring." The machine shop at Brest has no answers. "Be alert out there," is all that Flotilla Chiefs Lehmann-Willenbrock and Winter (1st Flotilla) can offer.

Bahr eases U305 out of Brest harbour at dusk on 8 December 1943. There is no festive send-off—no military band, no *Blitzmädchen*, no flowers, no soldiers, no Todt Organization workers, just a smattering of fellow u-boat captains. An early evening departure soon translates into protective darkness, for a skipper has to be particularly sharp these days steaming through the Bay of Biscay. Three out of every five boats running the bay do not make it. Bahr and the crew are keenly aware of this dismal statistic: the British radio station "Calais" takes malicious delight in keeping the Germans abreast of bad news.

Time to deploy Aphrodite. Bahr has given this task to Third Watch Officer Dohrmann. Hell, he'll be twenty in two months; time to learn a trade! The Old Man and his Exec double up with laughter on the bridge as poor Dohrmann fills a balloon with bottled helium gas, attaches a long line to it, and then struggles to fasten a string of aluminum foils to the line. The wind twirls the foils in every direction and whips the balloon and line directly into his face. When Dohrmann finally has balloon, line, and foils attached to the sheet anchor, he loses his balance and nearly falls overboard as he hurls the gadget over the rails of the new *Wintergarten* deck.

No sooner has the teenager mastered Aphrodite than Bahr entrusts him with Thetis. But this time Dohrmann rises to the challenge: in masterful fashion he inserts the 16-foot wooden pole with the metal dipoles into the top side of the rectangular cork float, the 16-foot steel pole as counterbalance into the bottom of the other side, and with an elegant toss lands the device in the bay. "Wonder what the Tommies think of these bloody toys, Exec?" Sander has been to too many electronics courses to care.

Bahr has also picked up a new trick: whenever possible, *U305* first settles among French fishing boats for protection and later Spanish. A reverse convoy! British Bristol Beaufighters seem reluctant to strafe these boats. One of the xB-Dienst types gave Bahr the idea when he related how he sailed with fishing smacks to gather information on convoy sailings. It also helps to break up the familiar monotony of the *Gammelfahrt*. On 12 December Admiral u-boats informs all boats that one of their own, *U333* (Lieutenant Peter Erich Cremer), managed to survive being rammed and then depth charged by a destroyer for nine hours. "This performance shows what a well-disciplined crew can do. Thorough emergency drills for all boats."

What Dönitz does not tell his commanders is that they are now operating totally "blind." Convoys no longer receive and confirm steaming routes in degrees of latitude and longitude, but according to what xb-Dienst calls "distance between and sonar contact from unknown preordained positions"—which the merchant skippers most likely receive in sealed orders shortly before leaving port. In fact, the Gibraltar to North America UGS and GUS convoys in particular, which are wholly under the control of the US Navy, encipher their radio transmissions with the US electric cipher machine, which the xb-Dienst cannot crack. Admiral u-boats concedes that his calculations are based on "pure speculation" and that convoy sightings are "more or less a matter of luck." Operationally, he abandons wolfpacks in favour of dispersal in hopes of covering more of the Atlantic.

On 18 December Dönitz directs *U305* as part of the Coronel patrol line—named after the German naval victory over a British squadron in 1914—to quadrant BE5471 in hopes of intercepting a Gibraltar convoy. But it is the usual story: no sightings are made. Five Luftwaffe Focke-Wulf 200s fail to start owing to foul weather. Dönitz rejects an air force offer to fly the reconnaissance mission on 20 December since the convoy will be beyond the range of his boats by then. More and more, he sends the u-boats to the West Indies and Brazil, Africa and the Indian Ocean in a desperate attempt to locate Allied merchant ships.

On 20 December Admiral u-boats orders a new Borkum patrol line to form, with *U305* on its left point. There are thirteen boats in all: *U801*, *U305*, *U107*, *U667*, *U618*, *U541*, *U270*, *U962*, *U641*, *U415*, *U382*, *U645*, and *U275*. Given the lack of air support, the u-boats are to dive at first light and to run submerged. Their target southwest of the Bay of Biscay is a joined convoy, MKS33/SL142. *U962* drops out of the line within a day because of a lack of fuel. Reconnaissance by five Focke-Wulf 200s by day and a mammoth six-engine BV 222 Viking flying boat by night produces no sightings.

Then, on 22 December, Bahr cannot believe the Enigma decrypt that Ballmann brings him: a patrolling Luftwaffe plane at 2:35 p.m. has spotted an aircraft carrier, a destroyer, and several "unidentified escorts" in BE5579, heading in the general direction of Borkum. "Shit! Air cover at last! What have we done to deserve this?" Berlin orders Bahr and the other Borkum captains not to risk isolated attacks, as this will only give their positions away and draw enemy air attacks. Moreover, a southwest force 7 near-gale makes surface operations impossible that night.

No sooner has Rudolf recovered from his initial shock than the Luftwaffe on 23 December reports a second sighting of hostile vessels near the thirteen Borkum boats at 45° north, 22° west. Christmas has come early in 1943! Perhaps the U-boats will stand a chance to attack the enemy this time. What the Luftwaffe pilot has spotted is Task Group 21.14, a hunter-killer group centred on the aircraft carrier USS *Card* (CVE 11) and the escort destroyers USS *Leary*, USS *Schenck*, and USS *Decatur*. The *Card* is a Bogue Class escort carrier commanded by Captain Arnold J. "Buster" Isbell. Its primary function is to support convoy escorts threatened by U-boats. In fact, TG21.14 had been screening another convoy, GUS24, but had been apprised of Borkum's existence and position and ordered to attack. Move, countermove. The next move is up to Dönitz.

Admiral U-boats on 23 December orders Borkum to set a southwesterly course in order to be at BE8411 by 10 a.m. the next day. The mission has changed: the Luftwaffe has spotted the merchant ship *Orsono* trying to run the Allied blockade with a load of desperately needed raw rubber, tin, and tungsten from Kobe, Japan. But an F4F Wildcat fighter flying off the deck of the *Card* in foul weather damages the ship and Borkum is ordered at full speed to come to her rescue. *Orsono* eventually manages to limp into Bordeaux under cover of the 4th Torpedo-Boat Flotilla, but runs onto the wreck of a minesweeper and has to be beached along the banks of the Gironde River. In the meantime, the Borkum boats encounter the American Task Group around 9 p.m.

"Number One, grab the binoculars! What the hell can that mountain of a shadow on the horizon be?" Bahr has never seen anything larger than a 1200-ton destroyer or an 8000-ton freighter while on patrol. Even in the dark, this 14,000-ton behemoth is the size of a city block. Bahr and Sander cling to the boat's conning tower as they struggle to get a clear look at the shadow through the wailing wind and blowing foam of a force 7 near-gale. It's got to be a carrier, they decide.

At 12:09 a.m. Ballmann reports the sighting in BE7325 to Admiral U-boats. He repeats the signal at 12:49 a.m. in an attempt to home the other U-boats in on the carrier, bearing southwest. Bahr's tracking "nose" is back in business: *U305* is the first boat to sight the task group. His job now is to stalk the carrier and to coach in his fellow grey wolves.

"Alarm! Destroyer, bearing three-four-zero! Angle zero!" Sander is on the ball!

"Right full rudder! Double flank speed! Chief, take her down and be quick about it!" This one is worth a good try.

"Clear the bridge! Action Stations!" Bahr and the watch are through the tower hatch in a flash. Brenner has set the sternplanes at 15 and is already flooding the ballast tanks. The e-motors are humming in unison. The planesmen hang on their controls. As *U305* dips beneath the waves, her crew can hear the USS *Schenck*'s 20-mm Oerlikon guns spraying the superstructure. The heavier 3-inch shells splash all around them. Asdic pings bounce off the U-boat's hull. The *Schenck* has picked up *U305*'s two radio messages to Dönitz with her Huff Duff and is now bearing down hard on Bahr's boat. She has radar everywhere up top! Sonar beams! Asdic!

"Propeller noises, sir! Getting louder! Impulses amplitude three!" Then come the depth-charges, one after the other, and a crescendo of *Wabos*, real sledgehammer blows. The deck-plates rattle as always, the bulkheads groan, paint peels off the deck-head, and moisture drips from pipes and ducts. The lights went out long ago, but Brenner has switched over to the back-up system. Bahr orders the Chief to take *U305* down another 65 feet, to 550. Brenner rigs the boat for silent running. The only sound is the humming of the e-motors.

"Destroyer propeller getting louder, Herr Kaleu! Impulses amplitude four!" *Verdammt*! A second tin can is after us. This one is the destroyer USS *Leary*. For two hours the two escorts fire their hedgehogs and depth-charges at Bahr. And then, just as suddenly as they started, they leave him alone. Ballmann breaks the silence: "Screw noises getting fainter!" USS *Leary* and USS *Schenck* are moving off.

In fact, a hellish inferno is raging all around *U305*. Lieutenant Kurt Neide of *U415* manages to get within about 2 miles of the *Card* and to fire a fan shot of three FATs at her; all three appear to explode prematurely as they "loop" through the screen's wakes! Neide next fires a T5 at the destroyer USS *Decatur* and it, too, misfires. First Lieutenant Otto Ferro of *U645* sees the *Schenck* pounding *U305* with hedgehogs and launches a wren at her. It misfires. The *Schenck* abandons the hunt for *U305* and takes after Ferro's boat, which it destroys with depth-charges. At 5:05 a.m. Lieutenant Helmuth Bork's *U275* strikes the USS *Leary* with a T5. Finally, a wren that works! Fifteen minutes later *U382* (First Lieutenant Rudolf Zorn) gives the destroyer the *coup de grâce*.

During all this time, not a single Borkum boat gets so much as a good look at the convoy. It is too well screened, and the fight is strictly between escorts and u-boats. Captain "Buster" Isbell manages to evade the u-boats by zigzagging for much of the night. He radioes for assistance from Task Group 21.16 escorting convoy UGS27 out of Norfolk, Virginia.

The odds against Borkum attacking a convoy get even worse later that evening of 23 December 1943 when convoy ONS62/KMS36 approaches the patrol line from the north, for it is screened by Escort Group B1 as well as by another task group centred on the escort carrier HMS *Striker*. Neide and *U415* torpedo the lead destroyer HMS *Hurricane*, steaming at 20 knots, with a T5; the wren blows off the propellers and rudders, leaving the *Hurricane* easy prey for a straight-running T3 torpedo. But the convoy remains impenetrable to the u-boats. Bahr and his fellow commanders are outgunned and outnumbered by the hunter-killer groups and their air support.

As Christmas Eve yields to Christmas Day, the Great Lion remembers his cubs out on patrol with Season's Greetings:

> My u-boat men! My intention to spend Christmas at a front base has been frustrated. Thus my thoughts today are even more with you and your loved ones. The fifth Christmas of the war sees us— front as well as home—more determined and tougher than ever behind our Führer in the struggle to secure our future.

At 5:29 p.m. on Christmas Day, *U305* spies a shadow on the horizon and draws nearer. It is a hostile destroyer. "Would make a lovely Christmas present!" Bahr thinks out loud. But the tin can has got a full head of steam, so there is no sense pursuing it. At 6:50 p.m. Bahr spots another silhouette. This one turns out to be *U1534*—code-name for the 2700-ton German blockade-runner *Alsterufer*—about 500 nautical miles northwest of Cape Finisterre in northwestern Spain. Bahr mistakenly reports it as the *Osorno* to Admiral u-boats in the top secret *Offizier* code. Dönitz quickly catches the error and corrects it over the air waves.

Bletchley Park decodes Bahr's priority message within an hour, leading to *Alsterufer's* destruction by rockets from a B-24 Liberator heavy bomber of the 311th (Czech) Squadron based on the Azores. The Reich loses 344 tons of desperately needed tungsten concentrate.

In the meantime, Bahr, obviously unaware of these developments and informed that both the Kriegsmarine's 8th Destroyer Flotilla and the 4th Torpedo-Boat Flotilla are already steaming out of Bordeaux to escort the blockade-breaker *Alsterufer* in, sees no need to screen her. Then, just before sunset, a number of Borkum U-boats report shadows on the horizon. Believing them to be stragglers from OS62/KMS36 driven off course by heavy seas, Dönitz orders: "Borkum. Course 225°. Full speed. Attack!" None of the boats manages to get a glimpse of the convoy.

"Captain to the bridge! Destroyer in sight! Action stations!" It is Bogatsch who has spotted the hostile vessel.

Bahr immediately orders "Clear the bridge! Both emergency ahead!" and begins a submerged approach. The Huff Duff and the radar on the destroyer must be out of commission, since she does not react at all to the danger.

"Open outer doors 1 and 2! Flood torpedo tubes 1 and 2." Sander in the control tower enters the last-second calculations into the torpedo guidance system. Range. Speed. Angle.

"Tube 1: Ready . . . FIRE!" A jolt rocks the boat.

"Tube 2: Ready . . . FIRE!" Another jolt.

The tin can still has not seen Bahr, who remains at periscope depth. *Scheisse!* The damned wrens explode in the destroyer's wake. What the hell is wrong with these bloody "birds"? Several days later, Bahr radioes Admiral U-boats: "Suspect boats at insufficient speed." The wren needs loud, thrashing propeller noises—speeds of more than 8 knots—to home in on. The torpedo gang works feverishly to reload the bow tubes.

First Lieutenant Otto of *U270* also fires a T5 at a destroyer of the support group and, like Bahr, watches it explode harmlessly in the escort's wake. The "mystery" weapons that the Allies deploy against the *Zaun-könig* are simple, yet effective. The Royal Navy's are called "foxers," acoustic decoys towed in pairs, one off each quarter of an escort, designed to make more noise than the propellers and hence draw the wren to themselves. The Royal Canadian Navy's anti-gnat device is even better. Dubbed "Cat-gear," it consists of harmonically tuned iron bars streamed behind the stern of an escort where it creates loud rhythmic vibrations. It is cheaper, simpler to build, and just as effective as the RN's foxer. While these devices interfere with an escort's asdic/sonar, they nevertheless declaw the wren. The hit ratio of the T5 sinks to 6 percent.

On 26 December Dönitz orders the Borkum line to BE743, since a Luftwaffe reconnaissance flight has spotted a southbound convoy, MKS34/SL143. The patrol line is down to ten boats as *U667*, *U107*, and *U415* head for their home bases. En route, all three boats report firing T5s—without results. Hostile air cover continues to harass the U-boats, and Dönitz sends out new instructions: "Surface patrols by day and night only with greatest vigilance, care, and battle readiness. Carelessness by the watch when boats in remote areas one of the greatest dangers." It is another one of those superfluous messages that annoy the U-boat skippers.

Moreover, Dönitz is concerned that his commanders are no longer able to stalk targets at periscope depth because of enemy radar, tighter screens, and air cover. On 28 December he orders the boats to "shoot blind at great depths"; the new T5 and FAT torpedoes, after all, have been designed precisely for this task. Of course, since the wren is an acoustic torpedo, it can be fired only in ten-minute intervals from the FAT! And the boats will have to dive immediately to 150 or more feet to get away from "stray" torpedoes. Finally, the Great Lion instructs the skippers not to spare the ammunition: "Fire all eels from their tubes."

But the eels are ineffective. On 31 December *U275* and *U382* report sinking one destroyer each. In fact, the wrens again fail to strike their targets; what the commanders hear over the hydrophones are the T5s exploding in their victims' wakes. Bahr also reports sinking a destroyer that day, though, again, the report pertains to a premature detonation. Convoy MKS34/SL143 safely passes the Borkum line. Happy New Year!

Admiral U-boats has no solution for breaking the iron ring that surrounds the convoys. *U305* is forced to crash dive on 2 and 3 January 1944 as aircraft hound its every moment on the surface. The other boats are likewise driven into the cellar by hostile air; *U667* is attacked no fewer than seven times in a single day. Conversely, the U-boats sight not one of the ten convoys that sail close to them and they sink only one straggler.

On 2 January Dönitz orders the remaining nine boats—two are heading home and one has joined the line—to deploy their 3.7-cm Flak in unison against hostile aircraft. "Danger in Biscay as acute as ever; only prudent deployment will keep your backs free." Hardly a grey wolf needs this obvious reminder. The next day Dönitz cancels the order and, to make detection of the patrol line more difficult, subdivides Borkum into three small patrols of three boats each. *U305* joins *U270* and *U382* as Borkum I. Dönitz also hopes that several small groups will stand a better chance to evade enemy escorts and to prevent convoys from steaming around the larger "rakes."

By 5 January 1944 Borkum I lies off the northwest coast of Spain. The main office of the xB-Dienst in France has received an agent's report stating that a northbound convoy has left Gibraltar and that it should pass the patrol line by the 7th or 8th. Instead, the three boats run into the 5th Support Group consisting of the Royal Navy frigates HMS *Nene* and HMS *Tweed*, as well as the Royal Canadian Navy corvettes HMCS *Calgary*, HMCS *Snowberry*, HMCS *Edmundston*, and HMCS *Camrose*, deployed to intercept German blockade-runners. Escorts outnumber Borkum U-boats twenty to nine.

U758 manages to get a shot off at a Canadian corvette, but the T5 detonates prematurely again. On 6 January *U270* shoots down a Boeing B-17F Flying Fortress bomber of the RAF 120 Squadron, but is damaged in the process. The next day *U763* just manages to fight off an aircraft that almost blinds its crew with a radar-guided Leigh Lights. British air patrols over the Bay of Biscay are also extraordinarily frequent, and Dönitz concludes that the heavy loss of escort vessels has forced the Allies to rely more heavily on airpower! He moves Borkum 90 miles south and spaces the boats 30 miles apart to rake as large an area as possible, in hopes that the patrol line can intercept a northbound convoy, MKS35/SL144, which the xB-Dienst expects in the middle of quadrant CF by 10 January.

"Middle of CF quadrant?" How imprecise! Bahr is flabbergasted that his instructions from the "Koralle" in Bernau now encompass 3240 square miles of ocean. What has happened to the old precision? Instead, Bahr gets an admonition from Admiral U-boats to reload his batteries not "during the first and last hours of darkness"—a tactic which the enemy apparently has discovered to advantage—but only during the middle of the night. Yet, Dönitz radios upon reflection, since *U305* has the 3.7-cm Flak, it can also charge the e-cells during the day. So, which is it, Bahr asks Brenner?

"Alarm! Shadows off to port! Range 6000! Captain to the bridge!" Bahr races up the aluminum ladder. The shadows in the distance have a low profile: corvettes or frigates, most likely. He snaps the Zeiss binoculars into the TBT and studies the shadows more carefully.

"Alarm! Three escorts! Bow zero! Range 5000 metres!" *U305* is in quadrant BE7655. It is late afternoon, 7 January.

"Clear the bridge! Action stations! Rig for diving! Take her down to periscope depth, Chief!" Sander is already hunched over his dials in the control tower as Bahr takes his seat at the periscope. The Old Man rivets his gaze on the three warships. He knows the silhouettes all too well, two frigates and a corvette in line abreast, hunting, about 2 miles apart. No fancy circle patterns this time. Straight down their throats!

"Hold zero bearing!" The only sound in the boat is the hum of e-motors. The red emergency lights give off an eerie glow. Then asdic "pings" hit the hull like a burst of machine-gun fire.

"Open outer doors Tubes 2, 3, and 4! Flood tubes 2, 3, and 4!"

The torpedo gang snaps back: "Tubes 2, 3, and 4 flooded, sir!"

Bahr criss-crosses the hairs of the periscope on the middle ship, a frigate. She must be the leader. She is bearing down on *U305* at about 15 knots, her sharp bow slicing through the waters. The other two escorts are slightly behind and on either side of the frigate. This constellation calls for a fan shot. What did the Great Lion order? "Fire all eels from their tubes." Steady, steady, let them come right at us. Bahr glances at his watch: 5:11 p.m.

"Tube 2: Ready . . . FIRE!" Sander slams the firing button. A jolt.

"Tube 3: Ready . . . FIRE!" Same button. Same jolt.

"Tube 4: Ready . . . FIRE!" Button. Jolt.

"Dive! Dive! Take her down to 50 metres! Rig for silent running!" Bahr orders absolute silence in the boat. "Quiet, you buggers!" Ballmann is steadily counting off the seconds. Thirty. Forty. Fifty. Sixty. One minute. One minute ten seconds. One minute twenty.

The Royal Navy frigates *Nene* and *Tweed* and the Royal Canadian Navy frigate *Waskesiu* have had a busy night. For hours they have criss-crossed their assigned patrol area off the Azores hunting a U-boat first sighted by a patrolling bomber. They have stayed closed up at action stations from just after midnight until 10 a.m., when they were ordered off the search. Now, they are steaming at line abreast, with escort leader *Nene* in the centre flanked by *Tweed* to port and *Waskesiu* to starboard. They are steering a base course of 180 degrees, but zigzagging to port and starboard of the base course. Lieutenant-Commander R.S. Miller, RNR, is in his sea cabin just below *Tweed*'s bridge. He is tired, but not so tired that he does not worry that *Tweed* is totally unprotected against acoustic torpedoes in these waters. When he tried to stream his foxer gear at twilight the previous evening, his equipment had malfunctioned.

"Just make sure everyone in that asdic hut keeps especially alert, Number One," he ordered when he retired after action stations had been cancelled. "With *Nene* and *Waskesiu* so close about, we should be alright."

It is now 4 p.m. The watch changes on *Tweed*'s bridge.

"We're doing a Number 8 zigzag, Guns," the departing Officer of the Watch informs his relief. "We're due for a signal from the SOE in about fifteen minutes. And mind that the asdic's been acting up. Lots of fish about, I'm told. Anyway, they've been picking up false contacts for the past hour or so. I'd check twice before disturbing the Old Man. He had quite a night."

He hands over the large bridge binoculars and clambers down the ladder heading for the galley.

Guns is now in control. He scans the horizon slowly. He's had a good rest since going off action stations. The sky is azure, the sea calm, the air fresh. It's a beautiful day at sea. Below him the vibration of the engines and the smells and sounds of the warship brighten his spirits. He is in charge. He will be tired in a few hours, but he is fresh now and he has always loved the first minutes of his watch. The bridge asdic repeater pings relentlessly. He checks his watch as he lights a cigarette. Just a few minutes to the course change. It'll be a gentle 30 degree turn to starboard. He wants to execute it smartly. He warns the men in the wheel-house to get ready and he trains his glasses on *Nene*'s yardarm. He spots the flag climbing up.

"Bunts, their flag's up. Step lively, man." The rating quickly clips the course-change flag to the halyard and hoists it. It snaps in the breeze.

Any moment now the SOE's flag will race down and the course change will be executed. Guns gets ready to snap out the command. He never gets the chance.

"Bridge, asdic. Contact at 120. Range seems to be about 1000 yards."

Guns is irritated at the interruption. "What do you mean 'seems to be'? Aren't you sure? You have been getting false readings, haven't you?"

"Can't get the range, sir. Could be a sub, she's showing Doppler. No, wait. We've got something else—CHRIST, SIR, HIGH SPEED SCREWS COMING IN FAST."

Torpedo. Right at them. It is meant for *Nene*, but *Nene* and *Waskesiu* have just executed their turn to starboard. The deadly fish is bearing down on *Tweed*.

"HARD A STARBOARD. ACTION STATIONS. CAPTAIN TO THE BRIDGE. Get ready to fire an emergency pattern."

Alarm bells, running and shouting men, *Tweed* heeling sharply over, the bow starting to come about, but ever so slowly at this speed. Then their steel world shudders and shakes with the violence of the massive explosion, and their ears are assailed by the crushing volume of sound. Their bodies are thrown against railings, bulkheads, hatches, decks, guns, and depth-charge rails. A massive column of sea water, streaked with bunker fuel, rises from the port quarter. Bodies and body parts cartwheel slowly upward, then fall to the surface of the ocean. *Tweed* lurches to the right. Miller is on the bridge pulling on his life-belt. He can feel the deck sloping back and to starboard. Tons of sea water must be rushing into the frigate. The magazine is already flooded. She will not blow up instantly as others of her type have, but she is dying very quickly nonetheless.

Miller knows there is no way one of these frigates can survive such a massive thrust into her vitals. "Abandon ship, abandon ship."

Bahr hears a loud, booming detonation.

"All right, we've heard enough! Chief, take her down and level off at A2! Rig for depth-charges!" As *U305* glides down to 500 feet, sharp, cracking noises can be heard throughout the boat. What sound like metal parts are cascading down all around the U-boat. The two predators had been so close to each other! Then come two more explosions. Depth-charges, but they are nowhere near them, judging by the sound.

Up above, the two remaining escorts alter course, their screws slow. Bahr has expected this reaction. They will try to keep their speed under 8 knots to throw off the wrens. But where are the rest of the depth-charges? The pinging is loud and clear, and every now and then a beam sweeps over the hull. Surely they must take a pasting!

"Come on you bastards, let's get it over with."

Commander J.D. Birch is the Senior Officer of the Sixth Escort Group. He is in *Nene*'s charthouse when he is shaken by the concussion of *U305*'s torpedo thundering into *Tweed*'s side. He dashes to the bridge as the Officer of the Watch calls for action stations. It must be one of those gnats. He flips up the voice-pipe cover.

"Chief, slow her to 7 knots. Now!" Then he turns to the Chief Yeoman. "Make to *Waskesiu*: '*Tweed* Torpedoed, close the wreck, slow to 7 knots.'" Then, "make to Admiralty '*Tweed* torpedoed in position 44 deg. 18'N, 21 deg. 19'w.'"

As they close *Tweed*, the stricken ship's bow lifts skyward and she sinks into the depths, stern first. The air from inside her shoots out from her open hatches as she plunges to the bottom. Then, two explosions tear the surface of the ocean. There had been no time to render her ready depth-charges safe. In death, she is killing her own crew as they struggle in the water.

Where *Tweed* vanished there is heavy fuel oil on the surface of the sea. The corpses of the dead and the bodies of the survivors are covered with the thick black stuff. Wreckage floats everywhere, bobbing on the gentle swell. Groups of survivors huddle on a Carley float and on *Tweed*'s still-intact whaler. Others cling to bits of wood or corkboard, or whatever will keep them afloat. Birch worries about another attack. At these slow speeds, he and *Waskesiu* are sitting ducks. He has no idea where the submarine is. Then *Waskesiu* reports a contact and drops a full pattern about a mile and half to the west of *Tweed*'s last position. The charges rumble down. Nothing. Asdic beams probe and search. Contact again. More charges into the black depths. Still nothing. It will be dark in a few hours. Birch joins the hunt and orders a box search. Both ships zigzag, changing speeds constantly to throw off the deadly gnats, and drop charges to keep their adversary deep. If he's still there. Is he? There are no further contacts. Birch orders *Waskesiu* back and the two consorts pick up survivors. Miller is hauled out of the oily sea along with seven of his officers and forty-eight ratings. One rating is already dead; four more die later that night. Their bodies are sewn up in hammocks, weighted down with fire bars, and consigned to the deep in a brief dawn service.

Bahr takes *U305* up to the surface shortly after midnight. Fresh air! The ventilators engage, as do the bilge pumps. Brenner fires the twin diesels up and starts to replenish the nearly exhausted batteries. It is a clear night with stars overhead. While the torpedo gang reloads the bow tubes, the technical division and the seamen come up on deck in shifts. Feels good: another u-boat hunter cracked wide open!

On 8 January the search for the convoy in the Atlantic resumes. The xB-Dienst is now expecting MKS35/SL144 the evening of 10 January. Perhaps it will link up with another convoy, since there are too many escorts and carriers out there for just one. The Luftwaffe sends up a four-engine JU 290A-2 from the 5th Reconnaissance Group in search of the expected MKS convoy, but it makes no sighting. Dönitz moves Borkum I south by dead reckoning. Radio intelligence service now suspects two eastbound convoys and one westbound.

But where is that "Rotterdam device," Dönitz rhetorically questions in his war diary, which the Luftwaffe allegedly is developing as surface-to-air radar? And why are the dozens of Thetis buoys seeded in the Bay of Biscay not attracting enemy aircraft?

Late in the evening of 8 January, *U305*, at the end of the Borkum I group, sights convoy KMS38/OS64. It is screened by Escort Group B4, which includes HMS *Abelia*. At 4:27 the next morning, the Royal Navy corvette establishes contact with a submarine about 2800 yards astern of the starboard wing column. It is *U305*. HMS *Abelia* reduces speed immediately to 7 knots to foil the German T5 torpedoes, and at a range of 1700 yards classifies the contact as a submarine. Lieutenant-Commander

O.G. Stewart is not trailing the cumbersome foxer gear because he feels a near-gale is in the offing: large waves are beginning to form, white foam is streaking from their crests, winds are at force 5 to 6 and rising, and the glass is falling.

By 4:35 a.m. the corvette closes the range to 950 yards and charges *U305* at full speed. Stewart decides against a hedgehog attack because of the heavy seas breaking forward and because he believes the u-boat is deep. Instead, he fires a pattern charge of ten MK7 and MK9 depth-charges set for 200 feet. All explode, but none finds *U305*.

Bahr is desperate to get an eel off against the intruder, but he has only a single wren left and it is in the stern tube.

"Open door to Tube 5! Flood Tube 5!"

The Old Man is determined to manoeuvre his boat to discharge the last *Zaunkönig* left in the tubes. The distance between the two hunters is down to 850 yards.

"Tube 5: Ready . . . FIRE!" Sander sends the eel on its way.

In less than sixty seconds, Bahr hears a loud explosion. The T5 has slammed into the corvette's starboard quarter, blowing off the *Abelia*'s rudder and partially flooding her tiller flat. Stewart's decision to charge *U305* at full speed at a range of 950 yards gave the wren the opportunity to find the tin can. Stewart had not received in time the new Atlantic Convoy Instructions, Article 138, not to increase speed until the distance to target had been brought down to 700 yards!

For Bahr, there is no time to waste: "Dive! Dive! Chief, take her down to A2!" As Brenner once again guides the boat to a depth of 500 feet, Escort Group B4 searches for Bahr and *U305* in the heavy seas. But the search is in vain. Although Stewart determinedly guides HMS *Winchelsea* onto the target, the escort fails to find *U305* either with hedgehog or with depth-charges. The tug *Storm King* takes HMS *Abelia* in tow, bound for Milford Haven, Wales.

Bahr continues the patrol, taking time to reload the stern tube. On 9 January another JU 290 goes up. Contact! Thirty-nine ships are slowly wallowing through the rolling Atlantic west of Portugal in quadrant CG9311, bearing northwest. Dönitz orders every available Borkum boat—eight in all—to head to quadrants CF2945 to CF3556 at full speed to intercept the convoy. On 10 January three JU 290s start up: the first flight from 4 a.m. to 8:30 a.m., the second from 12:30 to 4:30 p.m., and the third from 7:30 p.m. to 11:30 p.m. They see nothing. Has the convoy evaded the patrol line towards the west?

In the dimming twilight, First Lieutenant Bogatsch, Second Watch Officer, spies a shadow between the clouds. He immediately orders rapid fire by the 3.7-cm Flak guns. It is the third Ju 290 flight! Bahr hastily exchanges recognition signals with the Luftwaffe machine and then dives. Nerves have become frayed at the sight of anything that flies—and it is almost never German.

The Luftwaffe sends up two more Ju 290s on 11 January. The morning patrol sights nothing and has to return to base owing to gear breakdown; the evening patrol fails to start owing to foul weather. Where is that bloody convoy? Fearing that the convoy has veered away to the west, Admiral U-boats sends his grey wolves under the sea to escape detection and to await further orders that night. Has MKS35/SL144 been routed to the west around the patrol line? Without radar, the U-boats are blind.

Dönitz concludes that the convoy has detoured towards the west. He orders Borkum to proceed to quadrant CF2447/2357 at full speed. Perhaps they can intercept the enemy the evening of the 11th? And he decrees that the boats run on the surface. Five have the new 3.7-cm Flak; let them use it!

At 6:19 p.m. the most westerly boat in the patrol line spots the convoy in quadrant CF2452. It is Bahr and his *U305*. The old "sniffer" is back in top form! *Der grosse Löwe* instructs all boats to rush to the spot of Bahr's sighting report. It will soon be dark.

"Alarm! Aircraft at 220°. Range 2000 metres!" Dönitz has ordered surface combat, Bahr lectures his Second Watch Officer, so that's what will be done. Dr Loytved will finally earn his keep, however meagre and modest that may be! Bogatsch and his three gunners once more man the 3.7-cm Flak and open fire, as do most of the other boats.

The enemy aircraft are from the carrier USS *Block Island* (CVE 21), commanded by Captain Logan C. Ramsey. "Christ's sake! How many do they have? First it was only the *Bogue*. Then the *Card*. And now the *Block Island*, all on one patrol! And our frigging *Graf Zeppelin* still has not even left the shipyard!" Worse still, the enemy TBF Avenger torpedo bombers are each equipped with eight deadly new Model 5 (3.5 inch) rockets. *U758* is first to experience their deadly sting.

The artillery duel is a Mexican standoff. Neither side does substantial damage, but the u-boats get no closer to the convoy. At 9:35 p.m. Bahr radioes the "Koralle" that he has sighted a destroyer in CF2423. Immediately comes the reply: "At him!" But the tin can has detected *U305* with his Huff Duff, and Bahr crash dives to avoid destruction by those damned *Igl* mortars. "Am turning away!" Bahr radioes Dönitz. But there is no pursuit by the tin can, and Bahr brings *U305* back up to the surface.

Having joined the watch on the bridge at 11 p.m., Bahr is jarred by flares on the horizon. They are from HMCS *Lunenburg*. The Canadian corvette sent up starshell as soon as a T5 from *U953* (First Lieutenant Karl-Heinz Marbach) exploded in her wake. Thereafter, Admiral u-boats receives no further signals from the Borkum patrol line. Every single boat has had to seek safety beneath the sea from the convoy's escort vessels and from the *Block Island*'s aircraft. There is nothing left to do at the "Koralle" but to hold a postmortem on Borkum.

Admiral u-boats cuts right to the chase. Borkum failed because of lack of aerial reconnaissance and because the prongs of the rake were spread too far apart. While acknowledging that Göring's grandiosely entitled Atlantic Air Command has finally provided reconnaissance by six Ju 290s, Dönitz argues that twice this number of aircraft are needed just for minimum cover. And by deploying the boats at 30-mile intervals, they were too far apart to rush to Bahr's sighting of the convoy. It's a vicious circle: you have to spread out the few boats available in order to rake as large a sector of the ocean as possible, but then you cannot concentrate them sufficiently quickly once a sighting has been made.

Above all, Dönitz is angry that the Borkum boats did not keep him properly informed, especially about air attacks, during the course of the operation. A terse general instruction admonishes all boats to report the following five categories when under attack by aircraft: 1) Date, time, and location of the u-boat. 2) The boat's speed and maritime phosphorescence. 3) Time and number of air attacks. Did they use a spotlight? What was the angle of approach? Did they drop bombs? 4) What radar detector did you use: *Naxos, Borkum, Wanze* 136 cm? And 5) Any special occurrences?

"Good bloody God!" Bahr hisses at Ballmann, "next he will want to know how many eggs and sausages we have left on board!" Ballmann replies that he has just received a new admonitory radio message in which Dönitz relates to his skippers a recent catastrophe due to the *Naxos* gear. The captain of a submarine forced to dive by air attack discovered that the *Naxos* cable caused the conning tower hatch to jam as it was being closed. The Commanding Officer ordered "blow tanks" and rushed to the bridge. "His order reached the control room too late, the boat dipped, the conning tower hatch was slammed from above, and the Commanding Officer was thrown overboard and not picked up." The moral: Never disrupt a dive; the water pressure will eventually "flatten out" the *Naxos* cable. "Wonder if the Tommies monitoring our radio traffic liked that one?" Bahr caustically queries Ballmann.

On 12 January *U305* sights what appears to be a destroyer in grid quadrant BE7697, but the distance is so great and the tin can is moving so fast that chase is out of the question. Two other boats, *U953* and *U382*, fire wrens at escort vessels, but neither finds the target. Later that day Dönitz demands a full report in light of his recent general instruction. *U645* does not respond. The patrol line has shrunk to just six boats. There are no new u-boats at Brest, St Nazaire, Lorient, or La Rochelle immediately ready to send out to reinforce the line. The garden rake has become a tuning fork. On 13 January Dönitz formally breaks off Borkum and orders the boats to set a northerly course at 30-mile intervals.

Under a new moon, *U305* proceeds to quadrant BE2859, due west of the English Channel. Admiral u-boats instructs Bahr to remain submerged by day, but in case of an enemy sighting to go up at once and to "operate energetically on the surface." "Wonder how the Great Lion expects us to detect a destroyer while submerged?" Bahr queries his Number One. Dönitz further lectures the u-boats that they are allowed to dive only "when the boat is endangered from the air." That, Bahr muses, is constantly! On 13 January an ancient Vickers Wellington long-range medium bomber from the RAF 172nd Squadron sinks *U231* with *Fliebos*. Apparently, Wenzel did not pay sufficient heed to Admiral u-boats's instructions! Further radio messages reveal that *U645*, *U426*, and *U757* are presumed lost.

All this time, Bahr and *U305* head ever closer to the waters surrounding the British Isles. "Perfidious Albion" at last! Raw irony: the patrol line is named for the Baltic Sea island, Rügen, where Bahr started his naval career.

Admiral U-boats has reached a decision: to gather all available boats singly and in varying concentrations in a giant arc from Brittany in the south to the Faeroe Islands in the north, with Ireland as the fulcrum. Eighteen boats of the Rügen group already in the area will be augmented by six new grey wolves arriving from France, as well as by the last four Borkum boats: *U305*, *U382*, *U377*, and *U641*. Dönitz posts two U-boats as distant scouts: *U386* in the North Channel and *U260* off Reykjavik. Finally, the "Koralle" sites three weather boats—*U544*, *U763*, *U960*—in the central Atlantic. The scouts and the weather boats will have to compensate for the lack of radar.

"Herr Kaleu! Come to the radio compartment. There is a message in *Offizier* cipher for you from Admiral U-boats!" Christ, what does he want now? The number of loaves of bread remaining? Or the time of my last bowel movement? None of the above! "*U305*. For Kapitänleutnant Bahr (Rudolf). Congratulations on the German Cross in Gold. Admiral U-boats." Must be belatedly for the *St Croix*. Nice touch! Bahr recalls that the *Deutsches Kreuz*, introduced in 1941 as a distinct award above the Iron Cross 1st Class but below the Knight's Cross, features a large black swastika in enamel, surrounded by a wreath of oak leaves, with a sunburst star radiating out from its centre. Bahr chuckles to himself as he remembers what Berlin wags call the new 2.5-inch-wide decoration: NSDAP Party Badge for the Nearsighted! Now, I need only 85,000 tons more for the Knight's Cross! Or perhaps another tin can?

As the reinforced Rügen group drifts north towards Ireland, Dönitz continues to pepper his commanders with instructions. Admonitory Radio Message No. 80 reminds the captains that the adversary's material "superiority" in the U-boat war can only be overcome by detailed attention to any and all orders from Admiral U-boats! The "broadcast" is yet one more piece in what some of the skippers deride as the "flood of never-ending and constantly changing orders and instructions." Now, Dönitz radioes, such admonitions to U-boat captains will not "cease until we have achieved a decided edge. Until then, the boats must wrestle with it." Only the central control command in Bernau can oversee all aspects of a complex operation. Stay tuned. Stay alert. And follow orders!

But the commanders are a stubborn lot. On 16 January Dönitz cryptically enters in his war diary, "Group Rügen no report," making a note of the insubordination for future reference. But he does not share with his commanders a devastating confidential report from the Naval War Staff, Second Division, Submarine Operations: *U284* lost on first patrol; *U391* lost on first patrol; *U648* lost on second patrol; *U849* lost on first patrol; *U850* lost on first patrol. Life expectancy in the U-boats has plummeted almost to a single patrol. Only 1 percent of U-boat crews survive two years at the front.

On 17 January 1944 a Luftwaffe HE 177 weather flight sights a convoy in quadrant AM4336, due west of Islay. The pilot reports twenty-five to thirty freighters, escorted by six destroyers and two light cruisers. Course 250 degrees, west-south-west; estimated speed 10 knots. A B-24J Liberator out of Northern Ireland is overhead and drives the HE 177 off. Bernau immediately orders the Rügen group to head for AM4336 "at full speed in order to position for attack by day or for attack by night on 19 January."

"Captain to the bridge! Shadows bearing two-five! Range 5000 metres!"

It is noon, 17 January 1944. *U305* is in position 49°39' north, 20°10' west, roughly 420 miles west-southwest of Clear Island at the southwestern tip of Ireland. The sea is rising rapidly and the wind is howling about the bridge. Spray and foam whip the watch, and Atlantic rollers crash against *U305*'s superstructure. Not a good day for hunting! "Clear the bridge! Half-ahead both engines!" Bahr yells. "Take her down to periscope depth, Chief!" No use bucking this storm. After all, what did Dönitz order? "Shoot blind at great depths." Good day to try it.

Bahr's lookout has spotted the RN Escort Group B1, homeward bound after searching for German blockade runners. On this day B1 consists of three old V & W Class destroyers—*Wanderer*, *Watchman*, and *Woodpecker*—and the new River Class Frigate *Glenarm*. The Senior Officer is aboard *Woodpecker*. The old destroyers are ghosts from a bygone era. Once the pride of the RN's destroyer fleet, their keels were laid during the First World War. They were built to launch high-speed torpedo attacks against the Imperial German navy's battleships and battle-cruisers. When the RN's grim struggle against Dönitz's U-boats began, they were

quickly pressed into service as escorts. By early 1944 they have been extensively modified. Boilers have been removed and replaced with additional fuel tanks—speed has been sacrificed for range. They sport the
latest British-designed radars: Type 271 to detect u-boats, Type 293 to
warn of enemy aircraft. Their new Type 144 asdics are the best in the
world, and they mount the deadly new hedgehog spigot mortar on their
forecastles. The converted destroyers have lost their torpedoes, but they
have more than enough firepower with two 4.7-inch guns and four 20-
mm Oerlikons to make quick work of a surfaced u-boat. *Wanderer*'s
crew has scrounged a fifth Oerlikon. In a pinch, these destroyers can lay
down a ten-charge pattern from their two twin depth-charge throwers,
one on either side near the stern, and their twin depth-charge rails.

The four warships are steering 57 degrees and steaming at 12 knots.
They are all anxious to return to Londonderry after many weeks at sea,
but the falling glass, the heavy swell, and the rising winds and mounting
waves dictate caution. They are 3 miles apart in line abreast, with *Glenarm* on the starboard wing and *Wanderer*, *Woodpecker*, and *Watchman* to
the left in that order. All three are sweeping the waters ahead with their
asdic beams, but the heaving seas and the presence of many shoals of fish
make asdic conditions less than ideal. All three destroyers are veterans.
Wanderer has completed more transatlantic crossings than her crew cares
to remember. She has also braved the run to Murmansk and helped to
keep the supply lines open to the Allied troops fighting in Sicily. In the
course of her duties, she has already sunk three of Dönitz's u-boats and
killed more than 120 of his men. Her captain is Reginald "Bob" Whinney, a man whose naval career was almost cut short in the early 1930s.

Son of a dashing but undistinguished major in the Oxford and Bucks
Light Infantry, young Bob had been sent to the Royal Naval College at
Dartmouth. There he soaked up Royal Navy tradition while also developing a healthy scepticism about the intelligence of some of his superiors. He became known as a maverick, not a good thing for a man
aspiring to a career as a naval officer. He further blotted his copy book
during the Invergordon Mutiny of 1931 when he dared suggest to his superiors that the mutineers—ratings who objected to the foul conditions
of service—had a point that ought to be addressed. That almost finished
him. Later, he added to his tarnished reputation by specializing in anti-
submarine warfare, which few upwardly mobile RN officers did in the

late 1930s. When the war broke out, Whinney had been on the China station as a flotilla ASW officer and was then assigned to *Cossack*, one of the navy's powerful Tribal Class destroyers. After *Cossack* it was fifteen long months in the hell hole of Freetown, on the west African coast, before word arrived to return to England to take command of *Wanderer*.

Whinney joined *Wanderer* in Devonport, England, in March 1943. He knew she had already killed *U147* in June 1941 and *U401* in August of that same year. He hoped to carry on the tradition, but *Wanderer* was scarcely in any shape for sea duty when Whinney first saw her at the bottom of her dry dock. Her innards were exposed and her deck was covered in wires, pipes, scrap metal, boxes, packing cases, tarpaulins, and steel plates. Men with jack hammers, welding equipment, and cutting torches swarmed all over her. But the job was done within two months, and *Wanderer* put to sea with her longer range and better gear to find and kill enemy submarines. Whinney did not disappoint his superiors, as he brought *U523* to the surface some 400 miles west of Spain on 25 August with a series of well-planned depth-charge and hedgehog attacks and sank it with gunfire. Notwithstanding this triumph, Whinney was convinced that hedgehogs were overrated as an ASW device. He believed that the most important ASW weapon on any ship was the Captain. It was his luck, his skill as a hunter, and his determination not to give up until every iota of hope of finding the enemy below was gone that told in the end.

Bahr is about to face his deadliest foe.

———————————

In *U305*'s control room, Bahr sits on the bicycle seat and slowly rotates the periscope on its axis. "Escorts, bow right! 1500 metres!" It's hard to make out the low profiles in these gigantic ocean rollers. One minute the scope is high above the horizon on the crest of a grey-green mountain, and the next it is submerged in the inky water. Darkness envelops the sea.

"Open outer doors Tubes 2 and 4! Flood Tubes 2 and 4!" Might as well give it a shot, Bahr muses.

"Tubes 2 and 4 flooded, sir!" the torpedo gang snaps back almost instantly. Sander begins to enter vital data into his torpedo calculator at a feverish pace: target speed, angle, range. Bahr keeps the cross-hairs of the periscope focused on the escorts as best he can. Damned hard to see anything except salt spray and ocean foam in this hurricane! And too little light to make anything out!

The Old Man barks out "One-third-ahead, both e-motors, Chief!" Sander rhythmically echoes "Angle zero! Range 1200! Speed 12 knots!" Still, Bahr cannot see anything but house-high dark, menacing Atlantic breakers.

Suddenly, a barrage of asdic pings bounce off *U305*'s hull—a thousand small hammer blows. "Impulses bearing dead ahead! Getting stronger!" It is 1:55 p.m.

"Chief, take her down to 80 metres!" Bahr roars. The asdic pebbles intensify in volume. *Verdammt*! Bahr knows this routine only too well: at least one of the warships has caught *U305* in its asdic. But if it is only one and he can squirm away from it quickly enough, not much will be lost.

Wanderer's asdic beam scans the waters around the ship every three seconds. With his heavy navy duffle coat wrapped about him, Sub-Lieutenant D.J. Kidd is standing his watch on the bridge, holding the bridge rail as *Wanderer* pitches and rolls in the mounting sea. Kidd is not only the Officer of the Watch but *Wanderer*'s Anti-Submarine Control Officer as well. In the event of action stations, Kidd's place is right here.

Low clouds scud across the seascape. Kidd can see about 5 miles, but only with great difficulty. It is 1:55 p.m. From the wooden asdic hut at the back of the bridge comes the voice of the operator: "We've got a contact of some kind bearing 240, range 1200 yards. There's no Doppler, sir, I'm not sure what it is."

Kidd knows the asdic beam is bending in the heaving seas. Fish shoals, cavities of air trapped between waves, different water temperatures at different depths in this northern extension of the gulfstream are all playing tricks with the asdic set. What would a sub be doing here? None have been reported. None were expected. Still, better call the captain.

"Captain, sir, bridge."

Whinney has been fighting a bad cold for days. He is dozing in his sea cabin when Kidd calls.

"Yes, Sub-Lieutenant, what is it?"

"Sir, we're getting a reading on the trace recorder bearing 240 degrees, range 1200 yards. We're not sure it's a sub, sir, but I thought I'd let you know."

Whinney can easily hear the asdic repeater from his bunk.

"Sounds like fish to me, but I'll be right there." Whinney is beside Kidd within seconds, pulling on his duffle coat:

"Send for Cocks and go have a listen yourself. I'll take the bridge in the meantime." Leading Seaman Cocks is the Higher Submarine Detector and an expert with the asdic.

"He's already in the cabin, sir," Kidd replies.

"So, what does he think, Mr Kidd, and what do you think?" Kidd looks at the asdic hut for a moment, then scans the heaving seas.

"There's lots of fish down there and the waves are affecting the beam. You can see all that on the recorder. But every now and then there's a good solid return as well. There's a definite pattern, sir. I think there's a sub there, somewhere."

Whinney quickly decides: "OK, Sub, that's good enough for me. Let's go right at it. Sound action stations."

The bells begin to ring all over the ship, and men quickly don helmets and life-jackets and rush to their action stations.

"Chief Yeoman, make to *Woodpecker*, repeat to Admiralty: 'Contact at 1355. Am attacking.' Give our course and speed and whatever information you can on the contact." He orders Kidd to increase speed to 18 knots, but to stand by to reduce speed to 14 when he gives the word. He knows this is dangerous, that it might bring a gnat tearing into his stern, but the helmsman will have trouble holding the ship's head in these seas at 8 knots. Whinney gambles that any gnat fired will be thrown off by the cavitation noises from the tumbling wave tops. Then, to the depth-charge officer Whinney shouts, "We'll give it five of our best, set them for 150 feet."

Even at 18 knots, *Wanderer* is slow to come about and close the contact in the heavy seas. With the ship's crew closed up to action stations, Whinney is now running the destroyer, but Kidd's place is still on the bridge. Kidd squeezes himself into the asdic hut to count down the range. The asdic repeater is pinging and the unmistaken sound of a metallic echo can clearly be heard among the false echoes. The solid returns get closer together as they near the contact. The trace recorder needle in the asdic hut scratches across the iodized paper. The depth-charge and hedgehog crews wait for their orders.

Kidd watches the trace recorder, then calls to Whinney: "We're coming up on the target, sir." Whinney orders speed reduced to 14 knots. Almost immediately, Kidd pushes the firing buzzer. Two depth-charges sail off their throwers, three more drop astern. Five columns of sea water burst the rough surface of the ocean and climb skyward, but there is no wreckage, no fuel oil. Is there a U-boat there? Whinney thinks so, but he's not completely certain. Asdic contact is lost as the exploding depth-charges stir the waters beneath the ship.

As *Wanderer*'s screws draw closer, Bahr orders a slow turn to port and instructs Brenner to rig for silent running. Five heavy explosions ahead of *U305* lift the boat and shake its every section, but there is no structural damage. Nine minutes later, the crew of *U305* hears the sound of destroyer screws again. "Propeller blades. Amplitude 4, Herr Kaleu!" Ballmann picks up slight noises on the hydrophone. They are twenty-four hedgehog mortars striking the water.

Wanderer swings around quickly after her depth-charge run.

"Contact seems to have turned to port at the last minute," Kidd yells from the asdic hut.

"Make ready on hedgehog."

"Hedgehog ready, sir."

"Contact, sir, fine on the port bow."

"How far out, Sub?" Whinney must know the range.

"Less than 1000 yards, sir."

"If you lose the trace, fire on estimate."

"Aye, aye, sir."

Kidd peers at the trace recorder. He can feel *Wanderer*'s powerful turbines pushing her through the sea. He hits the firing buzzer. The hedgehogs whoosh up and sail forward of the forecastle, striking the sea ahead within seconds. There are no explosions.

"Damned hedgehog, bloody thing's useless. I need a contact, Mr Kidd. Begin a box search."

Carefully, the Coxswain nurses *Wanderer* around in the dark and heaving seas. As she heads into the wind, Kidd yells: "There's been an explosion down there, sir."

"Are you sure?" Whinney asks. It's been at least ten minutes since the hedgehogs burrowed beneath the surface of the sea.

"There's no doubt, sir, but I can't hear any breaking up noises or anything to indicate a hit."

Whinney hates the hedgehog. "Well, nothing to do but keep looking."

"*Woodpecker* signalling, sir." It's the Chief Yeoman. "She can't pick anything up. The SOE suggests we do a line abreast search."

"Ha," thinks Whinney. "So the Old Man wants a piece of the action, does he? Well, it's not his call. I'm the ship in contact and the rules are clear: it's my show."

"No, Chief Yeoman, we'll not do that now, we'll lose that contact permanently in the time it'll take to bring *Glenarm* and *Watchman* up. Make to *Woodpecker*: 'Thanks for the offer, but I'm going to keep after it by myself. Request you stand by for help if needed.'" Then, almost as an afterthought, he raises the depth-charge crew on the voicepipe. "As soon as we regain contact, we'll head right for it and I want ten of the best as fast as possible."

The depth-charge crew will have a hard time manhandling the heavy TNT-filled barrels on to the rails for a ten-charge pattern with the destroyer heaving in these rolling seas.

For Bahr and his crew, the minutes are filled with tension and anxiety. Several times, Ballmann reports the approach of propeller blades, but Bahr detects no new depth-charge or hedgehog attacks. Have the tin cans abandoned the hunt? No such luck! At 2:48 p.m. asdic pebbles again bounce off *U305*'s steel hull. *Wanderer* has regained contact at 2600 yards and is beginning her attack run. At 2:59 p.m. the pings stop, but still Ballmann reports that the destroyer screws are coming closer. Bahr orders a slow turn to starboard. Ten muffled depth-charge blasts tear apart the seas above *U305*. The boat is hurled sideways and down. "Extremely violent vibrations!" Bahr shouts for the KTB. Deckplates rattle, steel ribs groan, lights flicker on and off. But again, there is no major damage. The *Wabos* were set at 150 and 300 feet—too shallow.

Brenner quickly makes his customary damage reports. The air in the boat is becoming a problem: a noxious mix of urine, chlorine gas from the batteries, and diesel fuel. Water drips off the cold steel hull as the humidity in the boat rises. But there is no chance to go up as long as the tin cans cruise overhead. Asdic rolls off *U305*'s hull again at 3:02 p.m. and nine minutes later it ends just as suddenly. Then it reappears at 3:39 p.m. Dogged pursuers, whoever they are, Bahr muses.

At 3:40 p.m. Ballmann barks out: "Destroyer screws 1500 metres; getting stronger!" Asdic again finds *U305*.

Glenarm has come up to help. *Wanderer* stands off to guide her consort to the spot where she has last had contact. The SOE is still dubious that they are chasing a submarine and Whinney also harbours some doubts. But he isn't about to give up, even though the early winter twilight and the heavy seas are making a coordinated search almost impossible. *Glenarm* picks up the contact at 3:40 p.m. bearing 350 at 1500 yards. She closes and fires her hedgehog.

Below, Ballmann reports another two dozen hedgehog mortars slicing through the water at 3:46 p.m.; they pass far ahead of *U305*. No damage. *Glenarm* has fired the salvo much too early. Up above, *Wanderer* regains contact. Whinney orders another ten-charge pattern. The SOE is getting edgy. The seas continue to mount and the sky to grow darker. He is convinced *Wanderer* is chasing a false echo. Whinney badly wants to prove him wrong. This will be another high-speed run. Damn the gnats! Kidd presses the firing buzzer. Four charges sail off the throwers, six rumble off *Wanderer*'s stern.

Bahr must time his manoeuvre carefully. He waits for what seems like an eternity. Then he orders a slow turn to starboard. Wham! A sudden, sharp blow near the bow section! Nine more heavy sledgehammer blows off to starboard at depths of 250 and 385 feet. The time is 3:51 p.m.

Bahr cannot believe the news from Brenner: "Battery Room 2: several cells leaking acid! Section IIK leaking! Diesel from Fuel Oil Tank 2 in the bilge!"

Brenner rushes his engine crew to the batteries to bypass the damaged cells and to stop the leaking. For the next half-hour, the Chief works feverishly to control the damage to the fuel-oil tank and Section IIK. Bahr's only choice is to creep along silently and to hope that the gale above will dissuade the hunters from their deadly task. He orders the boat down to 2A—500 feet. This fifth attack is the most serious yet.

At around 4 p.m., with the gale blowing up even stronger (force 9) and darkness fast approaching, the SOE considers calling off the hunt. "There is no U-boat there," he signals *Wanderer*. Spotters have seen plenty of gulls and fish, but the SOE cannot pick up a solid contact. Whinney insists there is a U-boat beneath his ship, but he is not 100 percent certain. The evidence points to a submarine. His Higher Submarine Detector insists that the contact has "submarine" qualities as to tone, firmness, small extent of target, and Doppler. And the plot of the target suggests it is not just fish. But at bottom Whinney knows there is a U-boat because he can feel it in his bones. He's not about to ask his Chief Yeoman to signal that to the SOE!

Wanderer opens to extreme range and leads *Glenarm* to the target. At 4:17 p.m. the frigate gains contact with *U305* moving on a course of 075°; eight minutes later, at a range of 400 yards, *Glenarm* puts ten charges down. Bahr's craft is pounded by the explosions:

"*Wabo* detonations! Continuous detonations! Four in the distance, below, in rapid succession! Another two! Four at close range!"

The slender steel tube is thrown about violently. *Glenarm* had set the depth at 350 and 550 feet, and the deeper *Wabos* nearly found their target. Damned close to accurate for depth and range!

Bahr and *U305* have now been playing a game of cat and mouse with the four tin cans above for nearly four hours. They have sustained six separate attacks by HMS *Wanderer* and HMS *Glenarm* and suffered serious damage to the bow section. Over and over, Bahr queries Ballmann: "Are they going away yet?" Each time he gets the same reply: "No change." The entire crew, all fifty men, have heard the staccato pings of the asdic on and off for 205 minutes. To Rudolf's incessant requests, "Stronger or weaker?" Ballmann simply shakes his head. "No change, Herr Kaleu!"

Every twenty or thirty minutes, the men brace themselves for the blows of the depth-charges and hedgehog mortars and their droning echoes. The lights have long ceased to function. The steel hull groans and cracks, and the bulkheads creak every time the blows rock the boat. No one is interested in the *Smutje's* offers of ersatz coffee and mildewy sandwiches. Brenner struggles heroically to trim the boat and to keep her keel level. At 500 feet, he cannot afford a single mistake—or the boat will slide 2.4 miles straight down to the ocean floor.

The inside of the hull is getting almost unbearable. Moisture drips in rivulets from cold pipes, ducts, and deck-head steel plates. The bilge runs wild with a vile darkish-brown swill. The humidity stands at 100 percent. Suddenly, the men notice that the pings and the pounding have stopped. It is 5 p.m., 5:30, then 6, and still there is no asdic. At 6:05 there are a few light pings, then nothing for another hour. Whinney tries to lead HMS *Woodpecker* on to the target, but fails. He and *Glenarm* continue the search.

––––––––––––

Bahr thanks God for the strong gale and the darkness! The stench in the boat now is almost unbearable, but soon it will be safe to break surface. There will be cold fresh air and welcome salt spray!

Chief Brenner finally has time to undertake a detailed damage assessment. His report is not encouraging:

"Leakage from the overhead exhaust manifolds!"

"Leakage from the overhead forward torpedo storage tubes!"

"Leakage from the bow torpedo flange!"

"Leakage from the forward galley hatch!"

Now, that sounds familiar. Bahr runs through his mind the Great Lion's reminder of 12 December concerning *U333* having survived nine hours of depth-charging: "What a well-drilled crew can do!" Damn it, so is mine!

"Propeller noises coming on strong!" *Scheisse*! Once more, asdic pebbles bounce off the hull in rapid succession. Damned tenacious bastards! Don't they know there is a strong gale howling out there, that it is pitch dark, and that they are endangering their crews? Bahr orders still another slow turn to port.

Kidd leans out of the asdic hut and yells into the wind and the driving spray: "Contact again, sir, bearing 010, range 1200 yards."

Whinney reacts quickly. "I want a sixteen-charge pattern. They'll have to step lively back there, but we may not get another chance. She must be very deep by now. Set half the charges at 350 and half at 500 feet. Give me revolutions for 14 knots."

Wanderer pushes through the heavy seas, slowing a few revolutions before Kidd hits the firing buzzer.

A few seconds after 7:16 p.m., *U305* is repeatedly hammered. The *Wabos* explode all around, as well as below and astern. It is the heaviest attack yet. The crew is jolted out of its dreamy confidence. But still there is no major damage. The modified barrage pattern from *Wanderer* is correct for line, but fired late. The Old Man seems to have a knack for turning his boat to port just at the critical moment.

Bahr inspects his boat. The men are near the limits of their physical and psychological endurance. They have been going through this dark, deadly hell for almost six hours now. Clouds of thin blue smoke— steam—fill the boat. The bilge sloshes over with the usual brine: diesel fuel oil, piss, and hydrochloric acid. Several cells in Battery 2 have sprung leaks—again—and sea water is reacting with the battery acid to produce deadly chlorine gas. The men stare at the Old Man through reddish eyes. How much longer?

Brenner had not been able to ventilate the boat, charge the batteries, or pump the bilge when last on the surface because of the high seas and 25-knot winds. The e-cells are on their last reserves. The needle of the amperage/hour meter is near zero. Even at "crawl speed"—*Schleich-fahrt*—there is a limit to what she can do. The stench in the boat is overpowering. Oxygen is at a premium.

"Break out the cartridges!" Bahr's order activates the crew. Each man on duty gets a potash cartridge to augment breathing. Each man clamps his nose, bites the mouthpiece of his black rubber hose, and exhales carbon dioxide into and draws hot air through the potash filter contained in a 2-lb black box strapped to his chest. Heavy coughing ensues and eyes burn. How much longer?

On the surface, night has fallen. The mountainous seas are throwing *Wanderer* around like a toy boat. The asdic is barely functioning. The radar is useless. *Glenarm* is still standing off, ready to lend a hand, *Woodpecker* and *Watchman* are somewhere close by, but hard to spot in the raging storm. *Wanderer's* crew has been at action stations for almost seven hours in the worsening weather. Even the most even-tempered among them are beginning to doubt Whinney's sanity, or at least his judgment. It is all young Kidd can do to keep the asdic operators concentrating on the search. They have long ago concluded that *Wanderer* is chasing a ghost. Whinney stands beside the captain's chair smoking cigarette after cigarette. He is drenched and cold and tired. He can hear the edge in the men's voices as they acknowledge orders. Kidd, too, seems to have lost faith.

It is 7:50 p.m. Kidd leans out of the asdic hut again: "Captain, contact bearing 190. Target is moving left. We've picked up her screws, sir. There's no doubt now."

A depth-charge attack in this raging sea is out of the question. Much as he hates to use hedgehog, Whinney has little choice. *Wanderer* pushes into the sea at 10 knots. Kidd hits the firing buzzer and the hedgehog mortar bombs sail up, over the bow, and plunge into the ocean.

"Reload hedgehog. Quickly now." No explosions.

"Target appears to have moved to port at the last minute, sir." Once again contact is lost in the raging sea.

"Sir, target seems to have come to a stop. We can't pinpoint its location."

Is the German playing dead? Or has he been damaged? Whinney takes *Wanderer* 1500 yards up-sea of the suspected U-boat. "As soon as we pick something up, we'll go in at 15 knots, down-sea. What's the status of the hedgehog?"

"About one minute to completing the reload, Captain."

It'll be a risky operation. What if the U-boat spots the destroyer and fires a gnat?

Asdic pebbles bounce off Bahr's boat again. The crew braces itself for a ninth attack. Since the tin cans seem to have set on 350 feet for their depth-charges, Bahr orders *U305* down another 65 feet: "Foreplanes down 10! Stern planes up 7!" Brenner slowly nudges the vessel down. Perhaps there is safety in greater depth.

"Herr Kaleu, the forward dive planes are stuck!" Just like the last two patrols! The forward dive plane mechanism as well as capstan and chain motors must have been damaged by the attack at 3:51 p.m. The planesmen throw their bodies against the levers of the foreplanes. Nothing. Ever so slowly, *U305* angles towards the ocean floor.

"Every man aft!" As many of the crew of fifty as can be spared from their stations rush towards the stern to help push it down. No use. The needle on the depth-gauge continues to fall: 180 metres, 185, 190, 195, 200. The depth-gauge is calibrated only to 200 metres! And the Flender-Werke in Lübeck gave *U305* a normal depth rating of just 150 metres! All the same, the boat's momentum carries it on a downward trajectory. The game is up.

"Full speed astern! Both e-motors!" Bahr decides to risk sonar detection and to bring the boat up over the stern planes. It is his only hope. Bahr has tried this manoeuvre twice before, once on the surface and once submerged. But never at such depths. Both motors jump into full reverse on the last available electric power. The crew rushes through the boat to their customary places. Slowly, the needle of the depth-gauge begins to rise: 195 metres, 190, 185, 180, 175. *U305* is on her way up.

"Sir, the sub's started up again." It is 8:45 p.m. Whinney cannot believe his luck: *Wanderer's* hydrophone is picking up "submarine" effect.

"Mr Kidd, attack on estimate." Then, as an afterthought, he adds: "We've waited this long, don't be too bloody eager." At 8:56 p.m. Kidd hits the firing buzzer and another hedgehog salvo sails into the darkness. The range to contact is just 220 yards. Fifteen seconds later, an explosion rends the sea below and forward of *Wanderer's* bows. Almost everyone forward of *Wanderer's* engine room can hear it. The asdic operator tells Kidd he thinks it was at a depth of 175 feet. It is obviously a solid hit on a real submarine. Whinney knows the battle is almost over.

———————

The son of a bitch upstairs just won't let go, Bahr fumes. Most of the men are now too weak to raise themselves up. Some just crouch on the deck-plates coughing incessantly. Some vomit. Some soil themselves. Streams of water pour into the boat through the leaking galley hatch, propeller packings, exhaust vents, and torpedo tubes.

"Hedgehog, Herr Kaleu!"

Ballman's scream echoes in Bahr's ears as a powerful blow jolts the submarine from somewhere up front. There is a loud roar as sea water pours into the mortal wound opened in the hull by one of the hedgehogs. The expanding volume of water pushes the remaining air into the undamaged sections of the hull. Bahr's eardrums disintegrate. As the pain explodes into his skull, he tries to remember what they taught him at U-boat School. A column of water 10 metres high exerts the pressure of one atmosphere (14.5 lbs per square inch). At a depth of 1000 feet, the pressure equals roughly thirty atmospheres, or 435 lbs per square inch. But at what level or at what atmosphere does a submarine become a crushed metal can? No one has ever returned to reveal this truth.

Time: 8:56 p.m. Date: 17 January 1944. Place: the North Eastern Atlantic Basin, 700 miles west-southwest of Clear Island, Ireland; 49°39' north, 20°10' west.

In the asdic hut on the bridge of the *Wanderer*, Kidd hears a second blast, much louder and heavier than the first, followed by smaller detonations and the creaking and grinding of metal. He reports simply and briefly to his Captain: "Breaking-up noises."

In a strong gale and heavy sea, and returning from patrol, *Wanderer*, aided by *Glenarm*, has snuffed out the lives of Rudolf Bahr and the fifty officers and men of *U305*. The destroyers and frigate of Escort Group B1 search for wreckage for more than two hours to make a positive identification—and then for survivors. They find neither.

In Brest, Third Machinist Mate Hans Bethke heads back to the Base Hospital for a final check-up on the abscessed tooth that had kept him from joining his mates for *U305*'s fourth patrol on 8 December 1943. He is the only "survivor" of *U305*.

The last entry into Grand Admiral Karl Dönitz's *Kriegstagebuch* concerning *U305* and her crew is for 17 January 1944. It is professional and laconic to a fault: "Lost in BE24 on 17. 1. 1944."

U305 is one of 736 "iron coffins" that rest on the ocean's floor. Lieutenant Rudolf Bahr and his crew are among the 30,000 officers and ratings who never returned from the longest battle of the Second World War.

On 15 May 1944 Margret Bahr in Landsberg on the Warthe River receives a small box containing the *Deutsches Kreuz* that Bahr never saw. Accompanying it is a black-bordered letter with a black Iron Cross as its masthead.

> Your beloved son, Kapitänleutnant Rudolf Bahr, along with all his crew died a hero's death on 17 January 1944 for Führer, Volk, and Fatherland. True to his oath of loyalty, he gave his life to the Fatherland, fulfilling his soldierly duty as a model officer. You, Mrs Bahr, have sacrificed what was dearest to you for the greatness and the future of our Volk.
>
> Heil Hitler!
> Werner Winter, Commander and Flotilla Chief.

Epilogue

Are they so very different now, HMCS *St Croix* and *U305*?

The crushed remains of Dobson's destroyer rest on the bottom of the Atlantic at roughly latitude 48°12' north, 40°56' west—at the northern end of the broad canyon that connects the Labrador and Newfoundland basins. The crushed remains of Bahr's U-boat lie on the bottom of the same ocean at roughly latitude 49°39' north, 20°10' west—in the middle of the West Europe Basin. Ironically, the sunken hulks lie at almost the same latitude, though 1000 miles apart. Equally ironically, *St Croix* is approximately 600 miles east of Newfoundland, while *U305* is some 600 miles west of England.

Were they so very different, then, these two vessels of war and the men who sailed, fought, and died in them? Now, many decades after the end of the Second World War, it is tempting to declare that they were brothers in arms while they were alive, and that they rest as brothers in the arms of the sea for all eternity.

There is an affinity that men of war show for each other when they become old warriors. In the more than half-century since the end of the greatest war in history, veterans from both sides—soldiers, sailors, airmen—have come together many times. They raise a glass to long dead comrades and they declare that the animosities of the battlefield have now given way to the mutual understanding of men who have faced death in combat.

There is no denying the sincerity of what they feel. They are different from the rest of us who have never faced the great physical and psychological tests that combat is. Those who have been under fire do have more in common with each other in some ways than they do with everyone else on Earth. But the worth, the value, the identity of a man or woman is not measured only by how close he or she was to the sound of the guns. There are many more measures of what human beings are, and what defines their attitude to, and relation with, the world around them.

St Croix and *U305* were both vessels of war, and the men who sailed aboard them were both engaged in the task of finding and killing their enemies. They were almost, without exception, just kids: men barely out of their teens; men who killed, risked death, and died before they had any experience of life at all. And even the old ones among them— men like Andrew Hedley Dobson—were neophytes at their deadly trade.

But there the similarity ends. Just as the majestic peaks of the greatest mountain range on Earth, the Mid-Atlantic Range, separate the graves of *St Croix* and *U305*, so, too, a mountain of difference separated the crews of those two warships in the cause they fought for.

After the end of the Second World War, German authors began to relate the tales of the grey wolves, the steel sharks, the iron coffins that went to sea for Germany between 1939 and 1945. Most of these authors brushed aside any questions of morality by declaring that the young men on the u-boat service were "just soldiers." They were only doing their duty to defend their country. Surely they cannot be held responsible for the launching of an aggressive war, for the mass war crimes, or for the crimes against humanity committed by the Third Reich. The same claim has been repeatedly made, after all, by others about the soldiers who fought in the Wehrmacht or the airmen who flew for the Luftwaffe.

There is a germ of truth to this rationalization: Rudolf Bahr never deliberately murdered a Jew out of racial hatred. But if Bahr had prevailed, if Dönitz had prevailed, if the u-boat offensive had succeeded, Hitler would have ruled half the world for a very long time. We have had enough dramatic evidence of what he and his helpers were able to accomplish in the territory they did rule, for only a few years, to know what a curse that would have been on humankind.

No doubt the crew of HMCS *St Croix*, and HMS *Itchen*, and all the other Allied escorts sunk in the Second World War contained a good selection of both saints and sinners. No doubt, too, they sailed against Hitler for many reasons. Some were just plain bored with civilian life and went for the adventure. Some joined the navy for three square meals a day and a warm place to sleep. Some signed up to defend home, nation, and what was then known as "the Christian way of life." But it does not matter why they volunteered, because the cause they were defending was the survival of civilized life as we know it.

So the hulks of the *St Croix* and *U305* are not very different. Both vessels were inanimate objects then; if we could see them now, we likely could not tell them apart in their silty graves at the bottom of the sea. But each of these hulks has been attached by history to a powerful symbolism. The submarine sailed under the swastika, a flag that was the scourge of almost all western, central, and eastern Europe, the Balkans, Scandinavia, and North Africa. The destroyer sailed under the Union Jack—a tattered banner of freedom and human dignity at a time when the lights had gone out in so much of the world.

May the souls of all their crews now rest in peace.

A Word on Sources

The reader of a docudrama or work of historical recreation such as this is entitled to know what is truth and what is fiction. In a nutshell, all actions at sea have been faithfully reconstructed from surviving archival materials; actual conversations and numerous undertakings ashore have by and large had to be reconstructed from available memoirs and other accounts or, quite simply, made up.

Technical details regarding the construction, operation, maintenance, mothballing, and recommissioning of USS *McCook* and other destroyers of her class were obtained from Records of the United States Navy (RG 80) at the National Archives in Washington (NAW) and from M.J. Whitley, *Destroyers of World War Two* (London 1988), John D. Alden, *Flush Decks and Four Pipes* (Annapolis 1989), and Arnold Hague, *Destroyers for Great Britain* (London 1988). Hague's book contains much information on the "destroyers for bases" agreement and the hand-over of the fifty destroyers. So does Phillip Goodhart, *Fifty Ships That Saved the World* (Garden City, NJ 1965). Original records of the hand-overs are available at the NAW in RG 80, at the National Archives of Canada (NAC) in RG 24, and at the Public Record Office (PRO) at Kew, United Kingdom.

With regard to Rudolf Bahr's career, the pertinent facts were taken from his official copy book or *Personalnachweis*, acquired from the Deutsche Dienststelle in Berlin, and from the *Rangliste der Deutschen Kriegsmarine* (Berlin 1934–44). Bahr's early days as a naval cadet were taken from Crew 1935, the official album of his class of 1935 at the Naval Academy, which included his trip on board the cruiser *Emden*. Mention should also be made of a superb treatment of the crew just prior to Bahr's: Eric Christian Rust, *Crew 34: Deutsche Marineoffiziere in und nach der Hitlerzeit* (Private publication 1987), which rendered numerous insights into life and education at the Naval Academy, Kiel-Mürwik.

Harry Kingsley's life and career until his appointment to command HMCS *St Croix* have been reconstructed from his personnel files at the Personnel Records Unit (PRU) of NAC, and especially his regular fitness reports, done every six months, and his summary of service. This information was supplemented with recollections from former crew members, accounts of the Halifax explosion, and accounts of junior officers' lives in the Royal Navy between the wars.

Andrew Hedley Dobson's life and career until his appointment to command HMCS *St Croix* were reconstructed from his PRU files, from information about his family supplied by his son and daughter and other family members, from records of the ss *Nascopie* and Dobson's personnel files from the Hudson's Bay Company Archives in Winnipeg, and an account of his service in ss *Foundation Franklin* contained in Farley Mowat's *Grey Seas Under* (New York 1958). His service in the RCN prior to *St Croix* is reconstructed from deck logs and other pertinent files about *Fleur de Lis* and *Napanee* at NAC.

Rudolf Bahr's patrol in *U69* as Executive Officer is based on the boat's official war log: "Kriegstagebuch (KTB) von U-69, 7. U-Flotille, St. Nazaire," U-Boot-Archiv, Cuxhaven-Altenbruch; this log was checked for accuracy against the captured microfilm version of the KTB, Admiralty PG30066, vols. 7–9. Bahr's assumption of command and first three patrols as skipper of *U305* between September 1942 and October 1943 likewise stem from the boat's official war log: "Kriegstagebuch (KTB) von U-305, 8. U-Flotille, Brest," U-Boot-Archiv, Cuxhaven-Altenbruch; again, these logs were checked against the Admiralty microfilms PG30388, vols. 1–5. Thus, all technical details, sea and wind conditions, action and after-action reports, damage reports, enemy sightings, naval engagements, and evaluations by Admiral U-boats have been taken verbatim from the KTB.

To place Bahr's experiences with *U69* and *U305* within the larger framework of the overall German naval effort, a number of sources were consulted at the Federal Military Archive (Bundesarchiv-Militärarchiv) in Freiburg, Germany. First off, the radio traffic between Bahr and Admiral U-boats was gathered from Admiralty Records PG30388/5, Auszug aus der Funkkladde "U305." This material, in turn, was compared with radio intelligence reports that affected Bahr and *U305*: RM7/743 B-Bericht 1942 and 1943. Next, the boat's movements were charted on the Kriegsmarine's official naval grid maps of the Atlantic: Quadratkarte Nr. 1833G, 1843G, and 1870G. Thereafter, Bahr's actions were plotted against the official war logs of Grand Admiral Karl Dönitz, Admiral U-boats: RM 87, Kriegstagebuch (KTB), Befehlshaber der U-Boote (BdU), vols. 7–10; these records were compared with the official Admiralty translations into English, received from the Directorate of History, National Defence Headquarters, Ottawa, as DHIST 79/446. Finally, to place both Bahr and Admiral U-boats within the highest German command structure, two further sources were consulted: the official monthly diary of the Naval Supreme Command, RM7/54, Kriegstagebuch (KTB) der Seekriegsleitung (Skl), vols. 1–53; and the record of discussions by the Navy's Commanding Admiral with Adolf Hitler, RM7/177, 1 Skl. KTB Teil C VII, Überlegungen des Chefs der Skl und Niederschriften über Vorträge und Besprechungen beim Führer. All photographs of Bahr and *U305* are courtesy of the U-Boot-Archiv at Cuxhaven-Altenbruch.

The many voyages of HMCS *St Croix* under the command of both Harry Kingsley and Andrew Hedley Dobson have been pieced together from a variety of sources. The National Archives of Canada holds all surviving files pertaining to *St Croix*'s acquisition by the RCN, its refittings, damages sustained at sea, and modifications to improve both seaworthiness and ASW capability. NAC also holds files pertaining to *St Croix*'s voyages while assigned to the WLEF, her message logs, and her movement cards.

The major source for *St Croix*'s history with the NEF and MOEF is the PRO, which holds the Admiralty files, and especially ADM 199 and ADM 237, the classification under which most North Atlantic convoy operations fall. ADM 237 contains the so-called convoy covers, which include all pertinent information about particular convoys, including SOE reports, Commodore's reports, radio messages, reports of attacks by and against U-boats, aircraft, surface vessels, convoy sailing orders, course alteration instructions, and track charts. This material was supplemented by the Admiralty's quarterly reports of the war at sea. The PRO also holds reports of attacks against RN/RCN vessels and courts of inquiry reports for each loss of an RN/RCN vessel through enemy action. Admiralty records on convoy operations were supplemented by information in Marc Milner, *North Atlantic Run: The Royal Canadian Navy and the Battle for the Convoys* (Toronto 1985), Geoffrey Jones, *Defeat of the Wolfpacks* (London 1986), Tony German, *The Sea Is at Our Gates: The History of the Canadian Navy* (Toronto 1990), and Dan van Der Vat, *The Atlantic Campaign* (New York 1988).

No one has yet written extensively about living and fighting in a Town Class destroyer such as *St Croix*, but many excellent memoirs are available from former commanders, including D.A. Rayner, *Escort: The Battle of the Atlantic* (London 1955), who commanded an S Class destroyer, not unlike *St Croix* in it being a "wet" ship. Other memoirs such as Hal Lawrence, *A Bloody War: One Man's Memories of the Canadian Navy* (Toronto 1979), Alan Easton, *Fifty North: An Atlantic Battleground* (Toronto 1963), Roger Hill, *Destroyer Captain* (London 1975), Nicholas Monsarrat, *Three Corvettes* (London 1972), Ronald C. Weyman, *In Love and War* (Toronto 1995), and James B. Lamb, *On the Triangle Run* (Toronto 1986) tell of life in port in Halifax, St John's, and Londonderry. *Salty Dips*, published by the Naval Officers' Association of Canada, provided many stories of life at sea, as did William H. Pugsley, *Saints, Devils and Ordinary Seamen* (Toronto 1945), and Mac Johnston, *Corvettes Canada* (Toronto 1994).

Published and documentary information about *St Croix* was supplemented by interviews, tapes, or letters from former members of *St Croix*'s company. These informants include Donald Bullock, Ross Carnduff, Dan T. Dunlop, William Fisher, John Haverstock, Lorne Hickson, Fred Hodgson (brother of a *St Croix* crew member), Bruce Jewers, Carl Johnston, James Kelley, J.R. Kimber, Howard D. Laatsch, Mrs Jean MacLean (widow of a *St Croix* crew member), Sydney McNevin, Peter Melrose, Edgar Pennefather, David Pearson (*Ingerfire* survivor), Douglas Pearson, J.E. Roue, A.F. Salter, Harry Stanley, and Ronald Weyman.

The story of *St Croix*'s last voyage was put together primarily from the extensive records at the PRO and NAC about convoys ONS18/ON202, the records of proceedings of the inquiries into the losses of HM ships

Polyanthus and *Itchen* and HMCS *St Croix*, as well as the recollections of the lone survivor, William Fisher. Bahr's fourth and final patrol was recreated from the official war log of Admiral U-boats (RM 87), from the navy's monthly diary (RM 7/54) of actions at sea, from the Admiralty files pertaining to the attacks against *U305* carried out by HMS *Wanderer* and HMS *Glenarm*, and from the memoirs of Bob Whinney, *The U-Boat Peril* (Poole 1986).

Bahr's activities and conversations while ashore, which are not in the boats' official war logs, were reconstructed by the authors on the basis of information gathered from numerous diaries of other U-boat skippers and crews that sailed either with Bahr or out of the same ports. Among the most useful were Fritz Brustat-Naval and Teddy Suhren, *Nasses Eichenlaub: Als Kommandant und F.d.U. im U-Boot-Krieg* (Herford 1983); Lothar-Günther Buchheim, *The Boat* (New York 1975); Jost Metzler, *The Laughing Cow: A U-Boat Captain's Story* (London 1955); and Erich Topp, *Fackeln über dem Atlantik: Lebensbericht eines U-Boot-Kommandanten* (Herford 1990). Also useful in trying to come to grips with Bahr's actions and moods as commander of *U305* was a sociological investigation into the mentalities of U-boat skippers in the final phases of the war: Gottfried Hoch, "Zur Problematik der Menschenführung im Kriege. Eine Untersuchung zur Einsatzbereitschaft von deutschen U-Boot-Besatzungen ab 1943," in *Die deutsche Marine: Historisches Selbstverständnis und Standortbestimmung* (Herford and Bonn 1983).

Technical details of the U-boat war were gleaned from a number of pertinent treatments: Heinz Bonatz, *Seekrieg im Äther: Die Leistungen der Marine-Funkaufklärung 1939–1945* (Herford 1981); Jochen Bennecke, *Die Wende im U-Boot-Krieg: Ursachen und Folgen 1939–1943* (Augsburg 1995); William Hackmann, *Seek & Strike: Sonar, Anti-Submarine Warfare and the Royal Navy, 1914–54* (London 1984); Erich Rössler, *Die Torpedos der deutschen U-Boote: Entwicklung, Herstellung und Eigenschaften* (Herford 1984); Robert Stern, *Type VII U-Boats* (Annapolis 1991); and Fritz Trenkle, *Die deutschen Funkpeil- und Horch-Verfahren bis 1945* (Ulm 1982).

Bahr's five patrols, first as Exec and later as Captain, were further traced in (and the accuracy of his KTB checked against) several standard works on Allied convoys: Peter Gretton, *Crisis Convoy: The Story of HX 231* (London 1974); Martin Middlebrook, *Convoy: The Battle for Convoy*

SC 122 *and HX* 229 (London 1976); Jürgen Rohwer, *The Critical Convoy Battles of March 1943* (Annapolis 1977); Jürgen Rohwer and Gerhard Hümmelchen, *Chronology of the War at Sea*, 2 vols. (London 1974); and David Syrett, *The Defeat of the German U-Boats: The Battle of the Atlantic* (Columbia, SC 1994).

Information on the Battle of the Atlantic owes much to three classic treatments of Ultra and the war at sea: Patrick Beesley, *Very Special Intelligence: The Story of the Admiralty's Operational Intelligence Centre, 1939–1945* (London 1977); F.H. Hinsley et al, *British Intelligence in the Second World War*, 3 vols. (London 1979–90); and especially David Kahn, *Seizing the Enigma: The Race to Break the German U-Boat Codes, 1939–1943* (Boston 1991).

Index